The Comparative International Politics of Democracy Promotion

Though scholarly attention to democracy promotion is increasing, there is still little comparative and theoretically-based work on the protagonists of democracy promotion. This book investigates the motives that drive democracy promotion in a comparative and theoretically oriented manner, exploring how democracy promoters deal with conflicting objectives and the factors that shape their behaviour. It also addresses the more policy-oriented debate on the contemporary challenges to democracy promotion, focusing on US and German policies towards three kinds of challenges: the emergence of 'radical' leftist governments in Bolivia and Ecuador, the political rise of Islamist movements in Turkey and Pakistan, and the consolidation of (semi-)authoritarian rule in Belarus and Russia. In each case, North-Western democracy promoters have been confronted with serious conflicts of objectives between security, economic interests and democracy promotion. The analysis and comparison of such situations, in which democracy promoters have to deal with competing objectives and make tough decisions, provides powerful evidence as to the factors that shape democracy promotion.

The Comparative International Politics of Democracy Promotion will be of interest to students and scholars of international relations, comparative politics, democratization studies and foreign policy.

Jonas Wolff is senior research fellow at the Peace Research Institute Frankfurt (PRIF), Germany.

Hans-Joachim Spanger is member of the executive board and head of the research department 'Governance and Societal Peace' at the Peace Research Institute Frankfurt (PRIF) Germany.

Hans-Jürgen Puhle is Professor Emeritus of Political Science at Goethe University Frankfurt am Main, Germany.

Democratization studies
(formerly democratization studies, Frank Cass)

Democratization studies combines theoretical and comparative studies with detailed analyses of issues central to democratic progress and its performance, all over the world.

The books in this series aim to encourage debate on the many aspects of democratization that are of interest to policy-makers, administrators and journalists, aid and development personnel, as well as to all those involved in education.

1. **Democratization and the Media**
   Edited by Vicky Randall

2. **The Resilience of Democracy**
   Persistent practice, durable idea
   Edited by Peter Burnell and Peter Calvert

3. **The Internet, Democracy and Democratization**
   Edited by Peter Ferdinand

4. **Party Development and Democratic Change in Post-communist Europe**
   Edited by Paul Lewis

5. **Democracy Assistance**
   International co-operation for democratization
   Edited by Peter Burnell

6. **Opposition and Democracy in South Africa**
   Edited by Roger Southall

7. **The European Union and Democracy Promotion**
   The case of North Africa
   Edited by Richard Gillespie and Richard Youngs

8 **Democratization and the Judiciary**
   Edited by Siri Gloppen, Roberto Gargarella and Elin Skaar

9 **Civil Society in Democratization**
   Edited by Peter Burnell and Peter Calvert

10 **The Internet and Politics**
   Citizens, voters and activists
   Edited by Sarah Oates, Diana Owen and Rachel Gibson

11 **Democratization in the Muslim World**
   Changing patterns of authority and power
   Edited by Frederic Volpi and Francesco Cavatorta

12 **Global Democracy: For and Against**
   Ethical theory, institutional design and social struggles
   Raffaele Marchetti

13 **Constructing Democracy in Southern Europe**
   A comparative analysis of Italy, Spain and Turkey
   Lauren M. McLaren

14 **The Consolidation of Democracy**
   Comparing Europe and Latin America
   Carsten Q. Schneider

15 **New Challenges to Democratization**
   Edited by Peter Burnell and Richard Youngs

16 **Multiple Democracies in Europe**
   Political culture in new member states
   Paul Blokker

17 **Globality, Democracy and Civil Society**
   Edited by Terrell Carver and Jens Bartelson

18 **Democracy Promotion and Conflict-based Reconstruction**
   The United States and democratic consolidation in Bosnia and Afghanistan
   Matthew Alan Hill

19 **Requisites of Democracy**
   Conceptualization, measurement, and explanation
   Jørgen Møller and Svend-Erik Skaaning

20 **The Conceptual Politics of Democracy Promotion**
Edited by Christopher Hobson and Milja Kurki

21 **Ethnic Politics and Democratic Transition in Rwanda**
David Kiwuwa

22 **Democracy and Democratization in Comparative Perspective**
Conceptions, conjunctures, causes and consequences
Jørgen Møller and Svend-Erik Skaaning

23 **The Comparative International Politics of Democracy Promotion**
Edited by Jonas Wolff, Hans-Joachim Spanger and Hans-Jürgen Puhle

The Comparative International Politics of Democracy Promotion

Edited by Jonas Wolff,
Hans-Joachim Spanger and
Hans-Jürgen Puhle

LONDON AND NEW YORK

First published 2014
by Routledge

Published 2014 by Routledge
2 Park Square, Milton Park, Abingdon, Oxfordshire OX14 4RN

Simultaneously published in the USA and Canada
by Routledge
711 Third Avenue, New York, NY 10017

Routledge is an imprint of the Taylor and Francis Group, an informa business
First issued in paperback 2015

© 2013 Jonas Wolff, Hans-Joachim Spanger and Hans-Jürgen Puhle for selection and editorial matter; individual contributors their contribution.

The right of Jonas Wolff, Hans-Joachim Spanger and Hans-Jürgen Puhle to be identified as the authors of the editorial material, and of the authors for their individual chapters, has been asserted in accordance with sections 77 and 78 of the Copyright, Designs and Patents Act 1988.

All rights reserved. No part of this book may be reprinted or reproduced or utilized in any form or by any electronic, mechanical, or other means, now known or hereafter invented, including photocopying and recording, or in any information storage or retrieval system, without permission in writing from the publishers.

Trademark notice: Product or corporate names may be trademarks or registered trademarks, and are used only for identification and explanation without intent to infringe.

British Library Cataloguing in Publication Data
A catalogue record for this book is available from the British Library

Library of Congress Cataloging in Publication Data
The comparative international politics of democracy promotion / Edited by Jonas Wolff, Hans-Joachim Spanger and Hans-Jürgen Puhle.
    pages cm. – (Democratization studies)
    Includes bibliographical references and index.
    1. Democratization–International cooperation–Case studies.
    I. Wolff, Jonas. II. Spanger, Hans-Joachim. III. Puhle, Hans-Jürgen.
    JC423.C6615 2013
    327.1–dc23   2013011305

ISBN 978-0-415-82694-5 (hbk)
ISBN 978-1-138-95648-3 (pbk)
ISBN 978-1-315-88987-0 (ebk)

Typeset in Times New Roman
by Wearset Ltd, Boldon, Tyne and Wear

Contents

Notes on contributors ix
Preface x
Acknowledgements xii
List of abbreviations xiv

PART I
A comparative perspective on democracy promotion 1

1 Democracy promoters' conflicting objectives: the research agenda 3
   JONAS WOLFF AND HANS-JOACHIM SPANGER

2 Freedom Fighter versus Civilian Power: an ideal-type comparison of US and German conceptions of democracy promotion 37
   ANNIKA E. POPPE, BENTJE WOITSCHACH AND JONAS WOLFF

3 Norms versus interests: the determinants across the cases 61
   DANIEL SCHEWE AND JONAS WOLFF

PART II
Case studies on German and US democracy promotion 75

4 Democracy promotion in Bolivia: the 'democratic revolution' of Evo Morales 77
   JONAS WOLFF

5 Democracy promotion in Ecuador: the 'citizens' revolution' of Rafael Correa 107
   JONAS WOLFF

6 Democracy promotion in Turkey: the rise of political Islam 103
CEMAL KARAKAŞ

7 Democracy promotion in Pakistan: the rise and fall of
General Musharraf 161
NIELS GRAF AND IRIS WURM

8 Democracy promotion in Belarus: dealing with 'Europe's
last dictatorship' 191
AZAR BABAYEV

9 Democracy promotion in Russia: the ambivalent challenge
posed by Putinism 222
HANS-JOACHIM SPANGER

PART III
Results and conclusions 251

10 Democracy promotion as international politics: comparative
analysis, theoretical and practical implications 253
JONAS WOLFF

Index 289

Contributors

Azar Babayev is a research fellow at the Azerbaijan Diplomatic Academy in Baku. He holds a PhD from the University of Mannheim, Germany. Between 2009 and 2012 he was a research fellow at the Peace Research Institute Frankfurt (PRIF) in Germany.

Niels Graf studies political science at Goethe University Frankfurt, Germany. Between 2010 and 2012 he worked as a research assistant at the PRIF and Goethe University Frankfurt.

Cemal Karakaş is a research associate at the PRIF. He holds a PhD from Goethe University Frankfurt where he also worked as a research fellow between 2008 and 2011.

Annika E. Poppe is a research associate at the PRIF and a PhD candidate at Goethe University Frankfurt. Between 2009 and 2010 she worked as a research assistant at PRIF.

Hans-Jürgen Puhle is Professor Emeritus of Political Science at Goethe University Frankfurt. He holds a PhD from Free University Berlin and a habilitation from the University of Münster.

Daniel Schewe has studied international studies/peace and conflict research at Goethe University Frankfurt. In 2010 and 2011 he worked as a research assistant at the PRIF and Goethe University Frankfurt.

Hans-Joachim Spanger is a member of the executive board and head of research department at the PRIF. He holds a PhD from Goethe University Frankfurt.

Bentje Woitschach is a policy officer for education for sustainable development at Germanwatch in Bonn, Germany. Between 2009 and 2011 she worked as a research assistant at Goethe University Frankfurt and the PRIF.

Jonas Wolff is a senior research fellow at the PRIF. He holds a PhD from Goethe University Frankfurt.

Iris Wurm is a staff member at Goethe University Frankfurt. Between 2006 and 2011 she was research associate at the PRIF. She holds a PhD from Goethe University Frankfurt.

Preface

Democracy promotion carries a bold promise: to reconcile the competing claims of democratic norms and national interests. As Strobe Talbott once put it, in international democracy promotion 'American values and interests reinforce each other'. Indeed, in the 1990s quite a few politicians and scholars subscribed to the harmonizing notion of democracy promotion as a foreign policy strategy that was both rational and intrinsically good. Yet, democratization processes and external efforts to support them are invariably neither straightforward nor smooth. The (manifold) norms and the (multiple) interests that guide the foreign policy of established democracies like the United States may indeed at times reinforce each other. But frequently they compete or openly collide. Dealing with conflicting objectives is therefore part and parcel of the day-to-day practice of democracy promotion. This book, which presents the results of a comprehensive comparative research project, provides a detailed analysis of how democracy promoters go about doing this.

Our starting point is the proposition that democracy promotion is systematically confronted with conflicting objectives. Democratization is both a complex and also a conflict-laden process of redistributing political power that resists being steered from the outside. Moreover, as promoting democracy implies fostering self-determination, even in cases of successful democratization, elected governments may well adopt a political course or take decisions that threaten the economic or security interests of the external actors engaged in democracy promotion. As a result, the desire to support democracy regularly clashes with more traditional 'national' interests, and quite frequently proves inherently contradictory. In selected case studies, this volume examines how Germany and the United States of America have dealt with conflicting objectives of this kind in their democracy promotion policies.

In this endeavour we were less interested in the outcome or the impact of external democracy promotion on transformations in each 'recipient country', a topic that is itself worthy of research. Instead, we chose to focus our attention on the determinants, the motives and impulses that guide the behaviour of those promoting democracy. In short: we asked how the contradiction between norms and interests is articulated in international democracy promotion – and what that means for the practice of democracy promotion.

Our research shows that democracy promotion as a project of global transformation is, in fact, an ambivalent and contradictory undertaking. In the political practice analysed in this volume, these ambivalences and contradictions manifest themselves in a pattern of reaction to conflicting objectives that we call 'alternatively conditioned double standards'. This pattern holds for both the 'Civilian Power' Germany as well as the United States, whose democracy promotion policy fits less neatly into a single ideal type. The double standards that characterize the way democracy promoters deal with conflicting objectives also draw attention to the necessarily reflexive character of democracy promotion. Only if democracy promoters systematically reflect upon the ambivalences and limits of their project of global democratization will they be able to avoid the muddling through that we have observed.

Instead they might better heed the basic principle of *quidquid agis prudenter agas et respice finem*: whatever you do, be careful, and think about the consequences.

Hans-Jürgen Puhle, Hans-Joachim Spanger and Jonas Wolff
Frankfurt, Germany, February 2013

Acknowledgements

First and foremost, we wish to thank the numerous experts and practitioners in Bonn, Berlin and Washington, DC, in Moscow, La Paz and Quito, in Ankara and Minsk, who made themselves available for interviews and background briefings. To name them all is impossible and, in any case, many wish to remain anonymous. But we certainly would not have been able to conduct this study without the cooperation of officials in embassies and ministries on the 'donor' as well as the 'recipient' side, of representatives from developmental agencies, political foundations and nongovernmental organizations, as well as of academic experts and experienced practitioners throughout the world.

Our special thanks go to Jörg Faust, Tina Freyburg and two anonymous scholars who acted as external referees and made valuable suggestions for improving this book. We thank Peter Burnell, Milja Kurki, Wolfgang Merkel, Marina Ottaway, Peter W. Schulze and Laurence Whitehead for their critical and constructive suggestions at our project's closing workshop in Frankfurt, and Thomas Carothers for his manifold support. Our thanks also go to the members of the German research network 'external democratization policy' and (of necessity in blanket form) to the numerous colleagues who commented on our papers at various national and international conferences. As always, we owe many important observations to several of our colleagues at the Peace Research Institute Frankfurt (PRIF). When the concept for the project was being developed, Lothar Brock was particularly helpful, as was at a later stage Harald Müller, who did a critical review of the entire manuscript.

Finally it has to be mentioned that this book is an updated version of a German volume (*Zwischen Normen und Interessen: Demokratieförderung als internationale Politik*) published in 2012 in PRIF's book series at Nomos, Baden-Baden. It is based on a cooperative project between PRIF and the Institute of Political Science of Goethe University Frankfurt am Main. In addition to the three editors of this book, Azar Babayev, Cemal Karakaş and Iris Wurm were also members of the project team, which conducted intensive discussions and reached consensus on many issues. This also applies to Bettina Benzing, Kim Kohlmeyer, Annika E. Poppe, Vera Rogova, Daniel Schewe and Bentje Woitschach, who as research assistants made indispensable contributions, and particularly Niels Graf, who also participated in conducting one of the case studies. We have to thank them all. Matthew Harris translated four of the ten chapters, and greatly improved the language of the other six. We are indebted to Cornelia Heß for her careful editing and preparation of the final manuscript. Last but not least, we express our thanks to the German Research Foundation (DFG) for its generous financial support.

Abbreviations

AA	Auswärtiges Amt (Foreign Office), Germany
ADN	Acción Democrática Nacionalista (Nationalist Democratic Action party), Bolivia
ALBA	Alianza Bolivariana para los Pueblos de Nuestra América (Bolivarian Alliance for the Peoples of Our America), Latin America
AKP	Adalet ve Kalkınma Partisi (Justice and Development Party), Turkey
ANAP	Anavatan Partisi (Motherland Party), Turkey
ASPA	American Service-Members Protection Act, USA
ATPDEA	Andean Trade Promotion and Drug Eradication Act, USA
BMVg	Bundesministerium der Verteidigung (Federal Ministry of Defence), Germany
BMZ	Bundesministerium für wirtschaftliche Zusammenarbeit und Entwicklung (Federal Ministry for Economic Cooperation and Development), Germany
CBJ	Congressional Budget Justification, USA
CDU	Christlich Demokratische Union (Christian Democratic Union), Germany
CHP	Cumhuriyet Halk Partisi (Republican People's Party), Turkey
CIM	Centrum für Internationale Migration (Centre for International Migration), Germany
CINC	Composite Index of National Capability, Correlates of War Project
CIPE	Center for International Private Enterprise, USA
CIS	Commonwealth of Independent States
CONAIE	Confederación de Nacionalidades Indígenas del Ecuador (Confederation of Indigenous Nationalities of Ecuador), Ecuador
CONAM	Consejo Nacional de Modernización del Estado (National Council for the Modernization of the State), Ecuador
CSF	Coalition Support Fund, USA
CSU	Christlich Soziale Union (Christian Social Union), Germany

DAAD	Deutscher Akademischer Austauschdienst (German Academic Exchange Service), Germany
dbg	Deutsch–belarussische Gesellschaft (German–Belarusian Association), Germany
DCG	Defense Consultative Group, USA/Pakistan
DEA	Drug Enforcement Administration, USA
DED	Deutscher Entwicklungsdienst (German Development Service), Germany
DFG	Deutsche Forschungsgemeinschaft (German Research Foundation), Germany
DSCA	Defense Security Cooperation Agency
DYP	Doğru Yol Partisi (True Path Party), Turkey
ENF	Economic Freedom Network Pakistan, Pakistan
ENP	Europeran Neighbourhood Policy, EU
ESDP	European Security and Defence Policy, European Union
EU	European Union
FATA	Federally Administered Tribal Areas, Pakistan
FDI	Foreign direct investment
FES	Friedrich-Ebert-Stiftung, Germany
FIDEM	Fortalecimiento de Instituciones Democráticas (Strengthening of Democratic Institutions programme), USAID/Bolivia
FMF	Foreign military financing, USA
FNS	Friedrich-Naumann-Stiftung (für die Freiheit), Germany
FOL	Forward operating location (military facility), USA
FP	Fazilet Partisi (Virtue Party), Turkey
FSA	Freedom Support Act, USA
FUNDAPPAC	Fundación de Apoyo al Parlamento y a la Participación Ciudadana (Foundation for Parliamentary and Citizen Participation Support), Bolivia
FUNDEMOS	Fundación Boliviana para la Capacitación Democrática y la Investigación (Bolivian Foundation for Democratic Capacitation and Investigation), Bolivia
GAO	Government Accountability Office, USA
GDP	Gross domestic product
GIZ	Deutsche Gesellschaft für Internationale Zusammenarbeit (German Agency for International Cooperation), Germany
GTZ	Deutsche Gesellschaft für Technische Zusammenarbeit (German Agency for Technical Cooperation), Germany
HBS	Heinrich-Böll-Stiftung, Germany
HSS	Hanns-Seidel-Stiftung, Germany
HRDF	Human Rights and Democracy Fund, USA
IBB	Internationales Bildungs- und Begegnungswerk (International Education and Exchange), Germany
ICC	International Criminal Court
IJC	Integrated justice centre

IMET	International Military Education and Training, USA
IMF	International Monetary Fund
InWEnt	Internationale Weiterbildung und Entwicklung gGmbH (Capacity Building International), Germany
IR	International relations
IRI	International Republican Institute, USA
ISAF	International Security Assistance Force, NATO/Afghanistan
ISI	Inter-Services Intelligence, Pakistan
ITT	Ishpingo–Tambococha–Tiputini (oil fields), Ecuador
JI	Jama'at-i Islami (Islamic Party), Pakistan
JUI	Jami'at-i Ulama-i Islami (Assembly of Islamic Clergy), Pakistan
KAS	Konrad-Adenauer-Stiftung, Germany
LFP	Liberal Forum Pakistan, Pakistan
MAS	Movimiento al Socialismo (Movement towards Socialism party), Bolivia
MCA	Millennium Challenge Account, USA
MCC	Millennium Challenge Corporation, USA
MIR	Movimiento de Izquierda Revolucionaria (Revolutionary Left Movement party), Bolivia
MMA	Muttahida Majlis-i Amal (United Council of Action), Pakistan
MNR	Movimiento Nacionalista Revolucionario (Revolutionary Nationalist Movement party), Bolivia
NDI	National Democratic Institute, USA
NED	National Endowment for Democracy, USA
NGO	Nongovernmental organization
OAS	Organization of American States
ODA	Official development assistance
OECD	Organisation for Economic Co-operation and Development
OSCE	Organization for Security and Cooperation in Europe
OTI	Office of Transition Initiatives, USAID
PADEP	Programa de Apoyo a la Gestión Pública Descentralizada y Lucha contra la Pobreza (Decentralized Governance and Poverty Reduction Support Programme), GTZ/Bolivia
PAIS	Patria Altiva I Soberana (Proud and Sovereign Fatherland party), Ecuador
PCCF	Pakistan Counterinsurgency Capability Fund, USA/Pakistan
PDC	Partido Demócrata Cristiano (Christian Democratic Party), Bolivia
PIPS	Pakistan Institute for Parliamentary Services, Pakistan
PML	Pakistan Muslim League (party), Pakistan
PML-N	Pakistan Muslim League-Nawaz (party), Pakistan
PML-Q	Pakistan Muslim League-Quaid-e-Azam (party), Pakistan
PODEMOS	Poder Democrático y Social (Democratic and Social Power party), Bolivia

PPP	Pakistan People's Party, Pakistan
PROMODE	Programa de Modernización y Descentralización (Modernization and Decentralization Programme), GTZ/Ecuador
RLS	Rosa-Luxemburg-Stiftung, Germany
RP	Refah Partisi (Welfare Party), Turkey
SPD	Sozialdemokratische Partei Deutschlands (Social Democratic Party), Germany
START	Strategic Arms Reduction Treaty
SWP	Stiftung Wissenschaft und Politik
UDC	Unión Demócrata Cristiana (Christian Democratic Union), Ecuador
UN	United Nations
UNDP	United Nations Development Programme
USAID	United States Agency for International Development
WEU	Western European Union

Part I
A comparative perspective on democracy promotion

Part 1

1 Democracy promoters' conflicting objectives
The research agenda[1]

Jonas Wolff and Hans-Joachim Spanger

George W. Bush did democracy promotion one favour at least: as much as he brought the global spread of democracy into disrepute, his years as president of the United States finally established democracy promotion as a major topic in international politics.[2] Today, the complaint that scholars were neglecting international democracy promotion (Carothers 2004: 2; Schraeder 2003: 21) is no longer justified. Research has increasingly begun to focus on the increase in foreign policy and development policy activities that are committed to promoting democracy.[3] However, there is still a dearth of theoretically informed comparative studies on democracy promoters. Why, to what extent and under which conditions do democratic states make the democratization of authoritarian regimes and the consolidation of fledgling democracies a focal point of their foreign and development policy? What factors are prevalent in international democracy promotion and how do democracy promoters balance out material interests, on the one hand, and normative dispositions, on the other?

This book devotes itself to these questions. By means of 12 case studies and the systematic comparison of these, it works out the determinants that shape democracy promotion by democratic states. The study focuses on the United States and Germany and the policy of these two countries towards six 'recipient' states: Belarus, Bolivia, Ecuador, Pakistan, Russia and Turkey. We will analyse the ways in which 'donors' deal with conflicting objectives and by doing so identify the factors that drive or hinder democracy promotion. Each case study investigates specific conflict situations, in the context of which democracy promotion becomes problematic for the 'donor' in various ways. When democracy promoters have to weigh up competing objectives and make difficult decisions, this allows for inferences as to the determinants that drive and shape democracy promotion. The book, thus, focuses on two research questions:

In descriptive terms, the case studies ask *how* democracy promoters deal with conflicting objectives. To what extent and in what form do the United States and Germany react to perceived contradictions, costs and risks of democracy promotion? How do they adapt their policies to changing circumstances? Do conflicting objectives lead donors to turn away from (or move towards) democracy promotion? Or, more generally: to what extent do donor reactions include changing priorities between the stated objective of promoting democracy and other foreign policy objectives?

In explanatory terms, we study the ways in which conflicting objectives are handled, and systematically compare these patterns of reaction in order to identify the factors influencing democracy promotion. This involves the question *why* democratic states carry out the kind of democracy promotion that we observe. What motives, what interests and norms drive – or hinder – democracy promotion? Why are the foreign and development policies that are carried out as democracy promotion so strikingly different from donor to donor, but also in the case of one and the same donor from recipient to recipient? These questions cannot be dealt with in simple, dichotomous terms. International democracy promotion, as a rule, is not about all-or-nothing decisions on whether democracy promotion in a given country should be continued or not. It is much more a matter of the priority and intensity, the combination of instruments (foreign and development policy, cooperative and confrontational), the resources, the time perspective and the strategic orientation with which democracy promotion is to be carried out in a given situation. This book aims to deepen our knowledge about the configurations of the factors that shape such complex decisions by means of detailed case studies and systematic comparative analysis.

This introductory chapter presents a research perspective that focuses on the determinants of, and the conflicting objectives in, democracy promotion. For this purpose, we first identify the conflicting objectives of democracy promotion that result from the inherent dilemmas of democratization, and then work out the potential determinants of democracy promotion that are suggested by different theoretical approaches. After outlining the research design, the chapter concludes by presenting an overview of the present volume.

Conflicting objectives in the promotion of democracy

With the 'third wave' of democratization (Huntington 1991) and the end of the Cold War, the global spread of democracy became a central goal and a key strategy in the foreign, security and development policies of established democracies. This happened by no means solely for the normative reason of having these countries' foreign relations guided by their own democratic values; it was rather the case that the academic paradigm of the democratic peace became a political programme. According to the democratic peace paradigm, democracies do not wage war against each other and, in general, are more peace-loving and inclined towards cooperation.[4] Promoting the global spread of democracy, therefore, directly serves international peace and the security interests of established democracies.[5] The paradigmatic rise of democratic peace in the 1990s was accompanied by a corresponding paradigm shift in development theory: democracy was no longer regarded as the final result of, but rather as an important condition for, economic and social development (Sen 1999). At the same time, critical scholars noted that spreading democracy (at least in the restrictive version of polyarchy, see Dahl 1998) directly served the economic interests of the leading capitalist powers; in the era of globalization, the 'despotic peace' no longer seemed capable of guaranteeing the political stability required by global capitalism (see Robinson 1996; Smith 2000).

These paradigm shifts enabled the return of a concept of liberal thought anchored in the Enlightenment: the assumption 'that all good things go together and that the achievement of one desirable social goal aids the achievement of others' (Huntington 1970: 5). In the global promotion of democracy, according to Strobe Talbott (1996: 49), 'values and interests reinforce each other'. The reality, however, quickly frustrated such lofty expectations. Democratization has proven far less smooth and tractable a process than was originally anticipated in the early 1990s. The promotion of democracy is, thus, regularly confronted with conflicting rather than complementary objectives (cf. Hurrell 2007: 158–60; Leininger et al. 2012; Spanger and Wolff 2007a, 2007b).

The root cause of these conflicting objectives in democracy promotion is a set of dilemmas inherent to democracy as an emancipatory project and to democratization as a deep-rooted transformation process. In democratic regimes, conflict is not suppressed – it is articulated openly. The virtue of democratic conflict resolution is that democracy offers institutions for peacefully dealing with conflict. As a 'system of ruled open-endedness, or organized uncertainty' (Przeworski 1991: 13), however, it is the nature of such democratic processes that their outcome is systematically unclear, i.e. indefinite. In the established welfare states of the global North-West, conflict is ubiquitous but it is reined in by reliable rules and institutions; uncertainty is organized in such a way as to become calculable. Yet, as empirical research on democracy has shown, the mere existence of democratic institutions as such does not guarantee such a balance between conflict and its peaceful resolution, between uncertainty and its regulated limitation (see Diamond 1990). In countries with only rudimentary democratic procedures, as well as those which are experiencing a process of democratization, uncertainty and tendencies to conflict outweigh democratic procedures (cf. Hegre et al. 2001; Mansfield and Snyder 2008; Spanger 2012).

This is expressed in three basic dilemmas of democracy that particularly affect 'young' democracies and regimes experiencing democratization. Democracy can, first, be endangered by escalating conflict that can no longer be settled by democratic means ('democracy versus stability'). Second, democratic regimes can be confronted by an excess of contradictory social demands that make effective democratic government impossible ('democracy versus governability'). Democratic procedures can, third, lead to majority decisions that violate basic principles of democracy ('democracy versus majority').

As a result of these dilemmas, external actors have to contend with competing objectives. Analytically, we distinguish between intrinsic and extrinsic conflicts of objectives. In the first case, the various dimensions, sub-goals and time perspectives of democracy come into conflict with each other; in the second case, the objective of promoting democracy collides with other policy objectives of donors.[6]

Democracy versus stability. Criticizing the harmonizing assumptions of classical modernization theories, Samuel Huntington (1970) emphasized that processes of social mobilization lead to increasing demands for political participation, which, in turn, can overload the acceptance and the capacity of existing political institutions. The successful establishment of a basically democratic regime does not solve this problem. Here too, an excess of contentious demands can lead to a situation where democratic institutions are no longer capable of maintaining political stability and peace. Under circumstances like these, repression or outright authoritarian rule can promise stability, at least in the short run. This, of course, would mean compromising the democratic character of the political regime in question. But holding on to the democratic rules of the game may itself threaten democracy: destabilization and conflict escalation can lead to state collapse and/or civil war, depriving the democratic regime of its basic foundation. Hence, in countries with rudimentary, 'defective' or still 'young' democratic institutions, more democracy can become a problem for political stability and internal peace. This is shown for example by quantitative research on democratic civil peace: large-N studies have found that both processes of democratization and 'semi-democratic' conditions significantly increase the probability of civil war (see Hegre *et al.* 2001; Mansfield and Snyder 2008; Spanger 2012).

For an external actor involved in democracy promotion, manifestations of this dilemma directly generate an intrinsic conflict of objectives. Does the long-term aim of democracy promotion require tolerating or even supporting forms of conflict management that are contrary to democratic principles (e.g. violent repression)? Or should democracy promoters try to block such violations through appeals, threats or sanctions – even if this principled stance may place the overall objective in danger? At the same time, other donor preferences may also be threatened, giving rise to extrinsic conflicts of objectives. Destabilization and conflict escalation can jeopardize economic relations (e.g. trade) and political cooperation in areas that are important to the donor (e.g. counterterrorism or counternarcotics). Political crises in a recipient country can also pose a direct threat to investments or citizens from the donor country and may give rise to fears of regional contagion and/or streams of migrants.

Democracy versus governability. Since Ancient Greece, the alleged irrationality of democracy has been a common complaint: when the purportedly unqualified masses dominate political decision-making, neither reasonable decisions nor effective implementation can be expected (cf. Buchstein and Jörke 2003: 475). In the 1970s, this argument emerged again in the conservative criticism of the 'ungovernability' of mass democracies in the First World (cf. Offe 2003). At that time, less participation was deemed necessary to safeguard democratic governability (Crozier *et al.* 1975). The same proposition was later applied to the rest of the globe, with economic shock therapies and technocratic decision-making pursued in order to enable comprehensive programmes of structural adjustment in the Second and Third World (see Haggard and Kaufman 1995: 335). The overarching argument is that rational government is inhibited by the pluralism, open competition and accountability mechanisms characteristic of democratic regimes, in other words: by the inclusive nature of democratic participation and representation, as well as by the complexity of democratic procedures. Under such circumstances, limiting democratic standards may be regarded as tenable or even desirable. This can, again, also be justified in democratic terms: in the long run, ungovernability arising from democratic blockades of 'rational' decision-making will undermine the democratic regime itself.

This dilemma gives rise to a conflict between the two forms of legitimization on which any democratic regime is based: input and output legitimization (Scharpf 1999). For democracy promoters, this implies an intrinsic conflict of objectives. The aim to support mechanisms that guarantee inclusive participation, fair representation and democratic controls collides with the goal to strengthen the actual performance of the democratic regime in terms of effective and efficient policy-making. Concrete expressions of this intrinsic conflict are: Promote a strong executive that is capable of effective action or support democratic checks and balances? Promote a relatively autonomous state apparatus, which is removed from direct democratic control, and support limits on political competition (e.g. by means of limiting the number of parties in parliament), or instead seek to make participation and competition more inclusive and representative? Support a strong centralized state or decentralization and federalism? Problems of (un-)governability also have a simultaneous negative effect on donor interests and, as a result, may give rise to extrinsic conflicts of objectives. In contrast to the first dilemma, where it is escalating instability and conflict that threaten donor interests, in this case it is 'merely' the (in-)ability to govern effectively or rationally. The recipient whose cooperation is wanted turns out to be unable to democratically decide on and implement certain measures desired by the donor.

Democracy versus majority. Another constant theme in the critique of democracy concerns the inherent danger of a tyranny of the majority, as prominently emphasized by Alexis de Tocqueville and John Stuart Mill. The core problem, here, is that majority decisions, even if taken in compliance with democratic rules, may substantially challenge the basic principles of democracy. 'Germany 1933' is the classic warning. The military coup in Algeria in 1992 is the currently most discussed variant of this problem: because it prevented an election victory of the Islamic Salvation Front, it was tolerated by the West (but led straight into a bloody civil war). Majority decisions directed against minorities are more commonplace forms of expression. Liberal democracies deal with this dilemma by constitutionally limiting the scope of majoritarian decisions. This limitation of the power of the majority protects the overall procedural minimum requirements of a democratic order as well as the rights of minorities specifically. There are, however, no objective criteria that would define the appropriate scope and limits of democratic majority decisions, the non-negotiable core norms of democracy or the unassailable rights of minorities. These are themselves contingent upon political decisions.

For donors, an intrinsic conflict of objectives arises when democratic decisions in a recipient country violate norms that are essential to the donor's conception of democracy. Extrinsic conflicts, by contrast, emerge when the sovereign democratic decisions by the recipient endanger the material interests of the donor. Unlike the first two dilemmas, in this case it is deliberate actions by the recipient that may lead to deviations from donor preferences. Intrinsic and extrinsic conflicts regularly coincide. This is exemplified by the debate concerning the danger of an electoral takeover by Islamist forces that flared up in Palestine after the 2006 victory of Hamas. Although resulting from a democratic election, the victory of a political force that was perceived as fundamentally undemocratic and anti-Western was rejected by most Western governments both as a threat to democracy (intrinsic conflict) and to their (and Israel's) security and strategic interests (extrinsic conflict).

The emphasis on conflicts of objectives is a clear departure from the notions of democracy promotion as an undertaking that can be readily implemented with little difficulty. The emphasis on intrinsic conflicts implies abandoning the assumption that democratization is a 'natural process in which countries move from dysfunctional dictatorship to peaceful pluralism without great upheaval, violence or doubt,' as Thomas Carothers (2000: 194–5) critically summed up the basic assumptions of the US approach of 'institutional modelling'. Such a linear and teleological notion of transition describes the exception, not the rule (Carothers 2002).[7] At the same time, extrinsic conflicts challenge the notion that democracy promoters can anticipate immediate gains from their activities. Instead, the instrumental value of democracy varies, and potential benefits have to be weighed against potential costs (Spanger and Wolff 2007b).

In conflict situations, the 'standard synthesis' (Peceny 1999: 3) of democracy promotion is confounded: all good things do *not* go together. Differing objectives and instruments must be weighed against each other, and priorities specified. Hence 'tough choices' have to be made, of which Fareed Zakaria (2003: 118) has cited a few, with the alternatives of 'order and instability, liberalism and democracy, and secularism and religious radicalism'. As a result, the international hegemony of the democracy discourse and the proclamation of democracy promotion as a central foreign policy goal find only limited expression in practice. Commitment to democratic standards may have become almost a precondition for international acceptance, and democracy promotion a firmly established international norm (McFaul 2005). But when it comes to actually promoting democracy in individual cases, the harmonious alliance of democratic norms and foreign policy interests is regularly replaced by conflicting objectives that arise from the inherent dilemmas of democratization.

It is, therefore, not surprising that the practice of promoting democracy since 1990 has scarcely lived up to its claim to universality. Researchers unanimously agree that democracy promotion is neither universally pursued nor is it continuously pursued as a high priority. Variance and inconsistency characterize the field of democracy promotion – and this holds true for the political practice of individual promoters over time and in various target countries as well as for the comparison of different democracy promoters.[8] Up to now, however, we lack systematic knowledge about the causes that explain these variations in democracy promotion and, more specifically, about the factors that shape the ways of coping with conflicting objectives.

Existing studies have rarely tried to explain and/or theorize the behaviour of democracy promoters. Research that treats democracy promotion as one of many factors in democratization obviously focuses on the recipient countries, i.e. on the impact made by democracy promotion.[9] Theoretically, these studies rely, *inter alia*, on transition studies for conceptualizing the causal mechanisms through which external actors try to influence the internal processes of regime change. Analyses of democracy promotion from the perspective of international relations (IR) share this focus Here, democracy promotion is studied especially within the framework of concepts such as 'compliance' and 'international socialization'.[10] Generally, theoretical and explanatory efforts have thus far concentrated very much on the effects and the 'logics of influence' of external democracy promotion.[11]

Research that analyses the protagonists of democracy promotion is largely descriptive. Existing explanations mostly are not based on a theoretical framework and/or do not use comparative designs aimed at the systematic identification of determinants.[12] Nonetheless, these studies on individual democracy promoters provide two important starting points for the research agenda outlined here. First, some researchers have identified differing national patterns of democracy promotion and attributed these differences to specific national interests and values of donors.[13] Specifically, one international comparative research network (Schraeder 2002, 2003) identified the following differences: the United States is dominated by security interests, Germany and Japan by economic interests, and the Scandinavian states by 'humanitarian' interests. Generally speaking, comparative research points to at least gradual differences between the United States and Europe.[14] Thus, it is argued that European, and especially German, democracy promotion relies predominantly on an evolutionary understanding of democratization guided by modernization theory[15] as well as on cooperative strategies of engagement (Youngs 2004: 31–7).[16] In the case of the United States, by contrast, a 'missionary' understanding of democracy promotion (Monten 2005) is linked to its instrumentalization in terms of national security (Smith 1994: 4; see Muravchik 1991).[17] This is accompanied by a focus on (early) elections and institutional modelling (Carothers 2000: 194–5; see Carothers 1999: 85–122) as well as by a willingness to apply confrontational and offensive means (Youngs 2004: 31–7) – all the way to an 'imposition of democracy' (Whitehead 1991: 234). Whether these supposed differences can be confirmed by a systematic comparative analysis, however, remains to be examined – as does the question of which explanatory factors (different political cultures? different profiles of interests?) they are to be attributed to.

A second research finding concerns the dealing with conflicting objectives. Here, the mainstream opinion is ambivalent. Scholars largely agree that democracy promotion, since 1950, has become an important objective and instrument that is generally seen to correspond to both the foreign policy interests and the identity of democratic states. Yet, in comparison with other directly relevant foreign policy interests, it is of a 'soft' nature and in cases of conflict is relegated to the background. As a consequence, there is a broad consensus that the normative aim to promote democracy regularly takes second place to the usual national interests.[18]

To distinguish between the 'soft' democracy norm and 'hard' foreign policy interests may be analytically useful. As an explanation it is, however, not very convincing. As already mentioned, the prevailing standpoint among politicians and academics is that foreign policy interests and democratic values are very closely intertwined in democracy promotion. Yet, characterizing US democracy promotion as a 'national grand strategy' (Doyle 2000: 21) is scarcely compatible with the thesis that it can only lay claim to relevance when no interests stand in its way. If democracy promotion today is no longer regarded as a 'purely soft, idealistic interest', but as a 'pragmatic interest that reinforces other interests' (Carothers 1999: 60), it is not plausible that governments should regularly sacrifice 'strategic objectives such as democracy promotion' in favour of immediate security or economic interests (McFaul 2005: 158).[19]

In addition, it is unclear how this finding can be reconciled with the observation that democracy and democracy promotion have become increasingly established as international norms. This shift in international norms may primarily be a result of – and depend on – changes at the level of nation-states: the spread of democratization on the one hand, of democracy promotion practices on the other. Still – in a regulative sense – it should also have a reinforcing effect on international politics and thus limit arbitrary and purely interest-based deviations from norm-consistent behaviour (McFaul 2005: 160; see Lutz and Sikkink 2000).[20]

Obviously, the international politics of democracy promotion defy simple theoretical explanations. The analytic distinction between interests and norms should not obscure the fact that, empirically, we are not confronted with the question of whether 'hard' interests prevail over 'soft' norms or not. The task is rather to understand and explain political decision-making on conflicting objectives as a process in which utilitarian and normative considerations interact.[21]

The present volume thus adopts a configurational perspective that does not attempt to measure the causal effects of discrete 'independent variables'. Instead, we track down the complex interaction of determinants by means of in-depth case studies and their comparative analysis (see Ragin 2004). Conflicts of objectives offer an ideal opportunity for an analytical focus, making it possible to investigate how various utilitarian and normative considerations play out, reinforce or block each other in shaping democracy promotion.

Determinants of democracy promotion

The research on democratic peace offers a useful theoretical starting point for studying the determinants of democracy promotion. The democratic peace is not only the most popular academic approach that is specifically concerned with democratic foreign policy; as we have seen, it also serves as one of the most prominent justifications for democracy promotion. This holds true regardless of whether the monadic or the dyadic variant of democratic peace is adopted: the former regards democracies as generally more peaceful than any other type of political regime; the latter merely considers the democratic peace as limited to relations between fellow democracies. At first sight, both perspectives support the claim that democracy promotion should satisfy both the interests and the values of democratic states. On closer examination, however, this statement needs to be differentiated. In line with critical analyses of the democratic peace that have demonstrated its contradictions ('antinomies') (see Geis *et al.* 2006; Müller 2004; Müller and Wolff 2006), a review of the various approaches to democratic peace reveals sound arguments both *in favour of* and *against* democracy promotion.

In the following two sections, we will discuss rationalist and reflective perspectives on democratic peace, as well as related IR theories.[22] The aim is to work out a range of potential determinants of democracy promotion.

Rationalist perspectives: democracy promotion as an instrument

The utilitarian explanation of the democratic peace draws on Immanuel Kant's essay on the 'Perpetual Peace'. Democracies, according to this reasoning, are prone to peace because they realize the will of their citizens who fear for their lives and worldly goods (Czempiel 1996: 80). It is, therefore, non-democratic states that cause war – which makes democracy promotion an effective strategy in terms of international peace and national security.[23] This notion of an instrumental value of democracy is reinforced by the additional argument that democracies are also particularly inclined towards political cooperation and economic exchange (see Mansfield *et al.* 2002; Russett and Oneal 2001).

A more thorough cost–benefit analysis of democratic states, however, shows that the opposite conclusions are equally plausible (see Bueno de Mesquita and Downs 2006: 631–2). The basic problem is constituted by the risks and imponderables of democratization as a protracted and conflict-laden process of political transformation. First, democratization, by its very nature, is a long-term project whose benefits can only be gained in the relatively distant future; the costs, however, are incurred immediately.[24] Second, the success of democracy promotion is by no means guaranteed; democratization is not only an internal process but, as research shows, democratization processes seldom lead directly to stable liberal democracies (see Carothers 2002; Schmitter 1995). Third, democratization poses inherent risks – especially a typical risk of conflict, which can give rise to related costs (see above).[25]

Fourth, democracy promotion is only rational in utilitarian terms when the external actor can achieve a tangible effect with an appropriate level of effort. The net impact of external democracy promotion on democratization, however, 'is likely to be only marginal ... and, hence, singularly difficult to measure and predict' (Schmitter and Brouwer 1999: 11; see Goldsmith 2008: 136–44). Fifth, this problem draws attention to the significance of relative power positions

(Monten 2005: 118): only in the case of significant power asymmetries between donor and recipient can the former expect a discernible effect from appropriate effort.

In principle, the research on democratic peace tells us that democracies should prefer international partners whose political systems are also democratic. Still, efforts to actively promote democracy are rational only under highly specific circumstances: when the prospects of success are relatively good and short-term, risks are limited, and the power differentials between donor and recipient are marked. As a result, the rationalist perspective draws attention to four potential determinants of democracy promotion:

1   *Relative power.* From a rationalist point of view material power asymmetries between donor and recipient are generally regarded as a prerequisite for democracy promotion (see Monten 2005).[26] More specifically, a high power asymmetry in favour of the democracy promoter increases its willingness to take on the risks of democratization, as they can be controlled by the ability of the donor to project power. A relatively balanced, or even negative, power relationship, on the other hand, encourages restraint on the part of the donor. In such cases, provided that donors engage in democracy promotion at all, conflicting objectives should lead donors to quickly return to *realpolitik*.
2   *Security interests.* To the extent that democratic governments buy into the empirical proposition of the democratic peace, they regard democracy promotion as a contribution to national security. Considering its long-term effects and its instrumental character, however, democracy promotion represents a 'soft' objective only. When coming into conflict with 'hard', immediately effective, security objectives, it will be relegated to the background. In such a modified realist perspective, democracy promotion is an instrument that is applied (or not) in entirely opportunistic ways (see Schweller 2000).[27] Democracy promotion is thus only practised as long as democracy is regarded as relevant for security policy towards a given recipient country. It is terminated as soon as the extrinsic conflicts of objectives adversely affect the security interests of the donor.
3   *Economic interests.* According to economic liberalism,[28] democracy promises conditions favourable for economic cooperation in trade and investment: political stability, predictability and good governance based on the rule of law and, in particular, the protection of private property rights. In this sense, democracy promotion serves economic interests (see Moravcsik 1997: 528–9; Doyle 2008: 60–1).[29] Given its positive effect on economic cooperation and interdependence suggested by democratic peace research, democracy promotion can be regarded as part of a strategy for implementing economic interests (Ikenberry 1999) – but once again only from a long-term and clearly instrumental point of view. As with security interests, donor interest in democracy promotion is shaped by two factors: the extent to which democracy in the recipient country is regarded as helpful for

economic cooperation; and the extent to which the extrinsic conflicts of objectives impact the economic interests of donors.

4   *Domestic special interests.* From the perspective of republican liberalism (Moravcsik 1997), on which democratic peace research draws directly, the foreign policy of democratic states results from the pluralistic interaction among collective bearers of interests and values within society (see Müller and Risse-Kappen 1993: 32–8). Which preferences prevail remains unspecified as 'the precise policy of governments depends on which domestic groups are represented' (Moravcsik 1997: 530).[30] Democracy promotion is thus one foreign policy objective among several, and its relevance depends upon the extent to which organized proponents (interest groups, NGOs, state agencies) with more or less privileged access to political decisions and more or less support from the general public can exert their influence.[31] For the analysis of bilateral donor policies it is therefore decisive how far (and in which way) domestic interest and advocacy groups pay particular attention to an individual recipient country. The direction in which such domestic groups can be expected to impact on democracy promotion in a given case – in simplified terms: whether they advocate or inhibit democracy promotion – cannot be hypothesized in the abstract, but only in regard to particular pairs of states.

Reflective perspectives: democracy promotion as a norm[32]

According to the normative or cultural explanation of the democratic peace, democracy is characterized by norms of peaceful conflict resolution. In their international relations, democratic states are inclined to externalize these norms (Risse-Kappen 1995: 501). To do this, however, they are dependent upon partners who also favour cooperative behaviour and the peaceful solution of conflicts. Thus, the more democratic the partner the better democracies can live out their democratic 'nature' and build relationships characterized by cooperation and trust (cf. Risse-Kappen 1995: 501–6; Doyle 1983: 230). In addition, by promoting democratization around the world, democracies support the spread of the norms and values they regard as universal. As a result, democracy promotion can be seen as part of a 'mission' based on moral imperative embedded in democratic – or liberal – culture (Sørensen 2006: 259; see Jahn 2005; Müller 2004; Smith 1994).

Two arguments are opposed to this notion of a clear-cut normative preference for democracy promotion. They are also rooted in liberal-democratic norms but reject external intervention in processes of political change. First, democracy promotion by definition represents an intervention in the internal affairs of other states and, therefore, collides with the norm of collective self-determination – a basic principle of democratic thinking. As such intervention is never neutral, democracy promoters violate liberal-democratic norms, which, in accordance with the right to an independent political development, call for restraint (see Doyle 2009: 352–4; Rawls 1999: 62; Sørensen 2006: 258–9). The US tradition of 'exemplarism' corresponds to such a stance of restraint.[33]

Second, there are tensions between democracy promotion and the preference for international cooperation, which is also assumed to guide democracies. In a world that does not consist exclusively of democracies, maintaining international peace requires reliable cooperation also with non-democracies (Czempiel 1996: 97–8). Yet, if established democracies seek to disempower non-democratic partners, support democracy movements and make international cooperation contingent upon political conditions, they will generate mutual distrust and conflicts. By pursuing this approach, democracies provoke ingroup–outgroup dynamics and, thus, increase the risk of war (see Hermann and Kegley 1995; Kahl 1999).[34]

The normative perspective reinforces the utilitarian reasoning that democracies can be expected to prefer their international environment to be made up of fellow democracies. Again, however, the normative appropriateness of democracy promotion depends on specific conditions. On the donor side, the question is whether a militant interpretation of liberal norms dominates, or norms of restraint, non-intervention and/or exemplarism. In the first case, the normative tensions mentioned are decided in favour of a policy of actively promoting democracy; in the second, the government forgoes such attempts to intervene.[35] If the recipient government is democratically legitimate and shares the objective of deepening or consolidating its democracy, these normative contradictions vanish into thin air. Much the same is true when donor and recipient have agreed upon common norms of democracy (promotion) and have institutionalized these within the framework of joint international organizations. This yields two further potential determinants in democracy promotion:

5   *Political culture.* The argument that democracies externalize their norms in their foreign relations corresponds to an actor-centred constructivism in IR. This theoretical perspective emphasizes the importance of national self-images, roles and identities, or generally of political cultures for the foreign policy of states (Harnisch 2003: 340).[36] Accordingly, it is a specific national political culture that determines whether, to what extent and in which form a given state will promote democracy. The determinant 'political culture' is, of course, notoriously broad and vague. We will therefore restrict ourselves to a narrowly defined aspect of particular importance for the topic at hand: conceptions of democracy promotion. For individual donors, these conceptions encompass their particular assumptions concerning universal values, understandings of democratization and rules of appropriateness in democracy promotion (see Chapter 2 for further discussion).

6   *International norms.* Whereas actor-centred constructivism emphasizes sociocultural contexts within states, sociological institutionalism in IR (Katzenstein 1996) focuses on the influence of 'international cultural environments' on foreign policy (Jepperson *et al.* 1996: 34). For our topic, it is international democracy-related norms that should shape democracy promotion. To the extent that a commitment to democracy is established as a norm in the international community of (democratic) states, democracies can be expected to follow a corresponding 'logic of appropriateness' (March and

Olsen 1998): to pursue their national interests within the limits of democratically 'appropriate' behaviour (see Boekle *et al.* 2001: 120).[37] On a general level, democracy-related norms are universally anchored within the framework of the United Nations, especially in the Universal Declaration of Human Rights and the Human Rights Conventions (see Chapter 3). Yet, the commitment to a universal democracy norm, or even to a 'right to democracy', is still highly controversial, as is the legitimacy of intervention in the internal affairs of other states in the name of democracy (see Carothers 2010; Fox and Roth 2000; Hurrell 2007: chapter 6; but see McFaul 2005). At the regional level, the specification and institutionalization of democracy norms is, in part, much more advanced – most notably, in Europe (EU, Council of Europe) and the Americas (Organization of American States, OAS) (see Hawkins 2008: 392–4; Herman and Piccone 2003: 229–39). Thus, what is pivotal for democracy promotion is the extent to which donor–recipient relations are shaped by shared international norms that commit both sides to democracy and legitimize democracy promotion: the stronger such norms, the more we can expect states to actively promote democracy and to hold fast to this goal even in cases of conflicting objectives.

The eclectic perspective: configurations and contexts

The above discussion on the coalescence of interests and values in democracy promotion suggests that it is not very promising to analyse democracy promotion either from a purely rationalist or an entirely reflective perspective. An alternative theoretical perspective is offered by what Rudra Sil and Peter Katzenstein refer to as 'analytic eclecticism'. The aims of analytic-eclectic research are: 'to reflect, rather than simplify, the complexity and multi-dimensionality of social phenomena'; to pay 'attention to the multiplicity, heterogeneity, and interaction of causal mechanisms and processes that generate phenomena of interest'; and to contribute not only to academic scholarship but also to 'enrich policy debates and normative discussions beyond the academe' (Sil and Katzenstein 2010: 19–20, 22).[38] More specifically, this book investigates how states 'pursue their material and ideal preferences within given environments' without a priori giving ontological primacy to the actor or structure, material or ideational factors (Sil and Katzenstein 2010: 21; see also Kurki 2008: 285). The determinants of democracy promotion addressed here are thus not analysed as independent variables. To be sure, across the case studies, we will identify and isolate the individual determinants and their causal relevance. The determinants also serve the purposes of analytic differentiation and systematization of the investigation. But when it comes to explaining the phenomena of interest, we will focus on the interaction of causal factors. As with analytic eclecticism, our goal is not to establish a parsimonious grand theory of democracy promotion that claims to yield comprehensive explanations, but to develop a complex causal explanation that is located at the level of middle-range theory (Sil and Katzenstein 2010: 208).

The six determinants outlined and their configurative interaction constitute the explanatory framework of the present study. Yet, the qualitative case studies, which form the core of the investigation, will not be limited to this theoretically deduced set of determinants: the case studies also permit to inductively identify additional relevant factors that deviate from our explanatory model (see George and Bennett 2005: 20–1). In keeping with the eclectic perspective, those idiosyncratic contextual conditions that influence the effects and interaction of determinants in specific cases are also to be taken into account. For the analysis of democracy promotion in bilateral relations, three general contexts can be identified:

The donor context. It is not simply 'the state' that defines the objectives and strategies of democracy promotion and then implements these in the different recipient countries. Instead, democracy promotion emerges from interactions among numerous actors in differing institutional and political settings.[39] In this sense, the choice of what foreign-policy objectives, strategies and measures to pursue is influenced by a series of dynamics within the donor state: changes in government, party politics, varying power relationships within the government (e.g. between ministries) or between government and parliament, the institutional assignment of relevant instruments and resources to different ministries and agencies (see below). In addition, democracy promotion is implemented by several state, quasi-state and non-state agencies, which partly cooperate, but also compete with each other – and regularly interact with different actors on the recipient side. The respective bureaucratic interests of these agencies and organizations as well as their behavioural routines and organizational cultures are thus potentially significant (see Spence 2005; Melia 2005).[40] The determinant 'domestic special interests' grasps one important facet of the donor context. The case studies and the comparative analysis will show whether general patterns transcending this determinant are to be included in the explanation, and whether further characteristics on the donor side can be isolated by inductive means as relevant determining factors.

The recipient context. Recipient countries confront democracy promotion with very different conditions. These conditions shape the possibilities and limits, the prospects of success and the risks of democracy promotion. Donors only very partially live up to the self-proclaimed aspiration to design their democracy promotion strategies in case- and context-sensitive terms (see BMZ 2005: 17; USAID 2005: 7). Still, there can be no doubt that it is impossible to define and implement activities of democracy promotion without taking the specific recipient context into account: for instance, the kind of political regime on the recipient side, or the availability of like-minded partners within the government, the political elite and civil society. Within the framework of the present study, the recipient context is generally characterized by a conflict situation that leads to conflicting objectives on the part of the donors. The focus on conflict situations involves both their emergence and the way they evolve over time. These dynamics in the recipient countries will be shaped, *inter alia*, by case-specific – and varying – correlations of forces. The extent to which such (shifting) power relations in recipient countries influence the interaction of determinants on the donor side will be examined in the empirical analysis.

The regional and global context. Finally, bilateral relationships between donor and recipient are embedded in international contexts (regional and global), which also shape the objectives, strategies and consequences of bilateral democracy promotion. Generally, the international promotion of democracy is part of the overall attempt to build a liberal world order. The upsurge in North-Western democracy promotion followed the end of the Cold War for a reason. In the same way, reverse phenomena such as the (re-)emerging power of authoritarian states and the so-called 'backlash' against democracy promotion are changing the overall discourse on democracy promotion (Carothers 2010; see Chapter 10). Such global changes have an impact on bilateral democracy promotion. On a smaller scale, this also holds true for regional trends and events such as the 'colour revolutions' (Stewart 2009). Finally, third parties can intervene directly in relations between donor and recipient. Democracy promotion in a given recipient country, for instance, can be influenced by the donor's relations with an important neighbouring state. The determinant 'international norms' identifies an important aspect of the regional context. Here, too, case studies investigate whether additional elements of a given regional (or global) context need to be considered that go beyond our rather narrow focus on the *inter-national*, i.e. inter-state, politics of democracy promotion.

The research design

This book investigates the determinants of democracy promotion. These can hardly be identified when looking at the day-to-day routine of democratic foreign and development policy. As long as everything works smoothly, there is no way to scrutinize the official declaration that donor policies are consistently guided by the aim to promote democracy, which at the same time serves all other 'national interests'. This study, therefore, analyses how democracy promoters deal with conflicting objectives. The case studies focus on specific conflict situations in recipient countries that challenge democracy promotion. By investigating and comparing the patterns of donor reactions to these conflict situations – and thus the ways in which conflicting objectives are dealt with – we can draw significant inferences about the determining factors that shape democracy promotion.

By analysing the democracy promotion policies of the United States and Germany, the present study deliberately adopts a state-centred perspective.[41] The United States is certainly the most important player in the field of democracy promotion. As 'the world's most powerful democracy with unrivalled global reach and capabilities' (Herman and Piccone 2003: 210), US policies decisively influence the discourse on, and the practice of, international democracy promotion. The United States is also most explicit about its support of democracy and makes the most resources available for this endeavour (see Azpuru *et al.* 2008; Herman and Piccone 2003: 210–16). Germany presents an ideal case for comparison in order to facilitate potentially generalizable statements about the factors determining democracy promotion. On the one hand, Germany displays a broad and strong commitment to democracy promotion (Herman and Piccone 2003: 83–8). Together with the United Kingdom, Germany is the most important European donor in this area (Youngs 2008: 160–1). On the other hand, German foreign policy and, specifically, German democracy promotion are generally regarded as contrasting those of the United States. Germany is usually described as a Civilian Power that is guided more by economic than by security interests, and characterized by a multilateral orientation that tends to exercise political restraint (see Chapter 2). By focusing on Germany, this study deviates from mainstream democracy promotion research. In addition to the United States, existing work mostly investigates the EU,[42] and predominantly compares these two democracy promoters.[43] As a multilateral supranational player *sui generis*, however, the EU is inappropriate for the kind of analysis of the determinants of democracy promotion by states that is being conducted here.

As regards recipients, six countries are analysed: Bolivia and Ecuador, Turkey and Pakistan, Belarus and Russia. As shown in Figure 1.1 and discussed further in Chapter 3, the combination of the selected donors and recipients yields a broad range of differing determinant configurations. While highly different, the six recipient countries were selected based on three general criteria. First, since 1990, they have introduced basic institutions of democracy, at least temporarily.[44] Second, prior to the emergence of the conflict situation, none of the countries was in a confrontation with the United States and/or Germany. In the early 1990s, the outlook for external democracy promotion was thus relatively positive. However, political developments in all countries in the 1990s and 2000s turned out to be less easy and more contradictory than expected immediately after the end of the Cold War. Thus, third, the six recipient countries demonstrate the failure of linear and teleological conceptions of transition (Carothers 2002). Specifically, they represent three currently relevant conflict situations in which the dilemmas of democratization discussed above come to the fore and, correspondingly, confront democracy promoters with conflicts of objectives.

1   Pakistan and Turkey represent a conflict situation that primarily affects the (broadly defined) region of the Greater Middle East. The rise of Islamist political forces not only challenges the existing political regimes in the region, but also the North-Western states that cooperate with the respective governments. Among the predominantly Islamic countries in the region, Pakistan and Turkey are the only countries that display the political dynamic relevant to our study. The starting point for the case studies is characterized by the existence of basic democratic institutions as well as cooperation with and democracy promotion by 'the West'. Later, an emerging conflict situation characterized, *inter alia*, by ever stronger Islamist political forces leads to conflicting objectives and calls for a response from donors. When comparing the two recipient countries, the conflict situation and the conflicting objectives are far less severe in Turkey than they are in Pakistan.

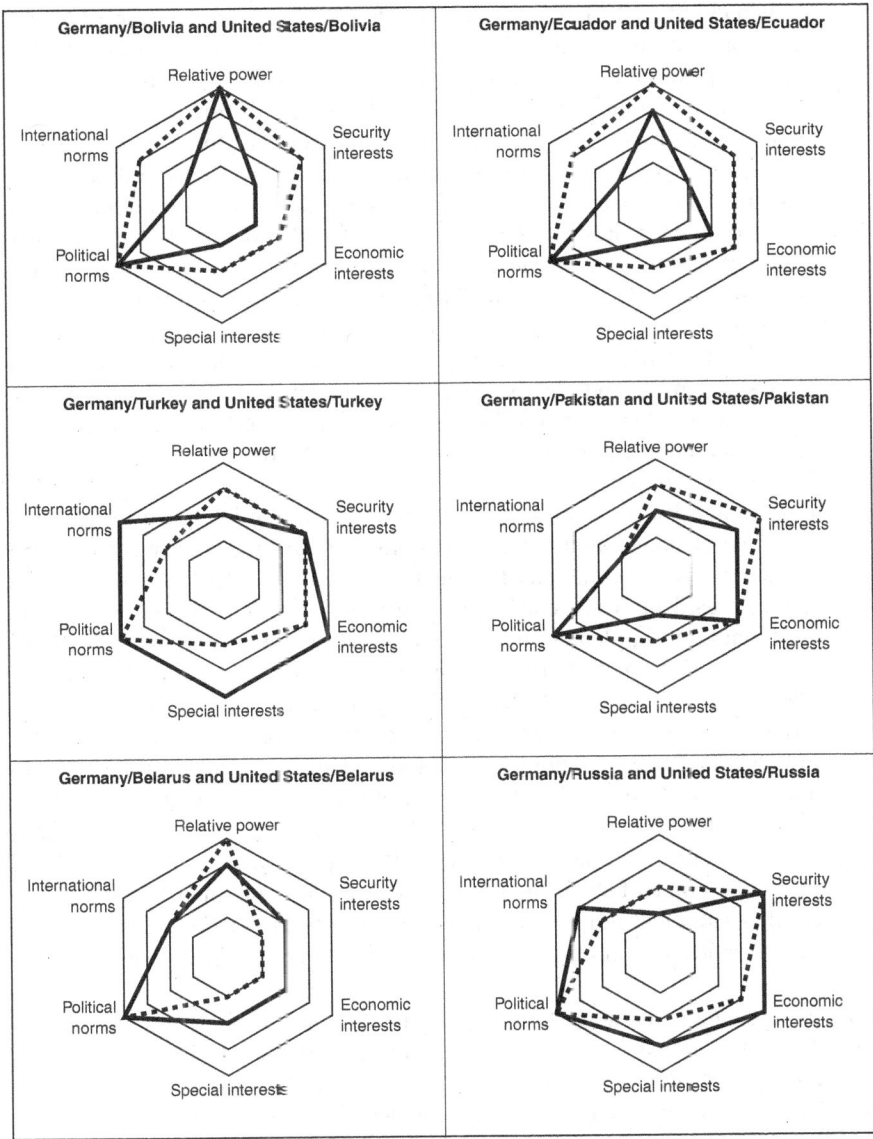

Figure 1.1 Overview of the 12 pairs of states (source: figure by the authors, created by Daniel Schewe, based on data presented in Chapter 3).

Note
As described there, all determinants are assigned a value from 1 (inner circle) to 4 (outer circle) on an ordinal scale. In this purely quantitative presentation the factor 'political culture' for the United States and Germany is assigned a 4 (high) rating, as a result of which qualitative differences in conceptions of democracy promotion are not represented.
Solid line: Germany/recipient; dashed line: United States/recipient.

2   Since the turn of the century, political regimes in South America have been challenged as well. Here, mass protests and social movements turned against the supposed constraints of neoliberal globalization and brought down a series of governments. In the course of a regional 'Leftist turn', the popular rejection of (neoliberal) capitalism, real-existing democracy and external 'imposition' (by the United States, the International Monetary Fund (IMF) and the World Bank) led to the election of a series of left and centre-left governments. Bolivia and Ecuador represent those South American countries in which protests against liberal market democracy found their way into corresponding government policies. New governments in these two countries have initiated a transformation of the existing political regimes and turned away from neoliberal recipes. While these changes take place in a generally democratic context, they have been accompanied by serious domestic conflict and clearly constitute a challenge to the norms and interests promoted by the North-Western donor community. The conflict situation and conflicts in objectives are significantly more pronounced in Bolivia than in Ecuador.

3   Belarus and Russia represent a conflict situation that is typical for the post-soviet space constituted by the Commonwealth of Independent States (CIS). Following the introduction of democratic rule in the early 1990s, across the region presidents have come into power who have used their democratic legitimation to implement increasingly authoritarian policies. The predominant result is 'semi-authoritarian' regimes (Ottaway 2003), political systems that range somewhere between 'defective democracies' and clearly authoritarian rule (see Merkel *et al.* 2006). Belarus and Russia are prime examples: in both countries, a temporary transition to democracy has been followed by a process of de-democratization. In the meantime, they are classified as 'not free' by Freedom House (2006). The establishment of an authoritarian regime occurred earlier and is more clear-cut in Belarus than in Russia.[45] From the point of view of the United States and Germany, however, the conflict situation and the conflicting objectives in Russia are significantly more serious than in Belarus, which has far less political relevance.

The three conflict situations imply significant conflicts of objectives that display both intrinsic and extrinsic dimensions. In all cases, democratic procedures – and specific majority decisions – have led to results that the donors regard as problematic for or even threatening to democracy (intrinsic conflict of objectives: 'democracy versus democracy'). At the same time, they affect the security and/or economic interests of the donors (extrinsic conflict: 'democracy versus donor interests'). In dealing with the growing influence of Islamist forces in Turkey and Pakistan, this poses the question whether donors should tolerate or even support restrictions on democratic standards ranging all the way to an outright coup. While problematic in democratic terms, such measures might be perceived as necessary to maintain a secular and pluralist order (intrinsic), to secure cooperation with 'the West' (extrinsic), and to uphold intra-societal peace (intrinsic

Introduction 21

and extrinsic). The election of left-wing governments in Bolivia and Ecuador confronted democracy promoters with the question of whether to tolerate or even support a gradual abandonment of universally conceived standards of liberal democracy and a market economy (intrinsic), which also threatened donor interests (extrinsic) and political stability (intrinsic and extrinsic), but could also be regarded as expressing democratic self-determination. Belarus and Russia, finally, raise the question of how to deal with governments that implement gradual re-authoritarianization, but base this policy on relatively widespread support within society, including in elections and referendums (intrinsic), and whose international cooperation and internal political stability is of great interest, at least when it comes to Russia (extrinsic).

The combination of two donor states and six recipient countries yields 12 cases that are studied in individual case studies and by way of a comparative analysis. The topic of this study – democracy promotion – is defined in broad terms. All measures by external actors that aim at establishing, strengthening or defending democracy in a country are regarded as part of democracy promotion (Azpuru *et al.* 2008: 151; see Schmitter and Brouwer 1999: 9). The range of instruments thus extends from development cooperation ('democracy assistance') through political conditions and sanctions, all the way to military force (Schraeder 2003: 26). Generally, democracy promotion concerns the entire range of foreign and development policy, including international economic and security policies. Systematically, we distinguish between five dimensions of democracy promotion that represent the different kinds of instruments available: international observation, foreign aid, diplomacy, international cooperation, and military intervention. For each individual dimension the extent to which and the form in which the measures adopted are aimed at democracy promotion will be examined (Table 1.1).[46]

The diversity of instruments of democracy promotion leads to a no less broad range of actors (see Burnell 2000; Schraeder 2002). Even democracy promotion by states, which is the focus here, still includes a variety of players. This first concerns the different government units that primarily shape external relations: the foreign and defence ministries, the White House or the Chancellor's Office, as well as the US Agency for International Development (USAID) or the German Federal Ministry for Economic Cooperation and Development (Bundesministerium für wirtschaftliche Zusammenarbeit und Entwicklung, BMZ). In the case of Germany, the quasi-state agencies charged with implementing official development cooperation are also included. In the area of democracy promotion, the German Agency for Technical Cooperation (Deutsche Gesellschaft für Technische Zusammenarbeit, GTZ) is of particular interest; further agencies include the German Development Service (Deutscher Entwicklungsdienst, DED) and the KfW Development Bank.[47] Finally, there are parastatal organizations that, in both donor countries, have traditionally played an important role in democracy promotion. In Germany, these are the political foundations: Konrad-Adenauer-Stiftung (KAS), Friedrich-Ebert-Stiftung (FES), Hanns-Seidel-Stiftung (HSS), Friedrich-Naumann-Stiftung (FNS), Heinrich-Böll-Stiftung

Table 1.1 Dimensions of democracy promotion: the research heuristic

Dimension	Logic of influence/ mechanism	Research question	Sub-dimensions
International observation	Transparency	To what extent and in what way do external actors observe democratic processes?	Observation of elections
			Observation of other kinds of political processes (e.g. of negotiations in political crises)
Foreign aid	Aid (technical and financial)	To what extent and in what way does foreign/ development aid focus explicitly on democracy promotion?	Political institutions*
			Political actors (political parties, political segments of civil society)*
Diplomacy	Appeal (normative)	To what extent and in what way do public statements, political dialogue and bilateral documents focus explicitly on democracy promotion?	Unilateral public statements on democracy*
			Democracy-related topics in political dialogue*
			Democracy-related statements in bilateral agreements and treaties
International cooperation	Incentives (material)	To what extent is international cooperation linked to political conditions or restricted by political sanctions (democracy-related positive or negative incentives)?	Placing conditions on political cooperation
			Placing conditions on military cooperation
			Placing conditions on economic cooperation
			Placing conditions on development cooperation
Military intervention	Coercion (physical)	To what extent is the use of physical force (or the threat of its use) aimed at promoting democracy?	Pro-democratic paramilitary use of force
			Pro-democratic military intervention

Note
In the sub-dimensions marked with *, in addition to the basic orientation to democracy promotion, it has also to be specified whether democracy-related measures take place (*a*) in cooperation with or in support of the government; (*b*) neutrally, i.e. supporting neither the government nor the opposition (or both); or (*c*) without the agreement of the government and/or in a form directed against the government.

(HBS), and Rosa-Luxemburg-Stiftung (RLS).[48] In the case of the United States, the National Endowment for Democracy (NED) and its four core grantees are of interest: the National Democratic Institute (NDI) and the International Republican Institute (IRI), the Center for International Private Enterprise (CIPE) and the American Center for International Labor Solidarity (Solidarity Center).[49]

Overview of the volume

The present book consists of three parts. Beginning with a comparative overview, it continues with detailed case studies and then returns to the comparative perspective.

In Part I, this introductory chapter is followed by two chapters that operationalize and measure the determinants outlined above. In Chapter 2, Annika E. Poppe, Bentje Woitschach and Jonas Wolff examine whether it is plausible to assume that US and German democracy promotion are characterized by differing understandings of democratization and democracy promotion. They present a typology that distinguishes between two ideal-type conceptions of democracy promotion: the Civilian Power and the Freedom Fighter. On the basis of a qualitative content analysis of official government sources, they argue that German and US rhetoric on democracy promotion roughly matches these two types. In Chapter 3, Daniel Schewe and Jonas Wolff present a quantitative assessment of the six determinants, including the one involving 'political culture' qualitatively analysed in Chapter 2. The values measured for each of the individual factors are converted into ordinal scales. The result is a comparative overview of the configurations of determinants for the 12 pairs of states.

The case studies presented in Part II form the heart of the book. In six chapters, these case studies examine German and US democracy promotion in relation to a particular recipient country. Jonas Wolff analyses the policies towards Bolivia (Chapter 4) and Ecuador (Chapter 5) and Cemal Karakaş does the same regarding policies vis-à-vis Turkey (Chapter 6). Niels Graf and Iris Wurm study democracy promotion in Pakistan (Chapter 7). In Chapters 8 and 9, Azar Babayev looks at Belarus and Hans-Joachim Spanger analyses the case of Russia.

All case study chapters start by outlining the conflict situation in the recipient country and summarize the conflicting objectives that emerge for the donors. The following sections on Germany and the United States each begin with brief profiles of bilateral relations in general, and democracy promotion in particular. The way democracy promoters deal with the conflict situation and conflicting objectives is examined in two further steps: in perception analyses, the authors work out how donors perceive and evaluate political developments in the recipient country; reaction analyses investigate how democracy promotion policies evolve over time and respond to conflicting objectives. At the level of these individual case studies, process-tracing (George and Bennett 2005: chapter 10) is applied in order to give preliminary answers to the explanatory question: to what extent and in which specific configuration do the determinants explain continuity and change in democracy promotion?

Finally, Part III presents the overall findings of the study. In Chapter 10, Jonas Wolff integrates the results of the 12 case studies into a structured and focused comparison (George and Bennett 2005: chapter 3). Corresponding with the two research questions outlined above, the primary aim of the concluding chapter is to systematically describe and explain the empirical patterns of democracy promotion across our cases. This also includes more general conclusions as to the interrelation of interests and norms in democracy promotion. In addition, the rich empirical evidence offered by the case studies will be used to discuss implications of our study for political practice.

The primary aim of this book is certainly academic. Yet, in-depth knowledge about the motives and factors driving democracy promotion, about the ways in which democracy promoters deal with conflicting objectives, and about the inherent contradictions with which democracy promotion is confronted 'on the ground', is also crucial for improving, if not rethinking democracy promotion.

Notes

1 We thank Niels Graf for assistance in preparing the original German version of this chapter.
2 See Carothers (2010); Desch (2007); Goldsmith (2008); Hassan and Ralph (2011); Ish-Shalom (2006); Monten (2005); Smith (2007); Whitehead (2009).
3 For obvious reasons, research on US democracy promotion emerged relatively early and continues to grow (see most recently Callaway and Matthews 2008; Collins 2009; Hill 2010; Monten 2005; Shaw 2007; Smith 2007; Whitaker 2007). In the meantime, there are quite a number of case studies on various 'donors' and 'recipients' (see most recently Arceneaux and Pion-Berlin 2007; Bicchi 2009; Börzel *et al.* 2008; Carothers 2009; Cooper and Legler 2006; Grävingholt 2007; Grimm 2010; Hawkins 2008; Kapstein and Converse 2008; Kneuer 2007; Legler *et al.* 2007; Mitchell 2009; Newman and Rich 2004; Pospisil 2009; Reiber 2009; Richter 2009; Schimmelfennig *et al.* 2006; Schlumberger 2008; Warkotsch 2009; Youngs 2004). There are also quantitative large-N studies, especially on the impact of democracy promotion (see Finkel *et al.* 2007; Knack 2004; Scott and Steele 2005); edited volumes that look at various 'donors', 'recipients' and topics (see most recently Barany and Moser 2009; Burnell and Youngs 2010; Erdmann and Kneuer 2009; Grimm and Merkel 2008; Hobson and Kurki 2012; Jünemann and Knodt 2007; Kapstein and Converse 2009; Magen *et al.* 2009; Magen and Morlino 2009; Stewart 2009; Youngs 2006); analyses of the ideas and ideologies that underpin democracy promotion (see Crosston 2009; Desch 2007; Guilhot 2005; Hobson 2008; Ish-Shalom 2006; Smith 2007); as well as countless works centred on practical matters or political aspects of this research topic.
4 See Maoz and Russett (1993); Müller and Wolff (2006); Risse-Kappen (1995); and Russett and Oneal (2001).
5 See Cox *et al.* (2000); Ish-Shalom (2006); Smith (2007); Spanger and Wolff (2007a, 2007b). This practical turn of the democratic peace is not an innovation of the US administration under George W. Bush (Bush 2006) but already appears in Clinton's democratic enlargement strategy (Talbott 1996) as well as in places outside the United States (see Burnell 2000: 45–7; Schraeder 2003: 31).
6 In political reality, the three dilemmas, as described below, will normally result in conflicting objectives of both types.
7 Interestingly, the simplistic assumptions of the transition paradigm as criticized by Carothers are found in the political programmes of, and in the academic research on, external democracy promotion more often than in the general literature on regime change and democratization. The latter, from the outset, has also emphasized the uncertainties and hazards of these processes (see O'Donnell and Schmitter 1986; Merkel and Puhle 1999; Merkel *et al.* 2003). For a critical discussion of the problematic role of transition studies in the discourse on and practice of democracy promotion, see Guilhot (2005: chapter 3) and Smith (2007: chapter 5).

Introduction 25

8 See Burnell (2000); Carothers (2009); Gerrits (2007); Hazelzet (2007); Kopstein (2006); Nau (2000); Schraeder (2002); Smith (1994); Youngs (2004, 2006).
9 See Erdmann and Kneuer (2009); Kneuer (2007); Levitsky and Way (2005); Pridham (1991); Schmitz and Sell (1999); Whitehead (1996).
10 See Cowles et al. (2001); Freyburg et al. (2009); Schimmelfennig et al. (2006); Schimmelfennig and Sedelmeier (2005).
11 A recently published edited volume on US and European strategies of democracy promotion (Magen et al. 2009) is also based on an analytical framework that refers to the 'logics', 'targets' and 'pathways' of influence (Magen and McFaul 2009: 11–16). Several other studies that compare US and European (and here in particular EU) democracy promotion policies share this focus (see Carothers 2009; Durac and Cavatorta 2009; Hawkins 2008; Huber 2008).
12 See Carothers (1999); Magen et al. (2009); Schraeder (2003); Smith (1994); Youngs (2006, 2004). Two exceptions, which combine a theoretical framework and an explanatory interest, are earlier studies by Mark Peceny (1999) and William Robinson (1996). Both, however, focus entirely on the United States – Peceny with a view to democracy promotion in the context of US military interventions, Robinson from a neo-Gramscian perspective.
13 See Schraeder (2002); Burnell (2000); Hanisch (1996); Youngs (2004: chapter 2).
14 See Carothers (2009); Kopstein (2006); Youngs (2004: 31–7). However, a recent edited volume found evidence for a certain convergence between US and EU democracy promotion (Magen et al. 2009).
15 For example, Rüland and Werz (2002: 74) emphasize that in the German 'policymaking establishment' economic growth is seen as a precondition for the emergence of liberal-democratic regimes in the Third World.
16 These differences, on the one hand, are attributed to specific interests, in the case of Germany to the predominance of economic interests (Rüland and Werz 2002: 73–4; Betz 1996: 207–8). On the other, scholars highlight that the forms, experiences and perceptions of democracy and democratization also differ between the United States and Europe/Germany (Nau 2000: 147–8; see Carothers 1991: 258; Ralph 2000: 200).
17 Some critical scholars emphasize economic interests as the driving force behind US democracy promotion (Smith 2000: 78; Gills 2000). Others argue that the US interest in upholding global hegemony implies that security and economic interests generally complement each other (see Robinson 1996; Cavell 2002).
18 See Hanisch (1996: 29, 39); Schraeder (2003: 33, 41); Youngs (2004: 184). For the United States, see Carothers (1999: 16); Hook (2002: 109); Lowenthal (1991: 277); Whitehead (1991: 236); for Germany, see Betz (1996: 207–8); Mair (2000: 132); Rüland and Werz (2002).
19 Carothers (1999: 16) calls this pattern – with a view to the practice of US democracy promotion – a 'semi-realist approach to democracy promotion' (Carothers 1999: 16). This, however, does not solve (and does not attempt to solve) the theoretical problem at hand.
20 The same problems apply to critical studies that identify (neoliberal) market democracy as a key trait of the new hegemonic world order (see Gills et al. 1993; Robinson 1996; Gills 2000). While emphasizing the ideational dimension of hegemony, they nevertheless tend to reduce democracy promotion to an instrument that is deliberately manipulable and deployable by those forces exercising global hegemony (see Guilhot 2005: 15–18; Geis and Wolff 2007).
21 Whenever we refer, in this book, to 'explaining' and/or 'understanding', we do not refer to the traditional distinction between positivist causal explanation and allegedly non-causal, hermeneutic interpretation. Instead, we follow the argument that causal analysis, in the end, always aims at both explaining and understanding a given empirical phenomenon (cf. Kurki 2008).

22 The distinction between rationalist and reflective perspectives on international relations is taken from Keohane (1988). For overviews of the diverse theories of democratic peace, see Müller and Wolff (2006) and Risse-Kappen (1995). In the following sections, we will focus on utilitarian and normative explanations of the democratic peace. The institutionalist perspective will be taken up later in this chapter. The following sections draw on Wolff and Wurm (2011).

23 The same logic applies for the rationalist explanation of dyadic democratic peace offered by Bueno de Mesquita et al. (1999). Here, democracies do also initiate war, but only because of the irrational decisions taken by non-democratic governments.

24 In a rationalist model, however, the utilitarian citizen weighs the immediate costs and benefits when casting votes, and democratic governments focus only on getting re-elected (see Bueno de Mesquita et al. 1999).

25 Research shows that countries that get stuck in the grey zone between autocracy and democracy scarcely have any prospects of a dividend in terms of peace or welfare (see Goldsmith 2008; Hegre et al. 2001; Spanger 2012; Spanger and Wolff 2007b).

26 Here the bilateral distribution of power in the donor–recipient relationship is of interest, unlike neo-realist foreign policy theory, which also emphasizes relative power but derives its statements about the foreign policy of states from their overall position in the international system.

27 In theoretical terms, this corresponds to the view of neo-classic realism which, unlike common (structuralist) neo-realism, takes the significance of perceptions and ideas seriously (Harnisch 2003: 323; see Rose 1998: 157–8).

28 The categories of economic and republican liberalism (see below) largely correspond to the distinction between commercial and republican liberalism outlined by Moravcsik (1997). Ideational liberalism, his third variant of liberal theory, is discussed in the section on reflective perspectives (subsumed by actor-centred constructivism), because the emphasis on a 'configuration of domestic social identities and values as a basic determinant of state preferences' (Moravcsik 1997: 525) goes beyond a rationalist perspective.

29 In this context, it does not matter whether economic interests are understood in terms of maximizing national welfare or in terms of individual profit seeking within capitalist societies. In this broad sense, traditional Marxist approaches and international political economy in general (see Frieden and Martin 2002) all share such an economic conception of foreign policy (Moravcsik 1997: 522, note 23).

30 Because either utilitarian or normative considerations can motivate intra-societal groups, republican liberalism is a hybrid approach that combines rationalist and reflective assumptions (Wolff and Wurm 2011: 85).

31 To the extent that the influence of domestic special interests depends on their public resonance in the general population, this determinant also includes the role of public opinion. We chose not to include an independent determinant 'public opinion' because, in the field of democracy promotion, it most plausibly has merely an indirect effect (which, in a similar manner, comes into play again via the determinant of 'political culture'). The reason is that the general interest of the population in democracy promotion – compared to, for example, military intervention – can be deemed rather low (on the United States, see Holsti 2000).

32 Unlike rationalist perspectives, reflective approaches generally emphasize that actor preferences are socially constructed and encompass not only material interests but also ideas, norms and values. The focus of the present study is on specific democratic norms and their relevance for the foreign policy of democratic states.

33 In this tradition, US attempts to shape the world according to its own image have to be limited to the force of its example. By contrast, an 'activist foreign policy may even corrupt liberal practices at home, undermining the potency of the US model' (Monten 2005: 113; see Brands 1998).

34 This is what Jahn (2005: 202–4) calls the 'specifically liberal security dilemma'.

35 This argument draws on work that has shown liberal norms to be ambivalent: they can justify both interventionism and a foreign policy of restraint. In this sense, Müller (2004) distinguishes between 'pacifist' and 'militant' democratic cultures; Sørensen (2006) discusses a 'liberalism of restraint' and a 'liberalism of imposition'; and Monten (2005) contrasts 'exemplarism' with 'vindicationism'.
36 See in greater detail the discussion and references in Chapter 2 of this volume.
37 To be sure, such international norms do not determine actions, but provide a normative framework only (Finnemore 1996: 158).
38 In terms of meta-theory, analytic eclecticism is agnostic about the epistemological trench warfare of competing paradigms (Sil 2000).
39 To a certain extent, this emphasis on actor pluralism and institutional complexity, which characterize democratic foreign policy, links up with the first generation of institutionalist approaches to democratic peace. The latter also underscored the cumbersome nature and the complexity of democratic institutions and procedures (see, for example, Maoz and Russett 1993). More recent institutionalist theories, however, explain the democratic peace mostly through democracy-specific processing of information, signalling, and audience costs (see the overview in Müller and Wolff 2006: 49–58).
40 In this context, Burnell (2000: 34) has cautioned that the quantity and diversity of organizations and approaches may make it difficult to identify 'the real agenda behind international democracy promotion' or to develop a 'valid and comprehensive general theory' of democracy promotion.
41 The focus on states as democracy promoters results from the theoretical and explanatory aim that guides this study. In linking up with democratic peace and related IR theories, we are interested in the foreign policy determinants of democratic states. It is highly unlikely that a unified theoretical framework can plausibly be applied to identify the determinants of state, multilateral and non-state democracy promotion in one structured and focused comparative design. State actors, international organizations (as well as the EU as a partially supranational entity *sui generis*) and NGOs are just too different for such an endeavour to hold promise.
42 See Börzel *et al.* (2008); Börzel and Risse (2009); Freyburg *et al.* (2009); Jünemann and Knodt (2007); Kneuer (2007); Magen and Morlino (2009); Schimmelfennig *et al.* (2006); Warkotsch (2009). Other regional organizations, especially the OAS, are also the subject of democracy promotion research (see Arceneaux and Pion-Berlin 2007; Cooper and Legler 2006; Hawkins and Shaw 2007; Richter 2009).
43 See Carothers (2009); Kopstein (2006); Magen *et al.* (2009); Youngs (2004).
44 The precise criterion for case selection was that a country, since 1990, had at least temporarily reached a minimum of seven points on the polity IV scale (see Marshall and Jaggers 2006).
45 For instance, the 2010 Bertelsmann Transformation Index still classified Russia as a highly defective democracy, whereas Belarus was termed a moderate autocracy (Bertelsmann 2009: 146).
46 This framework draws on Magen and McFaul (2009: 11–14). Their analytical framework also includes democracy promotion dimensions that go beyond democracy assistance ('control' and 'material incentives'), and they also distinguish between normative appeals ('normative suasion') and foreign aid ('capacity-building').
47 In January 2011, GTZ and DED as well as InWEnt were merged into the Deutsche Gesellschaft für Internationale Zusammenarbeit (GIZ) or German Agency for International Cooperation. As this merger occurred after the period being investigated in this study, this book still refers to GTZ and DED.
48 Germany's political foundations are among the longest-standing actors in the area of democracy assistance (Burnell 2000: 36; see Mair 2000; Pinto-Duschinsky 1991). Each of them is affiliated with a political party represented in the German Bundestag. Their international work is financed through federal grants, with the share of the

overall budget allocated to each foundation proportional to its party representation in the Bundestag. However, all development cooperation funds allocated by BMZ must be additionally applied for in the form of individual programmes and projects with the BMZ, and must be accepted by the Foreign Office (Mair 2000: 130). Despite their formal independence and relative autonomy vis-à-vis the respective ruling government, foundations are officially considered instruments of German foreign and development policy.

49 The NED was founded in 1983 as a publicly funded but private endowment. It is formally independent of the government, but its budget is determined each year by the US Congress. Republican and Democratic party representatives are on its board of directors, as well as representatives of the US Chamber of Commerce and US labour unions. These four institutions are also the primary recipients of NED grants – through the four institutes mentioned, which were designed roughly along the model of the German party foundations. The NED itself does not implement democracy assistance activities but instead awards grants – to the four core grantees, but also to civil society organizations in recipient countries (see Burnell 2000: 37; Pinto-Duschinsky 1991: 47–8). Critical scholars consider the NED and its subsidiary institutes direct instruments of the US government (see Robinson 1996: 71–116). Carothers, by contrast, emphasizes that US Congress – through its annual budget decisions – has a far more direct influence, whereas he sees the approval of NED projects by the State Department more as a formal act (Carothers 1991: 232–3).

References

Arceneaux, C. and Pion-Berlin, D. (2007) 'Issues, Threats, and Institutions: Explaining OAS Responses to Democratic Dilemmas in Latin America', *Latin American Politics and Society*, 49 (2): 1–31.

Azpuru, D., Finkel, S.E., Pérez-Liñán, A. and Seligson, M.A. (2008) 'Trends in Democracy Assistance: What Has The United States Been Doing?', *Journal of Democracy*, 19 (2): 150–9.

Barany, Z. and Moser, R.G. (eds) (2009) *Is Democracy Exportable?*, Cambridge: Cambridge University Press.

Bertelsmann Stiftung (ed.) (2009) *Transformation Index 2010. Politische Gestaltung im internationalen Vergleich*, Gütersloh: Bertelsmann Stiftung.

Betz, J. (1996) 'Die Demokratieexportpolitik der Bundesrepublik Deutschland', in R. Hanisch (ed.) *Demokratieexport in die Länder des Südens?*, Hamburg: Deutsches Übersee-Institut.

Bicchi, F. (2009) 'Democracy Assistance in the Mediterranean. An Overview', *Mediterranean Politics*, 14 (1): 61–78.

BMZ (2005) *Förderung von Demokratie in der deutschen Entwicklungspolitik. Unterstützung politischer Reformprozesse und Beteiligung der Bevölkerung. Ein Positionspapier des BMZ*, Bonn: BMZ.

Boekle, H., Rittberger, V. and Wagner, W. (2001) 'Constructivist Foreign Policy Theory', in V. Rittberger (ed.) *German Foreign Policy since Unification: Theories and Case Studies*, Manchester: Manchester University Press.

Börzel, T.A. and Risse, T. (2009) 'Venus Approaching Mars? The European Union's Approaches to Democracy Promotion in Comparative Perspective', in A. Magen, T. Risse and M.A. McFaul. (eds) *Promoting Democracy and the Rule of Law: American and European Strategies*, Houndmills: Palgrave Macmillan.

Börzel, T.A., Pamuk, Y. and Stahn, A. (2008) 'The European Union and the Promotion of Good Governance in its Near Abroad. One Size Fits All?', *SFB-Governance Working Paper 18*, Berlin: SFB 700.

Brands, H.W. (1998) *What America Owes the World: The Struggle for the Soul of Foreign Policy*, Cambridge: Cambridge University Press.

Buchstein, H. and Jörke, D. (2003) 'Das Unbehagen an der Demokratietheorie', *Leviathan*, 31 (4): 470–95.

Bueno de Mesquita, B. and Downs, B.W. (2006) 'Intervention and Democracy', *International Organization*, 60 (3): 627–49.

Bueno de Mesquita, B., Morrow, J.D., Siverson, R.M. and Smith, A. (1999) 'An Institutional Explanation of the Democratic Peace', *American Political Science Review*, 93 (4): 791–807.

Burnell, P. (2000) 'Democracy Assistance: Origins and Organization', in P. Burnell (ed.) *Democracy Assistance: International Co-operation for Democratization*, London: Frank Cass.

Burnell, P. and Youngs, R. (eds) (2010) *New Challenges to Democratization*, London: Routledge.

Bush, G.W. (2006) *President Discusses Freedom and Democracy in Iraq*, George Washington University, 13 March. Online, available at: http://georgewbush-whitehouse.archives.gov (accessed 2 March 2010).

Callaway, R.L. and Matthews, E.G. (2008) *Strategic US Foreign Assistance: The Battle between Human Rights and National Security*, Hampshire: Ashgate.

Carothers, T. (1991) *In the Name of Democracy: US Policy toward Latin America in the Reagan Years*, Berkeley, CA: University of California Press.

Carothers, T. (1999) *Aiding Democracy Abroad: The Learning Curve*, Washington, DC: Carnegie Endowment for International Peace.

Carothers, T. (2000) 'Taking Stock of US Democracy Assistance', in M. Cox, G.J. Ikenberry and T. Inoguchi (eds) *American Democracy Promotion: Impulses, Strategies, and Impacts*, Oxford: Oxford University Press.

Carothers, T. (2002) 'The End of the Transition Paradigm , *Journal of Democracy*, 13 (1): 5–21.

Carothers, T. (2004) *Critical Mission: Essays on Democracy Promotion*, Washington, DC: Carnegie Endowment for International Peace.

Carothers, T. (2009) 'Democracy Assistance: Political vs. Developmental?', *Journal of Democracy*, 20 (1): 5–19.

Carothers, T. (2010) 'The Continuing Backlash against Democracy Promotion', in P. Burnell and R. Youngs (eds) *New Challenges to Democratization*, London: Routledge.

Cavell, C.S. (2002) *Exporting 'Made-in-America' Democracy: The National Endowment for Democracy and US Foreign Policy*, Lanham, MD: University Press of America.

Collins, S.D. (2009) 'Can America Finance Freedom? Assessing US Democracy Promotion via Economic Statecraft', *Foreign Policy Analysis*, 5 (4): 367–89.

Cooper, A.F. and Legler, T. (2006) *Intervention without Intervening? The OAS Defense and Promotion of Democracy in the Americas*, New York, NY: Palgrave Macmillan.

Cowles, M.G., Caporaso, J. and Risse, T. (eds) (2001) *Transforming Europe: Europeanization and Domestic Change*, Ithaca, NY: Cornell University Press.

Cox, M., Ikenberry, G.J. and Inoguchi, T. (eds) (2000) *American Democracy Promotion: Impulses, Strategies, and Impacts*, Oxford: Oxford University Press.

Crosston, M. (2009) 'Neoconservative Democratization in Theory and Practice: Developing Democrats or Raising Radical Islamists?', *International Politics*, 46 (2/3): 298–326.

Crozier, M.J., Huntington, S.P. and Watanuki, J. (1975) *The Crisis of Democracy: Report on the Governability of Democracies to the Trilateral Commission*, New York, NY: New York University Press.

Czempiel, E.-O. (1996) 'Kants Theorem', *Zeitschrift für Internationale Beziehungen*, 3 (1): 79–101.

Dahl, R.A. (1998) *On Democracy*, New Haven, CT: Yale University Press.

Desch, M.C. (2007) 'America's Liberal Illiberalism. The Ideological Origins of Overreaction in US Foreign Policy', *International Security*, 32 (3): 7–43.

Diamond, L. (1990) 'Three Paradoxes of Democracy', *Journal of Democracy*, 1 (3): 48–60.

Doyle, M.W. (1983) 'Kant, Liberal Legacies, and Foreign Affairs', *Philosophy and Public Affairs*, 12 (3): 205–35.

Doyle, M.W. (2000) 'Peace, Liberty, and Democracy: Realists and Liberals Contest a Legacy', in M. Cox, G.J. Ikenberry and T. Inoguchi (eds) *American Democracy Promotion: Impulses, Strategies, and Impacts*, Oxford: Oxford University Press.

Doyle, M.W. (2008) 'Liberalism and Foreign Policy', in S. Smith, A. Hadfield and T. Dunne (eds) *Foreign Policy: Theories–Actors–Cases*, Oxford: Oxford University Press.

Doyle, M.W. (2009) 'A Few Words on Mill, Walzer, and Nonintervention', *Ethics and International Affairs*, 23 (4): 349–69.

Durac, V. and Cavatorta, F. (2009) 'Strengthening Authoritarian Rule through Democracy Promotion? Examining the Paradox of the US and EU Security Strategies: the Case of Bin Ali's Tunisia', *British Journal of Middle Eastern Studies*, 36 (1): 3–19.

Erdmann, G. and Kneuer, M. (eds) (2009) *Externe Faktoren der Demokratisierung*, Baden-Baden: Nomos.

Finkel, S., Pérez-Liñán, A. and Seligson, M.A. (2007) 'The Effects of US Foreign Assistance on Democracy Building, 1990–2003', *World Politics*, 59 (3): 404–39.

Finnemore, M. (1996) 'Constructing Norms of Humanitarian Intervention', in P.J. Katzenstein (ed.) *The Culture of National Security: Norms and Identity in World Politics*, New York, NY: Columbia University Press.

Fox, G.H. and Roth, B.R. (eds) (2000) *Democratic Governance and International Law*, Cambridge: Cambridge University Press.

Freedom House (2006) *Freedom in the World* (Webpage). Online, available at: www.freedomhouse.org (accessed 28 August 2006).

Freyburg, T., Lavenex, S., Schimmelfennig, F., Skripka, T. and Wetzel, A. (2009) 'EU Promotion of Democratic Governance in the Neighbourhood', *Journal of European Public Policy*, 16 (6): 916–34.

Frieden, J. and Martin, L.L. (2002) 'International Political Economy: Global and Domestic Interactions', in I. Katznelson and H.V. Milner (eds) *Political Science: The State of the Discipline*, New York, NY: W.W. Norton.

Geis, A. and Wolff, J. (2007) 'Demokratischer Frieden, Demokratischer Krieg und das Projekt globaler Demokratisierung. Hegemonietheoretische Überlegungen aus neogramscianischer Perspektive', in S. Buckel, and A. Fischer-Lescano (eds) *Hegemonie gepanzert mit Zwang. Zivilgesellschaft und Politik im Staatsverständnis Antonio Gramscis*, Baden-Baden: Nomos.

Geis, A., Brock, L. and Müller, H. (eds) (2006) *Democratic Wars: Looking at the Dark Side of Democratic Peace*, Houndmills: Palgrave Macmillan.

George, A.L. and Bennett, A. (2005) *Case Studies and Theory Development in the Social Sciences*, Cambridge, MA: MIT Press.

Gerrits, A. (2007) 'Is there a Distinct European Democratic Model to Promote?', in: M. van Doorn and R. von Meijenfeldt (eds) *Democracy: Europe's Core Value? On the European Profile in World-wide Democracy Assistance* Delft: Eburon.

Gills, B. (2000) 'American Power, Neo-liberal Economic Globalization, and Low-Intensity Democracy: An Unstable Trinity', in M. Cox, G.J. Ikenberry and T. Inoguchi (eds) *American Democracy Promotion: Impulses, Strategies, and Impacts*, Oxford: Oxford University Press.

Gills, B., Rocamora, J. and Wilson, R. (eds) (1993) *Low Intensity Democracy: Political Power in the New World Order*, London: Pluto Press.

Goldsmith, A.A. (2008) 'Making the World Safe for Partial Democracy? Questioning the Premises of Democracy Promotion', *International Security*, 33 (2): 120–47.

Grävingholt, J. (2007) 'Ohne Gewähr. Demokratieförderung in Zentralasien', *Osteuropa*, 57 (8/9): 401–16.

Grimm, S. (2010) *Erzwungene Demokratie. Politische Neuordnung nach militärischer Intervention unter externer Aufsicht*, Baden-Baden: Nomos.

Grimm, S. and Merkel, W. (eds) (2008) *War and Democratization: Legality, Legitimacy and Effectiveness*, London: Routledge (Democratization Special Issue).

Guilhot, N. (2005) *The Democracy Makers: Human Rights and International Order*, New York, NY: Columbia University Press.

Haggard, S. and Kaufman, R.R. (1995) *The Political Economy of Democratic Transitions*, Princeton, NJ: Princeton University Press.

Hanisch, R. (1996) 'Internationale Demokratieförderung: Gründe, Motive, Instrumente, Möglichkeiten und Grenzen', in R. Hanisch (ed.) *Demokratieexport in die Länder des Südens?*, Hamburg: Deutsches Übersee-Institut.

Harnisch, S. (2003) 'Theorieorientierte Außenpolitikforschung in einer Ära des Wandels', in G. Hellmann, K.D. Wolf and M. Zürn (eds): *Die neuen Internationalen Beziehungen. Forschungsstand und Perspektiven in Deutschland*. Baden-Baden: Nomos.

Hassan, O. and Ralph, J. (2011) 'Democracy Promotion and Human Rights in US Foreign Policy', *International Journal of Human Rights* 15 (4): 509–19.

Hawkins, D. (2008) 'Protecting Democracy in Europe and the Americas', *International Organization*, 62 (3): 373–403.

Hawkins, D. and Shaw, C.M. (2007) 'The OAS and Legalizing Norms of Democracy', in T. Legler, S.F. Lean and D.S. Boniface (eds) (2007) *Promoting Democracy in the Americas*, Baltimore, MD: The Johns Hopkins University Press.

Hazelzet, H. (2007) 'Carrots or Sticks? EU Reactions to Human Rights Violations in the Nineties and Beyond', in M. van Doorn and R. von Meijenfeldt (eds) *Democracy: Europe's Core Value? On the European Profile in World-wide Democracy Assistance*, Delft: Eburon.

Hegre, H., Ellingsen, T., Gates, S. and Gleditsch, N.P. (2001) 'Toward a Democratic Civil Peace? Democracy, Political Change, and Civil War, 1816–1992', *American Political Science Review*, 95 (1): 33–48.

Herman, R.G. and Piccone, T.J. (eds) (2003) *Defending Democracy. A Global Survey of Foreign Policy Trends 1992–2002*. Online, available at: www.demcoalition.org (accessed 22 September 2006).

Hermann M.G. and Kegley, C.W. (1995) 'Rethinking Democracy and International Peace: Perspectives from Political Psychology', *International Studies Quarterly*, 39 (4): 511–33.

Hill, M.A. (2010) 'Exploring USAID's Democracy Promotion in Bosnia and Afghanistan: a "Cookie-cutter Approach"?', *Democratization*, 17 (1): 98–124.

Hobson, C. (2008) 'Democracy as Civilisation', *Global Society*, 22 (1): 75–95.
Hobson, C. and Kurki, M. (eds) (2012) *The Conceptual Politics of Democracy Promotion*, London: Routledge.
Holsti, O.R. (2000) 'Promotion of Democracy as Popular Demand?', in M. Cox, G.J. Ikenberry and T. Inoguchi, T. (eds) *American Democracy Promotion: Impulses, Strategies, and Impacts*, Oxford: Oxford University Press.
Hook, S.W. (2002) 'Inconsistent US Efforts to Promote Democracy Abroad', in P.J. Schraeder (ed.) *Exporting Democracy: Rhetoric vs. Reality*, Boulder, CO: Lynne Rienner.
Huber, D. (2008) 'Democracy Assistance in the Middle East and North Africa. A Comparison of US and EU Policies', *Mediterranean Politics*, 13 (1): 43–62.
Huntington, S.P. (1970) *Political Order in Changing Societies*, New Haven, CT: Yale University Press.
Huntington, S.P. (1991) *The Third Wave: Democratization in the Late 20th Century*, Norman, OK: University of Oklahoma Press.
Hurrell, A. (2007) *On Global Order: Power, Values, and the Constitution of International Society*, Oxford: Oxford University Press.
Ikenberry, G.J. (1999) 'Why Export Democracy? The "Hidden Grand Strategy" of American Foreign Policy', *Wilson Quarterly*, 23 (2): 56–65.
Ish-Shalom, P. (2006) 'Theory as a Hermeneutical Mechanism: The Democratic-Peace Thesis and the Politics of Democratization', *European Journal of International Relations*, 12 (4): 565–98.
Jahn, B. (2005) 'Kant, Mill, and Illiberal Legacies in International Affairs', *International Organization*, 59 (1): 177–207.
Jepperson, R.L., Wendt, A. and Katzenstein, P.J. (1996) 'Norms, Identity, and Culture in National Security', in P.J. Katzenstein (ed.) *The Culture of National Security: Norms and Identity in World Politics*, New York, NY: Columbia University Press.
Jünemann, A. and Knodt, M. (eds) (2007) *Externe Demokratieförderung durch die Europäische Union*, Baden-Baden. Nomos.
Kahl, C.H. (1999) 'Constructing a Separate Peace: Constructivism, Collective Liberal Identity, and Democratic Peace', *Security Studies*, 8 (2/3): 94–144.
Kapstein, E.B. and Converse, N. (2008) *The Fate of Young Democracies*, Cambridge: Cambridge University Press.
Katzenstein, P.J. (ed.) (1996) *The Culture of National Security: Norms and Identity in World Politics*, New York, NY: Columbia University Press.
Keohane, R.O. (1988) 'International Institutions: Two Approaches', *International Studies Quarterly*, 32 (4): 379–96.
Knack, S. (2004) 'Does Foreign Aid Promote Democracy?, *International Studies Quarterly*, 48 (1): 251–66.
Kneuer, M. (2007) *Demokratisierung durch die EU. Süd- und Ostmitteleuropa im Vergleich*, Wiesbaden: VS Verlag für Sozialwissenschaften.
Kopstein, J. (2006) 'The Transatlantic Divide over Democracy Promotion', *Washington Quarterly*, 29 (2): 85–98.
Kurki, M. (2008) *Causation in International Relations. Reclaiming Causal Analysis*, Cambridge: Cambridge University Press.
Legler, T., Lean, S.F. and Boniface, D.S. (eds) (2007) *Promoting Democracy in the Americas*, Baltimore, MD: The Johns Hopkins University Press.
Leininger, J., Grimm, S. and Freyburg, T. (eds) (2012) *Do all Good Things Go Together? Conflicting Objectives in Democracy Promotion*, London: Routledge (Democratization Special Issue).

Levitsky, S. and Way, L.A. (2005) 'International Linkage and Democratization', *Journal of Democracy*, 16 (3): 20–34.
Lowenthal, A.F. (1991) 'The United States and Latin American Democracy: Learning from History', in A.F. Lowenthal (ed.) *Exporting Democracy: The United States and Latin America. Case Studies*, Baltimore, MD: The Johns Hopkins University Press.
Lutz, E.L. and Sikkink, K. (2000) 'International Human Rights Law and Practice in Latin America', *International Organization*, 54 (3): 633–59.
McFaul, M. (2005) 'Democracy Promotion as a World Value', *Washington Quarterly*, 28 (1): 147–63.
Magen, A. and McFaul, M.A. (2009) 'Introduction: American and European Strategies to Promote Democracy – Shared Values, Common Challenges, Divergent Tools?', in A. Magen, T. Risse and M.A. McFaul (eds) *Promoting Democracy and the Rule of Law: American and European Strategies*, Houndmills: Palgrave Macmillan.
Magen, A. and Morlino, L. (eds) (2009) *International Actors, Democratization and the Rule of Law: Anchoring Democracy?*, London: Routledge.
Magen, A., Risse, T. and McFaul, M.A. (eds) (2009) *Promoting Democracy and the Rule of Law: American and European Strategies*, Houndmills: Palgrave Macmillan.
Mair, S. (2000) 'Germany's Stiftungen and Democracy Assistance: Comparative Advantages, New Challenges', in P. Burnell (ed.) *Democracy Assistance: International Co-operation for Democratization*, London: Frank Cass.
Mansfield, E., Milner, H. and Rosendorf, B.P. (2002) 'Why Democracies Cooperate More. Electoral Control and International Trade Agreements', *International Organization*, 56 (3): 477–513.
Mansfield, E.D. and Snyder, J. (2008) 'Democratization and Civil War', *Saltzman Working Paper 5*. Online, available at: www.columbia.edu (accessed 31 August 2009).
Maoz, Z. and Russett, B. (1993) 'Normative and Structural Causes of Democratic Peace, 1946–1986', *American Political Science Review*, 87 (3): 624–38.
March, J.G. and Olsen, J.P. (1998) 'The Institutional Dynamics of International Political Orders', *International Organization*, 52 (4): 943–9.
Marshall, M.G. and Jaggers, K. (2006) *Polity IV Project: Political Regime Characteristics and Transitions, 1800–2003*. Online, available at: www.cidcm.umd.edu (accessed 15 December 2011).
Melia, T.O. (2005) *The Democracy Bureaucracy: The Infrastructure of American Democracy Promotion*, September 2005. Online, available at: www.wws.princeton.edu (accessed 23 June 2006).
Merkel, W. and Puhle, H.-J. (1999) *Von der Diktatur zur Demokratie. Transformationen, Erfolgsbedingungen, Entwicklungspfade*, Opladen: Westdeutscher Verlag.
Merkel, W., Puhle, H.-J., Croissant, A., Eicher, C. and Thiery, P. (2003) *Defekte Demokratie. Band 1: Theorie*, Opladen: Leske+Budrich.
Merkel, W., Puhle, H.-J., Croissant, A., and Thiery, P. (2006) *Defekte Demokratie. Band 2: Regionalanalysen*, Wiesbaden: VS Verlag für Sozialwissenschaften.
Mitchell, L.A. (2009) *Uncertain Democracy: US Foreign Policy and Georgia's Rose Revolution*, Philadelphia, PA: University of Pennsylvania Press.
Monten, J. (2005) 'The Roots of the Bush Doctrine: Power, Nationalism, and Democracy Promotion in US Strategy', *International Security*, 29 (4): 112–56.
Moravcsik, A. (1997) 'Taking Preferences Seriously: A Liberal Theory of International Politics', *International Organization*, 51 (4): 513–53.
Müller, H. (2004) 'The Antinomy of Democratic Peace', *International Politics*, 41 (4): 494–520.

Müller, H. and Risse-Kappen, T. (1993) 'From the Outside In and from the Inside Out: International Relations, Domestic Politics, and Foreign Policy', in D. Skidmore and V.M. Hudson (eds) *The Limits of State Autonomy: Societal Groups and Foreign Policy Formulation*, Boulder, CO: Westview Press.

Müller, H. and Wolff, J. (2006) 'Democratic Peace: Many Data, Little Explanation?', in A. Geis, L. Brock and H. Müller (eds) *Democratic Wars: Looking at the Dark Side of Democratic Peace*, Houndmills: Palgrave Macmillan.

Muravchik, J. (1991) *Exporting Democracy: Fulfilling America's Destiny*, Washington, DC: AEI Press.

Nau, H. (2000) 'America's Identity, Democracy Promotion and National Interests: Beyond Realism, Beyond Idealism', in M. Cox, G.J. Ikenberry and T. Inoguchi (eds) *American Democracy Promotion: Impulses, Strategies, and Impacts*, Oxford: Oxford University Press.

Newman, E. and Rich, R. (eds) (2004) *The UN Role in Promoting Democracy: Between Ideals and Reality*, Tokyo: United Nations University Press.

O'Donnell, G. and Schmitter, P.C. (1986) *Transitions from Authoritarian Rule: Tentative Conclusions about Uncertain Democracies*, Baltimore, MD: The Johns Hopkins University Press.

Offe, C. 2003 [1979] '"Unregierbarkeit". Zur Renaissance konservativer Krisentheorien', in: C. Offe, *Herausforderungen der Demokratie. Zur Integrations- und Leistungsfähigkeit politischer Institutionen*, Frankfurt a.M.: Campus.

Ottaway, M.S. (2003) *Democracy Challenged: The Rise of Semi-Authoritarianism*, Washington, DC: Carnegie Endowment for International Peace.

Peceny, M. (1999) *Democracy at the Point of Bayonets*, University Park, PE: The Pennsylvania State University Press.

Pinto-Duschinsky, M. (1991) 'Foreign Political Aid: the German Political Foundations and their US Counterparts', *International Affairs*, 67 (1): 33–63.

Pospisil, J. (2009) *Die Entwicklung von Sicherheit. Entwicklungspolitische Programme der USA und Deutschlands im Grenzbereich zur Sicherheitspolitik*, Bielefeld: Transcript.

Pridham, G. (ed.) (1991) *Encouraging Democracy: The International Context of Regime Transition in Southern Europe*, London: Leicester University Press.

Przeworski, A. (1991) *Democracy and the Market: Political and Economic Reforms in Eastern Europe and Latin America*, Cambridge: Cambridge University Press.

Ragin, C.C. (2004) 'Turning the Tables: How Case-oriented Research Challenges Variable-oriented Research', in: H.E. Brady and D. Collier (eds) *Rethinking Social Inquiry: Diverse Tools, Shared Standards*, Lanham, MD: Leicester University Press.

Ralph, J.G. (2000) '"High Stakes" and "Low-Intensity Democracy": Understanding America's Policy of Promoting Democracy', in M. Cox, G.J. Ikenberry and T. Inoguchi (eds) *American Democracy Promotion: Impulses, Strategies, and Impacts*, Oxford: Oxford University Press.

Rawls, J. (1999) *The Law of Peoples*, Cambridge, MA: Harvard University Press.

Reiber, T. (2009) *Demokratieförderung und Friedenskonsolidierung. Die Nachkriegsgesellschaften von Guatemala, El Salvador und Nicaragua*, Wiesbaden: VS Verlag für Sozialwissenschaften.

Richter, S. (2009) *Zur Effektivität externer Demokratisierung: Die OSZE in Südosteuropa als Partner, Mahner, Besserwisser?*, Baden-Baden: Nomos.

Risse-Kappen, T. (1995) 'Democratic Peace – Warlike Democracies: A Social Constructivist Interpretation of the Democratic Peace', *European Journal of International Relations*, 1 (4): 491–517.

Robinson, W.I. (1996) *Promoting Polyarchy: Globalization, United States Intervention and Hegemony*, Cambridge: Cambridge University Press.
Rose, G. (1998) 'Neoclassical Realism and Theories of Foreign Policy', *World Politics*, 51 (1): 144–72.
Rüland, J. and Werz, N. (2002) 'Germany's Hesitant Role in Promoting Democracy', in P.J. Schraeder (ed.) *Exporting Democracy: Rhetoric vs. Reality*, Boulder, CO: Lynne Rienner.
Russett, B. and Oneal, J.R. (2001) *Triangulating Peace: Democracy Interdependence, and International Organizations*, New York, NY: W.W. Norton.
Scharpf, F.W. (1999) *Governing in Europe: Effective and Democratic?*, Oxford: Oxford University Press.
Schimmelfennig, F. and Sedelmeier, U. (eds) (2005) *The Europeanization of Central and Eastern Europe*, Ithaca, NY: Cornell University Press.
Schimmelfennig, F., Engert, S. and Knobel, H. (2006) *International Socialization in Europe: European Organizations, Political Conditionality and Democratic Change*, Basingstoke: Palgrave Macmillan.
Schlumberger, O. (2008) *Autoritarismus in der arabischen Welt. Ursachen, Trends und internationale Demokratieförderung*, Baden-Baden: Nomos.
Schmitter, P.C. (1995) 'Transitology: The Science or the Art of Democratization?', in J.S. Tulchin (ed.) *The Consolidation of Democracy in Latin America*, Boulder, CO: Lynne Rienner.
Schmitter, P.C. and Brouwer, I. (1999) 'Conceptualizing, Researching and Evaluating Democracy Promotion and Protection', *EUI (European Institute Florence) Working Paper SPS 99/9*. Online, available at: http://cadmus.iue.it (accessed 15 September 2005).
Schmitz, H.P. and Sell, K. (1999) 'International Factors in Processes of Political Democratization', in J. Grugel (ed.) *Democracy without Borders: Transnationalization and Conditionality in New Democracies*, London: Routledge.
Schraeder, P.J. (ed.) (2002) *Exporting Democracy. Rhetoric vs. Reality*, Boulder, CO: Lynne Rienner.
Schraeder, P.J. (2003) 'The State of the Art in International Democracy Promotion: Results of a Joint European–North American Research Network', *Democratization*, 20 (2): 21–44.
Schweller R.L. (2000) 'US Democracy Promotion: Realist Reflections', in M. Cox, G.J. Ikenberry and T. Inoguchi (eds) *American Democracy Promotion: Impulses, Strategies, and Impacts*, Oxford: Oxford University Press.
Scott, J.M. and Steele, C.A. (2005) 'Assisting Democrats or Resisting Dictators? The Nature and Impact of Democracy Support by the United States National Endowment for Democracy, 1990–99', *Democratization*, 12 (4): 439–60.
Sen, A. (1999) 'Democracy as a Universal Value', *Journal of Democracy*, 10 (3): 3–17.
Shaw, C.M. (2007) 'The United States: Rhetoric and Reality', in T. Legler, S.F. Lean and D.S. Boniface (eds) *Promoting Democracy in the Americas*, Baltimore, MD: The Johns Hopkins University Press.
Sil, R. (2000) 'The Foundations of Eclecticism: The Epistemological Status of Agency, Culture, and Structure in Social Theory', *Journal of Theoretical Politics*, 12 (3): 353–87.
Sil, R. and Katzenstein, P.J. (2010) *Beyond Paradigms: Analytic Eclecticism in the Study of World Politics*, Houndmills: Palgrave Macmillan.

Smith, S. (2000) 'US Democracy Promotion: Critical Questions', in: M. Cox, G.J. Ikenberry and T. Inoguchi (eds) *American Democracy Promotion: Impulses, Strategies, and Impacts*, Oxford: Oxford University Press.

Smith, T. (1994) *America's Mission: The United States and the Worldwide Struggle for Democracy in the Twentieth Century*, Princeton, NJ: Princeton University Press.

Smith, T. (2007) *A Pact with the Devil: Washington's Bid for World Supremacy and the Betrayal of the American Promise*, London: Routledge.

Sørensen, G. (2006) 'Liberalism of Restraint and Liberalism of Imposition: Liberal Values and World Order in the New Millennium', *International Relations*, 20 (3): 251–72.

Spanger, H.-J. (ed.) (2012) *Der demokratische Unfrieden. Über das spannungsreiche Verhältnis zwischen Demokratisierung und innerer Gewalt*, Baden-Baden: Nomos.

Spanger, H.-J. and Wolff, J. (2007a) 'Universales Ziel – partikulare Wege? Externe Demokratieförderung zwischen einheitlicher Rhetorik und vielfältiger Praxis, in: A. Geis, H. Müller, and W. Wagner (eds) *Schattenseiten des Demokratischen Friedens. Zur Kritik einer Theorie liberaler Außen- und Sicherheitspolitik*, Frankfurt a.M.: Campus, 261–84.

Spanger, H.-J. and Wolff, J. (2007b) 'Why Promote Democratisation? Reflections on the Instrumental Value of Democracy, in: M. van Doorn and R. von Meijenfeldt (eds) *Democracy: Europe's Core Value? On the European Profile in World-wide Democracy Assistance*, Delft: Eburon, 33–49.

Spence, M. (2005) 'Policy Coherence and Incoherence: The Domestic Politics of American Democracy Promotion', *CDDRL Working Paper 31*. Online, available at: http://iisdb.stanford.edu (accessed 18 April 2005).

Stewart, S. (ed.) (2009) *Democracy Promotion before and after the 'Colour Revolutions'*, London: Routledge (Democratization Special Issue).

Talbott, S. (1996) 'Democracy and the National Interest', *Foreign Affairs*, 75 (6): 47–63.

USAID (2005) *At Freedom's Frontiers: A Democracy and Governance Strategic Framework*, Washington, DC: USAID.

Warkotsch, A. (2009) 'The European Union's Democracy Promotion Approach in Central Asia: On the Right Track?', *European Foreign Affairs Review*, 14 (2): 249–69.

Whitaker, B.E. (2007) 'Exporting the Patriot Act? Democracy and the "War on Terror" in the Third World', *Third World Quarterly*, 28 (5): 1017–32.

Whitehead, L. (1991) 'The Imposition of Democracy', in: A.F. Lowenthal (ed.) *Exporting Democracy: The United States and Latin America: Case Studies*, Baltimore, MD: The Johns Hopkins University Press.

Whitehead, L. (ed.) (1996) *The International Dimensions of Democratization: Europe and the Americas*, Oxford: Oxford University Press.

Whitehead, L. (2009) 'Losing "the Force"? The "Dark Side" of Democratization after Iraq' *Democratization*, 16 (2): 215–42.

Wolff, J. and Wurm, I. (2011) 'Towards a Theory of External Democracy Promotion: A Proposal for Theoretical Classification', *Security Dialogue*, 42 (1): 77–96.

Youngs, R. (2004) *International Democracy and the West: The Role of Governments, Civil Society, and Multinational Business*, Oxford: Oxford University Press.

Youngs, R. (ed.) (2006) *Survey of European Democracy Promotion Policies 2000–2006*, Madrid: FRIDE.

Youngs, R. (2008) 'Trends in Democracy Assistance: What Has Europe Been Doing?', *Journal of Democracy*, 19 (2): 160–9.

Zakaria, F. (2003) *The Future of Freedom: Illiberal Democracy at Home and Abroad*, New York, NY: W.W. Norton.

2 Freedom Fighter versus Civilian Power

An ideal-type comparison of US and German conceptions of democracy promotion

Annika E. Poppe, Bentje Woitschach and Jonas Wolff

Research on external democracy promotion has generally revealed diversity, not uniformity. Different actors seem to promote democracy in differing ways, preferring different strategies and instruments.[1] Two findings suggest that this variance is rooted in varying political conceptions of democracy promotion. First, one field of research emphasizes the importance of collective role conceptions, identities and cultures that shape the external policies of states.[2] Because it forms a part of foreign and development policy, this should also apply to democracy promotion. Second, democracy is a much contested concept and democratization a highly complex process, so that even a broadly shared normative preference for liberal democracy and its promotion can imply that how democracy, democratization and democracy promotion are perceived can be starkly different.[3] How a democracy promoter conceptualizes democracy, conceives of the democratization process and defines the appropriate role of external actors is all shaped by the historical experiences of a specific country and, more generally, its political culture and tradition of foreign policy practice.[4]

In this chapter, we explore whether and to what extent US and German conceptions of democracy promotion differ; doing so allows us to assess 'political culture' as a determinant, as described in the introduction to this book. The chapter first outlines the theoretical framework, which draws on the broader discussion about political and cultural determinants of foreign policy, in order, then, to focus on conceptual differences and develop two ideal-type conceptions of democracy promotion, namely those of the Freedom Fighter and the Civilian Power. As a second step, the plausibility of this conceptual distinction is probed as we empirically assess whether the United States and Germany do, in fact, fit these ideal types in their respective democracy promotion conceptions. After briefly reviewing the state of the art, we present the results of a qualitative content analysis that systematically explores the conceptual differences in government documents. The focus of our attention, thus, is the official rhetoric of

US and German governments and the specific conceptions of democracy promotion that are reflected in these government discourses.

Theoretical framework

Political culture as a determinant of foreign policy

The argument that the foreign policy of states is shaped by the domestic social context in which it is formulated and practiced is generally based on a constructivist perspective on international relations. Taking ideational factors at the national level as our point of reference, we draw on an actor-centred or societal constructivism, as distinguished from institutionalist or transnational constructivism. Whereas the latter emphasizes the characteristics of the international environment as crucial factors shaping foreign policy, the former stresses the importance of the domestic normative setting (Boekle *et al.* 2001: 121, 116; cf. Harnisch 2003: 340). In general, it is against the background of particular, culturally embedded patterns of thought that national interests and foreign-policy preferences are defined, and against which the environment and external events are perceived and evaluated. In the broadest terms, this domestic ideational context has been conceptualized in terms of political culture (Duffield 1999). National role conceptions and national identities refer to specific key elements of political culture, including foreign policy; the former emphasizes the perceived function of states in the international environment (including both internal and external role expectations), while the latter focuses on 'images of individuality and distinctiveness' (Becker *et al.* 2008: 818–19).[5]

Duffield has identified four ways in which political culture influences collective (external) behaviour: political culture (1) 'helps define the basic goals of the collectivity'; (2) 'shapes perceptions of the external environment'; (3) 'conditions the types of options that are seen to exist' and 'defines the instruments and tactics that are judged acceptable, appropriate, or legitimate within the broader set of those that are imaginable'; (4) 'can strongly influence the evaluation of the seemingly available options and thus the choices that are made among them' (Duffield 1999: 771–2). Political culture as a determinant of foreign policy, then, does not determine specific foreign-policy decisions but, as in Anthony Giddens's theory of structuration, operates by both enabling and constraining (Müller 2007: 306). The overall effect of culture is 'to predispose collectivities toward certain actions and policies rather than others' (Duffield 1999: 772). One merit of cultural analysis is that it tells us what types of foreign policy options would be considered impossible for a given country (Hudson 2007: 121).[6]

This chapter is not concerned with political culture – or national role conceptions or identities – in a broad sense, but only with a specific part of it: particular conceptions of democracy promotion. The assumption is that although, since the end of the Cold War, a broad consensus has emerged among North-Western democracies that it is normatively appropriate and strategically prudent to actively support the advancement and stabilization of democracy around the world,[7] divergent understandings prevail about what this abstract preference actually means for democracy promotion practice. From the perspective of cultural analysis, such variance is due to specific historical experiences with democracy and democratization and is related to general norms of appropriate (foreign policy) behaviour embedded in the political culture of the given country.[8]

Two ideal-type conceptions of democracy promotion

According to constructivist explanations of democratic peace, democracies tend to externalize their internal norms (Maoz and Russett 1993: 625; Risse-Kappen 1995: 501). In a general sense, this implies that established democracies are (culturally, normatively) predisposed to spread democracy globally. Yet, even if there is such a general predisposition, this still leaves considerable latitude for quite different understandings of the aim that is to be reached (democracy), of the path that may lead to this end point (democratization), and of the appropriate role of external actors in this process (see Hobson and Kurki 2012; Wolff and Wurm 2011: 81–2). In order to achieve a heuristic grasp of possible conceptions of democracy promotion, it seems reasonable to start with empirically observed conceptions.

In this regard, the distinction made by Carothers between two approaches to democracy assistance is a useful starting point. The political approach, according to this leading expert on democracy promotion, is characterized by 'a relatively narrow conception of democracy – focused, above all, on elections and political liberties – and a view of democratization as a process of political struggle in which democrats work to gain the upper hand in society over non-democrats'. Correspondingly, democracy assistance is directed 'at core political processes and institutions ... often at important conjunctural moments and with the hope of catalytic effects'. The developmental approach, by contrast, 'rests on a broader notion of democracy, one that encompasses concerns about equality and justice and the concept of democratization as a low, iterative process of change involving an interrelated set of political and socioeconomic developments'. Democracy assistance, here, 'pursues incremental, long-term change in a wide range of political and socioeconomic sectors, frequently emphasizing governance and the building of a well-functioning state' (Carothers 2009: 5).

In order to further develop and systematize this typology, we propose distinguishing between two ideal-type conceptions of democracy promotion – the Freedom Fighter and the Civilian Power – along four major dimensions (see Table 2.1).[9] Regarding the guiding universal values (1), the Freedom Fighter is characterized by an explicit and narrow focus on liberal democracy, clearly emphasizing civil liberties and political rights. The Civilian Power is guided by rather abstract and broad values, emphasizing international human rights in general. The mode of democratization (2) is conceived of either as a fairly short-term, quasi-revolutionary process of regime change (Freedom Fighter) or as a long-term, evolutionary process of transformation involving a series of gradual steps (Civilian Power). Concerning the attitude towards actors perceived as opponents to democracy or non-democrats (3), the Freedom Fighter, bound to a Manichean worldview, favours strategies of exclusion and confrontation towards the 'enemies' of democracy. The Civilian Power, bound to the notion of 'change through rapprochement', prefers pragmatic strategies of (institutional) cooperation and inclusion. Finally, the Freedom Fighter's style of democracy promotion (4) is proactive; assertive action on the part of external actors is legitimate and, at times, needed in order to enforce democratic standards. The Civilian Power, by contrast, is relatively reluctant to meddle openly in other states' affairs and to infringe on their rights to sovereignty and collective self-determination.

These four dimensions represent the major normative questions that democracy promoters have to deal with. Is promoting democracy about enforcing a universal right to democracy or 'only' about value-oriented support for processes of political change (Schraeder 2003: 25–6; cf. Fox and Roth 2000)? Can democracy promotion usefully rely on the notion that democratization involves a demarcated transition from authoritarian to democratic rule, even if a rather long-term process of consolidation may follow, or not (Carothers 2002; cf. Smith 2007: chapter 5)? Does promoting democracy require containing and fighting its enemies, or engaging and thereby transforming its opponents (Wolff and Wurm 2011: 81; cf. Jahn 2005)? And, finally, should external actors actively promote democracy at all, thus by definition intervene in another state's affairs, or should they prefer indirect, less 'political' means (Schraeder 2003: 25–6; cf. Doyle 2009)? The Freedom Fighter, then, represents the radical, pro-democracy edge in the contemporary debate on democracy promotion, whereas the Civilian Power stands for the least intrusive position that still strives to spread democracy.

Table 2.1 Conceptions of democracy promotion: two ideal types

	Freedom Fighter	*Civilian Power*
(1) Guiding universal values	Explicit (civil and political rights)	Abstract (broad human rights)
(2) Mode of democratization	Revolutionary ('big bang')	Evolutionary (gradualism)
(3) Attitude towards non-democrats	Manichaean (exclusion/confrontation)	Pragmatic (inclusion/engagement)
(4) Style of democracy promotion	Proactive (emphasis on democratic standards)	Reserved (emphasis on self-determination)

Source: authors' compilation.

US versus German democracy promotion: the state of the art

It is a commonplace that the United States and Germany have very different foreign policy profiles. In seeking to shape world order as a superpower, the United States has historically alternated between unilateral and multilateral internationalism on the one hand and isolationism on the other while laying claim to its status as leader of the (free) world and securing its interests where this was deemed necessary in military terms. By contrast, German foreign policy is usually seen as very much shaped by the export orientation of its economy; not least due to its recent history, Germany usually takes a moderate and reserved stance on the world political stage, is part of a tightly-knit regional integration framework, and its foreign policy since 1945 has been characterized mainly by multilateral and non-military behaviour.

Whether these broad distinctions are useful for understanding the foreign policy behaviour of these two states and whether and how they have shaped conceptions of democracy promotion are, however, still open questions. In the following, we assess how far the general characteristics of US and German democracy promotion in fact correspond with expectations regarding the two ideal types. As will be shown in this section, US democracy promotion has been frequently characterized as missionary, assertive and, if need be, coercive. In contrast, Germany's foreign policy in general has been found to closely correspond to the general role conception of a Civilian Power, and, in terms of democracy promotion, Germany has been described as reluctant, late-coming and selective.[10]

US democracy promotion: a Freedom Fighter?

Democracy promotion is – at least according to official declarations – a fundamental pillar of US foreign policy.[11] The American impulse to endow the world with freedom and democracy originated in the colonial period, and has become a deeply-entrenched expression of national identity (Brocker 2006; Monten 2005: 119–20; Smith 1994). This impulse derives its legitimacy not only from the perceived exceptionalism of 'God's own nation', but also responds to the assumed responsibility the United States has for the world; a world, which is thought to expect and rely upon the special role of the United States as a force for freedom and as liberator to the oppressed. While democracy promotion in early US history was conceivable only as a passive endeavour of a nation that considered itself a 'city upon a hill' and a 'beacon' to the world, but was still only a minor power on the global political stage, this policy took a more active turn with President Wilson's call to 'make the world safe for democracy'. After only selectively promoting democracy during the Cold War and sometimes undermining it under the prerogative of the containment strategy, democracy promotion became a major foreign and development policy goal with President Reagan's 'crusade for freedom' and has remained a vital part of the US foreign policy agenda ever since (Carothers 1991, 1999; Schmitz 2006; Smith 1994, 2007).

To what extent does the literature on US democracy promotion emphasize features that conform to the Freedom Fighter ideal type? Conceiving of democracy as a universal value is indeed a major characteristic of the US political creed (Monten 2005: 123); every human being, regardless of their origin or tradition, strives for the same rights and holds the same liberal values, which are best realized under democratic rule. This conviction is based on an optimistic liberal tradition postulating democracy not only as a universally strived for but also a universally achievable value. From the US liberal perspective, the implementation of democracy from the outside is also a relatively smooth process, which yields benefits for everyone involved while fostering peace (Desch 2007: 20–5).[12] Accordingly, long-term resistance to democratization in principle either stems from 'moral defect or malign intent' (Desch 2007: 32), thus informing a Manichaean world view as well as exclusion strategies with regard to those opposing democracy (cf. Smith 2007).

Also in line with the ideal-type conception of a Freedom Fighter is the determinedly proactive style that is usually ascribed to US democracy promotion (Youngs 2004: 31–7). External democracy promotion has become a persistent element of US foreign policy and is referred to emphatically, although the implementation of this policy does not often quite follow the rhetorical emphasis. Democracy promotion by force may not be the general rule for the United States, but, in the US political tradition, 'the "imposition" of democracy is no contradiction in terms' (Whitehead 1991: 234). The United States is seen to be 'far more willing to adopt tough punitive measures on democratic grounds' (Youngs 2004: 31), including resorting to military force (Peceny 1999). The forced regime changes in Afghanistan and Iraq furthermore point to the perceived possibility of externally induced democratic 'revolutions' (Kopstein 2006; Smith 2007).

With regard to different conceptions of how democracy promotion is to be conducted and under what circumstances it leads to a successful outcome, it is also worth noting the American proclivity to focus on the quick realization of elections and the establishment of institutions modelled according to the US example (Carothers 1999: 85–122). US democratization efforts often centre on civil society as the main force for democratic development and democratic breakthroughs; once an authoritarian regime has collapsed, US efforts shift to the organization of democratic elections and the designing of a constitution and democratic institutions (Kopstein 2006).[13]

Two factors account for the assertiveness of US democracy promotion. Beyond partisan lines and beyond differences in priorities, the majority of political actors share the conviction that democracy promotion is part of a genuine American mission, and that this endeavour serves the national interest (cf. Cox et al. 2000; Smith 1994; Poppe 2010). Democracy promotion thus not only constitutes an important element of a 'civil-religious impulse' (Brocker 2006: 216); following the liberal assumption that 'all good things go together', democracy and its promotion are also considered enabling factors for peace, prosperity and security (Desch 2007: 21–2).

This conviction gained strength in the 1990s, after the end of the Cold War and democracy's 'third wave' had fostered the belief in a long-term global victory of democracy. In this context, the US political elite readily absorbed democratic peace theory and attempted to make it operational in its policies (Cox 2000: 226; Ish-Shalom 2006; Smith 2007). The optimism about democracy's role and effects always had its critics, conflicts in policy implementation continued to exist and the declared primary goal of democracy promotion was often relegated to the back seat when it clashed with other interests (Carothers 1999: 3–5). The administrations after the Cold War, however, have firmly subscribed to the conviction that democracy promotion yields normative and material benefits. Accordingly, Clinton closely linked the promotion of democracy with the promotion of free market economies (Cox 2000), and Bush declared democracy promotion to be the most suitable weapon in the 'war on terror' (Carothers 2003) – in both cases, the global promotion of democracy played a central role on the general foreign policy agenda and also prominently found its way into the respective national security strategies. During the current US administration, Obama's initial attempt to downplay democracy promotion was met with severe criticism from different political camps and eventually led to an increased engagement with the issue on the part of the administration (Poppe 2010: chapter 5).

German democracy promotion: a Civilian Power?

The overall concept of a Civilian Power was developed by Hanns Maull in order to characterize German (and Japanese) foreign policy (Maull 1990; Kirste and Maull 1996: 297). From this perspective, the Civilian Power Germany basically aims at 'civilizing' international relations. Civilian Powers do not rule out 'meddling in the internal affairs of other states' (Kirste and Maull 1996: 302), but democracy promotion is not part of a Civilian Power's guiding principles. The latter include, in particular, constraining the use of force in handling political conflicts; strengthening international law, international norms and international regimes; intensifying multilateral cooperation with inclusive participation as well as a partial transfer of sovereignty; and promoting social justice at the global level (cf. Harnisch and Maull 2001b: 3–4).[14] Democracy promotion is, in this sense, part of a broader orientation towards universal rights and values and generally subordinated to a dominant focus on peaceful international cooperation.[15]

In fact, since the 1990s, German governments have increasingly emphasized human rights as an important guideline for their foreign and development policies and introduced democratic and human rights conditions in their development cooperation – but mainly as 'soft' criteria for observation and not as 'hard' conditionalities.[16] In the course of the 1990s, the GTZ (now GIZ) – the agency implementing German technical cooperation – adopted an increasingly political approach to governance assistance as part of German development cooperation (Erdmann 1996: 139). More than other donors, the German government has emphasized that democratization 'should not be limited to holding more or less free elections' but requires broader attention to human rights, the *Rechtsstaat* (rule of law) and civil society (Betz 1996: 204).

In general, the German approach to democracy promotion in the 1990s is described as being characterized by a reluctance to meddle politically in the internal affairs of other states: democracy assistance as part of German development cooperation focused on good governance, the rule of law, decentralization and administration, while the Development Ministry preferred to talk about human rights and not democracy promotion; the Foreign Office, if it considered democracy promotion at all, treated it as part of its broader human rights policy and limited democracy assistance to selective activities related to technical electoral support. This reluctance vis-à-vis an openly political approach to promoting democracy is well in line with the ideal type of a Civilian Power.

The same holds true for the German focus on capacity-building activities, i.e. on democracy assistance. In general, Germany is said to prefer dialogue and positive incentives as the means for exerting influence on other states' political development (Lerch 2007: 9; Rüland and Werz 2002: 86; Youngs 2006: 111).[17] Negative sanctions as a means of promoting (or protecting) democracy have been used only 'very selectively, occasionally half-heartedly, inconsistently, and situationally' (Betz 1996: 208). This cautious use of sanctions has traditionally been justified by an evolutionist, modernization-theory argument: the support for economic growth and reforms – e.g. in China – was supposed to lead to political reforms in the middle to long run (cf. Rüland and Werz 2002: 73–4, 76). According to Lapins (2007: 5), German democracy promotion is 'long term in conception', 'not missionary' but conceptualized 'as a policy of the good example'. The Foreign Office, in particular, prefers indirect measures, above all to avoid confrontation and being accused of interfering in other states' internal affairs (Rüland and Werz 2002: 80). Well in line with the Civilian Power concept, German human rights policy was far more consistent in strengthening international human rights norms than in terms of reacting to human rights violations in particular countries (Pfeil 2001; cf. Boekle 2001).

These features characterizing German democracy promotion since 1990 correspond not only to the culturally embedded profile of a Civilian Power, but also to the material interests of a middle power strongly dependent on its exports (Spanger and Wolff 2007: 284). Germany's cautious approach to democracy promotion quite obviously responds to considerations related to German trade and investment; political pressure and economic sanctions are regularly rejected when – as with China and Russia – such economic interests are threatened.[18]

US versus German democracy promotion: results of a content analysis

Data and methodology

In order to systematically analyse US and German conceptions of democracy promotion, a content analysis of official documents and speeches was conducted.

It draws on a selection of 20 primary sources issued by the respective governments of each case considered. Both subsamples include the most important official strategy papers and speeches that explicitly deal with democracy promotion as well as primary sources that outline the general guidelines of foreign, defence and development policy. US sources were chosen from the Clinton and Bush Administrations (1993–2009) and include speeches and documents from the President's Office (including the national security strategies), the State Department, and USAID (United States Agency for International Development). With regard to Germany, all German governments since 1990 (until 2009) and the four principal actors shaping foreign policy (Chancellory, Foreign Office, Defence and Development Ministry) are covered.

The qualitative content analysis was conducted as proposed by Mayring (2000). Following his approach of 'deductive category application', the four dimensions distinguishing the ideal-type conceptions of democracy promotion (see Table 2.1) were used to develop categories. In addition to these specific, theoretically derived categories, the coding scheme included broader categories in order to collect general statements about the concepts of 'democracy', 'democratization' and 'democracy promotion'.[19]

For assessing the (1) *guiding universal values*, we distinguished between – and respectively coded – statements that emphasize the universality of democracy on the one hand and the universality of general values and rights on the other. The recording units were text passages – ranging from a sentence to an entire paragraph – that contained a substantive statement on the issue under investigation.[20] For example, the statement 'Democracy and human rights are universal yearnings and universal norms, just as powerful in Asia as elsewhere' (White House 1995: 29) was coded as 'democracy universal', whereas the following text passage was coded as 'values/rights universal':

> We don't expect our partners to adopt the beliefs and institutions that have grown in the culture of the industrialized countries but to implement basic human rights and freedoms, which apply to all human beings and which, in their basic forms, are also common to all cultures.
> (Spranger 1998)

Similarly, the conceptual (2) *mode of democratization* was identified by considering all text passages in which the process of building democracy in general is either described or alluded to as being evolutionary/long-term or revolutionary/short-term. In gauging the (3) *attitude towards non-democrats*, at first all statements that characterize non-democratic actors as antagonists/'enemies' were collected, and, second, all strategies prescribed for dealing with non-democrats were examined as to whether they tended towards inclusion/engagement or exclusion/confrontation.

The (4) *style of democracy promotion* was analysed in a different manner, combining qualitative and quantitative content analysis. In order to assess whether government discourse is characterized by an explicit emphasis on democracy (promotion) or by a more reserved approach to this issue, two indicators were established. Drawing on the above-mentioned qualitative content analysis, the average number of codes assigned was counted for the US and German sources, respectively.[21] The assumption, here, is that a proactive approach to democracy promotion should imply more explicit references to democracy (promotion) and, therefore, a significantly higher number of statements to be coded. In an additional word frequency count, the occurrence rate of the terms 'democracy' ('*Demokratie*'), 'freedom' or 'liberty' ('*Freiheit*') and the 'rule of law' ('*Rechtsstaat*') in US and German documents was calculated. Again, in documents that represent a proactive style of democracy promotion we would expect more explicit references to 'democracy' while a reserved attitude would imply a relative preference for the less political 'rule of law'.

In general, the results of the content analysis were evaluated by combining quantitative and qualitative methods. On the one hand, the relative occurrence of statements for the different categories in the two subsamples (United States and Germany) was compared (see Table 2.2). This frequency analysis has the advantage of allowing for a systematic comparison between US and German rhetoric; the relatively small number of primary sources – even if encompassing the relevant spectrum of official documents (see above) – implies, however, that caution must be used regarding statistical differences. On the other hand, a comparative interpretation of the coded statements was conducted. By examining the specific wording and the context of the coded text passages, it was possible to identify typical rhetorical patterns in the two subsamples and to take a closer look at outliers.

Results

With regard to the basic definition and elements of democracy, US and German documents mostly agree. German rhetoric, however, is characterized by a close connection between democracy and the rule of law (*Rechtsstaat*) – two concepts often referred to together (cf. AA 2000: 5; BMZ 2008: 137; Fischer 2004; Kinkel 1996; Wieczorek-Zeul 2005). The normative principles that are mentioned as ones which guide German foreign policy include democratic values and human dignity as well as broadly understood (political, civil, economic, social and cultural) human rights – frequently with reference to internationally codified norms (cf. AA 2000: 5; BMZ 2005: 15; Kinkel 1996; Schröder 2002; Spranger 1998; Wieczorek-Zeul 2005).

Rule of law and human dignity play a crucial role in US documents as well (cf. Anderson 1999; Bush 2005, 2007; USAID 1998: 7, 2005: 8). In contrast to the German documents, there is, however, a strong tendency to emphasize the competitive and power-restraining nature of liberal democracy: free and fair elections (cf. USAID 1998: 11, 2002: 6, 43), the right to free speech, a free press and free assembly, an independent civil society, and political competition (cf. Albright 2000; Bush 2003; Christopher 1993; USAID 1998: 15, 2002: 43, 2005: 8; White House 2006: 5). US rhetoric also posits a direct link between political and economic freedom (cf. Anderson 1999; White House 2006: 4, 25), and, respectively, between democracy and the protection of private ownership rights (Bush 2003, 2007; Christopher 1993), the existence of a private market economy (Albright 2000; Bush 2003) as well as low transaction costs (USAID 2002: 7).

Table 2.2 summarizes the specific results for the four ideal-type dimensions. It shows that, in principle, the expected differences between the United States and Germany are confirmed: the former is generally closer to the ideal type of the Freedom Fighter, the latter to the Civilian Power-type conception of democracy promotion.

With regard to the *guiding universal values*, explicit references to the universality of democracy are much more frequent in US documents than references to abstract universal rights and values. US rhetoric invokes an 'imperative of self-government' (Bush 2005) and declares democracy and human rights to be 'universal norms' (White House 1995: 29). Accordingly, 'democratic development is always possible', regardless of 'culture, race, religion, and level of development' (Rice 2008: 10; cf. Anderson 1999; Bush 2002, 2003; White House 1995: 29, 2002: i–iii). In most instances, however, it is 'freedom' that is declared to be

Table 2.2 Results of the content analysis: the United States versus Germany, percentage (absolute number)

Indicators[a]	United States	Germany
(1) Guiding universal values		
Frequency of code 'democracy universal'[b]	12.3 (27)	5.0 (2)
Frequency of code 'values/rights universal'[b]	3.2 (7)	32.5 (13)
(2) Mode of democratization		
Frequency of code 'evolutionary'[b]	14.1 (31)	20.0 (8)
Frequency of code 'revolutionary'[b]	3.6 (8)	0.0 (0)
(3) Attitude towards non-democrats		
Frequency of code 'non-democrats as "enemy"'[b]	34.5 (76)	17.5 (7)
Frequency of code 'engaging non-democrats'[b]	5.0 (11)	10.0 (4)
Frequency of code 'excluding non-democrats'[b]	27.3 (60)	15.0 (6)
(4) Style of democracy promotion		
Frequency of coded text passages[c]	0.13 (220)	0.04 (40)
Frequency of terms:[c]		
• democracy (Demokratie)[d]	0.44 (723)	0.24 (226)
• freedom or liberty (Freiheit)[d]	0.30 (500)	0.10 (98)
• rule of law (Rechtsstaat)[d]	0.07 (112)	0.06 (57)

Notes
a The indicators reported here refer only to a part – namely, the categories dealing with conceptual issues – of a larger coding scheme developed for the overall research project.
b Relative frequency of statements in the given category as a percentage of all coded statements in the subsample (absolute numbers in brackets).
c Absolute frequency divided by the total word count for each subsample (US: 164,924 words; Germany: 94,615 words), displayed as relative occurrence per 100 words.
d Only the exact terms – not the respective adjectives such as 'free', 'democratic', etc. – were counted.

universal (cf. Bush 2002, 2003, 2005, 2007; White House 2002: i–iii, 2006: 2–3). Since 'democracy' and 'freedom' are generally used as interchangeable terms in official US rhetoric,[22] these statements were coded as 'democracy universal'. US documents do, however, emphasize that democracy is not to be imposed on anyone (cf. Anderson 1999; Bush 2003, 2005; White House 1995: 29).

In German documents, by contrast, references to rather abstract and broad universal values and rights predominate. Examples include references to 'human dignity' (BMVg 1994: 41; Merkel 2007), 'democratic values and basic principles' (BMZ 2005: 5) or human rights in general (BMZ 1998; Kinkel 1996; Spranger 1998). The Development Ministry (BMZ 2005: 6) explicitly emphasizes that Germany does 'not promote a particular form of democracy' but instead 'the implementation of democratic and rule-of-law principles'. The two references coded as declaring the universality of democracy, on closer examination, lend weight to this observation. In one instance, the BMZ (2005: 5) quotes then UN secretary-general Kofi Annan who called democracy a 'universal right' – but the ministry refrains from explicitly embracing this notion. Just as expectations of a Civilian Power would have it, the German government, thus, does not unilaterally proclaim a universal right to democracy but takes international norms – as represented by the UN Secretary-General – as the point of departure for conceiving its democracy promotion agenda. In the second text passage coded, the Defence Ministry emphasizes freedom, law and human dignity as the universally binding core of human rights (BMVg 1994: 41). This combination of concepts can be interpreted as an indirect, if substantial reference to democracy. Yet again, it is notable that democracy as such is not mentioned.

With a view to the *mode of democratization*, the relative frequency of references to democratization as being a gradual and 'evolutionary' process is roughly the same for the United States and Germany. In the US conception this is, however, only one part of the picture. Especially when it comes to 'help[ing] nations in transition move to a higher stage of democratic development' (Albright 2000), quasi-revolutionary changes come into play at certain crucial moments. US documents also talk about a 'revolution of democracy sweeping the continent [here: Africa]' (White House 1995: 31) and about a 'democratic revolution' in the twentieth century, in which 'tyrannies fell one by one and democracies rose in their stead' (White House 2006: 4). The clearest expressions in this regard come from USAID's Democracy and Governance Strategic Framework, which systematically includes 'democratic breakthroughs' – 'dramatic openings for democratization' like 'peaceful revolutions' – as crucial steps that make a 'democratic transition' possible and that require swift and focused action by democracy promoters (USAID 2005: 12). These different dimensions of democratization correspond to the identification of three phases – liberalization, transition and consolidation – according to the Transition Paradigm (Carothers 2002). Whereas the goal to 'expand freedom in authoritarian states' is considered a gradual and evolutionary process, at some point a revolutionary democratic breakthrough occurs, then to be followed by another 'long process' of 'democratic consolidation' (USAID 2005: 11–12; cf. USAID 1998).

To be sure, US documents also refer much more frequently to the 'evolutionary' than to the 'revolutionary' side of democratization. It is notable, however, that German documents include not a single reference to short-term transitions to democracy, revolutionary processes of change, or 'democratic breakthroughs'. Here, democratization is consistently characterized as a long-term process of gradual change that has to grow from within the respective society. According to the BMZ (1998: 28), democratization encompasses 'long-term structural changes that establish better preconditions so that projects and reforms in traditional sectors are viable and sustainable'. These are 'protracted processes' where setbacks are always possible (BMZ 2005: 5; cf. BMZ 2008: 139). Abandoning the Transition Paradigm, the Development Ministry's democracy promotion strategy does not mention the transition to democracy as a relevant phase of democratization (or as a noteworthy aim of democracy promotion), but speaks of 'hybrid' regimes only (BMZ 2005: 11–12).[23]

As concerns the *attitude towards non-democrats*, US documents frequently characterize those seen as opposing democracy as 'enemies' and tend clearly to emphasize exclusionary and confrontational strategies. Promoting democracy and freedom is a tool used against tyranny, slavery, despotism, torture and oppression or, simply, against 'evil' (cf. Bush 2002, 2003, 2005; White House 1995: 29).[24] This conception is not merely a consequence of the terror attacks of 9/11. Already the Clinton Government depicted the United States as being in 'a struggle between freedom and tyranny': a 'fight between those who would build free societies governed by laws and those who would impose their will by force' (White House 1995: 1–2). The dominant response to this kind of enemy correspondingly ranges from exclusion to outright confrontation.[25] USAID's 2005 conception of democracy promotion does not envisage cooperation with authoritarian governments at all. In principle, authoritarian regimes are not considered to be partners on whose evolution one should count; especially in those countries that reject the 'freedom agenda', the 'goal is to bolster credible reform forces wherever they are' (USAID 2005: 11–12; cf. USAID 2002: 10).[26] USAID in general resorts to emphasizing the linkage between support and 'concerted and consistent pressure' (USAID 2005: 2).

In comparison to US rhetoric, German documents relatively rarely characterize non-democratic countries or groups as 'enemies' and comparatively rarely argue in favour of their exclusion or marginalization. The fact that Germany advocates 'exclusion' more frequently than 'inclusion' is almost entirely due to references to terrorism (cf. BMVg 2003: 20, 2006: 16; Schröder 2002). When dealing with terrorists, Germany does adopt a non-inclusionary approach.[27] But if text passages related to terrorism are taken out, inclusion is the predominant strategy.[28] Exclusion is at best the very last option (Spranger 1998).[29] Confronted with 'countries in which the government impedes or hinders democratic will-formation by adopting arbitrary measures (violating human rights, freedom of opinion, etc.)', the Development Ministry provides for a policy dialogue in order to push the corresponding government 'to open or widen the scope for a socio-political reform discussion' (BMZ 1998: 29–30).

As long as authoritarian 'partner governments' refuse to become politically more liberal, official German democracy promotion as implemented by the government is to be restricted to indirect measures: it 'takes the existing order [in the partner country] as a starting point and, for the time being, accepts the given correlations of power'; official German democracy promotion, under these circumstances, has a 'long-term' orientation and aims at 'improvements in governance and administration' as well as at 'professionalization of the political system and the rule of law' (BMZ 2005: 18–19). Politically sensitive and potentially confrontational direct support for processes of political reform and liberalization is, under such conditions, 'first and foremost the business of non-state actors' (BMZ 2005: 19; cf. BMZ 2008: 139). In general, the official principles guiding German democracy promotion – 'dialogue', 'long-term commitment' and 'mutual trust' based 'on shared value orientations' – are focused entirely on cooperation (BMZ 2005: 10).

Regarding the *style of democracy promotion*, US documents address the issue of democracy (promotion) considerably more often and employ more explicit and straightforward language than German rhetoric does. One very salient example of this is Bush's (2005) declaration that 'it is the policy of the United States to seek and support the growth of democratic movements and institutions in every nation and culture, with the ultimate goal of ending tyranny in our world.' As previously mentioned, enemies of democracy and those opposing the goals of democracy promotion are clearly identified; this is particularly so in Bush's 'freedom agenda' (cf. Bush 2007; Fore 2008; USAID 2005), but already discernible under the Clinton Administration (White House 1995: 1–2; cf. Anderson 1999). Spreading democracy and freedom worldwide is, however, not 'only' a foreign policy goal, but is considered part of a genuine American mission (cf. Anderson 1999; Bush 2003, 2005; White House 2002: iii). Finally, US official rhetoric more directly and persistently depicts democracy promotion as beneficial to 'hard' interests – especially security but also economic interests – thus granting this policy a more immediate relevance for US foreign policy overall (cf. White House 1995, 2002, 2006).

The German reluctance to speak openly about democracy promotion noted above is confirmed by the general observation that relatively few text passages were coded at all. The whole issue – democracy, democratization, democracy promotion – is far less extensively present in German official rhetoric than in the US case. More specifically, the frequency analysis for the use of crucial terms reveals that US documents mention 'freedom/liberty' three times more often than German ones do, 'democracy' twice as often and 'rule of law' with nearly the same frequency. Correspondingly, German documents frequently avoid talking about democracy (promotion) as an aim by relying on indirect references that somehow imply democracy (cf. BMVg 1994: 41; BMZ 2005: 5–6; Merkel 2007; Steinmeier 2008). If democracy (promotion) is explicitly mentioned, it is usually depicted as situated in a broader context of societal development and as part of a general development agenda (cf. BMZ 2005: 6; Kinkel 1996).

Conceptual vagueness is further aggravated as German documents frequently refer to series of principles and aims which are not really delineated: 'freedom', 'law' and 'human dignity' (BMVg 1994: 41) or 'empowerment, participation and non-discrimination as well as transparency and accountability' (BMZ 2005: 6). Typical for Germany's cautious approach to democracy promotion is that not only 'direct' but also 'indirect' measures are included in the democracy promotion strategy. The purpose of such indirect democracy promotion is to contribute to the 'output legitimation' or the 'performance' of the state (BMZ 2005: 17) and is seen as particularly appropriate when dealing with authoritarian states that refuse to liberalize (BMZ 2005: 18–19).

Finally, for both the United States and Germany, there is preliminary evidence for changes taking place over time. For the period under investigation, the United States displays a clear tendency towards the ideal type of a Freedom Fighter. In this regard, the most conspicuous rhetoric comes, not surprisingly (cf. Monten 2005; Poppe 2010; Smith 2007), from the second Bush Administration. While Clinton's national security strategy still primarily focused on democracy promotion in states already on the path to democratic reforms (White House 1995: 7), the focus under Bush – at least rhetorically – shifted to the overthrow of tyrants (Bush 2007; White House 2006: 1).

In the German case, we find some evidence to support the observation reported in the literature review that Germany since 1990 has adopted – if reluctantly – an increasingly explicit stance on democracy promotion with more and more ministries, agencies, instruments and resources being geared in one way or other to this aim.[30] The first document explicitly laying out a strategy for democracy promotion was only published in 2005 (BMZ 2005). In general, the number of coded passages per document – meaning, the frequency of statements with regard to democracy and democracy promotion – increases over the years. Within the framework of the content analysis conducted here, such changes over time were, however, not systematically assessed. What can be said, though, is that the differences between US and German rhetoric remain distinct over time, even when comparing more recent German documents with US documents from the Clinton era. German governments are always more abstract with regard to their normative assumptions and more reserved with regard to the formulation of aims; moreover, the strategies espoused tend to be cooperative and oriented towards dialogue and inclusion, with Manichaean images missing entirely.

Concluding remarks

Different conceptions of democracy promotion characterize the foreign and development policies of the United States and Germany. The results of the qualitative content analysis confirm what the state-of-the-art suggests with regard to these two countries' democracy promotion profiles: the United States and the German government do indeed talk quite differently about democracy, democratization and democracy promotion, and these conceptual differences approach the ideal types of Freedom Fighter and Civilian Power.[31] While we do find indications for change over time in both document samples, differences remain clearly visible – regardless of what party is in power at a particular time.

Focusing on rhetoric – on official documents and speeches – has, on the one hand, allowed us to systematically assess the conceptual characteristics and differences of US and German democracy promotion in the form of a qualitative content analysis. On the other hand, differing conceptions of democracy promotion tell us nothing about democracy promotion practice. Whether the practice of democracy promotion in specific cases corresponds to the conceptions that we have found to characterize US and German general statements is one of the questions that inform the case studies in the second part of this book. The expectation that we draw from the analysis of conceptions is, however, abundantly clear: *ceteris paribus*, the Freedom Fighter United States is expected to explicitly and assertively advocate the promotion of liberal-democratic values and does not shy away from making use of negative or confrontational strategies, whereas Germany as a Civilian Power is expected to pursue democracy promotion in a more reserved and cooperative manner, focused on long-term results that favour support, dialogue and inclusion.

Notes

1 See Burnell (2000); Carothers (2009); Hazelzet (2007); Kopstein (2006); Nau (2000); Schraeder (2002); Youngs (2004, 2006). A recent edited volume, however, finds evidence for a convergence between US and European Union democracy promotion policies (Magen *et al.* 2009).
2 See Becker *et al.* (2008); Duffield (1999); Harnisch (2003: 329–40); Holsti (1970); Hudson (2007: 103–23); Katzenstein (1996); Kirste and Maull (1996); Müller (2007: 306–12).
3 See Burnell (2011: chapter 4); Carothers (2009); Kurki (2010); Hobson and Kurki (2012); Monten (2005: 113–14); Spanger and Wolff (2007); Wolff and Wurm (2011).
4 Carothers (1991: 258) has argued that 'the US national experience with democratic development, or at least the popular myths of the development of democracy in the United States, gives Americans a strongly institution-oriented view of democracy'. Nau (2000: 149) notes that Europeans 'advocate deep-seated, high-intensity reforms to transform class structures and state institutions' while US democracy programs 'emphasize private sector and local self-help initiatives', and attributes this difference to historical experiences.
5 National role conceptions have been introduced to IR by Holsti (1970: 245–6; see also Kirste and Maull 1996). National identity was emphasized most prominently by Katzenstein (1996; see also Joerißen and Stahl 2003).
6
> Well-known and well-practiced options, preferably tied in to the nation's heroic history, will be preferred over less well-known and less familiar options or options with traumatic track records – even if an objective cost–benefit analysis of the two options would suggest otherwise.
>
> (Hudson 2007: 121)

7 Cf. Azpuru *et al.* (2008); Magen *et al.* (2009); Schraeder (2002); Youngs (2006).
8 While some democratic countries may be characterized by a culture of restraint, non-intervention and/or exemplarism, in others a more activist – missionary or vindicationist – culture might prevail (Wolff and Wurm 2011: 82; cf. Monten 2005; Müller and Wolff 2006; Sørensen 2006).

9 The latter ideal type draws, of course, on the role conception of a Civilian Power developed by Hanns W. Maull (see section on 'German democracy promotion'). In contrast, the ideal type Freedom Fighter cannot draw on an established concept. The distinction between the two ideal-type conceptions of democracy promotion has been proposed by Spanger and Wolff (2007: 277–80).
10 Carothers discusses whether US and European democracy promotion policies correspond to the political and the developmental approach, respectively, and finds that there is too much institutional heterogeneity on both sides of the Atlantic and that one can find elements of both approaches on either side (Carothers 2009: 12–13). Yet, his brief comparison does point to a relative predominance of the political approach in the United States, and of the developmental approach in Europe (Carothers 2009: 14–18; see also Youngs 2004: 31–7; Kopstein 2006; but see Magen *et al.* 2009). We assume that comparing the United States with Germany – instead of Europe or the European Union – promises more precise results (see the introductory chapter to this volume).
11 The literature on US democracy promotion is, of course, vast. For overviews see, e.g. Azpuru *et al.* (2008); Cox *et al.* (2000); Hook (2002); Monten (2005); Poppe (2010: chapters 2–3); Robinson (1996); Smith (1994).
12 The US liberal tradition is, of course, not the only 'mindset' exerting influence on US foreign policy, and its versions and interpretations are diverse. It is, however, one of the dominant lenses through which the United States and its role in and for the world are perceived (Desch 2007; cf. Packenham 1973: chapter 3).
13 Analyses critical of US democracy promotion have emphasized the interventionist character of US democracy promotion. Specialized agencies like the NED have been identified as crucial instruments that use democracy promotion activities as a new form of 'political operations' (Robinson 1996: chapter 2).
14 Although the evolution of German foreign policy since 1990 – and, in particular, German participation in the Kosovo War in 1999 – provoked a debate on whether Germany was gradually abandoning its 'civilian' foreign policy culture, most observers see ' "modified continuity" rather than fundamental change' (Harnisch and Maull 2001b: 2; cf. Geis *et al.* 2010: 190–4; Harnisch and Maull 2001a; Rittberger 2001; Webber 2001).
15 A Civilian Power's prime interest is said to be in using international cooperation as a means of civilizing world politics, which implies both the inclusion of non-democratic regimes and the rejection of unilateral action. A Civilian Power's 'value-oriented foreign policy' (Kirste and Maull 1996: 302) can be expected to focus less on explicitly promoting democracy as a particular (and contested) type of political rule and more on supporting human rights in a rather broad notion of 'universal values' (Pfeil 2001: 88).
16 There are only a few studies on German democracy promotion, among them: Betz (1996); Erdmann (1996); Lapins (2007); Lerch (2007); Pospisil (2009); Rüland and Werz (2002).
17 The role of the German political foundations in implementing German democracy assistance adds to the Civilian Power character of German democracy promotion policy. Their work has traditionally been aimed at promoting dialogue, education and inclusive exchange with a view to enabling long-term processes of political development (cf. Mair 2000; Pinto-Duschinsky 1991).
18 Cf. Betz (1996: 205, 207–8); Pfeil (2001: 95–7); Rüland and Werz (2002: 73–4).
19 These general categories were used only for the qualitative interpretation of statements, not for the quantitative analysis of relative frequencies (see below).
20 If a document contained more than one statement on the same issue, the corresponding code was assigned several times as well. It was also possible to assign different codes to the same text passage – which happened whenever several issues were addressed together.

21 Since US documents as a general rule were more extensive than German documents, the average number of codes assigned was calculated relative to the total number of words in the corresponding subsample (codes per 100 words). The same constant ratio applies to the following indicator, the frequency of specific terms.
22 This is epitomized by the following statement by President Bush (2003): 'Time after time, observers have questioned whether this country or that people or this group are ready for democracy, as if freedom were a prize you win for meeting our own Western standards of progress.' See also Bush (2005, 2007); Powell (2003); White House (2002: i, 2006: 4–5).
23 The paper does mention 'transition countries' (*Übergangsländer*) but emphasizes that these regularly 'remain stuck in transitional structures' (BMZ 2005: 21–2, 8). The transition (from authoritarian rule and/or towards democracy) as a particular, rather short-term process of political change is not mentioned at all.
24 Clearly pointing out the 'enemies to democracy' goes hand in hand with distinct dichotomies, such as good/evil, tyranny/freedom, etc. (cf. Bush 2005, 2007; White House 1995: 1–2, 2002: i, 1, 2006: 1, 4, 9, 11).
25 See, *inter alia*, Bush (2002, 2003, 2005, 2007); Clinton (1999); Natsios (2004); Powell (2003); Rice (2008); USAID (2005: 3, 5); White House (1995: 1–2, 2002: i, 1, 7, 15, 2006: 1, 3–4, 11, 37).
26 In another document, however, the reality of US cooperation with authoritarian regimes is justified in terms of national security (Rice 2008: 13–14, 16).
27 In and of itself, this does not contrast with the Civilian Power concept. As Katzenstein (2003) has shown, the German approach to counterterrorism is about actively combating global terrorism but sees this largely as a fight against crime – not as a war, as the United States would have it.
28 Without references to terrorism, 'inclusion' (10.0 per cent) outweighs 'exclusion' (7.5 per cent).
29 A notable exception includes the following remark by Development Minister Wieczorek-Zeul, who called for telling 'those who still oppress their people, disregard freedom and human rights, and only pursue their own advancement, like Mugabe in Zimbabwe: you will fall too; your people will gain freedom too. We are working in pursuit of this aim' (Bundesregierung 2009: 8).
30 Youngs (2008: 161), for example, notes that the German Development Ministry's funding for democracy assistance 'increased from €180 million (6.2 per cent of bilateral ODA) in 2000 to €410 million (9 per cent) in 2006'.
31 This general finding is also supported by a comparative content analysis of parliamentary debates in Western democracies that identified the main arguments in favour of or against participation in the Gulf War in 1991, the Kosovo War in 1999, and the Iraq War in 2003. This study found that in US debates the relative incidence of references to 'power', 'enemy image' and 'democracy' was above average, while German discourse was characterized by frequent references to 'values', 'international law' and making sure all 'peaceful means' have been 'exhausted' (Geis *et al.* 2010: 190, 193).

References

AA (2000) *Rede des Bundesministers des Auswärtigen, Joschka Fischer, zur Eröffnung des Forums Zukunft der Auswärtigen Kulturpolitik*. 4 July, Berlin. Online, available at: www.ifa.de (accessed 23 February 2011).

Albright, M. (2000) *Sustaining Democracy in the Twenty-first Century*. 18 January, Washington, DC. Online, available at: www.atimes.com (accessed 16 February 2011).

Anderson, B. (1999) *Remarks to a USAID All-agency Meeting*. 17 November, Washington, DC. Online, available at: www.usaid.gov/press/spe_test/speeches/1999/sp991117_2.html (accessed 2 March 2009).

Azpuru, D., Finkel, S.E., Pérez-Liñán, A. and Seligson, M.A. (2008) 'Trends in Democracy Assistance: What Has the United States Been Doing?', *Journal of Democracy*, 19 (2): 150–9.
Becker, U., Müller, H. and Wisotzki, S. (2008) 'Democracy and Nuclear Arms Control – Destiny or Ambiguity?', *Security Studies*, 17 (4): 810–54.
Betz, J. (1996) 'Die Demokratieexportpolitik der Bundesrepublik Deutschland', in R. Hanisch (ed.) *Demokratieexport in die Länder des Südens?*, Hamburg: Deutsches Übersee-Institut.
BMVg (1994) *Weißbuch zur Sicherheit der Bundesrepublik Deutschland und zur Lage der Zukunft der Bundeswehr*, Berlin: BMVg.
BMVg (2003) *Verteidigungspolitische Richtlinien für den Geschäftsbereich des Bundesministers der Verteidigung*. Online, available at: www.bmvg.de (accessed 24 February 2011).
BMVg (2006) *Weißbuch zur Sicherheitspolitik Deutschlands und zur Zukunft der Bundeswehr*. Online, available at: www.bmvg.de (accessed 24 February 2011).
BMZ (1998) *Entwicklungspolitik der Bundesregierung zur Förderung von Menschenrechten, Demokratie und Rechtsstaatlichkeit*, Bonn: BMZ (Spezial, no. 090).
BMZ (2005) *Förderung von Demokratie in der deutschen Entwicklungspolitik. Unterstützung politischer Reformprozesse und Beteiligung der Bevölkerung. Ein Positionspapier des BMZ*, Bonn: BMZ.
BMZ (2008) *Auf dem Weg in die Eine Welt – Weißbuch zur Entwicklungspolitik*, Bonn: BMZ.
Boekle, H. (2001) 'German Foreign Human Rights Policy within the UN', in V. Rittberger (ed.) *German Foreign Policy since Unification: Theories and Case Studies*, Manchester: Manchester University Press.
Boekle, H., Rittberger, V. and Wagner, W. (2001) 'Constructivist foreign policy theory', in V. Rittberger (ed.) *German Foreign Policy since Unification: Theories and Case Studies*, Manchester: Manchester University Press.
Brocker, M. (2006) 'Demokratischer oder christlicher Missionarismus in der US-amerikanischen Außenpolitik?', in M. Brocker and T. Stein (eds) *Christentum und Demokratie*, Darmstadt: Wissenschaftliche Buchgesellschaft.
Bundesregierung (2009): *Regierungserklärung der Bundesministerin für wirtschaftliche Zusammenarbeit und Entwicklung, Heidemarie Wieczorek-Zeul*, Berlin: Bulletin der Bundesregierung (no. 12–1, 29 January).
Burnell, P. (ed.) (2000) *Democracy Assistance. International Co-operation for Democratization*, London: Frank Cass.
Burnell, P. (2011) *Promoting Democracy Abroad: Policy and Performance*, New Brunswick, NJ: Transaction Publishers.
Bush, G.W. (2002) *Graduation Speech at West Point*, West Point, NY, 1 June. Online, available at: http://georgewbush-whitehouse.archives.gov (accessed 15 February 2011).
Bush, G.W. (2003) *Remarks on the 20th Anniversary of the National Endowment for Democracy*, Washington, DC, 6 November. Online, available at: www.ned.org (accessed 15 February 2011).
Bush, G.W. (2005) *Second Inaugural Address*, Washington, DC, 20 January. Online, available at: www.washingtonpost.com (accessed 15 February 2011).
Bush, G.W. (2007) *President Bush Visits Prague*, Czech Republic, Discusses Freedom, Prague, 5 June. Online, available at: http://georgewbush-whitehouse.archives.gov (accessed 15 February 2011).

Carothers, T. (1991) *In the Name of Democracy: US Policy toward Latin America in the Reagan Years*, Berkeley, CA: University of California Press.

Carothers, T. (1999) *Aiding Democracy Abroad: The Learning Curve*, Washington, DC: Carnegie Endowment for International Peace.

Carothers, T. (2002) 'The End of the Transition Paradigm', *Journal of Democracy*, 13 (1): 5–21.

Carothers, T. (2003) 'Promoting Democracy and Fighting Terror', *Foreign Affairs* 82 (1): 84–97.

Carothers, T. (2009) 'Democracy Assistance: Political vs. Developmental?', *Journal of Democracy*, 20 (1): 5–19.

Christopher, W. (1993) *Statement at the Senate Confirmation Hearing*, Washington, DC, 13 January. Online, available at: http://dosfan.lib.uic.edu (accessed 16 February2011).

Clinton, W.J. (1999) *Remarks on Keeping America Secure in the 21st Century*, Washington, DC, 22 January. Online, available at: www.justice.gov (accessed 15 February 2011).

Cox, M. (2000) 'Wilsonianism Resurgent? The Clinton Administration and the Promotion of Democracy', in M. Cox, G.J. Ikenberry and T. Inoguchi (eds) *American Democracy Promotion: Impulses, Strategies, and Impacts*, Oxford: Oxford University Press.

Cox, M., Ikenberry, G.J. and Inoguchi, T. (eds) (2000) *American Democracy Promotion: Impulses, Strategies, and Impacts*, Oxford: Oxford University Press.

Desch, M.C. (2007) 'America's Liberal Illiberalism: The Ideological Origins of Overreaction in US Foreign Policy', *International Security* 32 (3): 7–43.

Doyle, M.W. (2009) 'A Few Words on Mill, Walzer, and Nonintervention', *Ethics and International Affairs*, 23 (4): 349–69.

Duffield, J.S. (1999) 'Political Culture and State Behavior: Why Germany Confounds Neorealism', *International Organization*, 53 (4): 765–803.

Erdmann, G. (1996) *Demokratie und Demokratieförderung in der Dritten Welt. Ein Literaturbericht und eine Erhebung der Konzepte und Instrumente*, Bonn: Deutsche Kommission Justitia et Pax.

Fischer, J. (2004) *Rede auf der 40. Münchner Sicherheitskonferenz*, Munich, 7 February. Online, available at: www.securityconference.de (accessed 23 February 2011).

Fore, H.H. (2008) *Remarks by Henrietta Fore, Director of US Foreign Assistance and Administrator, USAID*, Washington, DC, 8 October. Online, available at: www.usaid.gov (accessed 16 February 2011).

Fox, G.H. and Roth, B.R. (eds) (2000) *Democratic Governance and International Law*, Cambridge: Cambridge University Press.

Geis, A., Müller, H. and Schörnig, N. (2010) 'Liberale Demokratien und Krieg. Warum manche kämpfen und andere nicht. Ergebnisse einer vergleichenden Inhaltsanalyse von Parlamentsdebatten', *Zeitschrift für Internationale Beziehungen*, 17 (2): 171–202.

Harnisch, S. (2003) 'Theorieorientierte Außenpolitikforschung in einer Ära des Wandels', in G. Hellmann, K.D. Wolf and M. Zürn (eds) *Die neuen Internationalen Beziehungen. Forschungsstand und Perspektiven in Deutschland*, Baden-Baden: Nomos.

Harnisch, S. and Maull, H.W. (eds) (2001a) *Germany as a Civilian Power? The Foreign Policy of the Berlin Republic*, Manchester: Manchester University Press.

Harnisch, S. and Maull, H.W. (2001b) 'Introduction', in S. Harnisch, and H.W. Maull, (eds) *Germany as a Civilian Power? The Foreign Policy of the Berlin Republic*, Manchester: Manchester University Press.

Hazelzet, H. (2007) 'Carrots or Sticks? EU and EU Reactions to Human Rights Violations in the Nineties and Beyond', in M. Van Doorn and R. Von Meijenfeldt (eds)

Democracy: Europe's Core Value? On the European Profile in World-wide Democracy Assistance, Delft: Eburon.
Hobson, C. and Kurki, M. (eds) (2012) *The Conceptual Politics of Democracy Promotion*, London: Routledge.
Holsti, K.J. (1970) 'National Role Conceptions in the Study of Foreign Policy', *International Studies Quarterly* 14 (3): 233–309.
Hook, S.W. (2002) 'Inconsistent US Efforts to Promote Democracy Abroad', in P.J. Schraeder (ed.) *Exporting Democracy. Rhetoric vs. Reality*, Boulder, CO: Lynne Rienner.
Hudson, V.M. (2007) *Foreign Policy Analysis: Classic and Contemporary Theory*, Lanham, MD: Rowman & Littlefield.
Ish-Shalom, P. (2006) 'Theory as a Hermeneutical Mechanism: The Democratic-Peace Thesis and the Politics of Democratization', *European Journal of International Relations*, 12 (4): 565–98.
Jahn, B. (2005) 'Kant, Mill, and Illiberal Legacies in International Affairs', *International Organization*, 59 (1): 177–207.
Joerißen, B. and Stahl, B. (eds) (2003) *Europäische Außenpolitik und nationale Identität. Vergleichende Diskurs- und Verhaltensstudien zu Dänemark, Deutschland, Frankreich, Griechenland, Italien und den Niederlanden*. Münster: LIT.
Katzenstein, P.J. (ed.) (1996) *The Culture of National Security: Norms and Identity in World Politics*, New York, NY: Columbia University Press.
Katzenstein, P.J. (2003) 'Same War – Different Views: Germany, Japan and Counterterrorism', *International Organization*, 57 (4): 731–60.
Kinkel, K. (1996) *Rede anlässlich der 52. Sitzung der Menschenrechtskommission*, Geneva, 16 April.
Kirste, K. and Maull, H.W. (1996) 'Zivilmacht und Rollentheorie', *Zeitschrift für Internationale Beziehungen*, 3 (2): 283–312.
Kopstein, J. (2006) 'The Transatlantic Divide over Democracy Promotion', *Washington Quarterly*, 29 (2): 85–98.
Kurki, M. (2010) 'Democracy and Conceptual Contestability: Reconsidering Conceptions of Democracy in Democracy Promotion', *International Studies Review*, 12 (3): 362–86.
Lapins, W. (2007) *Demokratieförderung in der Deutschen Außenpolitik*, Berlin: Friedrich-Ebert-Stiftung. Online, available at: http://library.fes.de (accessed 29 May 2007).
Lerch, M. (2007) *Demokratie im Aufwind? Außenpolitische Strategien der Demokratieförderung*, Berlin: Friedrich-Ebert-Stiftung. Online, available at: www.fes.de (accessed 6 August 2007).
Magen, A., Risse, T. and McFaul, M.A. (eds) (2009) *Promoting Democracy and the Rule of Law: American and European Strategies*, Houndmills Palgrave Macmillan.
Mair, S. (2000) 'Germany's Stiftungen and Democracy Assistance: Comparative Advantages, New Challenges', in P. Burnell (ed.) *Democracy Assistance. International Cooperation for Democratization*, London: Frank Cass.
Maoz, Z. and Russett, B. (1993) 'Normative and Structural Causes of Democratic Peace, 1946–1986' *American Political Science Review* 87 (3): 624–38.
Maull, H.W. (1990) 'Germany and Japan: The New Civilian Powers', *Foreign Affairs*, 69 (5): 91–106.
Mayring, P. (2000) *Qualitative Content Analysis. FQS – Forum Qualitative Social Research 1(2)*. Online, available at: www.qualitative-research.net/fqs (accessed 22 January 2011).

Merkel, A. (2007) *Außenpolitische Grundsatzrede der Bundeskanzlerin in Abu Dhabi*, Abu Dhabi, 5 February. Online, available at: www.bundeskanzlerin.de (accessed 23 February 2011).

Monten, J. (2005) 'The Roots of the Bush Doctrine: Power, Nationalism, and Democracy Promotion in US Strategy', *International Security* 29 (4): 112–56.

Müller, H. (2007) 'Vorüberlegungen zu einer Theorie der Ambivalenz liberaldemokratischer Außen- und Sicherheitspolitik', in A. Geis, H. Müller, H. and W. Wagner (eds) *Schattenseiten des Demokratischen Friedens. Zur Kritik einer Theorie liberaler Außen- und Sicherheitspolitik*, Frankfurt a.M.: Campus.

Müller, H. and Wolff, J. (2006) 'Democratic Peace: Many Data, Little Explanation?', in A. Geis, L. Brock and H. Müller (eds) *Democratic Wars. Looking at the Dark Side of Democratic Peace*, Houndmills: Palgrave Macmillan.

Natsios, A. (2004) *Testimony before the Subcommittee on Foreign Operations, Committee on Appropriations of the US Senate*, Washington, DC, 21 April. Online, available at: http://pdf.usaid.gov (accessed 16 February 2011).

Nau, H. (2000) 'America's Identity, Democracy Promotion and National Interests: Beyond Realism, Beyond Idealism', in M. Cox, G.J. Ikenberry and T. Inoguchi (eds) *American Democracy Promotion: Impulses, Strategies, and Impacts*, Oxford: Oxford University Press.

Packenham, R.A. (1973) *Liberal America and the Third World. Political Development Ideas in Foreign Aid and Social Science*, Princeton, NJ: Princeton University Press.

Peceny, M. (1999) *Democracy at the Point of Bayonets*, University Park, PE: Pennsylvania State University Press.

Pfeil, F. (2001) 'Civil Power and Human Rights: the Case of Germany', in S. Harnisch and H.W. Maull (eds) (2001a) *Germany as a Civilian Power? The Foreign Policy of the Berlin Republic*, Manchester: Manchester University Press.

Pinto-Duschinsky, M. (1991) 'Foreign Political Aid: The German Political Foundations and their US Counterparts', *International Affairs*, 67 (1): 33–63.

Poppe, A.E. (2010) 'Whither to, Obama? US Democracy Promotion after the Cold War', *PRIF Report*, no. 96, Frankfurt a.M.: Peace Research Institute Frankfurt.

Pospisil, J. (2009) *Die Entwicklung von Sicherheit. Entwicklungspolitische Programme der USA und Deutschlands im Grenzbereich zur Sicherheitspolitik*, Bielefeld: Transcript.

Powell, C. (2003) *Remarks at the Elliott School of International Affairs*, Washington, DC, 5 September. Online, available at: http://en.epochtimes.com (accessed 15 February 2011).

Rice, C. (2008) 'Rethinking the National Interest: American Realism for a new World', *Foreign Affairs*, 87 (4): 2–26.

Risse-Kappen, T. (1995) 'Democratic Peace – Warlike Democracies: A Social Constructivist Interpretation of the Democratic Peace', *European Journal of International Relations*, 1 (4): 491–517.

Rittberger, V. (ed.) (2001) *German Foreign Policy since Unification: Theories and Case Studies*, Manchester: Manchester University Press.

Robinson, W.I. (1996) *Promoting Polyarchy: Globalization, United States Intervention and Hegemony*, Cambridge: Cambridge University Press.

Rüland, J. and Werz, N. (2002) 'Germany's Hesitant Role in Promoting Democracy', in P.J. Schraeder (ed.) *Exporting Democracy. Rhetoric vs. Reality*, Boulder, CO: Lynne Rienner.

Schmitz, D.F. (2006) *The United States and Right-wing Dictatorships, 1965–1989*, Cambridge: Cambridge University Press.

Schraeder, P.J. (ed.) (2002) *Exporting Democracy. Rhetoric vs. Reality*, Boulder, CO: Lynne Rienner.
Schraeder, P.J. (2003) 'The State of the Art in International Democracy Promotion: Results of a Joint European–North American Research Network', *Democratization*, 20 (2): 21–44.
Schröder, G. (2002) *Rede bei der 39. Kommandeurtagung der Bundeswehr*, Hannover, 8 April. Online, available at: http://archiv.bundesregierung.de/bpaexport/rede/83/75083/multi.htm (accessed 23 March 2009).
Smith, T. (1994) *America's Mission: The United States and the Worldwide Struggle for Democracy in the Twentieth Century*, Princeton, NJ: Princeton University Press.
Smith, T. (2007) *A Pact with the Devil: Washington's Bid for World Supremacy and the Betrayal of the American Promise*, London: Routledge.
Sørensen, G. (2006) 'Liberalism of Restraint and Liberalism of Imposition: Liberal Values and World Order in the New Millennium', *International Relations*, 20 (3): 251–72.
Spanger, H.-J. and Wolff, J. (2007) 'Universales Ziel – partikulare Wege? Externe Demokratieförderung zwischen einheitlicher Rhetorik und vielfältiger Praxis', in A. Geis, H. Müller and W. Wagner (eds) *Schattenseiten des Demokratischen Friedens. Zur Kritik einer Theorie liberaler Außen- und Sicherheitspolitik*, Frankfurt a.M.: Campus.
Spranger, C.-D. (1998) *Rede beim Entwicklungspolitischen Forum der Deutschen Stiftung für internationale Entwicklung (DSE)*, Berlin, 19 January.
Steinmeier, F. (2008) *Rede bei der Eröffnung der Deutschlandforschertagung der Bundeszentrale für Politische Bildung*, Berlin, 9 November. Online, available at: www.bpb.de (accessed 23 February 2011).
USAID (1998) *Democracy and Governance: A Conceptual Framework*, Washington, DC. Online, available at: www.usaid.gov (accessed 16 February 2011).
USAID (2002) *Foreign Aid in the National Interest: Promoting Freedom, Security and Opportunity*, Washington, DC. Online, available at: www.usaid.gov (accessed 16 February 2011).
USAID (2005) *At Freedom's Frontiers: A Democracy and Governance Strategic Framework*, Washington, DC. Online, available at: www.usaid.gov (accessed 16 February 2011).
Webber, D. (ed.) (2001) *New Europe, New Germany, Old Foreign Policy? German Foreign Policy since Unification*, London: Frank Cass.
Whitehead, L. (1991) 'The Imposition of Democracy', in A.F. Lowenthal (ed.) *Exporting Democracy: The United States and Latin America: Case Studies*. Baltimore, MD: Johns Hopkins University Press.
White House (1995) *A National Security Strategy of Engagement and Enlargement*, Washington, DC. Online, available at: www.au.af.mil (accessed 16 February 2011).
White House (2002) *The National Security Strategy of the United States of America*, Washington, DC. Online, available at: www.presidentialrhetoric.com (accessed 16 February 2011).
White House (2006) *The National Security Strategy of the United States of America*, Washington, DC. Online, available at: www.presidentialrhetoric.com (accessed 16 February 2011).
Wieczorek-Zeul, H. (2005) *A Year of Opportunities: UN Reform and Development Finance*, Washington, DC, 16 April. Online, available at: www.bmz.de/de/presse/reden/ministerin/2005/april/speech20050414.html (accessed 16 March 2009).

Wolff, J. and Wurm, I. (2011) 'Towards a Theory of External Democracy Promotion: A Proposal for Theoretical Classification', *Security Dialogue*, 42 (1): 77–96.

Youngs, R. (2004) *International Democracy and the West: The Role of Governments, Civil Society, and Multinational Business*, Oxford: Oxford University Press.

Youngs, R. (ed.) (2006) *Survey of European Democracy Promotion Policies 2000–2006*, Madrid: FRIDE.

Youngs, R. (2008) 'Trends in Democracy Assistance: What Has Europe Been Doing?', *Journal of Democracy*, 19 (2): 160–9.

3 Norms versus interests
The determinants across the cases[1]

Daniel Schewe and Jonas Wolff

The case studies constitute the empirical core of the research project that is presented in the present volume. The in-depth analysis of the 12 pairs of states (dyads) serves on the one hand to identify the effects and the interaction of the hypothesized determinants of democracy promotion. On the other, the case studies provide the material for the comparative analysis. Because there is wide variance in the configuration of determinants in the 12 cases, comparing them will allow for causal inferences. Indeed, the dyads selected are characterized in part by relatively symmetric, in part by extremely asymmetric, power relations; security considerations on the part of the donor are sometimes pivotal, sometimes irrelevant; economic interests are at times high, at times marginal; and a few pairs of states are joint members of international organizations with strong democracy-related norms, while others are not.

This chapter gives a comparative overview of the basic features of the cases, i.e. of the configurations of determinants for the 12 pairs of states. Thus, it presents and operationalizes the six determinants mentioned in the introduction: relative power position, security interests, economic interests, domestic special interests, political culture, and, finally, international norms. These determinants are 'measured' by drawing on both statistical data and qualitative assessments. All (sub-)indicators and determinants are ranked on an ordinal scale ranging from 1 (minimum) to 4 (maximum). Each ordinal scale is constructed to cover the empirical range constituted by the 12 pairs of states. All ranks given in the tables, thus, have to be read as relative within our set of cases, not as relating to the universe of state dyads in the contemporary world.

Relative power position

According to Realist approaches in IR, the relative position of power defined in terms of material power capabilities constitutes an important factor shaping democracy promotion in foreign policy (cf. Monten 2005). Only in cases of drastic asymmetries in relative power capabilities between donor and recipient country can efforts to promote democracy from the outside be regarded as rational in the sense of promising tangible effects at appropriate costs (Wolff and Wurm 2011: 80). At the same time, high power asymmetries enable the democracy promoter to control the risks of democratization. Relatively balanced power relations or even an asymmetry in favour of the recipient, on the other hand, should lead to reluctance or passivity on the part of the donor.

Established indicators that measure material power capabilities are the Composite Index of National Capability (CINC) compiled by the Correlates of War Project, and relative economic power as measured by gross domestic product (GDP). For each indicator, the ratio of donor to recipient measures the bilateral distribution of power (see Table 3.1).

Security interests

From a modified (neo-)Realist perspective, security interests drive democracy promotion to the extent that, following the democratic peace proposition, the democratic shape of other states' political regimes is seen by a given donor government as contributing to international peace and national security (Wolff and Wurm 2011: 82–3). In such a 'security-based approach' (Peceny 1999: 3), promoting democracy becomes a tool of security policy (cf. Smith 1994). However, because the positive impact on national security is long-term only, directly tangible security interests will prevail over the goal of democracy promotion

Table 3.1 Relative power position

	CINC*	GDP**	Total***	Ordinal scale****
United States/Bolivia	153.1	1,184.1	158.9	4
United States/Ecuador	94.5	436.2	77.6	4
United States/Belarus	54.1	423.9	56.5	4
Germany/Bolivia	31.4	298.1	36.4	4
Germany/Ecuador	19.4	106.4	17.1	3
Germany/Belarus	10.6	140.7	15.1	3
United States/Pakistan	11.2	122.1	14.1	3
United States/Turkey	10.2	30.7	7.2	3
Germany/Pakistan	2.4	30.9	3.3	2
United States/Russia	2.0	24.1	2.7	2
Germany/Turkey	2.1	7.7	1.6	2
Germany/Russia	0.4	5.8	0.6	1

Notes
* Ratio of the two countries' CINC according to COW (no date); average for the years 1991 and 2001.
** Ratio of the two countries' GDP according to World Bank (2011). Average for the years 1995, 2000 and 2005.
*** Average of both indicators. Since the average GDP ratio is higher than the average CINC ratio by a factor of 7.19, the former indicator was weighted accordingly: Total=$(CINC + [GDP/7.19])/2$.
**** The four categories were defined as follows: 1=negative power asymmetry (total<1); 2=low power asymmetry (1<total<5); 3=high power asymmetry (5<total<25); 4=extreme power asymmetry (total>25).

whenever both objectives clash. In general, democracy promotion, here, depends largely on the relevance of the particular recipient country for the security interests of the donor: this determines the extent to which democracy promotion as a long-term security strategy is of interest at all, as well as the extent to which serious extrinsic conflicts of objectives related to security issues can emerge.

To measure dyad-specific security interests, three indicators were chosen: the extent of security cooperation; possession of nuclear weapons by the recipient; strategic relevance of the recipient from the perspective of the donor (see Table 3.2). As to nuclear weapons, we distinguished between possession ('4') and non-possession ('1'). The overall strategic relevance of a given recipient cannot be measured objectively but only by drawing on subjective assessments on the part of the individual donors. With a view to this indicator, therefore, dyads were ranked according to qualitative assessments based on the bilateral profiles that were compiled at the beginning of the case studies.[2] For the United States, Pakistan, Russia and Turkey were ranked as of highest strategic relevance ('4'), Russia and Turkey in the case of Germany. Bolivia and Ecuador are strategically important recipients for the United States ('3'). For Germany, Pakistan is indirectly relevant strategically because of Germany's military involvement in Afghanistan, Belarus because of its geographical location ('2'). Finally, Bolivia and Ecuador are largely irrelevant to Germany, as is Belarus for the United States ('1'). With regard to the first indicator, the extent of security cooperation, dyads were ranked according to sub-indicators: military aid/presence and the extent of bi- and multilateral cooperation in security issues. The ranking, here, is justified as follows:

Table 3.2 Security interests

	Security cooperation	Nuclear weapons*	Strategic relevance	Total**
United States/Pakistan	3	4	4	4
United States/Russia	3	4	4	4
Germany/Russia	3	4	4	4
United States/Turkey	4	1	4	3
Germany/Turkey	4	1	4	3
Germany/Pakistan	2	4	2	3
United States/Bolivia	4	1	3	3
United States/Ecuador	4	1	3	3
Germany/Belarus	2	1	2	2
United States/Belarus	2	1	1	1
Germany/Bolivia	1	1	1	1
Germany/Ecuador	1	1	1	1

Notes
* Dichotomous ranking: massive increase in security interests in the case of possession of nuclear weapons (4) versus no security-related increase in importance in the case of non-possession (1).
** Rounded average of the three indicators.

The close security cooperation between the United States and Turkey ('4') can already be observed in purely quantitative terms by looking at the extent of military assistance, and especially military presence.[3] In qualitative terms, the joint membership in NATO and the US military base in Incirlik, near Adana, are to be mentioned (Migdalovitz 2008: 15–16). US security cooperation with Bolivia and Ecuador was also ranked as close. This refers mainly to bilateral cooperation in counternarcotics – which, from the US perspective, is a directly security-related issue. In the case of Bolivia, cooperation between the governments (and their security forces) has since the 1980s included US assistance in terms of equipment, personnel, money and expertise for the fight against coca cultivation, drug production and drug trafficking, and for some time also encompassed direct military cooperation (Ribando 2008a: 16–18).[4] In Ecuador, security cooperation has been primarily aimed at fighting drug trafficking and terrorism, in particular with a view to Ecuador's northern border to Colombia. The core element of US activities, from 1999 to 2009, was the US Forward Operating Location (i.e. the US military base) in Manta (Ribando 2008b: 5).[5]

US security cooperation with Pakistan and Russia was, by comparison, ranked as 'medium' ('3'). In the case of Pakistan, a significant amount of military aid notwithstanding, the military presence is much lower than in the case of Turkey.[6] Concerning Russia, data for both indicators are lower than in the case of US–Turkey relations.[7] Neither Pakistan nor Russia are members of NATO and neither hosts a US military base. Security cooperation, however, is still pronounced. In the case of Pakistan, this particularly concerns the US 'war on terror' (cf. Kronstadt 2009: 18–24). For security cooperation between the United States and Russia, the NATO–Russia Council, the Organization for Security and Cooperation in Europe (OSCE) and the UN Security Council are to be mentioned, as is bilaterally the area of arms control, for instance in the context of the Cooperative Threat Reduction programme (cf. Spanger 2008).

With regard to Germany, security cooperation with Turkey was ranked 'high', with Russia 'medium'. There is no significant amount of German military aid to, or military presence in, either of the recipient countries.[8] Only in the case of Turkey does joint membership in NATO imply the direct presence of German soldiers in the country.[9] Since the integration of the Western European Union (WEU) into the European Security and Defence Policy (ESDP), German–Turkish security cooperation under the umbrella of ESDP has to be added. Furthermore, with a view to intra-societal peace in Germany, there are bilateral agreements on the fight against pro-Kurdish and Islamist terrorism in Germany (cf. Karakaş 2011: 7). The cooperation between Germany and Russia includes, *inter alia*, joint activities in the context of the NATO–Russia Council and the OSCE as well as bi- and multilateral cooperation in the area of arms control (Cooperative Threat Reduction) (for further details, see the respective bilateral profiles in the chapters on Turkey and Russia).

US and German bilateral security cooperation with Belarus is insignificant. Some multilateral cooperation, however, does exist for both dyads because of NATO's Partnership for Peace programme. Military aid and presence is at best marginal.[10] Finally, there is no security cooperation involved in Germany's relations with Bolivia and Ecuador (cf. Bundesregierung 2009, 2010).

Economic interests

Concerning the factors that shape democracy promotion policies, besides security interests, it is economic interests that are mentioned most frequently in the literature. According to Economic Liberalism in IR, democratic regimes promise conditions (predictability, stability, rule of law) that are crucial for economic cooperation. In addition, democratic peace research emphasizes that democracies are particularly prone to increasing political cooperation and economic interdependence with each other (cf. Ikenberry 1999; Mansfield et al. 2002; cf. Wolff and Wurm 2011: 79–80, 83). Viewed from this perspective, democracy promotion directly serves economic interests – but democracy, again, is promoted for its instrumental value only. Democracy promotion should, therefore, take a back seat when it collides with the tangible economic interests of the donor.

Two indicators were selected to measure economic interests: the amount of a donor's foreign direct investment (FDI) in the respective recipient country and the amount of bilateral trade. Both indicators are measured as a percentage of total donor FDI/trade (see Table 3.3).

Table 3.3 Economic interests

	FDI*	Trade**	Total***	Ordinal scale****
Germany/Russia	0.2473	2.1230	0.3495	4
Germany/Turkey	0.3074	1.3279	0.2950	4
United States/Russia	0.1041	0.4604	0.1010	3
United States/Turkey	0.1297	0.2755	0.0942	3
United States/Ecuador	0.0904	0.1906	0.0655	3
United States/Pakistan	0.0523	0.1243	0.0394	3
Germany/Pakistan	0.0339	0.1114	0.0288	3
United States/Bolivia	0.0315	0.0205	0.0179	2
Germany/Ecuador	0.0176	0.0463	0.0137	2
Germany/Belarus	0.0043	0.0997	0.0128	2
Germany/Bolivia	0.0015	0.0084	0.0016	1
United States/Belarus	0.0002	0.0075	0.0009	1

Notes
* US and German FDI stocks in the recipient country as percentage of US and German total FDI stocks (UNCTAD 2011); average for the years 1995, 2000 and 2003.
** Share (in per cent) of bilateral trade (imports and exports) in total German/US trade (Statistisches Bundesamt Deutschland 2011; US Census Bureau 2011); average for the years 1995, 2000 and 2005.
*** Rounded and weighted average of the two sub-indicators. Since the average share of bilateral trade is higher than the average FDI ratio by a factor of 4.7, the former indicator was weighted accordingly: Total = $(FDI + [Trade/4.7])/2$.
**** The four categories are defined as follows: 1 = no economic interests (total < 0.01); 2 = low (0.01 < total < 0.02); 3 = medium (0.02 < total < 0.15); 4 = high (total > 0.15).

Domestic special interests

For the sake of this study, the introductory chapter has specified Republican Liberalism's general emphasis on the relevance of plural, societal interests for foreign policy. Here, we are interested only in those social groups in a donor country that specifically try to influence donor policies towards a given recipient country. At this general comparative level, the aim is to roughly operationalize the *strength* of such domestic special interests. This indicator, therefore, merely tells us whether this fourth determinant can be expected to be of any relevance for democracy promotion in a given pair of states. The shape and direction of this (expected) impact, however, can only be assessed qualitatively on a case-by-case basis. Immigrant/diaspora organizations as well as advocacy and interest groups that focus on an individual country may be of various shapes and take up very different (and quite heterogeneous) positions as to the (desired) political development of the recipient country.[11]

The overall strength of domestic special interests in a given recipient country was assessed by looking at two indicators (see Table 3.4). The first is based on the share of immigrants from the different recipient countries in the US and German total population.[12] The quantitative strength of a particular (ethnic/identity) group in the overall population, however, does not immediately translate into political influence. In addition, it is not only immigrant/diaspora groups that articulate specific recipient-related interests. Therefore, we look, second, at the organizational strength of interest groups and NGOs concerned with the respective

Table 3.4 Domestic special interests

	Immigrants*	Immigrants**	Lobby groups	Total***
Germany/Turkey	2.4295	4	4	4
Germany/Russia	0.1408	2	3	3
United States/Turkey	0.0418	1	3	2
United States/Russia	0.9424	2	2	2
United States/Ecuador	0.1148	2	2	2
United States/Pakistan	0.0899	2	2	2
Germany/Belarus	0.0112	1	2	2
United States/Bolivia	<0.04	1	2	2
Germany/Pakistan	0.0450	1	1	1
Germany/Ecuador	0.0044	1	1	1
Germany/Bolivia	0.0021	1	1	1
United States/Belarus	<0.04	1	1	1

Notes
* Share (in per cent) of population with ancestry (US) or foreign citizenship (Germany) of the respective recipient country in total US/German population (US Census Bureau 2004; Statistisches Bundesamt Deutschland 2003); data for 2000.
** The figures in the first column were ranked as follows: 1=no (share<0.05); 2=low (0.05<share<1); 3=medium (1<share<2); 4=high (share>2).
*** Rounded average of the two indicators.

recipient country. This can only be assessed in a qualitative way. Without a doubt, organized domestic special interests are clearly strongest ('4') for German–Turkish relations (cf. Karakaş 2011). Significantly less influential, but still relatively strong ('3'), is the heterogeneous spectrum of lobby groups in the United States that are interested in US–Turkey relations; these groups include the 'anti-Turkey' Greek and Armenian lobbies as well as the Turkish and (until recently) the traditionally 'pro-Turkey' Israel lobby groups (cf. Yilmaz 2004). For the German–Russian dyad, organized special interests were also ranked as relatively important ('3'). These groups range from the German Business Committee on Eastern European Economic Relations to advocacy groups 'that are concerned with Russia's democratic deficits or its war in Chechnya' (Spanger 2005: 4). While organized special interests can be termed non-existent ('1') for German relations with Belarus, Bolivia, Ecuador and Pakistan as well as for US relations with Belarus, for the remaining pairs of states there exist at least some lobby groups ('2').[13]

Political culture

From the perspective of an actor-centred Constructivist approach to IR, political culture constitutes an important determinant of foreign policy. The theoretical expectation, here, is that culturally rooted national self-perceptions, role conceptions or identities shape the perception and evaluation of the outside world as well as the formulation and implementation of foreign-policy preferences and strategies (see Chapter 2). From this perspective, the relevance of the determinant 'political culture' is expected to be consistently high and, therefore, ranked as '4' for both donors across all recipient countries.

This ranking implies the assumption that US and German democracy promotion policies are characterized by general, culturally rooted notions of democratization and democracy promotion. Chapter 2 suggests that we should expect these notions to differ significantly between the United States and Germany. Whether a donor is guided by the ideal-type conception of the Civilian Power or follows the script of the Freedom Fighter, should, of course, make a significant difference – in both cases, however, the 'political culture' thesis implies that particular conceptions of democracy promotion should generally shape foreign (and development) policy independently of specific recipient countries.

International norms

To a certain extent, democracy-related norms are established at the global level of the United Nations (UN). Yet, at the level of regional organizations, norms concerning democracy and democracy promotion are in part much stronger (cf. Piccone 2005). The strength of 'democracy norms' is assessed, first, by looking at the extent to which a group of states has institutionalized democracy as a common, binding principle: is a democratic political regime a condition for membership, and do violations result in sanctions going so far as the suspension of membership and exclusion from the organization? The second question refers to the extent to which an international (regional) organization defines the active promotion of democracy as a legitimate objective of the organization and/or its member states and the extent to which it establishes instruments for this purpose. In order to measure the strength of such democracy-related international norms for a given pair of states, the joint international (regional) organization with the highest democracy standards for the dyad was consulted.

The strength of democracy-related norms in international organizations ranges from the UN ('1') on the one hand to the European Union ('4') on the other. Norms concerning democracy and democracy promotion as established within the UN (cf. Newman and Rich 2004) constitute the global minimum standard. The EU, for its part, is most advanced in the institutionalization of democracy-related norms – this holds both for the common obligation to maintain democracy as well as with a view to instruments to protect and promote democracy (both internally and externally) (cf. Piccone 2005: 116; Youngs 2010). Although with a lower intensity than in the case of the EU, explicit norms related to democracy and democracy promotion including mechanisms for sanctions are also established by the Council of Europe (2007) and the OAS (cf. Boniface 2002; Piccone 2005: 103–8). In principle, NATO also requires its members to be democracies, but there is no 'formal democracy clause designed to protect democracy [in member states] from unconstitutional threats' (Piccone 2005: 113).

The members of the OSCE have, since 1990, codified commitments to democratic practices in a series of agreements. On paper, the OSCE also provides for

Table 3.5 International norms

	Joint organization with the strongest 'democracy norms'	Strength of the shared 'democracy norms'
Germany/Turkey	EU*	4
Germany/Russia	Council of Europe	3
United States/Bolivia	OAS	3
United States/Ecuador	OAS	3
United States/Turkey	NATO	2
Germany/Belarus	OSCE	2
United States/Belarus	OSCE	2
United States/Russia	OSCE	2
United States/Pakistan	UN	1
Germany/Pakistan	UN	1
Germany/Bolivia	UN	1
Germany/Ecuador	UN	1

Note
* Turkey is, of course, not yet an EU member state. In the framework of the ongoing EU accession process, however, Turkey – and, especially, German policy towards Turkey – has committed to the EU's democracy-related norms.

Norms versus interests 69

(soft) mechanisms to implement these standards. But in actual fact being a democracy is clearly not a condition for OSCE member states, and the existing mechanisms to enforce compliance are rarely used and consist mainly in naming and blaming (Piccone 2005: 114–16). Even lower is the strength of democracy-related norms in the framework of the NATO–Russia Council, which only indirectly commits its members by affirming the obligations made within the UN and OSCE (cf. NATO 1997).

Results: the configurations of determinants

The results of this chapter consist in a comparative overview of the determinants that characterize the 12 pairs of states that are studied in the present volume. Table 3.6 summarizes the respective configurations of determinants that arise from the above analysis (see also Figure 1.1 in the introductory chapter).

At one end of the spectrum are those dyads that combine marginal donor interests, high power asymmetries and a low level of shared democracy-related norms (Germany/Bolivia, Germany/Ecuador, United States/Belarus). In these cases, one would expect democracy promotion to be largely shaped by the specific political culture of the individual donor country. Conflicting objectives, here, would be expected to mainly be intrinsic in nature – i.e. pitting sub-dimensions of democracy or sub-targets of democracy promotion against each other – and donors would be expected to deal with these conflicts following a

Table 3.6 Configurations of determinants

	Determinant 1 Relative power	*Determinant 2 Security interests*	*Determinant 3 Economic interests*	*Determinant 4 Special interests*	*Determinant 5 Political culture**	*Determinant 6 International norms*
Germany/Bolivia	4	1	1	1	4 (CP)	1
United States/Bolivia	4	3	2	2	4 (FF)	3
Germany/Ecuador	3	1	2	1	4 (CP)	1
United States/Ecuador	4	3	3	2	4 (FF)	3
Germany/Turkey	2	3	4	4	4 (CP)	4
United States/Turkey	3	3	3	2	4 (FF)	2
Germany/Pakistan	2	3	3	1	4 (CP)	1
United States/Pakistan	3	4	3	2	4 (FF)	1
Germany/Belarus	3	2	2	2	4 (CP)	2
United States/Belarus	4	1	1	1	4 (FF)	2
Germany/Russia	1	4	4	3	4 (CP)	3
United States/Russia	2	4	3	2	4 (FF)	2

Note
* CP: Civilian Power; FF: Freedom Fighter. See Section 'Political culture' and Chapter 2.

logic of normative appropriateness that is defined by their particular ideological predispositions.

At the other end of the spectrum are those dyads in which one would expect donor policies to be determined by strong 'national interests'. Particularly in the cases of US policy towards Pakistan and Russia, this concerns powerful security interests. In German relations with Turkey economic interests predominate. One would expect German policy towards Russia to be driven by a combination of security and economic interests. In all these cases, significant extrinsic conflicts of objectives are to be expected, and donors would likely adapt their policies in line with their foreign-policy interests – if need be by going against their normative preferences. This expectation also holds for Germany's policy towards Pakistan: although German security and economic interests in Pakistan are somewhat lower than in Turkey or Russia, efforts at actively promoting democracy are additionally circumscribed by a relatively balanced power relationship.

Security and economic interests notwithstanding, in the case of German relations with Turkey strong democracy-related international norms as established by the EU enlargement process should prevent a purely interest-driven policy. Even if perceived German interests opposed promoting Turkish democracy, we would expect the international normative setting to push Germany towards a relatively coherent stance on democracy promotion and, at least, prevent an open disavowal of democracy (promotion) standards. The same holds for US policy towards Bolivia and Ecuador. Here, strong donor interests (mainly security-related), on the one hand, and political culture and international norms, on the other, indicate that an acute competition between interests and norms may potentially result. Finally, in the case of German–Turkish relations an additional factor is to be added that exists in none of the other dyads: the quite considerable domestic special interests due to the large segment of the population in Germany of Turkish ancestry.

Notes

1 Valuable research assistance by Katinka von Kovatsis, Jari Trabert and Annika E. Poppe is acknowledged.
2 These bilateral profiles are summarized at the beginning of each case study (see Chapters 4–9).
3 US security assistance to Turkey (US foreign assistance in the area 'Peace and Security') was $19.8 million in fiscal year 2007 and $53.0 million in 2002 (US Department of State 2008, 2003). US military presence of 1,586 (end 2007) and 1,873 men (late 2002) reflects the close cooperation within NATO (US Department of Defense 2007, 2002). For the other dyads, compare the data in notes 4–7 and 10.
4 US security assistance to Bolivia was, for example, $63.1 million in 2007 and $88.8 million in 2002 (US Department of State 2008, 2003); the number of military personnel was calculated at 13 (late 2007) and 24 (late 2002) (US Department of Defense 2007, 2002).
5 US security assistance to Ecuador – significantly lower than to Bolivia – was $16.8 million in 2007 and $29.0 million in 2002 (US Department of State 2008, 2003). Due to the military base, there was, however, a larger number of military personnel: 38 in late 2007 and 32 in late 2002 (US Department of Defense 2007, 2002).

Norms versus interests 71

6 US security assistance to Pakistan was $333.0 million in fiscal year 2007 and $176.5 million in 2002 (US Department of State 2008, 2003). The military personnel strength was 36 (late 2007) and 32 (late 2002) (US Department of Defense 2007, 2002).
7 US security assistance to Russia was $4.7 million in 2007 and $1.5 million in 2002 (US Department of State 2008, 2003). The number of military personnel was 72 (end 2007) and 76 (end of 2002) (US Department of Defense 2007, 2002).
8 According to the German government (Bundesregierung 2010: 17–18), in recent years no 'military consultants' were sent to any of the recipient countries and none of the recipients' armed forces received military equipment aid. Germany provided aid in terms of police equipment to Belarus, Bolivia, Ecuador, Pakistan and Turkey, but no military assistance (see Schürkes 2010: 15; Bundesregierung 2010: 17). There are no regular missions of the Bundeswehr in any of the countries, an exception being the participation of the Bundeswehr in disaster relief and humanitarian assistance to Pakistan and Turkey (cf. Bundesregierung 2009: 9; ZIF 2008). The presence of military attachés in the German embassies in Belarus, Pakistan, Russia and Turkey (Bundesregierung 2009: 10), however, points to certain security interests in these countries.
9 The close multilateral cooperation between Germany and Turkey is demonstrated by a German military presence as part of NATO staff (Bundesregierung 2009: 3).
10 US security assistance to Belarus was $150,000 (2007) and $0 (2002) (US Department of State 2008, 2003), military personnel strength stood at 2 (end of 2007) and 0 (end of 2002) (US Department of Defense 2007, 2002). Unlike in Bolivia and Ecuador, there is a military attaché at the German embassy in Belarus (Bundesregierung 2009: 10).
11 This will be analysed, as appropriate, in the individual case studies (see the respective sections on the profiles of bilateral relations in the case-study chapters).
12 As the best data available that roughly approximate what the indicator 'immigrants' is supposed to measure, we chose, for the United States, data on the size of groups within the total population that share a particular ancestry (US Census Bureau 2004) and, for Germany, data that refer to the size of groups living in Germany that share a particular foreign citizenship (Statistisches Bundesamt Deutschland 2003). Data, in both cases, are for 2000 but, in any case, do not vary much over the years.
13 Although there are no significant organizations in the United States that are specifically interested in Bolivia or Ecuador, there are at least organizations that are generally concerned with Latin America and influence US Latin American policy (such as the Inter-American Dialogue or the Washington Office on Latin America). With regard to Russia, there are certain organizations in the United States that are, in a narrow sense, specialized on this recipient country. In addition, there are organizations – such as some Washington think tanks – that follow political developments in Russia and US relations with that country and try to influence US Russia policy. The latter also applies for the US–Pakistan dyad. For Germany and Belarus, the German–Belarusian Society (deutsch–belarussische Gesellschaft) can be mentioned.

References

Boniface, D. (2002) 'Is there a Democratic Norm in the Americas? An Analysis of the Organization of American States', *Global Governance*, 8 (3): 365–82.
Bundesregierung (2009) *Auslandsaufenthalte der Bundeswehr ohne Mandat des Deutschen Bundestages. Antwort der Bundesregierung* (BT-Drs. 16/13861, 31 July), Berlin: Deutscher Bundestag.
Bundesregierung (2010) *Deutsche Beteiligung an Ausbildung und Ausrüstung von Sicherheitskräften im Ausland und zu Sicherheitssektorreformen. Antwort der Bundesregierung* (BT-Drs. 17/766, 22 February), Berlin: Deutscher Bundestag.

Council of Europe (2007) *Memorandum of Understanding between the Council of Europe and the European Union*. Online, available at: www.coe.int (accessed 31 May 2011).
COW (Correlates of War) (no date given) *National Material Capabilities (v3.02)*. Online, available at: www.correlatesofwar.org (accessed 21 April 2011).
Ikenberry, G.J. (1999) 'Why Export Democracy? The "Hidden Grand Strategy" of American Foreign Policy', *Wilson Quarterly*, 23 (2). 56–65.
Karakaş, C. (2011) 'Promoting or Demoting Democracy Abroad? US and German Reactions to the Rise of Political Islam in Turkey', *PRIF Report*, no. 106, Frankfurt a.M.: Peace Research Institute Frankfurt.
Kronstadt, K.A. (2009) 'Pakistan–US Relations', *CRS Report for Congress*, no. RL33498, 6 February.
Mansfield, E.D., Milner, H.V. and Rosendorff, B.P. (2002) 'Why Democracies Cooperate More: Electoral Control and International Trade Agreements', *International Organization*, 56 (3) 477–513.
Migdalovitz, C. (2008) 'Turkey: Selected Foreign Policy Issues and US Views', *CRS Report for Congress*, no. RL34642, 29 August.
Monten, J. (2005) 'The Roots of the Bush Doctrine. Power, Nationalism, and Democracy Promotion in US Strategy', *International Security*, 29 (4): 112–56.
NATO (1997) *Founding Act on Mutual Relations, Cooperation and Security between NATO and the Russian Federation*. Online, available at: www.nato.int (accessed 31 May 2011).
Newman, E. and Rich, R. (eds) (2004) *The UN Role in Promoting Democracy. Between Ideals and Reality*, Tokyo: United Nations University Press.
Peceny, M. (1999) *Democracy at the Point of Bayonets*, University Park, PE: Pennsylvania State University Press.
Piccone, T.J. (2005): 'International Mechanisms for Protecting Democracy', in M.H. Halperin and M. Galic (eds) (2005) *Protecting Democracy. International Responses*, Lanham, MD: Lexington.
Ribando Seelke, C. (2008a) 'Bolivia: Political and Economic Developments and Relations with the United States', *CRS Report for Congress*, no. RL32580, 14 November.
Ribando Seelke, C. (2008b) 'Ecuador: Political and Economic Situation and US Relations', *CRS Report for Congress*, no. RS21687, 21 November.
Schürkes, J. (2010) 'Deutsche Aufbauhilfe für Repressionsorgane. Eine Auswertung verschiedener Antworten der Bundesregierung auf Kleine Anfragen im Bundestag', *Ausdruck. Magazin der Informationsstelle Militarisierung*, 2: 14–16.
Smith, T. (1994) *America's Mission. The United States and the Worldwide Struggle for Democracy in the Twentieth Century*, Princeton, NJ: Princeton University Press.
Spanger, H.-J. (2005) 'Paradoxe Kontinuitäten. Die deutsche Russlandpolitik und die koalitionären Farbenlehren', *HSFK-Report*, no. 12, Frankfurt a.M.: Peace Research Institute Frankfurt.
Spanger, H.-J. (2008) 'Between Ground Zero and Square One: How George W. Bush Failed on Russia', *PRIF Report*, no. 82, Frankfurt a.M.: Peace Research Institute Frankfurt.
Statistisches Bundesamt Deutschland (2003) *Bevölkerung und Erwerbstätigkeit. Ausländische Bevölkerung sowie Einbürgerungen* (Fachserie 1/Reihe 2). Online, available at: www.destatis.de (accessed 15 February 2011).
Statistisches Bundesamt Deutschland (2011) *Außenhandel*. Online, available at: www-genesis.destatis.de (accessed 3 August 2011).
UNCTAD (2011) *FDI Statistics*. Online, available at: www.unctad.org (accessed 11 January 2011).

US Census Bureau (2004) *Ancestry 2000: Census 2000 Brief.* Online, available at: www.census.gov (accessed 3 August 2011).
US Census Bureau (2011) *Foreign Trade Statistics.* Online, available at: www.census.gov (accessed 11 January 2011).
US Department of Defense (2002) *Active Duty Military Personnel Strengths by Regional Area and by Country,* 31 December. Online, available at: http://siadapp.dmdc.osd.mil (accessed 21 April 2011).
US Department of Defense (2007) *Active Duty Military Personnel Strengths by Regional Area and by Country,* 31 December. Online, available at: http://siadapp.dmdc.osd.mil (accessed 21 April 2011).
US Department of State (2003) *Congressional Budget Justification for Foreign Operations.* Online, available at: www.state.gov (accessed 21 April 2011).
US Department of State (2008) *Congressional Budget Justification for Foreign Operations.* Online, available at: www.state.gov (accessed 21 April 2011).
Wolff, J. and Wurm, I. (2011) 'Towards a Theory of External Democracy Promotion: A Proposal for Theoretical Classification', *Security Dialogue,* 42 (1): 77–96.
World Bank (2011) *World DataBank, World Development Indicators and Global Development Finance.* Online, available at: http://databank.worldbank.org (accessed 20 January 2011).
Yilmaz, S. (2004) 'Impact of Lobbies on Turkish–American Relations', in M. Aydin, M. and C. Erhan (eds) *Turkish–American Relations. Past, Present and Future,* London: Routledge.
Youngs, R. (ed.) (2010) *The European Union and Democracy Promotion. A Critical Global Assessment,* Baltimore, MD: Johns Hopkins University Press.
ZIF (Zentrum für Internationale Friedenseinsätze) (2008) *World Map Crisis Prevention and Peace Operations 2008.* Online, available at: www.zif-berlin.org (accessed 31 May 2011).

Part II
Case studies on German and US democracy promotion

4 Democracy promotion in Bolivia
The 'democratic revolution' of Evo Morales[1]

Jonas Wolff

The victory of Evo Morales in the December 2005 elections was a sign of the success of Bolivian democracy. For the first time since the introduction of universal suffrage in the 1952 revolution a president moved into the presidential palace who, like the majority of Bolivians, represented the indigenous population. Morales promised to ensure the rights of the country's indigenous peoples, who had been discriminated against for centuries, to improve the quality of an until then rather formal democracy, to combat poverty and inequality, and to enhance the sovereignty and independence of Bolivia.

Such an agenda would be expected to be completely acceptable to external actors who – like Germany and the United States – were committed to promoting democracy in Bolivia. Indeed, since the 1990s, both German and US institutions have worked actively for the empowerment of the poor and indigenous majority of the population, supported anti-poverty strategies and sought to strengthen democratic institutions. The electoral victory of Morales and his political movement 'Movimiento al Socialismo' (MAS) was, however, by no means greeted with undivided approval in Berlin and Washington. For the way the Morales government intended to implement the general goals of democratic emancipation and the fight against poverty were in part diametrically opposed to the expectations and interests of these donors. As an umbrella organization for social and indigenous movements, the MAS stood for the demand for radical change in power and wealth relationships in the country, for a fundamental reconstruction of democratic institutions and for a significant change in course in economic, social, drug and foreign policy.

The 'democratic revolution' called for by Morales thus confronted Germany and the United States with serious conflicts of objectives. After a brief summary of the conflict situation in Bolivia, this chapter will analyse the way Germany and the United States handled this challenge.

Bolivia's 'democratic revolution' as a conflict situation

At the end of the 1990s Bolivia was regarded internationally as a model of success in which a synthesis of political democratization and stability, as well as economic structural adjustment had succeeded particularly well, despite difficult conditions (see Mayorga 1997; Puhle 2001). After a turbulent transition to democracy and a difficult economic crisis in the first half of the 1980s, since 1985 a system of 'pacted democracy' (*democracia pactada*) had developed which was dominated by three major parties – 'Acción Democrática Nacionalista' (ADN), 'Movimiento de Izquierda Revolucionaria' (MIR) and 'Movimiento Nacionalista Revolucionario' (MNR) – and brought the country previously unknown political stability as well as profound economic and political reforms under a (neo-)liberal banner.

From the beginning of the new millennium, however, this model came under increasing pressure (see Wolff 2004). Mass protests against the privatization of water in Cochabamba in 2000 marked the beginning of a series of social conflicts and political upheavals, culminating in 2003 in the overthrow of the elected president, Gonzalo Sánchez de Lozada. As his successor in office, interim president Carlos Mesa also had to yield to widespread protests in 2005. These protests were driven by a broad spectrum of social and indigenous movements (see Crabtree 2005; Van Cott 2005: chapter 3; Yashar 2005: chapter 5). They were directed against the historic discrimination of the indigenous majority population of Bolivia,[2] against 'neoliberalism' as well as in general against mass poverty and a development model that reproduced social inequality. This also included contesting a political system that, while formally democratic, was in reality quite exclusive in nature as well as rejecting external actors who profited from Bolivia's natural riches (such as international oil and gas companies), forced the government to adopt austerity measures (IMF and World Bank) or pushed for a counternarcotics strategy based primarily on forced coca eradication (United States).

During this wave of social conflicts the indigenous union leader and coca grower, Evo Morales, and his political movement MAS succeeded in establishing themselves at the head of the various protest movements. In December 2005, Morales was elected the first indigenous president of Bolivia, with 54 per cent of the vote. Since then he has introduced comprehensive political change, which the government refers to as a 'democratic revolution'.[3] Core elements of the changes are a transformation of the democratic system by means of a Constituent Assembly and a change in the course of economic, social and drug policy.

The Constituent Assembly, which Bolivia's indigenous movements had demanded for many years, was elected in July 2006 and met until December 2007. It was marked by bitter confrontations between the government camp and the opposition, and ended with a scandal: the text of the constitution only obtained the required support of a two-thirds majority because the most important opposition group was not present when the vote was held. Only after a major internal political crisis, which brought Bolivia to the brink of civil war (see below), was a compromise reached between the government camp and moderate elements of the opposition. In October 2008, the Bolivian parliament – although not authorized by law to do so – carried out a detailed revision of the draft of the constitution; this ultimately provided the two-thirds majority of the parliament required for holding a constitutional referendum (see Romero *et al.*

2009). In January 2009, 61 per cent of the population voted in favour of the new constitution. At the end of the year, Morales was clearly confirmed in office with 63 per cent of the vote, and the MAS won two-thirds of the seats in the new parliament, the 'Asamblea Legislativa Plurinacional'. Direct elections for the new Supreme Court (see below), by contrast, only took place in October 2011. Following a series of resignations starting in May 2009, the previous judicial organs were in fact unable to make decisions until President Morales, in an extremely controversial decision, nominated provisional judges at the beginning of 2010.

On the one hand, the new constitution guarantees classical political and civil rights while maintaining the traditional institutions of representative democracy. On the other hand, however, significant modifications of the liberal-representative concept of democracy can be seen. Indigenous justice is recognized as the legal system of the indigenous peoples, with status equal to state justice, and indigenous collective rights are recognized and make possible autonomous forms of indigenous self-government according to customary laws and practices; indigenous rural minorities receive special seats in the parliament; mechanisms of direct democracy such as recalls and other types of referendums as well as citizens' legislative initiatives are established; in addition to the government and parliament the highest judicial organs are also elected by popular vote; 'organized civil society' receives vaguely defined but potentially far-reaching rights of participation in and monitoring of public administration; finally, social and economic human rights are extended and in return the scope for privatization of, for example, public services is limited and private property (e.g. rural property) restricted (see Wolff 2013).

In economic and social policy, the MAS government relied particularly on extending the economic role of the state (see Kaup 2010; Mendonça and Santaella 2010). In May 2006 Morales announced the 'nationalization' of natural gas. This resulted in foreign companies being forced into new contracts that extended state control – and that of the state natural gas company, YPFB – and massively increased the federal tax revenues from such companies. Further nationalization took place in the mining and telecommunications sectors but was confined to individual companies. Increasing government income was used to raise public investment and to introduce a series of social programmes.[4] In the so-called 'war on drugs' the Morales government ended the US-driven focus on the forced eradication of coca crops: the new coca and drug policy acknowledges, on the one hand, that the coca leaf is part of Bolivia's indigenous culture, promotes legal trade, and presses for the international legalization of coca; on the other hand, coca growing is to be restricted through cooperation with the unions of the coca growers (*cocaleros*) while repressive measures are concentrated on drug production and trading (see Farthing and Kohl 2010; Ledebur and Youngers 2008).

Within Bolivia these policies have been extremely controversial. Resistance to the Morales government came primarily from regional autonomy movements in the departments of the south-eastern lowlands (the so-called *media luna*). These were led by the elected department governors and citizen's committees at the departmental level ('comités cívicos') and were based especially on the 'old' elites. In response to the MAS project of constitutional change, they promoted comprehensive (and unconstitutional) autonomy statutes. The conflicts between the government and the social movements supporting it and the regional autonomy movements mainly involved the redistribution of power and prosperity pursued by the government. This specifically included the distribution of income from the natural gas fields concentrated in the lowlands (Santa Cruz, Tarija); the division of powers between the central government in La Paz and the *departamentos* seeking autonomy; the land reforms being promoted by Morales, which were a direct threat to the large landowners in the lowlands; and the goal of the government to promote, within the framework of establishing a 'pluri-national state', the political recognition and participation of the indigenous majority at the expense of the traditional elites and the non-indigenous middle classes. In September 2009 the protests of the autonomy movements in the lowlands escalated: cities, roads and gas pipelines were blocked, local institutions of the central state were occupied and looted, and there were violent clashes between opposition groups and groups close to the government (see Peñaranda 2009: 152–65).

At the centre of the following case studies is the first phase of this 'democratic revolution' in Bolivia, which extends from Morales's first election at the end of 2005 to the constitutional referendum and his re-election in 2009. The political changes in those years represent almost paradigmatically the three basic dilemmas of democratization outlined in the introduction to this volume. The democratic empowerment of the previously marginalized indigenous majority provoked resistance, and escalating conflicts endangered political stability and internal societal peace (democracy versus stability). At the same time, clear majorities in the population opposed 'neoliberal' recipes which, from a technocratic standpoint, are portrayed as the only option available. These large majorities resulted in changes in economic and social policy, changes which – not least from the point of view of the donors – appear irrational. The advent of a government that sees itself as a 'government of social movements' also meant that the technical quality of government suffered from elected officials with little administrative experience (democracy versus governability). Finally, Morales's 'democratic revolution' received the support of clear majorities in a series of democratic elections and referenda, but it also involved a partial rejection of liberal-democratic standards (democracy versus majority).

On the part of external promoters of democracy – here Germany and the United States – this results in both extrinsic and intrinsic conflicts of objectives:

1   *Democracy versus donor interests (extrinsic)*. In accordance with a normative pledge to democracy promotion the new set of economic and drug policies mentioned above, which is widely approved of in Bolivia, should be tolerated as an expression of democratic self-determination. However, the donors' material interests oppose this. In the case of the United States this mainly involves the 'war on drugs', which is regarded as a national security issue. In the case of Germany, a German company (Oiltanking) was hit by

expropriation as part of nationalization policy. In general, the rejection of a neoliberal economic policy focused on free trade and investors' rights runs counter to German and US economic interests. In the area of foreign policy, this also applies to the diversification of international relations being vigorously pursued by Morales, which among other things includes cooperation with Venezuela, China, Russia and Iran.

2 *Democracy versus democracy (intrinsic).* Especially with regard to the new constitution and the partial rejection of liberal-democratic standards it includes, the normative respect for democratic procedures conflicts with the substantive insistence on specific principles of liberal democracy, good governance and the rule of law. Furthermore, the new government has on the one hand committed itself to the political inclusion of the indigenous majority and thus to a deepening of democracy. With the political rise of the MAS, Bolivia's democratic institutions became much more representative, and political participation much more inclusive. In pressing ahead with its political project, however, the government was not willing to accept institutional constraints as imposed by the existing political system. As part of the constitutional reform, established democratic institutions were gradually dismantled and checks and balances largely eliminated, while alternative institutions had yet to be built. This also resulted in difficult questions regarding the relationship between democracy and peace/stability. To the extent that the Morales government (and oppositional resistance against it) is seen as endangering societal peace, the democratic objective of supporting a process of political emancipation and inclusion can work in opposition to the preference for conflict prevention and political stability. Looked at the other way round, the Morales government may be seen as a threat to democracy, but at the same time – in terms of peace and stability – considered the only option for containing the protests by social and indigenous movements. Finally, the process of rewriting the constitution posed the question of whether violations of procedural rules and informal deals should be rejected as undemocratic or accepted as a pragmatic form of conflict resolution.

Germany: cooperative adaptation and pragmatic support for the revolution

Profile of bilateral relations

Relations between Germany and Bolivia are focused on development policy. In terms of foreign policy Bolivia is, from the German standpoint, not a relevant power. But, as one of the poorest and most highly indebted countries in Latin America, it is a central partner in German development cooperation. Apart from development cooperation, German–Bolivian relations are shaped by Germany's activities in the area of culture and education (German schools, Goethe Institutes, German–Bolivian cultural societies) as well as by the presence of a

'German colony' (see Vogl 2006: 550–1). Economic relations are negligible. The limited activity of German companies in the Bolivian market mainly results from their presence in the far larger economies of Brazil, Chile and Peru in the region.

Germany's strong development policy engagement is closely linked to the fact that in the 1990s Bolivia was able to establish itself as a model of successful international development efforts, including in the framework of the international debt reduction initiative HIPC (see Spanger and Wolff 2003: 28–38). The starting point was the first democratic change of government in Bolivia in 1985, which was accompanied by a swing to a neoliberal structural adjustment policy. Since 1987, Bolivia has been a priority country among German development cooperation counterparts and remained so when, at the end of the 1990s, Germany began to reduce the number of partner countries. Bolivia is one of the 20 primary recipients of German bilateral official development assistance (ODA) (OECD 2006: 92).

Profile of German democracy promotion in Bolivia

Since the beginning of the 1990s, German development cooperation in Bolivia has been explicitly active in the area of democracy promotion. In fact, Bolivia was the first country in the world in which the BMZ placed emphasis on modernization of the state (Ströbele-Gregor 1996: 48). Since 2001 Germany has concentrated on three priority areas including 'state and democracy' (BMZ 2007: 7); the other two are water supply and sanitation as well as sustainable agricultural development. According to OECD (Organisation for Economic Cooperation and Development) categories, between 1999 and 2008 just under 20 per cent of total German commitments to Bolivia were earmarked for 'governance and civil society'; since 2003 the share of this sector in annual ODA disbursements has fluctuated between 20 and 30 per cent (OECD 2010; own calculations).

At the level of the individual organizations responsible for Germany's official development cooperation, this development is reflected in the fact that during the period under review practically all so-called implementing agencies in Bolivia were also active in the area of democracy promotion (see Wolff 2010: 9–10; Zilla 2006: 15–17). The DED was focused on promoting civil society, especially through organizational and institutional strengthening of disadvantaged social groups. The Integrated Experts of the Centre for International Migration (CIM) supported the decentralization process in Bolivia as well as the administration at the subnational level. The KfW Development Bank concentrated its efforts in the area of decentralization on supporting poverty reduction and public finances.

The most important player in German democracy aid was the GTZ, which ran a comprehensive programme on 'decentralized governance and poverty reduction support' in Bolivia from 2002 to 2011. In 2002, this 'Programa de Apoyo a la Gestión Pública Descentralizada y Lucha contra la Pobreza' (PADEP) merged individual projects in the areas of decentralization, planning, administrative reforms, municipal development, land-use planning, and development funds. Alongside the key areas of decentralization and community development, the programme focused on two especially poor regions (Norte de Potosí and Chaco). The first phase of the programme ran until 2005, the second was from 2006 to 2009 and the third and final phase was from 2010 until 2011 (see GTZ 2010).

Among Germany's political foundations, the FES, the KAS and the HSS have offices in Bolivia. Following a focus on cross-party dialogue forums in the phase of 'pacted democracy', since the end of the 1990s the FES has been emphasizing decentralization. Starting in 1997, it supported the Bolivian Congress and civic education on parliamentary issues. Through conferences, workshops and its own series of publications the FES offered a forum for political reflection. The KAS worked in the areas of parliamentary advising and modernization of the state, social participation in political processes, justice and constitutional reform, social and economic issues and environmental protection. A permanent partner in the explicitly political area was the 'Fundación de Apoyo al Parlamento y a la Participación Ciudadana' (FUNDAPPAC), a Bolivian foundation that offered cross-party advice to the parliamentary parties and supported the political participation of civil society. The HSS worked primarily with a Bolivian political foundation as well, the 'Fundación Boliviana para la Capacitación Democrática y la Investigación' (FUNDEMOS). FUNDEMOS generally supported political, business and civil-society leaders, but operated mostly as a think tank with a clear party affiliation: initially to the conservative ADN, and from 2005 to Poder Democrático y Social (PODEMOS), the alliance opposing Morales. For the FES and the KAS, by contrast, the collapse of the traditional party system meant that they had largely lost their institutional partners among the parties (MIR and MNR) (see KAS 2008: 17–18).

In addition to democracy promotion through development assistance, the policy dialogue between the two governments included a 'sector dialogue on state and democracy' (BMZ 2007: 10). In 2006 the responsible regional officer for Bolivia, Ecuador and Peru in the Foreign Office emphasized that 'the main objective of our political relations' is 'to support Bolivia on its path to democratic stability and in this way to contribute to the stability of the Andean region'. This included 'above all strengthening the democratic institutions and promoting orientation towards the common good and equality among the various groups in the population' (Vogl 2006: 549).

In a general overview of German democracy assistance in Bolivia, Claudia Zilla (2006: 6) concluded that its objective was 'strengthening the capacity of institutions' through the 'promotion of good governance' (see also Bundesregierung 2008: 5–6). In this sense, support for civil society in the priority area of 'state and democracy' also aimed at strengthening state institutions. Traditionally, all this was largely focused on 'the local level of cities and municipalities' (Zilla 2006: 15). Until the election of Morales, German development cooperation considered the national level mostly in terms of its significance for deepening decentralization (see Gómez 2006).

Perception analysis

From a development policy standpoint, the German government unequivocally welcomed the objectives of the Morales government. This especially concerned the goals of reducing poverty and the inclusion of the indigenous majority population (BMZ 2007: 1; see Bundesregierung 2006: 9–10; Knill 2006; Vogl 2006). With regard to conflict escalation, human rights and the standards of democracy, certain misgivings were expressed about the strategies with which the Bolivian government sought to pursue these objectives. Above all, however, the structural barriers that stood in the way of implementing government policy were emphasized (see BMZ 2007: 1, 8, 3; Bundesregierung 2008: 1–7). The basic democratic legitimacy of the government and its political project was not questioned, but it was clearly stated that the political situation was prone to conflict. The new constitution was greeted by Development Minister Wieczorek-Zeul as an 'important signal for strengthening the rights of the indigenous population' (BMZ 2009; see also Bundesregierung 2008: 5). By contrast, the new orientation of economic policy was viewed with ambivalence.[5]

The assessment among individual German parties and party foundations was in part significantly more critical. After a year of the Morales government the then representative of the KAS in Bolivia pronounced that the promised 'democratic and cultural revolution' had 'revealed itself as an authoritarian political project' (Behrens 2007: 1).[6] In their Latin America strategy, the parliamentary group of the Christian Democratic Union and the Christian Social Union (CDU and CSU) (2008: 8, 6, 4) explicitly regarded Bolivia as a part of the Hugo Chávez-led group of 'radical and left-populist' countries run by dirigiste governments 'with authoritarian tendencies'.[7] In order to justify continued development cooperation with Bolivia, however, the Union parliamentary group also drew attention to the 'participatory mobilization of the indigenous populations', which was referred to as Morales's 'greatest success', as well as to 'notable progress' in the area of 'acknowledgment of their rights and their role in political life' (Bundestag 2008a: 15407).

The attitude of the Social Democrats and the FES (as well as the Greens) largely corresponded to the – significantly more positive – official government view. The Social Democratic Party (SPD) staunchly avoided mentioning Bolivia under Morales in the same breath as Venezuela, but as a rule completely avoided mentioning the country at all.[8] The SPD described the autonomy referendums of the opposition as 'illegal' and in addition called for 'supporting the legally elected government' (Bundestag 2008b: 17011).[9] President Morales was described as pursuing 'a self-confident policy for the poor of his country'; criticism could be directed 'against certain parts of his policy' to be sure, but it had to be 'accepted that Bolivia had elected this president' (Bundestag 2008a: 15408). The local representative of the FES saw the Morales government as indisputably democratically legitimized and as a chance for Bolivian democracy, albeit with risks (see for instance Hölscher 2009). Prior to the election, however, the FES had followed the rise of Morales and the MAS with critical distance (see Quiroga 2003: 5–6; Toranzo 2006: 15–58).

Reaction analysis

The German government's official reaction to Morales winning the election was explicitly positive. In February 2006, Development Minister Wieczorek-Zeul promised continued support of Bolivia (BMZ 2006b), and two months later travelled to La Paz in order to 'signal that Germany is a reliable partner for Bolivia and that we support the efforts of the new government, especially in combating poverty, protecting the environment and strengthening the rights of the indigenous population' (BMZ 2006c).

In government negotiations in June 2006 the two countries agreed on the continuation of German development cooperation in the existing priority areas and – in the democracy area – on German support of the prospective Constituent Assembly (BMZ 2006a). Interviews and background talks indicate that the (non-public) assessment of the German Foreign Office was more critical than that of the BMZ, but the German embassy in La Paz reacted mainly in a sympathetic and supportive way (see Riedler 2009).

A glance at the data on German ODA for Bolivia confirms the supportive stance. After the change of government, Germany, in intergovernmental negotiations, committed itself to increasing development aid: after €42 million in 2001/2 and €51 million in 2003/4, the German government promised €72 million (2006/7), €52 million (2007/8) and €62 million (2009/10) (Wolff 2010: 40). According to OECD data, German ODA to Bolivia increased significantly again after the year of crisis in 2005, and reached – adjusted for inflation – approximately the level of previous years; after a low ebb in 2007, ODA disbursements returned to normal levels (OECD 2010). The resources spent on democracy assistance remained relatively constant throughout – both in their absolute amount as well as their relative proportion. In accordance with the German focus on strengthening governance capacities (Zilla 2006), between 2006 and 2008 around 75 per cent of these resources were channelled to the area of 'government and civil society' through the public sector. The funds approved in 2008 document an increasing orientation towards government: the share of the 'government administration' subsector here amounts to about 60 per cent, whereas just about 17 per cent of the funds were destined for justice and civil society respectively (OECD 2010; own calculations). In the following sections German reactions are examined more closely, with special emphasis on the examples of the GTZ programme PADEP and the work of the political foundations.

In response to the election of Morales, Germany's most important programme in the area of democracy assistance was adjusted to the new political situation. Within the framework of the GTZ's PADEP, the national level had a noticeably greater significance – relative to the subnational units –, and significantly more activities were aimed at structural political reforms beyond decentralization than originally intended. Thus, with the Constituent Assembly, a new component was added to explicitly support the most important political project of the Morales government.[10] This cooperation involved assistance to the presidential entity formed in March 2006 to prepare the 'Asamblea Constituyente', as well as direct support to the assembly itself (GTZ 2008).[11] After the closure of the Constituent Assembly the PADEP component shifted its focus to supporting the transition process from the old to the new constitution, the implementation of the new Magna Carta and the work of the new parliament. Within PADEP's 'decentralization' component, among other institutions, GTZ worked closely with the Bolivian Ministry for Autonomy to support the changed decentralization process, now being run under the label of 'autonomies'. At the request of the Bolivian government support for the national planning system was temporarily upgraded to an independent (sixth) PADEP component.[12]

A process of adaptation is also evident in greater awareness regarding conflict on the part of German development cooperation in Bolivia (see Kampffmeyer and Helmchen 2006: 228–9). This closer focus on crisis prevention and conflict management came after the escalation of social conflicts after 2000, and reflected a general trend in German development cooperation, but was emphasized even more given the special situation under the new government. In 2007, Germany's Civil Peace Service started a programme in Bolivia. PADEP had been active in the area of conflict resolution and crisis prevention since 2002. Among other programmes, it developed a comprehensive early warning system for social conflicts. In PADEP's third phase, one of the three components covered the topic of conflict management (GTZ 2010). In 2007 German development cooperation in Bolivia began reviewing prospective projects for any effects that might provoke conflict (GTZ 2009). In the area of democracy promotion, too, awareness increased that – in the highly politicized context of Bolivia – even a cooperative project conceived of as 'technical' had to consider systematically its political and conflict-related ramifications (see GTZ 2008; Kampffmeyer and Helmchen 2006: 239–40). As a specific reaction, PADEP's cooperation with political institutions (central and subnational governments, the parliament, the Constituent Assembly) shifted, at least in part, away from technical consultation to encouraging processes of dialogue. One important example is the unofficial role played by Germany in facilitating negotiations between the central government and the opposition, which ultimately paved the way for an agreement on constitutional reform in Congress in October 2008.[13] Two more recent GTZ projects followed this shift to a dialogue-based approach: a programme entitled 'Strengthening Concertation and the Rule of Law' (Programa de Fortalecimiento a la Concertación y al Estado de Derecho – CONCED) funded by the German Foreign Office in 2009 and 2010 and a BMZ project called 'Supporting the Development of an Intercultural Legal System in Accordance with the Rule of Law' (Proyecto de apoyo al desarrollo de un ordenamiento jurídico intercultural en el marco de un Estado de Derecho democrático – PROJURIDE, 2010–12).

German democracy promotion through GTZ was mainly orientated to its partner government. To the extent that it involved (party) political actors, as for example in the case of the Constituent Assembly, it was at pains to adopt a 'cross-party orientation' in order to maintain a 'neutral image' (GTZ 2008: 50). The political foundations, on the other hand, adopted an explicit political position as part of their purpose. In the case of the Morales government, the task of the Social-Democratic FES was to develop a relationship with the MAS (see Zuazo 2009). Because the FES had worked closely with previous governments and the traditional parties, developing such a relationship was not easy, especially as it involved a break with the previous (general German)[14] position of not cooperating with the opposition movement represented by Morales and the MAS. In the changed context, however, a policy of engaging the MAS fit well into the overall decision of the German government to engage the new government.[15] However, this policy of rapprochement did not imply that the FES explicitly supported the MAS and its political positions; in accordance with its sceptical attitude towards the government, the FES limited itself largely to cross-party activities that now included representatives of the MAS.[16] The general orientation of the FES was similar to government-run development assistance: cooperation with the government and the government camp focused on 'moderate' or 'democratic' forces and persons within the cabinet and the MAS.

On the other side of the political spectrum, the CSU-affiliated HSS supported PODEMOS, the only remaining opposition party after the 2005 elections. In fact, this was done from an explicitly partisan stance, even if indirectly through HSS support of FUNDEMOS. The work of the Christian-Democratic KAS, by contrast, remained essentially neutral. In addition to specific supporting measures for small centre-right parties and temporary contacts with a regional autonomy party from Santa Cruz,[17] support through FUNDAPPAC was significantly expanded, above all for cross-party parliamentary support (KAS 2008: 17–18). This contrasts with clearly oppositional statements of the KAS, and may be attributed not least to a lack of potential (party) political cooperation partners. At the regional level, since 2006 the KAS has been carrying out a programme that promotes indigenous participation by strengthening (moderate) political leaders from the indigenous population – a project focused on elites explicitly conceived of as a counterweight to the dominance of left wing and revolutionary positions in indigenous movements in Bolivia and Ecuador (see Meentzen 2007). From their respective political positions, the three political foundations also contributed to the process of constitutional change, especially by supporting discussions and critical analyses, as well as – in the case of the FES – through support for cross-party dialogue.[18]

Germany's basic attitude of support did not mean, however, that the German government refrained from expressing criticism on the state of democracy under Morales. This was also on the official agenda of political dialogue between the governments (BMZ 2007: 10), but remained almost exclusively limited to non-public interventions and exchange.[19] In some instances, however, Germany also reacted with direct measures. When, for example, procedural irregularities and conflicts within the Constituent Assembly came to a head in December 2006 and again in the final months of the assembly in 2007, Germany – in accordance with a joint policy of the European Union – terminated its support of the process. As a reaction to the highly controversial passage of the draft constitution in December 2007, Germany cancelled its original plan to help with the public dissemination of the draft. GTZ reacted in the same way to the unconstitutional passage of 'autonomy statutes' by the opposition-led departments: PADEP temporarily stopped every new cooperation initiative with the departmental governments, made cooperation with them conditional upon the agreement of the central government, and limited support to areas that made no contribution to the process of regional autonomy.

A further case involved the German company that was affected by the 'nationalization' of the gas sector. In support of Oiltanking, the German embassy continually called on the Bolivian government to find a negotiated solution (i.e. an 'appropriate' level of compensation). At the EU Latin America Summit in Lima in May 2008, Chancellor Merkel apparently spent a large part of her talks with President Morales on this topic. As a direct sanction the German government finally suspended an environmental project in the climate and energy area – but beyond that the dispute had no perceptible effects on bilateral relations and German development cooperation (see Riedler 2009: 14).

The United States: ambivalent flexibility and reactive confrontation

Profile of bilateral relations

Relations between the United States and Bolivia are marked by extreme power asymmetry and by a history of far-reaching US interference in Bolivia's internal affairs (see Gamarra 1999; Lehman 1999). Since the late 1980s, cooperation in the US 'war on drugs' has been 'Washington's overriding policy focus' (Crandall 2008: 102). From the US point of view, production of drugs and illegal drug trade is a direct threat to national security (Gamarra 1999: 180).

Until the Morales government came to power Bolivia was regarded as 'a close US ally in the fight against illegal narcotics' (Ribando 2008: 16). The close cooperation in combating coca farming and drug trade in Bolivia involved substantial technical, material and personnel support of the government, and the Bolivian security forces in particular, and included military cooperation. In addition to the US State Department, the Department of Defense, US Southern Command and the Drug Enforcement Administration (DEA) were involved.

The strategic significance of Bolivia in the 'war on drugs' was also the main reason behind US development assistance. For years Bolivia had been among the main recipients of US foreign aid (Tarnoff and Nowels 2004: 12–13). The priority area for assistance was once again combating drugs. Of a total of about $150 million in US foreign aid to Bolivia in 2004, over $90 million was for counternarcotics assistance – and of that just under $50 million for direct measures against drug production and trafficking, the rest for promoting alternative development (CBJ 2006: 502; Ribando 2008: 18). Both US development aid (Foreign Assistance Act) and trade preferences (Andean Trade Promotion and Drug Eradication Act – ATPDEA) are contingent upon ongoing cooperation by Bolivia in combating drugs. If, in the course of the annual 'certification' process, the US president decides that a country relevant to drug policy has not fulfilled its responsibilities adequately, US development aid and trade preferences are at risk (see Gamarra 1999: 188; Ledebur and Walsh 2008).

US economic interest in Bolivia is marginal: the Bolivian market is small, its economic integration limited, and only a small number of US companies operate in the country. After Venezuela, Bolivia has the second largest natural gas reserves in South America, but it exports natural gas mainly to Brazil. The main investors in this sector come from Brazil (Petrobras) and Spain (Repsol-YPF) (Ribando 2008: 10–11).

Profile of US democracy promotion in Bolivia

Alongside combating drugs and fighting socioeconomic exclusion, official statements include the strengthening of democratic institutions and processes as US priorities in Bolivia (see CBJ 2008: 603, 2006: 502). From 1992 to 2002 a total of $63 million was allotted to democracy aid (US GAO 2003: 6). The primary areas were rule of law, support of the parliament, electoral assistance as well as – since 1996 – support of municipal governance (US GAO 2003: 27, 47, 52).

USAID is the most important player in US democracy aid in Bolivia. For many years, democracy promotion has been one of the 'strategic objectives' of USAID in the country (see USAID 1997, 2005). Before Morales took office, the country strategy envisaged four components: continued support for justice reform, strengthening political parties and participatory municipal governance as well as an additional focus on anti-corruption (USAID 2005: 15). For many years, the United States has also delivered electoral assistance: USAID supported the establishment of a politically neutral National Electoral Court in 1988 and the registration and provision of information to voters between 1991 and 1999 (US GAO 2003: 90).

In 2004 the two US party institutes, the NDI and the IRI, opened offices in Bolivia. The starting point was a USAID initiative on strengthening political parties. Whereas NDI was responsible for direct support of political parties, IRI initially concentrated on cross-party assistance for women and indigenous peoples as well as on supporting electoral organs and election-related educational measures. In 2003 the NED supported the initial NDI support for Bolivian parties, and in 2004 the assistance to the Chamber of Industry and Commerce of Santa Cruz through the CIPE (see NED 2003, 2004). In the following years, the NED massively expanded its range of activities (see below). Further players in the area of democracy assistance in Bolivia have been the USAID Office of Transition Initiatives (OTI, between 2004 and 2007) and the Millennium Challenge Corporation (MCC, between 2004 and 2008).

At the level of rhetorical appeals as well as policy dialogue, representatives of the US government and the US embassy regularly express their views on political developments in Bolivia, and warn against what they see as problems of and threats to democracy. Traditionally, this included direct interference in political and personnel-related decisions – for which, once again, combating drugs was the central motivation (see Crandall 2008: 102–18; Gamarra 1999). For the present analysis, the US intervention in the 2002 presidential election is of greatest relevance. At that time, assistant secretary of state Otto Reich and US ambassador Manuel Rocha openly threatened that cooperation between the two countries and, more specifically, US aid for Bolivia would be jeopardized if Bolivians were to elect Morales (Campbell 2002; Van Cott 2003).[20]

Furthermore, US security and military cooperation also have components that impact on democracy and human rights issues. The International Military Education and Training (IMET) programme, for instance, includes activities in areas such as 'civil–military relations' and 'democratic institution building' (CBJ 2007: 539). In general, human rights constitute one topic in the capacity building carried out by the US military for the Bolivian armed forces (US Embassy La Paz 2009).

Perception analysis

Before the 2005 elections there was no doubt in Washington that Morales, if elected president, would endanger both democracy and vital US interests in Bolivia. Then commander of US SouthComm, General James Hill (2004), saw the actual danger of the *cocalero* Morales turning Bolivia into a 'narco-state'. And quite a few officials in Washington even regarded Morales as the 'Osama bin Laden of Latin America' (Rieff 2005: 72). During the 2005 election campaign, however, the US government refrained from making any public assessments.

In an internal cable in March 2006 the US ambassador characterized President Morales as a 'pragmatic leader' 'with strong anti-democratic tendencies' (US Embassy La Paz 2006). In general terms the US embassy assessed Morales's 'stated goal of social inclusion' to deserving of support, but expressed serious doubts about 'his commitment to democracy and to the rule of law' (US Embassy La Paz 2007a). In particular, attacks on the judiciary and the 'aggressive' behaviour of the MAS in the Constitutive Assembly were read as signalling an active threat to democracy (US Embassy La Paz 2007b). In June 2006 USAID officially concluded that the new Bolivian government had, 'on several occasions, demonstrated inclinations to consolidate executive power and promote potentially anti-democratic reforms through the Constituent Assembly and other means' (Franco 2006: 19). At the beginning of 2007 the director of national intelligence, John Negroponte, regarded Bolivian democracy, alongside that of Venezuela, as the 'most at risk' in the region. Negroponte added that Chávez and Morales were 'taking advantage of their popularity to undercut the opposition and eliminate checks on their authority' (Negroponte 2007: 9).

Critical voices in the US Congress mainly complained about counternarcotics, nationalization policy and the rhetoric of the Morales government criticizing the United States. On the part of members of the Republican party, Morales, mostly together with Hugo Chávez in Venezuela and Fidel Castro in Cuba, was regarded as a socialist opponent of freedom, whereas Democrats tended to draw attention to the fact that Morales was democratically elected and that his objectives of fighting poverty and including the indigenous population were legitimate (see for instance US Congress 2009; Wolff 2011: 26–9).

Reaction analysis

The US government reacted to the election of Morales in December 2005 with a wait-and-see approach. In official language the United States congratulated the Bolivian people on a 'successful election' and announced that 'the behavior of the new government' would determine the future course of bilateral relations. This included an explicit reference to Morales having to 'govern in a democratic way' (White House 2005). Still, the US embassy in La Paz even indicated a certain willingness to rethink a counternarcotics policy that had been focused on forced coca eradication (cf. Wolff 2011: 11).

In the first two years of the Morales government, the overall US attitude remained essentially cooperative. While criticizing Bolivia's new approach to counternarcotics,[21] in both 2006 and 2007 President Bush decided in favour of 'certifying' Bolivia. Trade preferences within the framework of ATPDEA were extended at regular intervals, and US foreign assistance showed only a slight reduction: from \$135 million (2005) to \$134 million (2006) and \$122 million (2007) (CBJ 2007: 538, 2008: 603, 2009: 659).[22]

The Congressional Budget Justifications (CBJs) issued by the State Department demonstrate that continued aid to Bolivia should not be understood as unqualified support of the democratically elected Morales government. On the one hand, US foreign assistance was justified on the grounds of continued need in Bolivia, above all in the areas of counternarcotics, poverty reduction and democracy promotion (see CBJ 2009: 659, 2008: 603, 2007: 538). On the other hand, it was regarded as necessary in order to protect US interests: in response to the election 'of a government that campaigned on promises that included decriminalizing coca and nationalizing private property' Washington expressed the need to demonstrate 'flexibility to protect our core interests'. Flexibility, here, meant trying to 'engage with the new government (as circumstances allow)', but also with 'the military and, particularly, the regional governments' (CBJ 2007: 538).[23]

In fact, a new USAID programme for the strengthening of democratic institutions ('Fortalecimiento de Instituciones Democráticas' – FIDEM) selected the *prefecturas*, i.e. the departmental governments, as its main partners (USAID 2009). Reacting to the first-time election of departmental governors (*prefectos*) in December 2005, USAID decided to abandon support for municipal governments and to concentrate in their place on the departmental level. This decision was made prior to the 2005 elections in which Morales won at the national level, whereas six of nine department elections were won by opposition candidates. However, the result was that FIDEM – when it commenced its work in October 2006 – gave direct support to Morales's most important opponents (even though it also supported MAS-ruled *prefecturas*).

The USAID OTI reinforced this trend. At the beginning of 2004 OTI responded to the political crisis surrounding the overthrow of President Sánchez de Lozada by launching a programme 'to help reduce tensions in areas prone to social conflict and to assist the country in preparing for key electoral events' (USAID 2007a). Initially, this meant a focus on the city of El Alto, which had played a central role in the protests against Sánchez de Lozada (USAID 2004). After the 2005 elections, however, OTI focused its programme on the newly elected departmental governments: between March 2006 and June 2007 the USAID office awarded about 100 grants, valued at just under $4.5 million, to 'technical support and training for prefecture staff', *inter alia*, 'to help departmental governments operate more strategically' (USAID 2007a).

In mid-2006 USAID had already proposed this kind of reorientation of US democracy promotion as a strategic response to the political dominance of Morales and MAS at the national level. Then USAID assistant administrator Adolfo Franco (2006: 18) argued that assistance should focus on 'the support of counterweights to one-party control such as judicial and media independence, a strong civil society, and educated local and state level leaders'. In accordance with this, in 2007 the State Department announced its objective of developing 'partnerships' with departmental and local governments, nongovernmental organisations (NGOs), the private sector and other non-executive branch entities, 'to prevent further erosion of democracy, to combat cocaine production and trafficking, improve health care and to increase educational opportunities' (CBJ 2008: 603). Programmes in the democracy and governance area were to 'strengthen the Congress as well as state and local governments', to 'encourage moderate national leaders', as well as to support 'an active, credible civil society' and political parties (CBJ 2008: 604; cf. Burron 2012: 122–7). In 2008 Bolivia was classified as a 'priority Freedom Agenda country' (CBJ 2009: 661), and the share of US aid for democracy promotion rose from about 10 per cent (2006–7) to 13.2 per cent (2008) and then to 17.5 per cent (2009) (CBJ various sources; own calculations).

At the same time, NED massively expanded its Bolivia programme and in this way placed the focus of US democracy aid more strongly on civil society and political parties (see NED various sources). The NED portfolio grew from $270,000 and three partner organizations (2005), through $560,000 and nine partners, to a good $1.3 million and 15 partner organizations (2009). The largest NED projects were carried out by NDI, IRI and CIPE. NDI and CIPE supported civil society inputs into the Constituent Assembly (2006), NDI supported political leaders (2007), and IRI focused on encouraging good governance and citizen participation at the municipal level (2007/9). What should be added to this is the work of IRI and NDI financed by USAID (see below).

However, the statement that the United States focussed on 'counterweights' to the Morales government has to be qualified. Washington continued to cooperate with the central government – and this cooperation went beyond assistance in counternarcotics and socioeconomic issues to also include democracy aid.[24] In addition, it was important for the United States – in view of a highly sensitive Morales government that regularly accused the United States of supporting the opposition – that its democracy promotion programmes should be framed and implemented 'in an apolitical, balanced manner' (US Department of State 2007: 13). As a result, support for departmental and local authorities included assistance for representatives from both the opposition and the ruling party (US Department of State 2007: 11; USAID 2008b). In addition, from 2007 on, the US-funded programmes supporting political parties were restricted 'to multi-party training events so as to ensure a clear public perception of an apolitical "balance"'. Training and consultations for individual parties, which had been a central element of the programme, were put on hold (US Department of State 2007: 13).

This latter move affected the US party institutes IRI and NDI the most. With USAID funding, IRI trained candidates for the Constituent Assembly until September 2007, while NDI organized debates between candidates from all parties for the assembly. Between October 2007 and July 2008 both institutes supported political parties, citizen groups and indigenous organizations by means of multi-party events and workshops that included MAS representatives (USAID 2009). Prior to USAID deciding not to carry out any measures with individual parties, IRI and NDI had already included MAS in their work (Burron 2012: 122).[25] At the time USAID planned its party-strengthening programme, however, the objectives of the US government were hardly apolitical or balanced: the 'planned USAID Political Party Reform Project' was explicitly intended to 'dovetail' with the then governing party, MNR, and to 'help build moderate, pro-democracy political parties that can serve as a counterweight to the radical MAS' (US Embassy La Paz 2002).

Starting at the end of 2007, USAID discussed an adjustment of its democracy programme to accommodate the demands of the Bolivian government. These adjustments included replacing the extremely controversial support of the regional *departamentos* by a priority programme for municipal governments (USAID 2007b, 2008a; CBJ 2010: 576). In addition, plans were made to expand the support for the Integrated Justice Centres, a programme implemented in close cooperation with the Bolivian Ministry of Justice (USAID 2008a; CBJ 2010: 575). Other planned measures were also intended as conciliatory gestures towards the Bolivian government.[26]

Implementing such an adjustment of the USAID programme was, however, blocked by the 'diplomatic breakdown' in 2008 (Gray 2009: 171–6). In June 2008, the *cocalero* movement and mayors in the Chapare, Bolivia's most important coca-growing region, declared that they would not sign any more agreements with USAID and essentially expelled the agency from the region – a decision endorsed by the Bolivian government. In September – in the midst of a serious internal political crisis provoked by the regional autonomy movements – President Morales expelled US ambassador Philip Goldberg from the country for supporting the opposition. The US government responded in kind by expelling the Bolivian ambassador to Washington from the country. A few days later Bush 'decertified' Bolivia because it had 'failed demonstrably' to fulfil its obligations concerning counternarcotics. Still, the US president avoided the automatic discontinuation of US foreign assistance to Bolivia by declaring ongoing programmes in Bolivia as 'vital to the national interests of the United States' (White House 2008). All the same, Bolivia lost its trade preferences within the framework of ATPDEA. Morales retaliated by expelling the US DEA.

As a direct consequence of the diplomatic crisis, in December 2008 Bolivia was cut off from being funded by the Millennium Challenge Account (MCA). In 2004, the country had been initially rated as eligible for MCA support, which included meeting conditions concerning 'ruling justly'. When the MCC board of directors decided in December 2008 that Bolivia no longer met those conditions, it was able to refer to a certain decline in some of the (World Bank) indicators used to assess the quality of governance (MCC 2009). However, a comparison with other MCA beneficiaries and interviews with relevant US officials show that the gradual decline in Bolivia's governance performance alone would hardly have led to the suspension of Bolivia.

In an attempt to rebuild bilateral relations with Bolivia, the new Obama Administration launched a bilateral dialogue between the two countries. First meetings were held in May and October 2009, but during the time under investigation the dialogue did not produce any measurable results. It was only in November 2011 that the two governments signed a framework agreement aiming at re-establishing full diplomatic relations (US Department of State 2011). At the time of writing, however, Obama has so far refused to reinstate trade preferences for Bolivia and continued to 'decertify' the country (Ledebur and Youngers 2012). When Obama for the first time confirmed Bush's 'decertification' decision, the Bolivian government countered by accusing the United States of continuing to support the opposition (cf. *La Prensa* 2009a, 2009b). In August 2009 the Morales government finally called on USAID to end its democracy programme, but signalled its willingness to accept the continued support of municipal governments.[27] USAID thus terminated its democracy programme, 'with the exception of some municipal strengthening activities' (CBJ 2011: 658). After an NDI application for registration was rejected, the party institute closed its office in the country in 2009. Like NDI, IRI lost its USAID funding, but was able to continue NED-financed support for four municipal governments. In 2010 NED funds were the only form of official US democracy aid in Bolivia.

Results

German and US policies in Bolivia are clearly oriented towards the declared objective of promoting democracy. This is particularly evident in the dimensions of foreign aid and diplomacy. Both donors emphasized support for democracy, governance and civil society as a priority area of their development cooperation – even if in the portfolio of US aid this area was clearly subordinated to counter-narcotics. In the case of diplomatic appeals, US representatives persistently expressed their views on matters related to democratic development. The German government, by contrast, exercised considerable restraint regarding this issue. In internal political dialogue, however, both donors emphasized democracy and human rights. Germany and the United States were indirectly involved in the dimension of international observation, with a focus on electoral processes: Germany through the EU,[28] the United States primarily through its support of local civil society elections monitors.[29]

Bilateral cooperation – in the areas of foreign policy, economic relations, development aid and, in the case of the United States, military cooperation – was and remains officially conditioned upon standards of democracy. Both Germany and the United States, in all probability, would have responded to any open rupture of the democratic order in Bolivia with corresponding sanctions – though this remains counterfactual speculation. The sanctions actually observed were, however, at best indirectly related to democracy promotion. The suspension of US trade preferences was explicitly justified in terms of counternarcotics. The exclusion from the MCA was officially explained by Bolivian deficits in the area of good governance, but, in actual fact, responded to the bilateral crisis. Germany's suspension of a development project in the area of climate and energy reacted to the expropriation (and protracted compensation) of a German company. When suspending democracy-related measures in the context of the process of constitutional change, Germany responded to disputed violations of rules, but these decisions were primarily attributable to the objective of conflict prevention and 'do no harm'.[30]

How did Germany and the United States deal with conflicting objectives? German policies in Bolivia were scarcely challenged by *extrinsic conflicts* according to the pattern democracy versus donor interests. Germany did not see the change in Bolivian counternarcotics policy as a grave problem because Berlin had been sceptical about the US 'war on drugs' anyway and had not actively participated in it. Sceptical comments notwithstanding, the German government also accepted the change in the course of economic policy and, specifically, the nationalization policy as a sovereign decision. The intensive efforts by the German embassy and chancellor in support of a single German company, which even included a concrete sanction in terms of a suspended development project, suggest, however, that Germany would scarcely have respected more drastic violations of their economic interests as a legitimate democratic decision by Bolivia.

On economic issues, the United States held a similar view. It is true that the nationalization policy was discussed critically – especially in the US Congress and in the context of the discussions on trade preferences. But, as no US company was affected, these critical remarks had no discernible political consequences.[31] Even in the area of counternarcotics, the United States initially reacted in a way surprisingly consistent with the objective of democracy promotion. The democratic election of a government openly opposed to the US 'war on drugs' was officially accepted, key portions of counternarcotics cooperation continued under these new auspices, and in 2006 and 2007, despite reservations, Bolivia was 'certified' again. The reduction of cooperation in this area was above all reactive, and it is entirely possible that Bolivia would have remained certified if the US ambassador and DEA had not been expelled. At the same time, the insistence on unilateral (de-)certification makes it clear that the United

States considers vital interests in combating drugs non-negotiable – security interests, which systematically limit US respect for democratic self-determination. In the same way, the observable inclination of the United States to support 'counterweights' clearly reflects the perception of Morales as being in opposition to US interests.

Both donors reacted to *intrinsic conflicts of interests* (democracy versus democracy) with general respect for the democratically legitimized deviations from liberal-democratic standards of good governance. On the one hand, this was made relatively easy for them by the fact that the basic features of a liberal-democratic order were never openly questioned. On the other hand, both governments (and the various agencies involved) had serious reservations about the transformation of Bolivian democracy – reservations that were clearly shaped by their own conceptions of liberal democracy and the rule of law. Politically, these misgivings only had a very limited impact. Thus, Germany directly supported the Morales government and, specifically, the process of restructuring the political system. The only exceptions were the German decisions to stop supporting the process of constitutional change in the event of especially drastic violations of rules.

The United States was prepared to make some concessions and institute some support measures – and negative US reactions primarily responded to disagreements about counternarcotics and to the diplomatic 'aggression' by the Bolivian government. The explicit strategy of the United States to contain the democratically legitimized process of political change by strengthening 'counterweights' can, however, also be interpreted as a specific attempt to safeguard what is regarded as a core element of liberal democracy ('checks and balances').

Generally, the clear support of the majority of the population for the Morales government and for all major steps of political change proved to be a central factor. This support made it almost impossible for external actors who have committed themselves to the promoting of democracy to openly confront the political project of the MAS. In the case of both donors, however, the relatively cooperative attitude was not simply due to the respect for democratic procedures, but also involved pragmatic adaptation. In working with a government that had the support of a broad majority of the population, continuing cooperation and engagement was clearly used as a strategy to contain deviations from liberal market democracy (especially in the German case) and from comprehensive counternarcotics (in the US case). With regard to the transformation of democracy, the United States, ultimately, remained more or less neutral (or ambivalent), whereas Germany openly supported it.

The perception that overthrowing the democratically elected Morales government would have caused open political chaos in the country certainly also contributed to the relatively cooperative attitude of the US government. This draws attention to the constraining effects of the recipient context. On the one hand, there was general consensus that returning to the political *status quo ante*, i.e. to the model of 'pacted democracy', was not an option. On the other, no relevant internal or external actor considered a turn to openly authoritarian rule as a viable solution for guaranteeing peace and/or political stability. In this context, neither Germany nor the United States insisted on democratic or constitutional principles as long as their violation – without any open break with democracy – seemed helpful in terms of peace and stability policy. This was unmistakable in the case of the German decisions to suspend/restart democracy-related aid activities (see above) and was confirmed by stronger focus on dialogue and compromise-building. For the United States, however, an opposite position was revealed. The focus on 'counterweights' to the dominance of the MAS in fact meant that democracy promotion (according to the US concept) enjoyed priority over a focus on conflict prevention. Although the support for federal and civil society checks and balances matched the US understanding of liberal democracy, it predictably exacerbated political polarization in the country (and also made the United States a party to the conflict).

To what extent can these patterns of reaction be explained by the profiles – i.e. the particular configurations of determinants (see Chapters 2 and 3) – that characterize the bilateral relations of the two donors with Bolivia? German policy largely corresponds to theoretical expectations. In the sense of a Civilian Power, Germany presented itself as guided by norms and values, but was reluctant to openly interfere with sensitive political issues in Bolivia. In particular, Germany tended to support consensus-based discussion processes, reacted in a generally cooperative way to political changes and flexibly adapted its democracy assistance to the changing preferences on the recipient side. As we have seen, this pattern of reaction was not 'disturbed' by significant German interests.

By contrast, US reactions reflect a clash of interests and norms, as was to be expected given the configuration of determinants at play in the country's relations with Bolivia. Security and economic interests, as perceived in Washington, clearly suggested that the US government would work towards (premature) failure of the Morales government. This was reflected in the shaping of bilateral relations (suspension from trade preferences and MCA funds) as well as in democracy assistance (reorientation towards civil society and the subnational level), although the real extent of support for the departmental opposition could not be determined exactly (see Burron 2012). However, the turn away from the government was ambivalent, hesitant and reactive, and remained embedded in continued efforts to maintain cooperation and dialogue with the Morales government (see Gratius and Legler 2009: 206).

It is impossible to say whether these constraints on a confrontational US approach can be attributed to a democracy norm anchored in its identity and/or in the Western Hemisphere. The pattern of reaction can just as convincingly be explained by a modified US assessment of its interests with regard to Bolivia and Latin America. Given the domestic strength and legitimacy of the Morales government, as well as its external support in the region, the prospects for success of an openly confrontational policy were limited, and the potential for collateral damage high. This is, at least, a plausible lesson the US government learnt in 2002, with its tentative support of the (ultimately failed) coup against

Venezuela's president Hugo Chávez (see Wolff 2011: 28). In any case, US reactions make one thing clear: the extreme power asymmetry between the United States and Bolivia, by objective (material) criteria, tells us very little about the current possibilities of exerting influence. Clearly, the opportunities the United States had available to influence the agenda and outcomes in Bolivia under Morales were quite limited.

In general terms, the US pattern of reaction corresponds to the ideal-type conception of the Freedom Fighter (see Chapter 2). Confronted with a government that, with a democratic legitimation, increasingly monopolized political power, the United States accepted, on the one hand, the elected government. On the other, it chose to support 'counterweights'. However, an explicit insistence on universal models contrasting with Germany's Civilian Power approach was only evident when MCA funding for Bolivia was suspended – and here the reference to governance standards served the purpose of legitimization only. For Germany, too, its particular conception of democracy was reflected in the dimension of justification. In the German understanding, private ownership rights form a genuine part of the constitutional state, while the *Rechtsstaat* and democracy are directly related to each other. In this sense, the suspension of a development project, in order to protect German economic interests, was justified as a value-oriented defence of the democratic constitutional state in Bolivia.

The significance of domestic power relations within Bolivia (recipient context) and the political situation in Latin America (regional context) have already been emphasized. An examination of the donor context demonstrates for both donors the pluralism of actors typical of democracy promotion. In the case of the United States, however, this had only limited consequences. In Bolivia the relatively clear integration of USAID within US foreign policy affected NDI and IRI too, to the extent that a major part of their activities was financed by USAID. Their behaviour reflected this – and so did their perception in Bolivia. Only NED carried out relatively independent activities. The change of government from Bush to Obama also had only limited effects on policy and on the relations between the United States and Bolivia. Despite certain diplomatic efforts to achieve a rapprochement, the Obama Administration generally continued to follow the same policy direction established under Bush (Wolff 2011, 2012).

In the case of Germany, the various sub-actors involved in democracy promotion acted in ways that were significantly more independent. De facto, however, their division of labour very closely matched the strategic goals of the German government. Entirely in line with the overall stance of the German government, the Ebert-Stiftung served as a bridge to the MAS and GTZ/PADEP as a partner of the new Bolivian government. At the same time, DED supported small civil-society organizations, and the Seidel-Stiftung supported the opposition. The framework that made these diverse strategies possible was the official German decision to generally support the Morales government. That Germany took such a clearly supportive stance can certainly be attributed, *inter alia*, to the fact that the BMZ played a significantly greater role in relations with Bolivia (vis-à-vis the Foreign Office) than in the case of most other recipient countries analysed in this volume and that, at the time Morales took office, this ministry was headed by a Social Democrat (who belongs to her party's left wing, and also took a personal interest in Bolivian politics).

Finally, both case studies have shown that the organizational self-interest of the implementing agencies on the ground is also a relevant factor. For instance, the responsiveness of GTZ to the Morales government meant that it directly assisted the dismantling of the very political institutions it had previously supported. Yet, this corresponded quite well with the internal logic and the particular interests of an organization that is dependent upon cooperation with the government and is interested in continuity in its work and in the flow of resources. The same is true for USAID, which temporarily showed an astonishing willingness to adapt its democracy-related activities to the preferences of the Bolivian government – even if this was not enough to prevent the closure of USAID's democracy programme in the country.

Notes

1 In addition to those mentioned in the preface, I wish to express my thanks to John Crabtree, Arthur Goldsmith and Richard Youngs for comments on earlier versions of this text. The chapter draws on results published in Wolff (2012a).
2 In Bolivia a majority of the population (about 60 per cent) are classified as indigenous. The two largest of the 35 indigenous peoples of Bolivia represent about a third (Quechua) and almost a quarter (Aymara) of the total population respectively. These two live mainly in the Andean region: the highlands (Altiplano) and the subtropical high valleys. In the southeastern lowlands there are numerous smaller indigenous groups (as well as *indígenas* who have migrated from the highlands), in the south mainly the Guaraní (Van Cott 2005: 50–2).
3 For an overview see Crabtree and Whitehead (2008); Ernst and Schmalz (2012); Kohl and Bresnahan (2010); Wolff (2012b).
4 Since 2006, parents receive financial support for elementary school-age children attending school (*Bono Juancito Pinto*); in 2008 a pension was introduced for people over 60 (*Renta Dignidad*); and since 2009 pregnant women and young mothers receive a payment if they participate in preventive care programs (*Bono Juana Azurday*).
5 Whereas Wieczorek-Zeul commented on the 'nationalization' of natural gas by emphasizing that every country must 'be able to decide autonomously how it organizes its natural resources sector' (*Der Spiegel* 2006: 19), Foreign Minister Steinmeier expressed his 'great scepticism' (*Die Welt* 2006: 5). Assessments by the German Development Ministry were ambivalent about the economic course taken by Bolivia (see BMZ 2007: 4; Knill 2006: 530).
6 The assessment by the HSS was similar (see HSS 2006).
7 See Bundestag (2009: 24111, 2007: 8643). In the FDP too, a development was noted 'which is quite clearly undemocratic and not in the sense of the constitutional state' – which is why 'German support should be questioned' (Bundestag 2008b: 17007; see also Bundestag 2008a: 15409–10).
8 See Bundestag (2008b: 17003–6, 2007: 8644–5, 2006: 3037–9); Steinmeier (2008); SPD (2008).
9 The Greens reached a similar conclusion (Bundestag 2008b: 17002). The Leftist party ('Die Linke') called more unequivocally for 'massive support for the constitutional process and the elected president of Bolivia' (Bundestag 2008b: 17001).

10 The original decision to support the preparation of a Constituent Assembly within the framework of PADEP had already been taken at the end of 2003 (GTZ 2008: 5). In fact, Germany supported – through GTZ as well as the political foundations – the preparatory process that started in November 2003 under Carlos Mesa (GTZ 2008: 10–18; see Gómez 2006: 25–7, 33).

11 The measures in PADEP included technical aid for the presidency, the directorate and the technical unit of the Constituent Assembly; support for 'territorial meetings' of assembly members with civil society groups in the nine *departamentos* of the country; advice to 13 of the 21 commissions of the *Constituyente;* and support for the (electronic) collection, documentation and public dissemination of discussions and suggestions (GTZ 2008: 37, 39, 43–5).

12 In the third PADEP phase, however, the components were again reduced to three: 'Reform of State Structure', 'New Public Management' and 'Constructive Conflict Management' (GTZ 2010: 2).

13 Even though Germany was not among the international observers that supervised the negotiations between the government and the regional opposition in Cochabamba (Peñaranda 2009: 178–80), GTZ/PADEP still made use of personal contacts within the central government and the opposition-led regional government of Tarija to initiate dialogue. GTZ was actually directly involved in talks through individual (ex-) colleagues.

14 According to interviews, this (previous) decision to not cooperate with the MAS and Morales was adopted by the Foreign Office, but also shared by those organizations not directly dependent on the government such as the political foundations.

15 At the same time, however, the opening up of the FES to the MAS was also consistent with the foundation's own interests: after all, from 2005 the MAS was the only relevant party in the centre-left spectrum with national reach.

16 At the same time, the FES temporarily supported an opposition initiative to build a new social democratic party.

17 Among the traditional parties these were the MNR and the Christian democratic 'Partido Demócrata Cristiano' (PDC). In dealing with the new regional opposition in Santa Cruz, which belongs to the conservative camp but, in part, displays secessionist and/or racist tendencies, KAS remained hesitant: after initial instances of cooperation with Santa Cruz-based 'Autonomía para Bolivia', it stopped support for this party at the beginning of 2008.

18 The KAS was much more directly involved in preparations for the Constituent Assembly under previous governments than in the context of the assembly itself (see Schwarzbauer 2007). The FES, on the other hand, made a central contribution *after* the assembly: it supported cross-party efforts for a compromise on the draft constitution; the personal relationships between key 'opponents' created in this way, as well as concrete suggestions for constitutional reform, formed an important basis for the dialogue that led to the constitutional agreement (Peñaranda 2009: 149, 162).

19 Isolated official statements relating to events in Bolivia remained neutral (see BMZ 2008, 2009).

20 In January 2002, the Bolivian Congress had decided to expel Evo Morales as a member of parliament for inciting violence against Bolivian anti-drug units. This decision was already attributed to the US government by many observers (Van Cott 2003: 772). Former Bolivian foreign minister Antonio Araníbar (2004: 210, note 5) describes how the US government, after the 1997 elections, worked in support of a coalition government led by ex-dictator Hugo Banzer that would implement a comprehensive and repressive counternarcotics strategy.

21 In September 2006, President Bush had already expressed concern 'with the decline in Bolivian counternarcotics cooperation' (White House 2006), and in the following year he complained about the neglect of 'essential complements [to drug interdiction, JW], especially coca crop eradication' (White House 2007).

22 Beyond official rhetoric, however, the US government did not react solely in a cooperative wait-and-see manner. For instance, a series of measures supporting alternative development in the coca growing region of Chapare were suspended at the beginning of 2006, and were only resumed during 2007 subject to the condition of prior coca crop reductions (Ledebur and Youngers 2008: 5).
23 Support for the Bolivian armed forces via IMET and the foreign military financing (FMF) was cancelled because of automatic sanctions related to the American Service-Members Protection Act (ASPA). ASPA requires states that have signed the Rome Statute of the International Criminal Court (ICC) to enter into a bilateral agreement with the United States in order to exempt US citizens from prosecution by the ICC. In 2007 the US government could resume IMET support in Bolivia by 'de-linking' it from ASPA sanctions, but abstained from reviving FMF because of 'competing priorities worldwide' (CBJ 2008: 606).
24 Thus, for example, the Administration of Justice programmes that included support of local integrated justice centres (IJCs) were continuously implemented in close cooperation with the Bolivian Ministry of Justice (see USAID 2005: 47). Although the US government was willing to continue with this programme (USAID 2008a; CBJ 2010: 575), in 2009 the Bolivian government insisted on phasing it out (*La Prensa* 2009c). The planned support of parliament by USAID within the framework of FIDEM was also cancelled at the request of the Bolivian government.
25 According to NDI statements, MAS representatives had been beneficiaries of NDI promotion activities since 2004.
26 This was the case with, for example, the idea of a 'management training programme for GOB [Government of Bolivia] officials' that 'could enjoy strong GOB support and would greatly facilitate bilateral coordination and implementation of our program'. Expansion of activities aimed at the 'harmonization of community justice systems with the formal justice system' – 'a high priority for our GOB counterparts' – was also planned (USAID 2008a).
27 See *La Prensa* (2009d) and *La Razón* (2009).
28 Election observation missions of the EU accompanied the elections to the Constituent Assembly in 2006, the constitutional referendum at the beginning of 2009 and the general elections in December 2009.
29 During the period under review, this support was carried out through the NED as well as USAID. In addition to this, independent election monitoring activities were carried out by the Carter Center (e.g. in 2009).
30 Decisive to the suspension or reinstatement of German support in these cases was the question of whether or not a concrete political process and a certain political behaviour were regarded as legitimate in the country, i.e. whether a majority of the population and a broad spectrum of the political actors expressed their agreement. Questions of formal legality or democratic correctness thus faded into the background.
31 In another area, the US embassy actively attempted to ensure that the Bolivian government did not harm 'US mining interests' – in other words: US companies active in the Bolivian mining sector – and was obviously successful (see US Embassy La Paz 2007a, 2007b).

References

Araníbar, A. (2004) 'Impacto de los cambios de la política exterior estadounidense en la región: el caso de Bolivia', in C. Fuentes S. (ed.) *Bajo la mirada del halcón. Estados Unidos-América Latina post 11/9/2001*, Buenos Aires: Biblos.

Behrens, P.-A. (2007) 'Ein Jahr Evo Morales in Bolivien – eine Bilanz', *Politischer Kurzbericht der Konrad-Adenauer-Stiftung*, La Paz: Konrad-Adenauer-Stiftung.

BMZ (2006a) 'Millenniumsziele und Verfassungsreform im Mittelpunkt der deutschen Unterstützung für Bolivien', *Press Release*, 26 June. Online, available at: www.bmz.de (accessed 27 March 2008).
BMZ (2006b) 'Wieczorek-Zeul sagt Bolivien weitere Unterstützung zu', *Press Release*, 27 February. Online, available at: www.bmz.de (accessed 27 March 2008).
BMZ (2006c) 'Bundesministerin Wieczorek-Zeul trifft bolivianischen Staatspräsidenten Morales', *Press Release*, 22 April. Online, available at: www.bmz.de (accessed 31 March 2008).
BMZ (2007) *Länderkonzept Bolivien*, Bonn: BMZ.
BMZ (2008) 'Wieczorek-Zeul: Konflikt in Bolivien im Dialog lösen', *Press Release*, 6 May. Online, available at: www.bmz.de (accessed 22 October 2009).
BMZ (2009) 'Wieczorek-Zeul begrüßt Verfassungsreferendum in Bolivien', *Press Release*, 26 January. Online, available at: www.bmz.de (accessed 22 October 2009).
Bundesregierung (2006) *Verhandlungen über die zukünftige Entwicklungszusammenarbeit mit der neuen bolivianischen Regierung* (BT-Drs. 16/1047), Berlin: Deutscher Bundestag.
Bundesregierung (2008) *Zur Menschenrechtssituation in den Ländern der Andengemeinschaft und Venezuela* (BT-Drs. 16/11297), Berlin: Deutscher Bundestag.
Bundestag (various years) *Stenografische Berichte. 16. Wahlperiode* (Plenarprotokolle 16/35 [2006], 16/85 [2007], 16/145 [2008a], 16/161 [2008b], 16/220 [2009]), Berlin: Deutscher Bundestag.
Burron, N. (2012) 'Unpacking US Democracy Promotion in Bolivia: From Soft Tactics to Regime Change', *Latin American Perspectives*, 39 (1): 115–32.
Campbell, D. (2002) 'Bolivia's Leftwing Upstart Alarms US. Washington Threatens to Cut Aid if Coca-growers' Leader becomes his Country's New President', *Guardian*, 15 July. Online, available at: www.guardian.co.uk (accessed 15 February 2006).
CBJ (various years): *Congressional Budget Justification: Foreign Operations*, US Department of State, several editions (CBJ 2009: Fiscal Year 2009, etc.), Washington, DC: US Department of State.
CDU/CSU (2008) *Lateinamerika, Deutschland und Europa: Partnerschaft für das 21. Jahrhundert. Lateinamerika-Strategie der CDU/CSU-Bundestagsfraktion*. Online, available at: www.cducsu.de (accessed 9 May 2008).
Crabtree, J. (2005) *Patterns of Protest: Politics and Social Movements in Bolivia*, London: Latin American Bureau.
Crabtree, J. and Whitehead, L. (eds) (2008) *Unresolved Tensions: Bolivia Past and Present*, Pittsburgh, PA: University of Pittsburgh Press.
Crandall, R.C. (2008) *The United States and Latin America after the Cold War*, Cambridge: Cambridge University Press.
Der Spiegel (2006) 'Jedes Land muss souverän entscheiden', *Der Spiegel*, 8 May, 19.
Die Welt (2006) '"Die Erwartungen an uns sind groß". Ein Gespräch mit Bundesaußenminister Steinmeier zum EU-Südamerika-Gipfel und der Rolle der Deutschen dort', *Die Welt*, 12 May, 5.
Ernst, T. and Schmalz, S. (eds) (2012) *El primer gobierno de Evo Morales: un balance retrospectivo*, La Paz: Plural.
Farthing, L. and Kohl, B. (2010) 'Social Control: Bolivia's New Approach to Coca Reduction', *Latin American Perspectives*, 37 (4): 197–213.
Franco, A. (2006) 'Statement of the Honorable Adolfo Franco', in US Congress *Democracy in Latin America: Successes, Challenges and the Future. Hearing before the Committee on International Relations*, House of Representatives, 21 June, Washington, DC, 14–21.

Gamarra, E.A. (1999) 'The United States and Bolivia: Fighting the Drug War', in V. Bulmer-Thomas and J. Dunkerley (eds) *The United States and Latin America: The New Agenda*, Cambridge, MA Harvard University Press.
Gómez, R. (2006) *Bolivien. Partizipation als Beitrag zu sozialer Gerechtigkeit*, Eschborn: GTZ.
Gratius, S. and Legler, T. (2009) 'Latin America Is Different: Transatlantic Discord on How to Promote Democracy in 'Problematic' Countries', in A. Magen, T. Risse and M.A. McFaul (eds) *Promoting Democracy and the Rule of Law. American and European Strategies*, Houndmills: Palgrave Macmillan.
Gray Molina, G. (2009) 'The United States and Bolivia: Test Case for Change', in A.F. Lowenthal, T.J. Piccone and L. Whitehead (eds) *The Obama Administration and the Americas: Agenda for Change*. Washington, DC: Brookings Institution Press.
GTZ (2008) *Asesoramiento en contextos altamente políticos. Experiencia del PADEP/GTZ en el proceso Constituyente en Bolivia*, La Paz: GTZ.
GTZ (2009) *Cooperación alemana en Bolivia diseña Estrategia de enfoque y acción sensible al conflicto*. Online, available at: www.padep.org.bo (accessed 25 January 2010).
GTZ (2010) *Experiencias destacadas para el proceso de cambio. Programa de Apoyo a la Gestión Pública Descentralizada y Lucha contra la Pobreza de la Cooperación Técnica Alemana PADEP-GTZ 2002–2010*, La Paz: GTZ.
Hill, J.T. (2004) *Testimony of General James T. Hill, United States Army Commander United States Southern Command before the House Armed Services Committee United States House of Representatives*, 24 March. Online, available at: http://armedservices.house.gov (accessed 21 January 2005).
Hölscher, K. (2009) 'Boliviens neue Verfassung: Spaltung trotz Einigung?', *Kurzbericht der Friedrich-Ebert-Stiftung*, Bonn: Friedrich-Ebert-Stiftung.
HSS (2006) 'Bolivien', *Monatsbericht der Hanns-Seidel-Stiftung*, 4/2006, La Paz: HSS.
Kampffmeyer, T. and Helmchen, C. (2006) 'Fragile Staatlichkeit in Bolivien – Konsequenzen für die Internationale Zusammenarbeit', in J. Calließ (ed.) *Fragile Statehood: Can Stability and Peace be Advanced from Outside?*, Rehburg-Loccum: Evangelische Akademie Loccum.
KAS (2008) *Parteien und Parteien-Kooperationen der KAS in Lateinamerika*, Berlin: KAS.
Kaup, B.Z. (2010) 'A Neoliberal Nationalization? The Constraints on Natural-Gas-Led Development in Bolivia', *Latin American Perspectives*, 37 (3): 123–38.
Knill, P. (2006) 'Bolivien auf dem Weg zum selbstbestimmten Entwicklungsmodell?', in F. Bopp and G. Ismar (eds) *Bolivien. Neue Wege und alte Gegensätze*, Berlin: Wissenschaftlicher Verlag.
Kohl, B. and Bresnahan, R. (eds) (2010) 'Bolivia under Morales', *Latin American Perspectives*, 37 (3–4).
La Prensa (2009a) 'Canciller Dice que Obama es Peor que Bush y Ahonda Tension', *La Prensa*, 8 July. Online, available at: www.laprensa.com.bo (accessed 22 December 2009).
La Prensa (2009b) 'Evo Afirma que USAID Financia la Campaña de Manfred y "Leo"', *La Prensa*, 7 September. Online, available at: www.laprensa.com.bo (accessed 22 December 2009).
La Prensa (2009c) 'Dinamarca Financiará el Plan de Justicia Tras Salida de USAID', *La Prensa*, 29 September. Online, available at: www.laprensa.com.bo (accessed 23 November 2012

La Prensa (2009d) 'El Ejecutivo y la Embajada de EEUU Negocian Para "Salvar" Algunos Proyectos', *La Prensa*, 19 September. Online, available at: www.laprensa.com.bo (accessed 21 December 2009).

La Razón (2009) 'El Gobierno pone fin a un programa de ayuda de Usaid', *La Razón*, 19 September. Online, available at: www.la-razon.com (accessed 22 December 2009).

Ledebur, K. and Walsh, J. (2008) *Decertifying Bolivia: Bush Administration 'Fails Demonstrably' to Make its Case: Comments Pertaining to the Review of Bolivia's Designation as a Beneficiary Country under the ATPA and ATPDEA*. Online, available at: www.wola.org (accessed 31 August 2009).

Ledebur, K. and Youngers, C.A. (2008) *Balancing Act: Bolivia's Drug Control Advances and Challenges*. Online, available at: www.wola.org (accessed 9 January 2009).

Ledebur, K. and Youngers, C.A. (2012) *Washington in Wonderland: United States Slams Bolivian Drug Control Efforts Lauded by UN*. Online, available at: www.wola.org (accessed 1 October 2012).

Lehman, K.D. (1999) *Bolivia and the United States: A Limited Partnership*, Athens, GA: University of Georgia Press.

Mayorga, R.A. (1997) 'Bolivia's Silent Revolution', *Journal of Democracy*, 8 (1): 142–56.

MCC (2009) *Scores: Bolivia FY09*. Online, available at: www.mcc.gov (accessed 14 December 2009).

Meentzen, A. (2007) 'La participación política indígena en América Latina: reconocimientos de nuevos sujetos políticos', *Diálogo Político*, 24 (2): 95–109.

Mendonça Cunha, C. and Santaella Gonçalves, R. (2010) 'The National Development Plan as a Political Economic Strategy in Evo Morales's Bolivia: Accomplishments and Limitations', *Latin American Perspectives*, 37 (4): 177–96.

NED (various years): *Annual Report*, several editions. Online, available at: www.ned.org (accessed 22 July 2010).

Negroponte, J.D. (2007) *Annual Threat Assessment of the Director of National Intelligence*. Online, available at: www.dni.gov (accessed 16 November 2009).

OECD (2006) *DAC Prüfbericht über die Entwicklungszusammenarbeit: Deutschland*, Paris: OECD.

OECD (2010) *Development Database on Aid Activities: CRS online*. Online, available at: www.oecd.org (accessed 13 January 2010).

Peñaranda, R. (2009) 'Crónica del proceso constituyente', in C. Romero, C. Böhrt and R. Peñaranda *Del conflicto al diálogo. Memorias del acuerdo constitucional*, La Paz: fBDM/FES-ILDIS.

Puhle, H.-J. (2001) 'Herausragende Transformations- und Entwicklungsleistungen in Bolivien', in W. Weidenfeld (ed.) *Den Wandel gestalten – Strategien der Transformation*, Volume 1, Gütersloh: Bertelsmann Stiftung.

Quiroga, Y. (2003) 'Bolivien. Eine Demokratie vor dem Zerfall?', *Analyse der Friedrich-Ebert-Stiftung*, Bonn: Friedrich-Ebert-Stiftung.

Ribando Seelke, C. (2008) 'Bolivia: Political and Economic Developments and Relations with the United States', *CRS Report for Congress*, no. RL32580, updated 14 November 2008.

Riedler, E. (2009) 'Ein Lotse geht von Bord. Ein Gespräch zum Abschied des deutschen Botschafters Erich Riedler', *Monatsblatt des Centro Cultural Alemán La Paz*, 2: 12–16.

Rieff, D. (2005) 'Che's Second Coming?', *New York Times Magazine*, 20 November: 72.

Romero, C., Böhrt, C. and Peñaranda, R. (2009) *Del conflicto al diálogo. Memorias del acuerdo constitucional*, La Paz: fBDM/FES-ILDIS.

Schwarzbauer, A. (2007) 'Supporting a Constitutional Reform Process in Bolivia', in BMZ (ed.) *Transforming Fragile States – Examples of Practical Experience*, Baden-Baden: Nomos.

Spanger, H.-J. and Wolff, J. (2003) 'Poverty Reduction through Democratisation? PRSP: Challenges of a New Development Strategy', *PRIF Report*, no. 65, Frankfurt a.M.: Peace Research Institute Frankfurt.

SPD (2008) *Gemeinsame Verantwortung und Zukunft: Lateinamerika und Karibik als strategische Partner für Deutschland und Europa. Lateinamerika-Strategie der SPD*. Online, available at: www.spd.de (accessed 9 May 2008).

Steinmeier, F.-W. (2008) 'Rede von Bundesaußenminister Frank-Walter Steinmeier in der Lateinamerika-Debatte des Deutschen Bundestages am 9. Mai 2008', in Bundestag (ed.) *Plenarprotokoll 16/161*, Berlin: Deutscher Bundestag.

Ströbele-Gregor, J. (1996) *Förderung von politischer Teilhabe in Lateinamerika. Regionalgutachten im Rahmen der F&E-Vorhabens*, Eschborn: GTZ.

Tarnoff, C. and Nowels, L. (2004) 'Foreign Aid: An Introductory Overview of US Programs and Policy', *CRS Report for Congress*, no. 98–916 F, updated 15 April 2004.

Toranzo Roca, C. (2006) *Rostros de la democracia: una mirada mestiza*, La Paz: Plural.

USAID (1997) *USAID Bolivia Strategic Plan FY 1998–2002*, La Paz: USAID.

USAID (2004) *USAID/OTI Bolivia Field Report June 2004*. Online, available at: www.usaid.gov (accessed 22 December 2009).

USAID (2005) *USAID/Bolivia Country Strategic Plan 2005–2009*, La Paz: USAID.

USAID (2007a) *USAID/OTI Bolivia Field Report Apr–June 2007*. Online, available at: www.usaid.gov (accessed 8 January 2009).

USAID (2007b) *Justification for Proposed Changes in USAID/Bolivia Democracy Office Budget*. Online, available at: www.jeremybigwood.net (accessed 31 August 2009).

USAID (2008a) *Budget Scenarios for USAID/Bolivia Democracy Program. Online, available at:* www.jeremybigwood.net (accessed 31 August 2009).

USAID (2008b) *USAID/Bolivia Planned FY 2008 Program Overview*. Online, available at: www.jeremybigwood.net (accessed 31 August 2009).

USAID (2009) *USAID/Bolivia* (webpage). Online, available at: http://bolivia.usaid.gov (accessed 7 January 2009).

US Congress (2009) *US–Bolivia Relations: Looking Ahead. Hearing before the Subcommittee on the Western Hemisphere of the Committee on Foreign Affairs, House of Representatives* (3 March 2009), Washington, DC: US Government Printing Office.

US Department of State (2007) *Bolivia 2007 Performance Report*. Online, available at: http://pdf.usaid.gov/ (accessed 8 January 2009).

US Department of State (2011) 'Joint Statement by the United States of America and the Plurinational State of Bolivia', *Media Note*, Washington, DC, 7 November.

US Embassy La Paz (2002) *Scenesetter: Bolivia's August 6 Transition, the Challenges Ahead, and the US Role*, Cable 2002LAPAZ02723. Online, available at: www.jeremybigwood.net (accessed 6 January 2010).

US Embassy La Paz (2006) *Evo and His Advisory Circle, Part 1 of 3*, Cable 06LAPAZ886, 30 March. Online, available at: http://213.251.145.96/cable/2006/03/06LAPAZ886.html (accessed 6 December 2010).

US Embassy La Paz (2007a) *Codel Nelson Scenesetter*, Cable 07LAPAZ383, 13 February. Online, available at: http://213.251.145.96/cable/2007/02/07LAPAZ383.html (accessed 6 December 2010).

US Embassy La Paz (2007b) *DEPSEC's Upcoming Meeting with Bolivian VP*, Cable

07LAPAZ2385, 29 August. Online, available at: http://213.251.145.96/cable/2007/08/07LAPAZ2385.html (accessed 6 December 2010).
US Embassy La Paz (2009) *Homepage*. Online, available at: http://bolivia.usembassy.gov, http://spanish.bolivia.usembassy.gov (accessed 7 January 2009).
US GAO (2003) *Foreign Assistance: US Democracy Programs in Six Latin American Countries Have Yielded Modest Results*, Washington, DC: US GAO.
Van Cott, D.L. (2003) 'From Exclusion to Inclusion: Bolivia's 2002 Elections', *Journal of Latin American Studies* 35 (4): 751–75.
Van Cott, D.L. (2005) *From Movements to Parties in Latin America: The Evolution of Ethnic Politics*, Cambridge: Cambridge University Press.
Vogl, D. (2006) 'Freundschaftlich und vertrauensvoll: Ein kurzer Überblick über die politischen Beziehungen Deutschlands zu Bolivien', in F. Bopp and G. Ismar (eds) *Bolivien. Neue Wege und alte Gegensätze*, Berlin: Wissenschaftlicher Verlag.
White House (2005) *Press Briefing by Scott McClellan*, 20 December. Online, available at: http://georgewbush-whitehouse.archives.gov (accessed 17 November 2009).
White House (2006) *Presidential Determination on Major Drug Transit or Major Illicit Drug Producing Countries for Fiscal Year 2007*, 18 September. Online, available at: http://georgewbush-whitehouse.archives.gov (accessed 17 November 2009).
White House (2007) *Presidential Determination on Major Drug Transit or Major Illicit Drug Producing Countries for Fiscal Year 2008*, 17 September. Online, available at: http://georgewbush-whitehouse.archives.gov (accessed 17 November 2009).
White House (2008) *President Bush Signs H.R. 7222, the Andean Trade Preference Act Extension*, 16 October. Online, available at: http://georgewbush-whitehouse.archives.gov (accessed 17 November 2009).
Wolff, J. (2004) 'Demokratisierung als Risiko der Demokratie? Die Krise der Politik in Bolivien und Ecuador und die Rolle der indigenen Bewegungen', *HSFK-Report*, no. 6, Frankfurt a.M.: Peace Research Institute Frankfurt.
Wolff, J. (2010) 'Demokratieförderung als Suchprozess. Die Bolivien- und Ecuadorpolitik Deutschlands in Zeiten demokratischer Revolutionen', *HSFK-Report*, no. 6, Frankfurt a.M.: Peace Research Institute Frankfurt.
Wolff, J. (2011) 'Re-engaging Latin America's Left? US Relations with Bolivia and Ecuador from Bush to Obama', *PRIF Report*, no. 103, Frankfurt a.M.: Peace Research Institute Frankfurt.
Wolff, J. (2012) 'Democracy Promotion, Empowerment, and Self-Determination: Conflicting Objectives in US and German Policies towards Bolivia', *Democratization*, 19 (3): 415–37.
Wolff, J. (2013) 'Towards Postliberal Democracy in Latin America? A Conceptual Framework applied to Bolivia', *Journal of Latin American Studies*, 45 (1): 31–59.
Yashar, D.J. (2005) *Contesting Citizenship in Latin America: The Rise of Indigenous Movements and the Postliberal Challenge*, Cambridge: Cambridge University Press.
Zilla, C. (2006) 'Externe Demokratieförderung in Bolivien. Die Politik Deutschlands und der Europäischen Union', *SWP-Studie*, no. 28, Berlin: SWP.
Zuazo, M. (2009) *¿Cómo nació el MAS? La ruralización de la política en Bolivia. Entrevistas a 85 parlamentarios del partido*, La Paz: Fundación Ebert.

5 Democracy promotion in Ecuador
The 'citizens' revolution' of Rafael Correa

Jonas Wolff

With Rafael Correa a ten-year phase of almost continuous political crisis in Ecuador has come to an end. Between 1997 and 2006 no elected president served a full term in office. President Correa, elected for the first time at the end of 2006, not only achieved this – in 2009 he was even confirmed in office in the first round of voting. The 'citizens' revolution' (*revolución ciudadana*) proclaimed by the new head of state made two promises: on the one hand, bringing the 'long night of neoliberalism' (Correa) to an end, which in specific terms amounted to strengthening state capacity as well as increasing the state's role in social and economic development of the country; on the other hand, introducing fundamental reform of the political system with the intention of weakening the power of the established political parties (*partidocracia*) and giving the citizenry more opportunities for participation. At the heart of the political changes initiated by Correa and his political movement 'Patria Altiva I Soberana' (PAIS) was, as in the case of Bolivia, constitutional reform through a directly elected Constituent Assembly.

Since the Correa Administration took office in 2007, external democracy promoters in Ecuador – such as Germany and the United States – have been confronted with difficult challenges. In many ways, these challenges are similar to the ones observed in connection with Bolivian development under Morales. The following analysis of the conflict situation in Ecuador and the conflicts of objectives for the United States and Germany thus runs parallel to Chapter 4. However, the conflict situation and conflicts of objectives in Ecuador are generally less acute than in Bolivia. This is reflected in particular in US reactions to the Correa government.

Ecuador's 'citizens' revolution' as a conflict situation

At the turn of the millennium, when Bolivia was still being celebrated as a model of democratic stability, Ecuador was already considered a Latin American country chronically engulfed in crisis. Elected in 1979, Ecuador's democratic regime was never considered particularly successful (see Conaghan 1995). In the second half of the 1990s, political instability in the country worsened considerably once again. The overthrow of President Bucaram in 1997 initiated a ten-year phase of recurrent mass protests and political crises, during which no elected head of state was able to serve a full term of office. Jamil Mahuad (2000) and Lucio Gutiérrez (2005) were also driven from office amid social protests, with the more or less active support of Congress and the military (see Wolff 2008: chapter 5).

The social conflicts that had been escalating since the mid-1990s were marked especially by the political rise of the indigenous movement in Ecuador, which united with other social movements, left wing groups and unions to form a broad protest alliance (see Van Cott 2005: chapter 4; Yashar 2005: 4).[1] These protests combined specific indigenous demands (for political and legal recognition), a rejection of neoliberal austerity and structural adjustment measures, as well as criticism of a democratic regime that was perceived as corrupt, scarcely representative and dominated by a small (party) political elite. Rafael Correa was not actively involved in these protests, but he embraced their agenda in establishing his political career. After a short interlude as economy and finance minister in 2005, the left-wing economist and political outsider won the 2006 presidential election with his promise to radically break with Ecuador's 'political class'. Correa's programme for a 'citizens' revolution' really did take up the most important demands of the social protests of earlier years: the ouster of the ruling parties and rebuilding of the political system through a Constituent Assembly;[2] the rejection of 'neoliberalism' in economic and social policy; and – in connection with this – an emphasis on national sovereignty vis-à-vis the IMF, World Bank and the United States (see *La Tendencia* 2009; Ospina 2009).

In order to convoke a Constituent Assembly, the resistance of the 'traditional' parties in Congress had to be overcome (see Conaghan 2008).[3] This was made possible by a controversial ruling handed down by the Supreme Electoral Tribunal that rescinded the mandates of the opposition majority in parliament. In a referendum, 82 per cent voted in favour of convening a Constituent Assembly, and subsequent elections confirmed a clear majority for Correa's PAIS. Endowed with 'full powers', the Constituent Assembly suspended Congress and – for the period between acceptance of the new constitution and new parliamentary elections – appointed a provisional legislature replacing the elected parliament. In a referendum in September 2008 64 per cent approved the new constitution. In the new elections that followed in April 2009, with 52 per cent of the vote Correa defeated his opponents by a clear margin. PAIS narrowly failed to gain an absolute majority in parliament.

Ecuador's new constitution displays many parallels to the new constitution of Bolivia (see Wolff 2012). It also combines the usual principles and norms of liberal democracy with elements that significantly modify them. Mechanisms of direct democracy (recall and other referendums, citizens' legislative initiatives) stand alongside classic institutions of representative democracy. In addition, select individuals appointed to a 'council of citizen participation and social control' are able to exercise some kind of control over government and administration. Political and civil rights are supplemented by a broad range of economic and social human rights. The privatization of public social services and 'strategic sectors' is restricted. In general, the market economy and private property are embedded in a mixed 'social and solidarity-based' economy. The constitution also introduces the completely new concept of the 'rights of nature'. It also strengthens the (collective) rights of the indigenous population – even if in this area it falls well short of the Bolivian constitution.

In the area of economic policy, the Correa government focused on strengthening the capacity and the role of the state. This involved expanding state activities related to development planning as well as the role played by public-sector companies. Continuing the policy decisions of his predecessor, Alfredo Palacio, in Ecuador's key oil sector, Correa introduced further tax increases on foreign companies and strengthened the role of the state-owned oil company, Petro-Ecuador. Already under the Palacio Administration, Ecuador had revoked the permits held by the US-based Occidental Petroleum (Oxy) in the country over alleged contract violations, and handed the oilfields in question over to Petro-Ecuador (Ribando 2008: 4). Correa used increasing government revenue, not least deriving from high oil prices, to heavily increase spending on public investment and social policies.[4]

Internationally, under Correa Ecuador is clearly striving towards national sovereignty and the diversification of foreign relations. Thus the newly elected president declared the representative of the World Bank a '*persona non grata*', paid off Ecuador's debts to the IMF and obtained relatively favourable restructuring of state bonds. As he had already announced in the election campaign, Correa refused to renew the contract, due to expire in 2009, which since 1999 had permitted the United States to use its forward operating location (FOL) in the Ecuadorean port of Manta. The government also refused to sign free trade agreements with either the United States or the European Union (EU). At the same time, Correa relied on more intensive cooperation within South America but also with countries such as Russia, China and Iran.

The following case study focuses on the first phase of the 'citizens' revolution' in Ecuador from the first election of Correa at the end of 2006 to his re-election in 2009. In these years, the basic dilemmas of democratization (see Chapter 1 of this volume) emerged in a significantly less acute form than in the case of Bolivia. The centre-right opposition proved to be too weak and fragmented to be able to openly resist the government. At the same time, the country's indigenous and social organizations on the left side of the political spectrum were for the most part aligned with the government – at least until the successful constitutional referendum. The process of constitutional reforms meant a far-reaching destabilization and, in fact, the decomposition of existing political institutions, which corresponds to the 'democracy versus stability' dilemma. However, in comparison with the phase between 1997 and 2006, the election of Correa ushered in a period marked by fewer social conflicts and less political instability.[5] The situation is similarly ambivalent with regard to tensions between democracy and governability. When seen from a technocratic and/or neoliberal perspective, Correa's economic and social policies might be considered 'populist': popular with the public, but economically unreasonable. At the same time, however, the general assessment is that the technical capacity and quality of governance has improved since Correa took office.

By contrast, the election of Correa clearly gave rise to the emergence of the 'democracy versus majority' dilemma. The convening of the Constituent Assembly was legitimized by an overwhelming majority in the referendum. It was accompanied, however, by what in effect was the dissolution of the democratically elected parliament and meant the (temporary) establishment of a political power subject to no horizontal controls. In general, the partial deviation from liberal democracy and Correa's 'plebiscitary' style of government also point to the tension between majority decisions and democratic principles (Conaghan 2008).

On the part of external democracy promoters – specifically Germany and the United States – these political changes have given rise to both extrinsic and intrinsic conflicts of objectives:

1   *Democracy versus donor interests (extrinsic)*. Both the change in economic course and the shutting down of the US military base in Manta were election promises made by Correa, for which he had received an unmistakable democratic mandate in the 2006 election. Ecuador's new 'hard' line against foreign (oil) companies, especially Oxy, was widely supported across the country. All these manifestations of democratic self-determination simultaneously affected the security (Manta) and economic (Oxy) interests of the United States. German interests, on the other hand, were only affected in an abstract manner: Ecuador's turning away from free market and free trade policies generally run counter to German economic preferences. This is also true for the United States, and also holds for both donors with regard to Correa's policy of diversifying Ecuador's international relations and increasing cooperation with Venezuela, China, Russia and Iran.
2   *Democracy versus democracy (intrinsic)*. Both the process and the results of the constitutional reform led to various sub-goals of democracy promotion coming into conflict with each other. The Constituent Assembly was a profoundly democratic undertaking that was democratically legitimized at every essential step. At the same time, it was based upon violations of basic norms of representative democracy (dismissal of parliament) and of the constitutional state (an assembly with absolute power). As occurred in Bolivia, in the course of constitutional reform, existing institutions were gradually dismantled, while new (albeit democratic) institutions had yet to be erected. Generally, a president who keeps election promises and by whom broad sections of the population feel represented is as much in accordance with the goals of external democracy promoters as the passage of a democratically legitimized constitution. At the same time, however, the focus on plebiscitary forms of legitimation meant limiting institutional controls: the new constitution's combination of a strong executive, direct democracy and participatory mechanisms led some observers to fear a weakening of parliament and the judiciary.

Germany: supportively biding its time

Profile of bilateral relations

From the German perspective, political relations with Ecuador are characterized by comprehensive insignificance. In economic terms, Ecuador is a little more relevant than Bolivia, but marginal all the same. German companies are mostly involved through trade and only in exceptional cases carry on production in Ecuador (BFAI 2007: 3). However, given the unique biodiversity in the country, particular on the Galapagos Islands and in the Amazon region, Ecuador attracts some interest in terms of environmental policy. In addition, a number of German or German–Ecuadorean institutions for cultural and educational cooperation exist.

In addition to these cultural relationships, the main focus of bilateral relations clearly lies in the area of development cooperation. Ecuador is not among Germany's high-priority partners, but, in terms of concentration on countries, was still chosen as one of ten Latin American partner countries. Since the 1980s Ecuador's share of bilateral German development cooperation with Latin America (ODA disbursements) has remained relatively constant at about 4 per cent (OECD 2010, own calculations). The main focus of German development cooperation lies in the area of environmental and resource protection, specifically with a view to protected areas.

Profile of German democracy promotion in Ecuador

In the 1980s, German development policy in Ecuador still focused entirely on 'classical' socioeconomic issues. In 1992, Germany established 'modernization of the state' as a priority area (Wolff 2010: 12). Since 2000, Ecuador's classification as a non-priority 'partner country' should have meant focusing German development cooperation on one main area. The Federal Ministry for Economic Cooperation and Development, however, decided to maintain two priority areas: 'Environment and Resource Protection' and 'Modernization of the State, Decentralization and Support of Local Governments' (BMZ 2007: 6, 2008). Nevertheless, the ministry stipulated 'giving priority' to environmental protection; cooperation in the area of democracy and governance is supposed to be discontinued 'in the long term' (BMZ 2007: 9, 7).

OECD data on ODA reflect this secondary focus on democracy. In the years 1999 to 2008, 15 per cent of German ODA commitments were in the 'Government and Civil Society' sector. When looking at actual disbursements between 2004 and 2008, this sector represented around 20 per cent of German ODA to Ecuador (OECD 2010, own calculations).

The usual range of agencies that implement German development cooperation is present in Ecuador. During the period under study, their activities in the area of democracy assistance placed special emphasis on decentralization and the sub-national level (see Wolff 2010: 12–13). The DED worked at the local level in the area of development planning with a view to supporting the participation of civil society. The CIM supported the decentralization process, for example through Integrated Experts in the associations of the various sub-national authorities. The KfW Development Bank concentrated its financial assistance on local and provincial governments, but did so with a focus on environment and resource protection matters.

The most important agency implementing German democracy assistance in Ecuador is the GTZ, now operating as the GIZ and including DED and InWEnt. In 2003, GTZ merged a series of individual projects into a major programme on modernization and decentralization. This 'Programa de Modernización y Descentralización' (PROMODE) was scheduled for ten years and its aim was to promote the transfer of duties, competencies, and resources to sub-national authorities (provinces, municipalities and parishes) in order to deliver services more efficiently, more closely linked to the needs and with greater participation of the population (GTZ 2005: 21). Core activities included the support of the decentralization process, advising sub-national authorities and their associations, and generally fostering efficiency and transparency in public financial management (see BMZ 2007: 8; GTZ 2006: 3).

Of the political foundations, the FES, the KAS and the HSS run their own offices in the capital, Quito.[6] In the area of democracy promotion, FES has been supporting democratic institutions, political and social organizations. Its work has been specifically focused on institutional reform (most recently the Constituent Assembly, see below), a dialogue among the left and centre-left forces (e.g. through the journal *La Tendencia*), and the strengthening and renewal of the parties within this spectrum. The activities of the KAS have generally focused on strengthening democratic institutions, the rule of law as well as societal and institutional modernization processes. In the area of party politics, the Christian Democrat 'Unión Demócrata Cristiana' (UDC) was a partner of the KAS for many years (KAS 2008: 29–30). Since the early 1990s, the HSS in Ecuador has concentrated on the education of the indigenous population, especially through a scholarship programme primarily orientated towards indigenous people. In addition, the HSS also put on political forums and ran training measures for young party members.

Apart from the foundations, the focus of German democracy assistance in Ecuador has clearly lain – and continues to lie – on the state. Even projects focused on civil society participation were ultimately aimed at strengthening and modernizing state institutions.[7] The sub-national level figured most prominently in this (see also Vega and Zimmermann 2006). The rationale behind this strategy was that political instability in Ecuador made it almost impossible to make lasting contributions at the national level, whereas at the provincial and municipal level the underlying conditions were significantly better (BMZ 2007: 6). As a result, an evaluation by PROMODE prior to the election of Correa concluded that the chances for successful policy advice at the national level were 'limited' and therefore the programme needed to be 'more strongly staffed at the regional/local level in the next phase' (GTZ 2006: 6, 8).

Perception analysis

It is against the background of a decade of political instability in the country that the BMZ evaluated the incipient Correa government. While the past ten years of crisis 'significantly hindered systematically fighting poverty', the new government signalled an earnest 'willingness' to make reforms and promote development (BMZ 2007: 1). Qualifying an overall positive assessment, the BMZ country concept also included areas of concern: the new government, for instance, might subordinate 'democratic principles' in order to push through its reform objectives; and the planned constitutional process could 'lead to new political unrest' (BMZ 2007: 1; cf. Bundesregierung 2008: 7–14). The ministry generally welcomed Correa's economic and social policy proposals, but warned against 'a bloated state apparatus' and adverse effects on 'private investors' (BMZ 2007: 2).

At the local office of the Adenauer Foundation, the election of Correa was pronounced 'another triumph of left-wing populism in Latin America' (Rothfritz 2006). After two-and-a-half years of experience with the government, the KAS concluded rather moderately that 'in terms of actual policies, hardly anything has happened' (Weig 2009: 39). With regard to Ecuador's relationship to Venezuela, the KAS representative in Quito stated that President Correa was seeking to 'keep his distance from Chávez' and striving 'on the whole to do things his own way' (Weig 2009: 40).[8] In Weig's assessment, the new constitution meant 'above all' that 'political power' in the country was being concentrated 'in the hands of the president' (Weig 2009: 45). Yet, his overall assessment of the constitution was differentiated and mainly emphasized the general absence of any substantial change. Correa's political style also seemed to be a continuation of well-known practices: 'like his predecessors' Correa was described as playing the role of 'the strong man' and 'mimicking Caudillo'. However, 'with his radical political rhetoric' Correa had 'deeply' divided the country (Weig 2009: 46–7).

Coming from a position that was, during the first year and a half, relatively close to the Correa government, the Ebert Foundation reached approximately the same conclusion. Before the 2009 elections concerns were voiced that the government could slip into 'authoritarianism' if it failed to achieve a majority in its own right (Detsch 2009: 1). Despite its own professed interest in participation, the government had 'until now not created any genuine space for linking or articulating with the social movements'; in fact, the president seemed 'at present not to be committed to this objective' (Detsch 2009: 4). Correa's social policies were, however, judged more positively than by the KAS; nevertheless, FES also warned against frightening off potential investors through 'a strong role of the state in planning and regulating the economy' (Detsch 2009: 4–5). The assessment of the new constitution was also generally more positive. It was seen as resulting from an effort 'to promote a socially just, participatory and self-determined development while acknowledging the cultural diversity and the historical roots of the country' (Langer 2008: 1). Looking at the risk of hyper-presidentialism, the FES did stress 'the expanded powers of the president', but at the same time drew attention to strengthened 'control functions of the parliament' as well as to the 'strengthening of the Constitutional Court' (Langer 2008: 2–3).

Reaction analysis

Germany's official reaction to Correa's election was to maintain a supportive wait-and-see stance. The Ministry of Development publicly stated that the German government supported 'the reform process in Ecuador' (BMZ 2008), but did not make declarations of sympathy as it had with Bolivia (see Chapter 4). Within the German government and among Germany's development cooperation agencies the suspension and later dissolution of parliament was regarded as a clear violation of democratic rules.[9] However, no discernible consequences for bilateral relations resulted. In view of the massive support for Correa and the Constituent Assembly in opinion polls and elections, Germany ultimately accepted the suspension of parliament.[10]

In terms of development cooperation, there is broad continuity. From 2003 to 2008 annual ODA disbursements varied between €21 million and €28 million, with an upwards trend in the first two years of the Correa government (2007–8). New commitments remained at a constant level between 2002 and 2010 (see Wolff 2010: 40). This was also the case for those ODA funds that, between 2004 and 2008, were earmarked for the 'government and civil society' sector (OECD 2010). In the intergovernmental negotiations in June 2008, Germany committed €23 million for 2008 to 2010, of which €3.5 million (about 15 per cent) was allocated for modernization of the state and, specifically, for the GTZ programme PROMODE (AGECI 2008).[11] In general, after the election of Correa, the share of German ODA in the sector 'government and civil society' that is channelled through the public sector increased; in turn, the share for 'civil society' was significantly reduced.[12]

In the area of democracy assistance, 'wait and see' was official policy. As specifically requested by the Correa government, Germany did continue work in the area 'modernization of the state', but at a relatively low financial level and only provisionally. This priority area, according to the BMZ (2007: 8), was only to be retained 'in the medium term' if and when 'structural improvements guarantee the effectiveness of development cooperation'. Correspondingly, the ministry abstained from updating the outdated strategy paper 'Modernization of the State, Decentralization and Promotion of Local Government' from 2004; in May 2010, it at least adopted a position paper (*Eckpunktepapier*) on the topic.

At the same time, German democracy promotion adapted flexibly to the preferences of the new Ecuadorean government. Directly as well as indirectly, Germany supported the Constituent Assembly. GTZ made constitutional reform a priority area of PROMODE and supported first the assembly itself, then the implementation of the new constitution. In addition to direct aid for the Constituent Assembly,[13] GTZ contributed indirectly by supporting input to the assembly from different local partners of PROMODE.[14] The German political foundations also supported 'the constitutional process through information and advisory seminars' (Bundesregierung 2008: 11). These special activities of the *Stiftungen* were financed through additional funds made available by the Foreign Office. The Ebert Foundation was particularly active – not least because Alberto Acosta, a former staff member of FES, had been elected president of the assembly. FES provided direct support to the assembly through advisory services.[15] The Seidel Foundation 'primarily' supported opposition members of the assembly from the centre-right.[16] The Adenauer Foundation abstained from directly contributing to the constitutional process and concentrated on promoting critical observation.[17]

The adaptation of GTZ democracy assistance in response to the new political situation went beyond the constitutional process. Specifically, the policy change under Correa required (and permitted) GTZ to focus more on the national level, on questions of state reform and on development planning. In terms of policy, this led to a new PROMODE component entitled 'state reform'. Institutionally, a change of the local executing partner was necessary. The Correa government dismantled the 'Consejo Nacional de Modernización del Estado' (CONAM), which under the previous government had been committed to a (neo-)liberal state modernization process and had been PROMODE's lead executing partner. With Correa, the new Planning and Development Secretariat SENPLADES became the central coordinating unit for state reform and development planning. German development cooperation adapted to this change and chose SENPLADES as its central partner and the lead executing agency of PROMODE. This meant that the strengthening of state planning capacity – in addition to the constitutional process and decentralization – became a central area of German support.[18]

Beyond support for the Constituent Assembly, adaptation by each of the political foundations reflected their respective party political profile. Especially in the first two years of Correa's presidency, the work of the Ebert Foundation corresponded closely to the agenda of the Correa government and, to a considerable degree, consisted in providing support and advice to the constitutional reforms. This was possible because FES in Ecuador had direct lines of communication with the government camp. Nonetheless, FES did not commit itself to the governing PAIS party as its partner.[19] The Adenauer and Seidel Foundations, by contrast, focused on the opposition right-of-centre spectrum, without having specific party partners there. Since the collapse of the Christian Democrat parties in Ecuador, the Adenauer Foundation had been without an institutional partner among the political parties. At the beginning of 2010, however, it concluded a cooperation agreement with the 'Partido Sociedad Patriótica', the party of former president Gutiérrez, which under Correa became the most important opposition force.[20] In its directly (party) political work, the Seidel Foundation cooperated with various partner organizations in which 'promising' individuals from the conservative camp who had left their respective political parties were working out new perspectives.[21]

Prior to Correa taking office, a trend had already emerged in German democracy promotion in Ecuador that can be interpreted as a reaction to the years of political instability. In view of the enormous difficulties in making sustainable contributions to democracy and governance at the national level, Germany concentrated on the sub-national level. However, the fact that decentralization also depends upon the national framework suggested reducing involvement in the entire area of 'state modernization'. Under Correa, this trend was temporarily halted and modified in some areas. But the general orientation was retained. Given the difficulties in reforming the democratic state, German development cooperation was inclined to withdraw from democracy promotion – and to concentrate on the less complicated environmental area and, specifically, on clearly demarcated protected areas (BMZ 2007: 7). The German decision to continue development cooperation in the area of state and democracy, if at a reduced level, can already be regarded as a leap of faith for Correa and can in fact be attributed to the Ecuadorean government, which insisted on the retention of this priority area.

Finally, an initiative in the area of environmental protection and climate change must be mentioned as it met with the strongest and most positive response in Germany. Shortly after assuming office, the Correa government communicated to the 'international community' that it would refrain from exploiting oil fields in the Ishpingo–Tambococha–Tiputini corridor (ITT) in Yasuní National Park if, in return, Ecuador received international compensation for half the income forfeited. This 'ITT initiative' received important support from Germany, initially from civil society, followed by support from the German parliament (see Bundestag 2008: 18366–71) and the government. GTZ supported feasibility studies to further develop the initiative.[22]

The United States: pragmatic continuity

Profile of bilateral relations

Before the election of Correa, Ecuador was regarded as a 'staunch US ally against narco-trafficking and terrorist violence' (CBJ 2007: 551). In Ecuador, there is neither significant coca farming nor drug production. However, the country's strategic location – between the two drug-producing countries of Colombia and Peru – gives it direct relevance to US drug and security policy. Until 2009, US cooperation in this area was focused on the Forward Operating Location in Manta. In 1999, Manta had replaced US military bases in Panama. Since then, the military base had been crucial for US counternarcotics and counterterror activities in the framework of Plan Colombia (see Pineo 2007: 210; Rivera 2005).

US foreign assistance to Ecuador clearly reflects the priority of counternarcotics (see Rivera 2005). From 2000 to 2008, combating drug trafficking was by far the most important element of foreign assistance (see Wolff 2011: 39–40). In addition, development cooperation was focused on the northern region bordering Colombia – from the US point of view, this support aimed at both fighting drug trafficking and the Colombian FARC guerrillas. US foreign assistance as well as trade preferences granted to Ecuador in the framework of the ATPDEA are linked to the annual 'certification' of Ecuador by the US president, i.e. to Ecuador's cooperation in the US 'war on drugs' (see Chapter 4).

From a US perspective, overall economic relations are insignificant. Yet, a series of US companies were (and are) active in Ecuador, especially in the oil-producing sector. In the case of Oxy, it involved investments of about $1 billion (Lettieri 2006). In response to the tax increases in the oil-producing sector imposed under Correa and his predecessor Palacio, three other US companies also initiated international arbitration proceedings against Ecuador with the World Bank's International Centre for Settlement of Investment Disputes (US Department of State 2009e).

Profile of US democracy promotion in Bolivia

In addition to environmental protection, securing the northern border with Colombia and combating poverty, strengthening of democratic institutions was a stated priority of US policy towards Ecuador (Ribando 2008: 5). Promoting democracy, in particular, was regarded as an instrument against 'Ecuador's chronic instability and its role as a major source of illegal immigration and drugs' (CBJ 2008: 625). At the end of the 1990s, phasing out the limited USAID measures in this area (justice reform and promotion of civil society) was still planned, together with the entire USAID programme (USAID 1997). The increasing significance of the country in connection with Plan Colombia, as well as the emerging phase of political instability, ultimately led to the USAID remaining active in Ecuador and initiating a comprehensive democracy programme.

Between 2004 and 2007, USAID's democracy programme encompassed four areas: strengthening the justice sector, supporting democratic local governance, fighting corruption, and supporting free and fair elections (see CBJ 2005: 484, 2006: 515, 2007: 552). In addition to the judiciary and local governments, a key partner was the local NGO 'Participación Ciudadana', which, in addition to elections monitoring, carried out watchdog and civic education measures (see USAID 2006: 9–10).

The NDI and the IRI started work in Ecuador in the context of the 2002 elections, which followed the ouster of President Mahuad in 2000. With USAID funds NDI supported the creation of 'Participación Ciudadana' – the election observation organization that later became the central partner organization of USAID (see above). In the same year, IRI carried out an international election observation mission. NDI opened an office in Quito in 2006 and, since then, has carried out a programme financed by the NED to strengthen political parties. In 2001 and 2002, IRI offered training of junior members of political parties (financed by NED); in 2009, it again commenced work in Ecuador (see below). In addition to NDI and IRI, between 2000 and 2008 the CIPE received regular NED funding for activities in Ecuador. A growing number of local organizations also received NED grants (NED various years).

In addition to US democracy assistance, the declared goal of democracy promotion is also reflected in regular rhetorical appeals by the US government and in the political dialogue between the two countries. A case in point is the rebellion-turned-coup in January 2000, during which an alliance of the indigenous movement with parts of the military overthrew President Mahuad. The US government immediately threatened the self-proclaimed 'Junta of National Salvation' with the cancellation of US aid as well as political and economic isolation, and in this way contributed to the Ecuadorean military leadership, declaring after a few hours that the coup was over (Wolff 2003: 83). By contrast, US reactions were much less swift in 2004/5 when President Gutiérrez, in a manner that was in part openly unconstitutional, removed and replaced a series of justices in the highest courts of the country. While these decisions set off a wave of protest that culminated in the toppling of Gutiérrez, the US government remained notably silent and supported the strongly pro-US president to the very end (see Edwards 2005).

Officially, security and military cooperation is also aimed at 'strengthening democratic institutions' and reinforcing principles of civilian rule and human rights (see CBJ 2003: 410–11, 2008: 625–6). This refers specifically to IMET (but see also Rivera 2005).

Perception analysis

During the campaign for the 2006 presidential elections, the US-educated economist Correa aroused significantly less anxiety in Washington than the Bolivian coca grower Morales. Nevertheless, his success was clearly perceived as a strengthening of the camp of anti-US left-wing governments grouped around Venezuela's president Hugo Chávez (see Wolff 2011: 19). In early 2006 the State Department had promised that US foreign assistance to Ecuador would be devoted to 'keeping the country on track in the face of regional and internal trends towards populist ideology and anti-Americanism' (CBJ 2007: 551). A cable from the US embassy in Quito explicitly identified Correa with this trend and called him a 'dark horse populist, anti-American candidate' (US Embassy Quito 2006a). However, the US government refrained from making any public statements.

The embassy reports published by WikiLeaks reveal an ambivalent US perception of the new Ecuadorean government.[23] On the one hand, the clear democratic legitimation of the elected president was as little in doubt as the broad support that he – and, specifically, his proposal for a Constituent Assembly – enjoyed among the population (see for example US Embassy Quito 2007a). The relative stability of the government after ten years of uninterrupted crisis, Correa's efforts at combating corruption and his relatively pragmatic attitude in areas such as economic policy were also viewed positively (see US Embassy Quito 2008a). On the other hand, Correa's political reform project, and above all his (authoritarian) style of government, was viewed with general scepticism. With regard to democracy, there were fears that a dominant president would weaken checks and balances (parliament, the judiciary) and would tend to intimidate or control private-sector media (see US Embassy Quito 2007a, 2007b).[24]

This ambivalence was also reflected in public statements. Immediately after Correa's election, assistant secretary of state Thomas Shannon spoke of 'a moment in which showing solidarity for Ecuador ... is going to be very, very important' (Shannon 2006). In early 2007, he emphasized that 'it is the peoples themselves who decide their way of organizing politically and economically' (*Miami Herald* 2007). At the same time, however, 'Correa's populist tendencies, his ties with Hugo Chávez of Venezuela, and his state-centered economic policies' were regarded with concern in Washington (Ribando 2008: 4). This is evident in, for instance, the assessment of the director of National Intelligence, who nonetheless differentiated his critical analysis of Ecuador:

> Inspired and supported by Venezuela and Cuba, leaders in Bolivia, Nicaragua, and – more tentatively – in Ecuador are pursuing agendas that undercut checks and balances on presidential power, seek lengthy presidential terms, weaken media and civil liberties, and emphasize economic nationalism at the expense of market-based approaches.
>
> (McConnell 2008: 33)

By contrast, there are no public statements by the US government concerning the suspension of the opposition majority in Congress and the subsequent dissolution of the entire parliament. The State Department's human rights reports merely referred to the conflicts between Correa and the private media and concluded rather sympathetically that 'the government, while critical of the media, generally respected these rights [freedom of speech and of the press] in practice' (US Department of State 2009b; see Wolff 2011: 23). Much harsher criticism, on the other hand, came from some Republican members of Congress and former members of the first George W. Bush Administration (see Wolff 2011: 29).

Reaction analysis

The immediate reaction of the US government to Correa's election victory corresponded to the cooperative wait-and-see style that the administration had chosen a year before with regard to Bolivia.[25] Both the US ambassador to Quito and President Bush made phone calls directly after the elections to congratulate Correa. In a communiqué, the embassy emphasized the willingness of the US government to continue 'successful cooperation with Ecuador' (*El Comercio* 2006). In contrast with US–Bolivian relations (see Chapter 4), relations between the US and Ecuador remained significantly better throughout Correa's entire first term of office – and beyond that. Not only bilateral cooperation but also development cooperation with Ecuador were characterized by much more continuity than change.[26]

Despite quite a number of serious differences between the two governments, diplomatic relations remained astonishingly friendly. In reference to the future of the US military base in Manta, the US administration declared that it would respect all decisions of the Ecuadorean government (US Department of State 2007).[27] At the end of 2009, the base was closed without this causing any noticeable irritations in bilateral relations. How Ecuador treated US companies aroused criticism – especially in US Congress; yet, trade preferences within the context of ATPDEA were continuously renewed nevertheless.[28] In 2006, when under President Palacio the contract with Oxy was declared void, the US government responded by breaking off negotiations on a bilateral free trade agreement (Ribando 2008: 4). The Correa government, however, had no interest in such an agreement anyway.

Even when Correa expelled two members of the US embassy in February 2009, the US government refrained from the usual retaliatory measures.[29] In November 2009 a second meeting of the bilateral dialogue between the two governments took place. This dialogue had started in the previous year as a 'forum to address issues of interest to both sides and to highlight and build on existing cooperation and positive engagement' (US Embassy Quito 2008b). A decisive factor from the US point of view was that the counternarcotics policy of the Correa government was judged to be relatively effective and cooperative (see US Embassy Quito 2008a; Wolff 2011: 21).[30] Added to this was significant US reluctance to drive Correa – who certainly was much more moderate and pragmatic than Chávez or Morales – to more closely align himself with the other two left-leaning South American rulers (see US Embassy Quito 2006b, 2009a). When in September 2010 police protests in Ecuador threatened to escalate into a coup (see note 5), the US Ambassador signalled explicit support not only for the country's democratic institutions, but also for President Correa personally (*Ecuador Inmediato* 2010).

US concerns about Ecuadorean democracy did not play a noticeable role in official relations at all. This topic was explicitly excluded from the bilateral dialogue, although (probably) discussed in general diplomatic exchanges. In particular, US concerns about threats to press and media freedom in Ecuador were publicly voiced. President Obama thus used his telephone call on the re-election of Correa not only to congratulate him and to express his desire for a deepening of bilateral relations; at the same time, he emphasized his support of a free and independent press (US Embassy Quito 2009b). Assistant secretary Arturo Valenzuela and secretary of state Hillary Clinton also discussed this topic during their visits to Quito (Wolff 2011: 23).

Political changes in Ecuador since the election of Correa have had scarcely any noticeable effect on US foreign assistance to the country. From fiscal year 2007 to 2008 the budget declined from $32 million to $26 million, but climbed again to about $35 million in 2009. The most important area of foreign assistance continued to be 'Peace and Security' with a clear focus on counternarcotics (see Wolff 2011: 39–40).

General budget cuts in fiscal year 2008 affected counternarcotics assistance, but also USAID's democracy programme. Specifically, USAID projects on justice reform and local governments were cancelled. In 2008 and 2009, the focus of USAID was thus on civil society and elections. Support for the local NGO 'Participación Ciudadana' was continued and, through the regional human rights institute IIDH-CAPEL, technical support was offered for Ecuador's electoral authorities.[31] The focus on civil society can be interpreted as a certain negative reaction to Correa – especially because 'Participación Ciudadana', while a highly regarded non-partisan watchdog NGO, tended to be critical of the government. As with the reduction in funding, this focus was also only temporary. When funding again increased significantly (and particularly benefited the area 'Governing Justly and Democratically'), the USAID portfolio was expanded and support for the judicial system and local governments resumed. The US government's budget request for fiscal year 2011 in the area of democracy and human rights was even criticized by Freedom House (2010: 3) for reducing the relative weight of civil society support in Ecuador – a reduction that corresponded to the preferences of the Correa government. The budget request for fiscal year 2012 emphasized the support of local governments and the judicial system (with a focus on counternarcotics measures) as the priority areas of US democracy assistance in the country – and did not apply for new funding in the area of 'civil society' (CBJ 2012: 752–4).

Significant growth was to be seen, however, in NED's Ecuador programme, although this had already begun prior to Correa's election. Between 2000 and 2005 NED annual funding for Ecuador ranged from $50,000 to $300,000. Since 2006 over $1 million per year has flowed to a significantly increased number of grant recipients.[32] NED support, *inter alia*, made the aforementioned activities of NDI and IRI possible. In 2008, NDI initiated a programme supporting political and civil society organizations at the local level in influencing ongoing reform processes. In its party work, the institute conducted multiparty workshops and activities with individual parties. The latter included a broad spectrum of parties, including Correa's PAIS. In 2009, IRI initiated a programme to foster discussion in four cities among civil society, parties, media and companies on implementation of the new constitution (see Wolff 2011: 22). Both US party institutes made a visible effort to adopt a non-partisan stance.

Results

As in the case of Bolivia, for Ecuador too US and German democracy promotion relied above all on development policy and, to a lesser extent, diplomacy. During the period under investigation, both donors had made democracy, governance and civil society an area of focus in their development cooperation. In both cases, however, this ranked behind a clear priority area – counternarcotics and counterterrorism (United States) or environmental protection (Germany). Both governments were sparing in the use of diplomatic appeals. Exceptions were the regular statements by the US government on freedom of the press and the – relatively neutral – EU communiqué on the conflict among state powers issued by the German ambassador at the beginning of the Correa Administration. In the framework of political dialogue, both governments apparently raised concerns about democracy and human rights issues. What is striking, however, is that official bilateral dialogue between the United States and Ecuador explicitly excluded this topic.

With regard to election observation, Germany was only indirectly involved through the EU.[33] For US democracy assistance, by contrast, elections were a major issue. US funds supported international election observation missions (e.g. by IRI), local election observation organizations ('Participación Ciudadana') as well as official electoral authorities.[34] This support went well beyond the dimension of simple observation and included capacity-building for civil society and state monitoring agencies.

As in the case of Bolivia, bilateral cooperation is officially linked to democratic conditionality. This refers to political, economic and development cooperation as well as, in the case of the United States, military cooperation. In terms of counterfactual reasoning, it is again plausible to assume that an open break with the democratic order in Ecuador would have prompted German and US sanctions. In its response to the ousting of President Mahuad in January 2000, the US government had in fact threatened direct consequences (suspending US assistance, isolating Ecuador). This, however, does not apply to individual decisions under the Correa government that the donors perceived as serious violations of democratic standards and the rule of law, but not as threatening democracy as such. Such decisions did not have any noticeable consequences for bilateral relations.[35]

How did Germany and the United States deal with conflicting objectives? In Ecuador, only the United States was confronted with *extrinsic conflicts* along the lines of democracy versus donor interests. Even in the case of the US government, however, the extent of conflicting objectives was clearly more limited than in US–Bolivia relations. The decisions of the Correa government that concerned US (oil) companies and the closure of the US military base in Manta provided clear grounds for the United States to openly oppose this democratically elected government. Yet, the US government considered Correa to be relatively credible and effective in the most important area for US security policy: the 'war on drugs', including securing the northern border with Colombia. Correspondingly, the United States made diplomatic efforts both to defend 'its' companies as well as on behalf of the air base in Manta. In the final analysis, however, the clear impairment of 'national interests' did not result in any perceptible consequences. This can at best be attributed in part to respect for Ecuador's right to self-determination; in addition, it obviously followed the strategic consideration that an openly confrontational stance would scarcely benefit US economic interests, but instead would contribute to further radicalizing the Correa government and endangering the still functioning cooperation (in counternarcotics in particular).[36]

Conversely, the strategic interest of the United States in cooperating with and engaging Correa stood in contrast to democracy-related appeals and measures in response to decisions perceived as undermining democracy. In this sense, the relatively reserved demeanour of the United States with regard to political change in Ecuador – and the largely cooperative adaptations in democracy assistance – can be traced back to such strategic reasoning. This is also the case for Germany. Here, the clear emphasis on cooperation and adaptation was reinforced both by the fact that no German security and/or economic interests were involved and by the strategic wish to avert a radicalization and distancing of Correa.

Intrinsic conflicts of objectives (democracy versus democracy) were clearly of a less fundamental nature and much more temporary than in the case of Bolivia. The extent to which Germany and the United States feared that Ecuador would fall away from liberal-democratic conceptions was significantly smaller. Correa's 'citizens' revolution' involved only limited changes in regard to indigenous self-government and indigenous customary law; mechanisms of direct democracy were expanded but did not – as in Bolivia – encompass popular election of the judiciary; and the introduction of new participatory rights, by focusing on the individual citizen, ultimately followed liberal ideas rather than collectivist notions related to the participation of social movements and organizations, as in Bolivia (see Wolff 2012).

An exception was the threat of an executive reinforced by plebiscites gaining dominance. Here, concern was stronger in connection with Ecuador and Correa than with Bolivia. However, the feared excessive power of the president was juxtaposed against the perception of developments that encouraged democracy. This most notably entailed relative political stability (after the series of overthrows of presidents between 1997 and 2005) as well as improved governability in terms of state capacity and political will. Since Correa and his government could simultaneously count on clear democratic legitimation and broad social support, a strategy of democracy promotion *against* Correa but *for* democracy was scarcely plausible.

In specific instances, temporary *intrinsic conflicts of objectives* emerged, for instance when the democratically legitimized process of constitutional reform (including the Constituent Assembly itself) clashed with the rights of the elected parliament. In this context, Germany and the United States eventually accepted the massive support of the population expressed in elections and referendums as decisive. They refrained from insisting on democratic and constitutional rules, which in any case had no chance of succeeding. Thus, in a cautious and as politically neutral manner as possible, donors tried to strengthen pluralism and checks on the government (as in the case of US support for 'Participación Ciudadana' and a broad spectrum of political parties) as well as to support inclusive processes of dialogue (as within the framework of the German PROMODE programme). In the case of Germany, however, the dominant approach was active support of the process of political change pursued by Correa.

To what extent can these patterns of reaction be explained by the profiles – i.e. the respective configuration of determinants (see Chapters 2 and 3) – that characterize the bilateral relations between Ecuador and the two respective donors? In their basic characteristics, the reaction patterns of both Germany and the United States closely correspond with the analysis for Bolivia. Existing differences in the patterns observed in Chapter 4 correspond with theoretical expectations. In the case of Germany, the limited 'disruptive factor' of a German company directly affected by Bolivia changing course regarding its economic policy was absent in relations with Ecuador. Germany's behaviour was thus even more characteristic of a Civilian Power.

On the part of the United States, the competition between interests and norms in Ecuador was significantly weaker than in Bolivia. A strong 'national interest' (in counternarcotics) and strategic considerations (engagement to prevent radicalization) as well as normative respect for democratic self-determination pointed in the same direction: cooperation. The fact that, unlike Germany, the US government did not adopt a clear stance in support of the political transformation initiated by Correa may be attributable in part to democracy-related concerns. Still, what was decisive here was probably the 'violations' of US economic and security interests (Oxy, Manta). The latter were reinforced by Correa's critical statements on the United States as well as, in general, by the ambivalent attitude of the Ecuadorean government to US cooperation in more 'political' matters. In this context, there were only extremely limited activities that could be viewed as attempts to actively shape the transformation of democracy under Correa in line with the Freedom Fighter conception of democracy promotion. In general, a US attitude towards Ecuador prevailed that corresponded both to central security and strategic interests as well as to international democracy norms established in the OAS. Insistence on specific, universally conceived standards of liberal democracy, rule of law and the free market economy were of lesser importance.

The contextual conditions of democracy promotion outlined in the introductory chapter are basically similar in Bolivia and Ecuador. Given the time lag between the election of Morales and Correa, the regional context in the case of Ecuador even more clearly induced Germany and the United States to choose a strategy of engaging Correa – in order to not drive him into the 'camp' of Chávez and Morales. Generally, the US-trained economist Correa seemed to be less 'foreign', and his relative distance from the Venezuela-led 'Alianza Bolivariana para los Pueblos de Nuestra América' (ALBA) reinforced this impression. Ecuador did not join this alliance until after Correa's re-election. The situation in Ecuador (recipient context) had a similar effect, with certain hopes of political stabilization and improved governability placed in the Correa Administration.

Considering the specific features of German policy towards Ecuador (donor context), the role of the BMZ was relatively strong, given the marginal foreign policy interests – although with a significantly lower level of German development cooperation in Ecuador (compared with Bolivia). However, the spectrum of German sub-actors was similarly broad and a certain division of labour was evident here too. Germany could thus cooperate with the government without too obviously choosing sides and support opposition forces without causing political confrontation. This is also true for the United States, though with significantly less support for the 'citizens' revolution'. In contrast to the German division of labour, US efforts to strike a balance manifested themselves more in various sub-actors, each pursuing non-partisan or multiparty activities.

Notes

1 Around 30 per cent of Ecuador's population is considered of indigenous heritage. The most important organization of the country's indigenous movement is the 'Confederación de Nacionalidades Indígenas del Ecuador' (CONAIE) founded in 1986.
2 Following the overthrow of Bucaram, a directly elected constituent assembly had already worked out a new constitution, which was adopted through a referendum in 1998. In the assembly at that time, however, representatives of the 'traditional' parties – in particular those from the centre-right spectrum – still had a dominant position.
3 Correa's PAIS movement had not taken part in the congressional elections in 2006 at all.
4 Directly after taking office. Correa doubled a conditional cash transfer to poor households (*Bono de Desarrollo Humano*), increased education and health expenditures, and expanded subventions for housing construction, nutrition and microcredit programmes.
5 Since 2008, however, conflicts between the Correa government and its former allies among the social (indigenous) movements, the unions and the centre-left have increased. At the beginning of 2009 a first massive protest of the indigenous movement against the government took place (directed against a new mining law). In September 2010 police protests against government austerity measures escalated to the point that President Correa was physically assaulted and held captive in a police hospital for several hours and had to be rescued by soldiers and a police special forces unit. The government assessed these events as an attempt at a *coup d'état* in which the most important opposition party *Sociedad Patriótica* of ex-president Lucio Gutiérrez was allegedly involved (see Ospina 2010).
6 In 2010, the RLS opened an office in Ecuador that is responsible for the Andean region. The work of this office lies outside the time period of the investigation, but its establishment shows clearly that the political changes initiated by Correa (as well as those promoted by Morales in Bolivia and Chávez in Venezuela) have prompted greater political interest in the region on the part of the RLS and the party DIE LINKE, with which the foundation is linked. This interest is closely related to the ruling governments even though key areas of work by the RLS on the ground focus on grass-roots social groups.
7 'To enable active participation by civil society and the private sector in the development process, German development cooperation also supports sub-national administration in working out development strategies that are participatory and focused on specific territories' (BMZ 2007: 8).
8 By contrast, the Seidel Foundation concluded that Correa was 'revealing himself more and more to be a clone of Hugo Chavez' (Senger 2009: 5). The FSS reports from Quito are generally concerned with providing information and rarely involve comment.
9 The extent to which this was discussed in the intergovernmental dialogue is not known. From the perspective of the BMZ (2007: 9), this political dialogue was to include, among other issues, the topic of 'Preservation or consolidation of democracy and the rule of law in the course of planned reforms of the state (including human rights and freedom of the press)'.
10 In a joint communiqué initiated and presented by the German ambassador, the EU ambassadors expressed their 'concern [...] about the complex political circumstances' and called upon government and opposition to commit themselves 'to the rule of law, separation of powers, independence of the judiciary and pluralism' (*Diario Hoy*

2007). The report of the German government already cited above contains no comment on these matters (Bundesregierung 2008: 7–14).
11 At the same time, PROMODE funds left over from the first phase of the programme were released, which significantly softened the effects of the reduced budget.
12 As a result, the 'government administration' subsector was continuously – and most recently again to an increasing degree – the dominant objective of German democracy assistance, significantly ahead of 'civil society' (OECD 2010).
13 The partner of GTZ was the assembly's coordination unit responsible for international relations, through which GTZ supported visits from international experts, advisory services for the commissions, workshops and discussion forums. In addition, the GTZ participated in coordinating the donors that supported the constitutional process.
14 These included, among others, the Planning and Development Secretariat SENPLADES and the Ministry of Finance at the central state level as well as organizations at the provincial, municipality and parish level. The DED also in part orientated its cooperation with civil society organizations – for instance with the indigenous umbrella organization CONFENIAE (Frank and Cisneros 2009) – towards influencing the constitutional process.
15 FES, on the one hand, supported cross-party efforts among the centre-left spectrum to prepare input for the process; on the other, it established a group of experts which de facto acted as a direct service provider to the presidency of the assembly.
16 Through the HSS partner organization 'Corporación Autogobierno y Democracia', 'groups from Ecuadorean civil society [...] as well as domestic and foreign experts on constitutional issues were given the opportunity of communicating their views and experiences to selected members of the Constituent Assembly' (HSS 2008).
17 Three local experts from the political spectrum of the KAS were sent to the site of the assembly and commented on events in weekly newspaper articles.
18 As in the case of Bolivia, GTZ also shifted towards support for political dialogue processes – in addition to 'conventional' technical support. In this case, however, German development cooperation reacted less to Correa than to the general experience of political instability since 1997. Even before Correa came to power, PROMODE had supported draft laws through the promotion of broader conciliation processes. Under Correa, related activities concerned the constitutional reform and the ensuing process of implementing the new constitution.
19 Since completion of the constitutional reform, FES, on the one hand, shifted towards general support to democratic institutions (such as the electoral court) and to the implementation of the constitution. On the other, it showed renewed vigour in promoting an interparty dialogue running across political camps within the centre-left. The latter also included the support of openly opposition-based processes of union reorganization.
20 In this way, KAS aligned itself with a political party whose time in government (2003–5) the local KAS representative himself had characterized as 'egomaniac' (*selbstherrlich*) and 'with strongly autocratic traits' (Weig 2009: 42). At the same time, in 2009 the KAS terminated the longstanding support of an NGO that is not located in the Christian-Democrat camp, but rather has a left wing profile: from 1997 CEDIME had carried out a KAS-funded, multi-party programme to promote the political participation of women.
21 In this way, HSS sought to again significantly strengthen the (party-)political profile of its work – following many years in which it had almost exclusively worked in the area of indigenous education (see above).
22 In 2010, however, the new minister for development, Dirk Niebel (FDP), announced that – contrary to earlier statements – the German government would not be contributing to the UNDP (United Nations Development Programme) Trust Fund, which had been set up in the meantime. In 2012, the two governments agreed a face-saving compromise: Germany promised additional funds to support the Yasuní national park –

but these funds would be administered in the framework of German bilateral development cooperation, without any relation to the UNDP fund and the ITT initiative (*El Comercio* 2012).
23 See the various cables from the US embassy in Quito published through WikiLeaks (no date).
24 The US embassy observed Correa's foreign policy in a similarly ambivalent way. Political rapprochement with countries like Venezuela and Cuba was regarded with concern. But at the same time the United States greeted cooperative signals in the relationship with the United States as well as the decision during Correa's first term of office not to become a member of the Venezuela-led ALBA – Ecuador, however, joined ALBA after Correa's re-election. In the area of economic policy, US criticism was levelled at infringements of private property rights – particularly of foreign investors – and also at the general focus on an economically strong and active state.
25 This was an explicit strategy:

> we recommend the Department issue or make a statement on November 27 congratulating Correa as the apparent victor, along the lines of what was issued after the Morales victory in Bolivia. We would gain points from many observers here for graciousness in the face of what is widely assumed to be an undesired result. Delaying such a statement would make us appear grudging, and risks starting us off badly with the incoming government to no benefit.
> (US Embassy Quito 2006b)

26 In April 2011, the US embassy cables published by WikiLeaks provoked a brief crisis in diplomatic relations. Responding to statements in these cables, the Correa government declared ambassador Heather Hodges to be *persona non grata*, and the US government retaliated by expelling the Ecuadorian ambassador. In September 2011, however, both governments nominated new ambassadors.
27 However, the US embassy requested additional funds from the State Department and the Department of Defense in order to conduct projects for the local population in Manta as well as a national media campaign. The aim was to rally support for the US air base and thereby prevent the closure of Manta (US Embassy Quito 2007c).
28 In February 2011 an impasse between Republicans and Democrats in Congress prevented the renewal of ATPDEA for some time. This inaction had nothing to do with Ecuador and also affected the close US ally, Colombia. It did, however, mean that trade preferences were not in force for a few months.
29 The two officials had been responsible for US cooperation with an Ecuadorean police special forces unit. The Correa Administration accused the two of interfering in internal security matters, and discontinued US cooperation with the unit. The State Department did nothing more than deny the accusations (cf. *Ecuador Inmediato* 2009).
30 After the Colombian military attacked a secret camp of Colombian FARC guerrillas on Ecuadorean territory in March 2008, an open diplomatic crisis broke out between Ecuador and the most important US ally in the region. The events led to diplomatic irritations between the United States and Ecuador and aroused US concerns over potential cooperation between parts of the Ecuadorean government and FARC (see US Congress 2008). Ultimately, however, the US government evaluated Correa's position vis-à-vis FARC as credible and his administration's policy on securing the northern border to Colombia as relatively successful (see US Embassy Quito 2008a).
31 According to the USAID website (no date) between 2007 and 2009 the democracy programme supported 'civil society oversight capacity through expanded and enhanced participation of citizens in political processes and effectively functioning institutions', promoted 'transparent and more inclusive elections' through election observation by civil society and worked to consolidate 'alliances among civil society groups to effectively promote democratic practices and principles'.

32 Only in 2007, grants temporarily shrank to $330,000 (NED various years).
33 In Ecuador, EU election observation missions monitored electoral processes in 2007, 2008 and 2009.
34 In addition, independent monitoring activities were carried out by the Carter Center. These involved the elections and referendums in 2007 and 2008 as well as the process of transition from the old to the new constitution.
35 Most important in this sense was the suspension of the opposition majority in Congress and the subsequent dissolution of the entire parliament in the course of the constitutional reforms.
36 That the US government broke off negotiations on a free trade agreement with Ecuador after the 'expropriation' of the US company Oxy was clearly due to economic interests – but had occurred under Correa's predecessor. In the case of the interim president, Palacio, who was domestically weak and made clear calls for US support, the US government obviously did not fear that sanctions of such a kind could result in Ecuador distancing itself from the United States and becoming more radical.

References

AGECI (Agencia Ecuatoriana de Cooperación Internacional) (2008) *Informe de las negociaciones intergubernamentales entre la República del Ecuador y la República Federal de Alemania desarrolladas del 9 al 12 de junio de 2008*. Online, available at: www.ageci.gov.ec (accessed 24 March 2010).

BFAI (Bundesagentur für Außenwirtschaft) (2007) *Wirtschaftsentwicklung Ecuador 2006*. Online, available at: www.bfai.de (accessed 24 April 2008).

BMZ (2007) *Länderkonzept Ecuador*, Bonn: BMZ.

BMZ (2008) 'Naturschutz und Staatsmodernisierung im Zentrum. Regierungsverhandlungen mit Ecuador abgeschlossen', *Press Release*, 11 June. Online, available at: www.bmz.de (accessed 15 January 2009).

Bundesregierung (2008) *Zur Menschenrechtssituation in den Ländern der Andengemeinschaft und Venezuela* (BT-Drs. 16/11297), Berlin: Deutscher Bundestag.

Bundestag (2008) *Plenarprotokoll 16/172*, Berlin: Deutscher Bundestag.

CBJ (various years) *Congressional Budget Justification: Foreign Operations, US Department of State*, several editions (CBJ 2009: Fiscal Year 2009, etc.), Washington, DC: US Department of State.

Conaghan, C.M. (1995) 'Politicians against Parties: Discord and Disconnection in Ecuador's Party System', S. Mainwaring and T.R. Scully (eds) *Building Democratic Institutions: Party Systems in Latin America*, Stanford, CA: Stanford University Press.

Conaghan, C.M. (2008) 'Ecuador: Correa's Plebiscitary Presidency', *Journal of Democracy*, 19 (2): 46–60.

Detsch, C. (2009) 'Was will Correa?', *Kurzbericht der Friedrich-Ebert-Stiftung*, Berlin: FES.

Diario Hoy (2007) 'Unión Europea Llama a Sostener Estado de Derecho', *Diario Hoy*, 11 May. Online, available at: www.hoy.com.ec (accessed 11 July 2011).

Ecuador Inmediato (2009) 'EE.UU. Evalúa su Respuesta a Ecuador', *Ecuador Inmediato*, 20 February 2009. Online, available at: www.ecuadorinmediato.com (accessed 20 February 2009).

Ecuador Inmediato (2010) 'Embajadora de Estados Unidos en Ecuador Reitera Apoyo a Presidente Correa', *Ecuador Inmediato*, 30 September. Online, available at: www.ecuadorinmediato.com (accessed 15 May 2013).

El Comercio (2006) 'Estados Unidos le Tiende Puentes a Rafael Correa', *El Comercio*, 28 November. Online, available at: www.elcomercio.com (accessed 5 February 2007).

El Comercio (2012) 'Alemania Dará a Ecuador 34,5 Millones de Euros Para Parque Amazónico', *El Comercio*, 3 May. Online, available at: www.elcomercio.com (accessed 12 November 2012).

Edwards, S.G. (2005) 'Outside the Rule of Law: Ecuador's Courts in Crisis', *WOLA (Washington Office on Latin America) Special Update*. Online, available at: www.wola.org (accessed 6 August 2005).

Frank, V. and Cisneros, P. (2009) *Buenas Prácticas. La CONFENIAE – Un actor indígena en procesos de concertación nacional – Experiencias de la cooperación con la Confederación de las Nacionalidades Indígenas de la Amazonía Ecuatoriana*, Eschborn: GTZ.

Freedom House (2010) *Investing in Freedom: An Analysis of the Obama Administration FY 2011 Budget Request for Democracy and Human Rights*, Washington, DC: Freedom House.

GTZ (2005) *Zusammenarbeit mit indigenen Völkern in Lateinamerika und der Karibik*, Eschborn: GTZ.

GTZ (2006) *Modernisierung und Dezentralisierung (PROMODE), Ecuador, Evaluierung laufender Vorhaben 2006 (Kurzbericht)*, Eschborn: GTZ

HSS (2008) *Hanns-Seidel-Stiftung berät die Verfassungsgebende Versammlung in Ecuador*. Online, available at: www.hss.de (accessed 8 April 2010).

KAS (2008) *Parteien und Parteien-Kooperationen der KAS in Lateinamerika*, Berlin: KAS.

Langer, M. (2008) 'Eine neue Verfassung für Ecuador? Eine Analyse des Verfassungsentwurfs', *Kurzbericht der Friedrich-Ebert-Stiftung*, Bonn: FES.

Lettieri, M. (2006) 'Ecuador Breaks with Washington over Occidental Petroleum', *Council On Hemispheric Affairs Memorandum to the Press 06.30*. Online, available at: www.coha.org (accessed 23 May 2006).

Miami Herald (2007) 'Shannon: Ecuador Puede Hacer lo que Quiera con su Deuda', *Miami Herald*, 23 January. Online, available at: www.miamiherald.com (accessed 24 January 2007).

McConnell, J.M. (2008) *Annual Threat Assessment of the Intelligence Community for the House Permanent Select Committee on Intelligence*, Washington, DC, 7 February. Online, available at: www.dni.gov (accessed 16 November 2009).

NED (various years) *Annual Report*, several editions. Online, available at: www.ned.org (accessed 22 July 2010).

La Tendencia, (2009) 'Programa anticrisis: legitimidad y eficacia' March/April. Online, available at: http://library.fes.de/pdf-files/bueros/quito/05108/tendencia2009,9.pdf (accessed 25 February 2013).

OECD (2010) 'Development Database on Aid Activities', *CRS online*. Online, available at: www.oecd.org (accessed 13 January 2010).

Ospina Peralta, P. (2009) 'El proyecto político de la revolución ciudadana: líneas maestras', *CEP (Comité Ecuménico de Proyectos Análisis de Coyuntura)*. Online, available at: www.cepecuador.org (accessed 4 June 2010).

Ospina Peralta, P. (2010) '¿Intento de golpe o motín policial?', *CEP (Comité Ecuménico de Proyectos) Análisis de Coyuntura*. Online, available at: www.cepecuador.org (accessed 24 November 2010).

Pineo, R. (2007) *Ecuador and the United States: Useful Strangers*, Athens, GA: University of Georgia Press.

Ribando Seelke, C. (2008) 'Ecuador: Political and Economic Situation and US Relations', *CRS Report for Congress*, no. RS21687, updated 21 November.

Rivera Vélez, F. (2005) 'Ecuador: Untangling the Drug War', in C.A. Youngers and E. Rosin (eds) *Drugs and Democracy in Latin America*, Boulder, CO: Lynne Rienner.

Rothfritz, H. (2006) 'Ein weiterer Sieg des Linkspopulismus in Lateinamerika: Rafael Correa ist neuer Präsident Ecuadors', *Länderbericht der Konrad-Adenauer-Stiftung*, Sankt Augustin: KAS.

Senger, H. (2009) 'Viele Baustellen und wachsender Widerstand', *Quartalsbericht III/2009 der Hanns-Seidel-Stiftung*, München: HSS.

Shannon, T.A. (2006) *Remarks at the Council of Americas*, 12 December. Online, available at: http://2001-2009.state.gov (accessed 19 November 2009).

USAID (no date) *Country Page Ecuador*. Online, available at: http://ecuador.usaid.gov (accessed 7 January 2009).

USAID (1997) *USAID/Ecuador Strategic Plan FY 1998–FY 2002*. Online, available at: http://pdf.dec.org (accessed 9 February 2006).

USAID (2006) *USAID/Ecuador Operational Plan FY 2006*. Online, available at: http://pdf.usaid.gov (accessed 20 November 2009).

US Congress (2008) *Crisis in the Andes: The Border Dispute Between Colombia and Ecuador, and Implications for the Region*, Briefing and Hearing before the Subcommittee on the Western Hemisphere of the Committee on Foreign Affairs, House of Representatives, 10 April. Online, available at: http://foreignaffairs.house.gov (accessed 24 November 2009).

US Department of State (2007) *Press Availability with Ecuadorian Media Outlets. John D. Negroponte, Deputy Secretary of State; Thomas A. Shannon, Assistant Secretary for Western Hemisphere Affairs*. Online, available at: www.state.gov (accessed 16 October 2007).

US Department of State (2009a) *2009 Investment Climate Statement – Ecuador*, February, Washington, DC. Online, available at: www.state.gov/e/eeb/rls/othr/ics/2009/117668.htm (accessed 18 November 2009).

US Department of State (2009b) 'Ecuador', in US Department of State (ed.) *Advancing Freedom and Democracy Report*. Online, available at: www.state.gov (accessed 18 November 2009).

US Embassy Quito (2006a) *Subject: Ecuador Election Update – Six Months Out*, Cable to Secretary of State, 10 May. Online, available at: http://centrodealerta.org (accessed 13 October 2010).

US Embassy Quito (2006b) *Election: Correa Wins Big, Noboa Fizzles*, Cable 06QUITO2898, 27 November. Online, available at: http://wikileaks.org (accessed 19 July 2011).

US Embassy Quito (2007a) *Referendum Wins Big, Boosting Correa*, Cable 07QUITO850, 16 April. Online, available at: http://wikileaks.org (accessed 19 July 2011).

US Embassy Quito (2007b) *Correa Escalates War Against the Press*, Cable 07QUITO1124, 16 May. Online, available at: http://wikileaks.org (19 July 2011).

US Embassy Quito (2007c) *Manta FOL – Request for DOS and DOD Financial Support*, Cable 07QUITO642, 29 March. Online, available at: http://wikileaks.org (accessed 19 July 2011).

US Embassy Quito (2008a) *Scenesetter for Codel McGovern*, Cable 08QUITO1043, 7 November. Online, available at: http://wikileaks.org (accessed 19 July 2011).

US Embassy Quito (2008b) *Launch of US–Ecuador Bilateral Dialogue*, Cable 08QUITO1128, 8 December. Online, available at: http://wikileaks.org (accessed 19 July 2011).

US Embassy Quito (2009a) *Whither Correa: A Shift Further Left*, Cable 09QUITO15, 14 January. Online, available at: http://wikileaks.org (accessed 19 July 2011).

US Embassy Quito (2009b) *President Obama's Call to President Correa Adds to Press*, Cable 09QUITO449, 15 June. Online, available at: http://wikileaks.org/cable/2009/06/09QUITO449.html (accessed 19 July 2011).
Van Cott, D.L. (2005) *From Movements to Parties in Latin America. The Evolution of Ethnic Politics*, Cambridge: Cambridge University Press
Vega, L.M. and Zimmermann, A. (2006) *Ecuador. Machtumverteilung und Inklusivität über kulturelle Grenzen hinweg*, Eschborn: GTZ.
Weig, B. (2009) 'Ekuadors „Bürgerrevolution" vor dem Stresstest. Das politische Projekt Rafael Correas zwischen Anspruch und Wirklichkeit', *KAS Auslandsinformationen*, 5: 33–51.
WikiLeaks (no date) Secret US Embassy Cables: Embassy Quito. Online, available at: http://wikileaks.org/origin/65_0.html (accessed 10 February 2012).
Wolff, J. (2003) *Bestimmungsfaktoren und Konsequenzen der offiziellen Dollarisierung in Lateinamerika. Eine politökonomische Analyse unter besonderer Berücksichtigung Ecuadors*, Hamburg: Institut für Iberoamerika-Kunde.
Wolff, J. (2008) *Turbulente Stabilität. Die Demokratie in Südamerika diesseits ferner Ideale*, Baden-Baden: Nomos.
Wolff, J. (2010) 'Demokratieförderung als Suchprozess. Die Bolivien- und Ecuadorpolitik Deutschlands in Zeiten demokratischer Revolutionen', *HSFK-Report*, no. 6, Frankfurt a.M.: Peace Research Institute Frankfurt.
Wolff, J. (2011) 'Re-engaging Latin America's Left? US Relations with Bolivia and Ecuador from Bush to Obama', *PRIF Report*, no. 103, Frankfurt a.M.: Peace Research Institute Frankfurt.
Wolff, J. (2012) 'New Constitutions and the Transformation of Democracy in Ecuador and Bolivia', in D. Nolte and A. Schilling-Vacaflor (eds) *New Constitutionalism in Latin America: Promises and Practices*, Farnham: Ashgate.
Yashar, D.J. (2005) *Contesting Citizenship in Latin America: The Rise of Indigenous Movements and the Postliberal Challenge*, Cambridge: Cambridge University Press.

6 Democracy promotion in Turkey
The rise of political Islam

Cemal Karakaş

Turkey is the only country in the Muslim community of states (*a*) in which Islam is not the official state religion while secularism/laicism is established in the constitution, (*b*) that is a member of NATO, and (*c*) that is a candidate for accession to the European Union (EU).

Among the Western community of states, the United States and Germany have the closest relations with Turkey in terms of foreign, security and development policy. The great interest taken by these two donor countries is reflected, among other things, in the extensive level of foreign aid and development cooperation – both countries are Turkey's most important donors in absolute terms (OECD 2012). Ever since 9/11, many politicians in Berlin and Washington, DC, have also regarded Turkey as a 'model' for other Muslim countries. At the same time, however, two political parties rose to power that were part of a political movement whose scope ranged from pro-Islamic to Islamist: the Welfare Party ('Refah Partisi', RP) in 1996–7 and the Justice and Development Party ('Adalet ve Kalkınma Partisi', AKP) in 2002. Basically, the two donors were faced with choosing one of two stances: either tolerate the omnipotent role of the Kemalist state elite in the interest of preserving both the secular nature of the state and Turkey's pro-Western stance; or remain true to their own democratic principles and respect the vote of the Turkish electorate and the takeover of governmental responsibilities by the Islamic parties as well as Turkey's right to self-determination – even at the risk that these governments were advancing a secret agenda of the Islamization of state and society and turning away from the West, if the Kemalists' predictions were to be believed.

This chapter examines the time period from 1995 to 2010[1] in terms of the RP's and AKP's policies and impact, as well as of how the United States and Germany dealt with the conflicting goals that emerged from the rise of political Islam[2] and the countermeasures by the Kemalist state elite.[3]

Rise to power and politics by the RP and AKP as a conflict situation

The RP was founded in 1983 and came to be seen as the political arm of the 'Milli Görüş' movement (National Outlook) initiated by Necmettin Erbakan in the early 1970s. This movement pursued the introduction of a 'just', i.e. Islamic, order in state, society and the economy (Yürüsen and Yala 1997). The RP won the municipal elections in March 1994, followed by the parliamentary elections in December 1995 with 21 per cent of the vote. It was able to benefit in particular from protest votes cast in the midst of a serious economic crisis (1994), from its support of charitable causes, its successful municipal politics as well as a greater-than-average share of votes from the underdeveloped and predominantly Kurdish southeast (Akıncı 1999).

After the fragile Kemalist conservative minority government under Prime Minister Mesut Yilmaz of the Motherland Party ('Anavatan Partisi', ANAP) and the True Path Party ('Doğru Yol Partisi', DYP) of Tansu Çiller stepped down in June 1996, RP leader Erbakan was elected the first Islamist prime minister of Turkey in a coalition with the DYP. During the electoral campaign, Erbakan had praised the advantages of the Sharia, had flaunted his anti-Americanism, anti-Zionism, and anti-Europeanism, and had spoken in favour of Turkey's withdrawal from NATO. In his inaugural speech, however, he pledged that he would respect Turkey's secular order and pro-Western stance. Nevertheless Prime Minister Erbakan did not make inaugural visits to the United States or Germany. Instead, he visited 'rogue states' such as Iran and Libya in order to deepen bilateral economic relations and to establish a Muslim economic community.

When Erbakan's Kurdish and financial policies failed, however, criticism within his own party grew, leading to a populist politicization of religion. For example, the RP restricted the sale of alcoholic beverages in the cafeterias of state agencies and asked for the repeal of the headscarf ban at universities that had been introduced after the *coup d'état* in 1980 – for the Kemalist state elite, the Muslim headscarf 'türban' was not a piece of clothing but a political, anti-secular symbol. Moreover, some RP mayors had 'indecent' sculptures removed from public squares while others demanded the introduction of the Sharia (Karakaş 2007).

Such actions heightened public disputes between Islamists and Kemalists. The Turkish military reacted in late February 1997 by having the National Security Council draw up a catalogue of political and legal measures to combat Islamism that Prime Minister Erbakan had to implement if he wanted to avoid a forced resignation (*FAZ* 1997a). The military's course of action entered the annals of history as a 'soft coup'. Paired with ever-growing pro-Kemalist mass demonstrations, the RP–DYP lost its majority in parliament. After just one year in office, Erbakan resigned in June 1997. The RP was banned in 1998, and Erbakan was banned from politics for five years (Akıncı 1999).

Following the ban of the RP and its short-lived successor, the opposition Virtue Party ('Fazilet Partisi', FP), the AKP was founded in the summer of 2001, emerging as a result of a rift in Erbakan's 'Milli Görüş' movement. The movement's reform-minded wing assembled under the leadership of Abdullah Gül (currently Turkey's president) and Recep Tayyip Erdoğan (the current prime minister) in the AKP. Both politicians had been critical of Erbakan's authoritarian leadership style, the RP's failures during its time in government as well as the Islamist rhetoric that had prompted the party ban (Dağı 2008; Yavuz 2003). This reversal was evidenced by the new party manifesto, in which the AKP officially pledged to promote democracy and human rights and asserted its respect for the fundamental principles of Kemalism. The most important issue in the party platform – and, at the same time, the most striking difference compared to the RP – was its clear endorsement of the Western community. Turkey's accession to the EU became a priority, and NATO and the United States were described as important partners.

Just one year after its creation, the AKP won the parliamentary elections of November 2002 with 34 per cent of the vote. The AKP was able to benefit from votes cast by the Islamic (Sunni) portion of the electorate, a dearth of political alternatives, protest votes resulting from a serious financial crisis (spring 2001), and also benefitted to a disproportionate degree from the 10 per cent electoral threshold, Europe's highest – with just one-third of the votes, it received almost two-thirds of the seats in parliament. The AKP was also able to win over voters who advocated EU membership, liberals, the business world as well as those with an Alevi or Kurdish background (Dağı 2008; Özel 2003). In the early parliamentary elections of July 2007, the AKP was able to increase its share of the vote to 46 per cent and again in June 2011 to 49 per cent.

Among the AKP's successes are: its policy of democratization, which included the abolition of the death penalty, greater legal equality for men and women, a liberalization of criminal law, and the reform of the National Security Council, all pursued in order to fulfil the 'Copenhagen Criteria', which allowed Turkey to begin accession negotiations with the EU; and its economic policies: privatizing state-owned enterprises and opening the domestic market to international investors led to the longest economic boom in Turkish history, from 2002 to the beginning of the international financial crisis in 2008. In addition, the Erdoğan government carried out a reform of the state-run retirement fund and put in place both state-run unemployment insurance and state-mandated health insurance – the latter of which found a positive reception especially among the poorer sections of the population.

Despite (or because of) the successes of the AKP's new Islamic elites, a cultural power struggle over the 'true' republic has broken out with the old secular Kemalist state elite over the last several years – on an even larger scale than was the case for the RP in the mid-1990s. According to the Kemalists, the AKP had been working towards Islamizing state and society. This claim arises out of both the AKP's one-party dominance beginning in 2002 and its appointment of party loyalists to key positions of the state apparatus (ministries, courts of law, police, etc.). Measures such as the bill to criminalize adultery (which has since been withdrawn), the expansion of state-run Koran schools and restrictions on the sale of alcoholic beverages in AKP-run municipalities (officially, for public health reasons) have given rise to fears of Islamization. These fears led to the threat of a *coup d'état* by the military against Abdullah Gül's candidacy for the office of president in April 2007, and also led to early parliamentary elections in July 2007. The AKP's attempt in spring 2008 to rescind the headscarf ban through a constitutional amendment resulted in proceedings before the Constitutional Court to ban the party that were later abandoned (Karakaş 2008). As part of the constitutional reforms of September 2010, the AKP government was able to have the headscarf ban for students largely revoked; civil servants continue to be banned from wearing headscarves.

With regard to minority rights, which had repeatedly been criticized by the EU as too feeble, Prime Minister Erdoğan was able to gradually strengthen the cultural rights of Kurds. Plans for further liberalization in this area have been thwarted since 2009 by sizeable public resistance by nationalist groups and by fears that were stoked regarding a threat to Turkey's territorial integrity. Moreover, the European Commission criticized the continued existence of limits imposed on the religious freedoms of the Christian and Alevi minorities and the violations of free speech and freedom of the press (EU Commission 2010).

The AKP government was also chastised for the 'Ergenekon' investigations, which have been under way since 2008 and in the course of which several hundred persons, including retired generals and journalists, have been arrested on suspicion of intent to overthrow the government. The government is said to have used the arrests to discredit critics and to weaken the military (Jenkins 2009; Müftüler-Baç and Keyman 2012). A further problem is the decision by the Erdoğan government not to lower the 10 per cent electoral threshold in the course of the constitutional reforms of September 2010, despite promises it had made to the contrary – ostensibly to safeguard political stability and prevent a fragmentation of the party system. In reality, the decision was made out of political calculation: the AKP wanted to continue to benefit from the 10 per cent threshold.

Not only domestic policy has undergone changes, however, but also foreign policy. The foreign policy doctrine of the AKP government ('strategic depth') postulates an active policy with the goal of 'zero problems' with Turkey's neighbours. In the process, Turkey is supposed to grow into the roles of being a stabilizing regional power and 'honest broker' (Davutoğlu 2005). This policy led, among other things, to an expansion of Turkey's relationship with Greece, Armenia and Iraq, and Ankara has mediated in Bosnia as well as in the conflicts between Israel and Palestine, and Israel and Syria. This new foreign policy, however, has also resulted in Turkish economic and security interests taking precedence over those of its NATO allies. For example, the AKP's members of parliament, together with MPs from the opposition Kemalist Republican People's Party ('Cumhuriyet Halk Partisi', CHP), refused in spring 2003 to allow US troops to invade Iraq from Turkish soil. At the same time, relations with the anti-Western regimes in Russia, Iran, and Syria were expanded under Erdoğan. Turkish resistance to the recognition of Cyprus, Turkey's sometimes harsh criticism of Israel and its Middle East policy, and the joint opposition by Brazil and Turkey in the summer of 2010 to UN sanctions against Iran's nuclear programme have enjoyed the support of a majority of the public as well as approval by the rapidly growing business sector. Taking such stances is designed to underscore Turkey's self-confidence and position it as a leading nation in the Islamic world (*The Economist* 2010).

The policies and achievements of both the RP and especially the AKP aptly reflect the three fundamental dilemmas of democratization, which are discussed in the introduction to this book: the Sunni majority of the population and its elites have developed a claim to shaping their own destiny, which they express self-confidently through their own government parties in the areas of domestic, economic and foreign policy; this has become a threat to political stability and domestic peace and resulted, among other things, in the government being nearly overthrown on two occasions, the banning of the RP, and attempts to ban the AKP (democracy versus stability).

Moreover, the Erdoğan government in particular has, under the pretence of wanting to ensure the country's governability, engaged in questionable political cronyism and been responsible for bringing the democratization process to a halt. Concretely, the 10 per cent electoral threshold remains in place, restrictions have been imposed on free speech and freedom of the press, and minorities have been denied further rights due to public pressure on the government (democracy versus governability).

When the RP and particularly the AKP, which won an absolute majority in three consecutive parliamentary elections, took control of government, they were able to rely on clear majorities that lent them democratic legitimacy. However, the Erdoğan government's earlier pursuit of a policy of democratization was later in part replaced by the adoption of a more authoritarian posture. By catering to the religious inclinations of its Sunni core constituency, the AKP stokes fears of an Islamization of both the public sphere and society as well as concerns about an erosion of the principle of secularism (democracy versus majority). This results in the following extrinsic and intrinsic conflicts of objectives challenging German and US democracy promotion in Turkey:

1   *Democracy versus donor interests (extrinsic).* If democracy promotion is understood as a value per se, then the changes in Turkish politics embarked upon by Erbakan in the mid-1990s and expanded by Prime Minister Erdoğan would have to be tolerated by the donor countries as expressions of democratic self-determination on the part of the recipient country, Turkey. However, both donors have vital interests at stake in their relations with Turkey. In the case of the United States the former consist primarily of geostrategic interests due to which the United States is confronted specifically with the conflicting goals of 'NATO member Turkey as pro-Western anchor of stability versus Turkey's leading nation ambitions' with regard to the Islamic world. In the case of Germany, which is home to the world's largest diaspora of Turkish origin, there is concern that an Islamization of Turkey could spill over to the diaspora in Germany, thereby (further) complicating its social integration and jeopardizing domestic peace *in* Germany. Berlin is interested in strengthening democracy and human rights and stabilizing the Turkish economy, which could both put an end to Turkish and Kurdish migration and temper Turkey's desire for EU membership. However, the latter is a contested issue among the political parties in Germany.

2 *Democracy versus democracy (intrinsic).* There is no question about the democratic legitimacy of both the RP and AKP governments. The takeover of governmental responsibility by these two parties has expanded the democratic legitimacy of the (Kemalist) state by giving political representation to large portions of the Sunni population and implementing many of their interests. However, the charge of Islamization, the partial halt to EU reform policies, more and more restrictions on free speech and freedom of the press as well as the continued presence of a few democratic deficiencies (especially the 10 per cent electoral threshold) run counter to the liberal democratic principles of both donors. In the case of Turkey, these conflicting goals are caused by tensions between democracy and secularism. The donors are confronted with the dilemma of advocating religious freedom *for* Muslims in Kemalist secular Turkey without wanting to see civil liberties restricted *by* religion (e.g. for non-Muslims) in a predominantly Muslim society. Another conflicting goal (one that could also be part of the extrinsic dimension) results from the two donors' amorphous idea of Turkey serving as a 'model' for other Muslim countries. Do the donors regard the idea of the Turkish model as an instrument for realizing their own material interests and/or normative values? Or do they see it as a political regime that integrates Islamic parties into the political system of a parliamentary democracy by means of free elections, moderating their stances and accepting their right to self-determination *grosso modo*?

Germany: inconsistent support

Profile of bilateral relations

Germany and Turkey maintain close relations, in which the 'traditional friendship' and the 'human factor' are officially regarded as playing a prominent role (German Embassy Ankara 2011). An important characteristic of German–Turkish relations is the interdependence of internal and external factors. It is a result of the fact that Germany is home to around three million people of Turkish origin, of whom 700,000 have German citizenship – making this the largest diaspora of Turkish origin in the world. These people do not, however, constitute a homogeneous group, but are divided along several sub-identities (Turks, Kurds, Alevis, Sunni, secularists, etc.), with each group's interests represented by its own related association. There are many examples for this interdependence, e.g. the xenophobic attacks on migrants of Turkish origin in the first half of the 1990s (e.g. in Solingen and Mölln); the use of German arms by the Turkish government in its fight against the Kurdish organization PKK; the more restrictive asylum law (1993); the spilling over of the Turkish–Kurdish conflict to the diaspora in Germany; the campaign against dual citizenship (1999); rising Islamophobia after the terror attacks of 9/11; and stricter rules for immigration and obtaining German citizenship (2007).[4]

These events not only caused turmoil in bilateral relations and led to calls for more democracy and human rights in Turkey, but also increased Turkey's relevance for domestic peace and security in Germany proper (Kramer 2004: 93; Steinbach 1994: 82). As a result, the Kurdish PKK was also outlawed in Germany (1993), a national 'Integration Summit' convened and the 'German Islam Conference' established. Germany's European policy is also characterized by strong domestic interests. Together with France and Austria, Germany is witnessing the most controversial debates about Turkish EU membership (Leggewie 2004).

Concerning the external dimension of German security interests, close German–Turkish cooperation within NATO is worth mentioning (German Embassy Ankara 2011). Apart from the United States, until the mid-1990s Germany was Turkey's most important NATO ally. Within the framework of NATO cooperation Ankara received German military aid in the amount of DM6.5 billion between 1964 and 1995 (Kramer 2004: 93).

Furthermore, security cooperation can also be observed at the EU level. Since the Western European Union (WEU) was integrated into the EU by the Nice Treaty, as a former WEU member, Turkey has participated in numerous EU peacekeeping operations in the Balkans (Hofmann and Reynolds 2007).

Economic relations have been without friction. Germany is Turkey's most important trading partner. In 2010 the combined number of German and Turkish companies operating in Turkey with a German equity stake was around 4,000. Foreign trade between the two countries was worth around €26.1 billion in 2010, with Germany generating a trade surplus of €6.3 billion. Another important area within bilateral foreign trade relations is tourism. Of the 27 million tourists in 2009 who spent their holidays in Turkey, more than 4.4 million came from Germany (DTR-IHK 2011; GTAI 2011).

Profile of German democracy promotion in Turkey

The good bilateral relations between Germany and Turkey are reflected in their development cooperation; Germany is Turkey's largest donor. Development cooperation between Germany and Turkey began in 1958, and between 1990 and 2010 approximately $3.6 billion in ODA were disbursed (OECD 2012). However, due to Turkey's positive socio-economic development and the beginning of EU accession negotiations (2005) no new commitments have been made (German Embassy Ankara 2011).

Development cooperation is led by the Federal Ministry for Economic Cooperation and Development (BMZ) and implemented mainly by the GTZ (now GIZ), and the KfW Development Bank. Their main goal in the 1990s was the reduction of socio-economic inequalities, among other objectives in order to curb the appeal of Islamist and Kurdish extremist organizations among poverty-stricken sections of the population, as well as to reduce migration flows within Turkey and to Germany (cf. BMZ 1995). Since 2000, the GTZ and KfW have been supporting municipal infrastructure and environmental projects in particular, but also providing assistance to medium-sized businesses and more effective administrative capacity. The main goals were environmentally compatible municipal development, business development, decentralization, and the reduction of regional disparities between Turkey's industrialized west and the underdeveloped Kurdish southeast (BMZ 2009).

While the BMZ is primarily committed to Turkey's socio-economic development, the Foreign Office (AA, Auswärtiges Amt), particularly via the German embassy, has focused on political issues, such as human rights, the rule of law, and religious freedom, and has been engaged in a 'Dialogue with the Islamic World' (German Embassy Ankara 2011).

Other relevant actors are the party-affiliated political foundations: in Turkey, the KAS, the FES, the FNS and the HBS run liaison offices.[5] The work of these foundations focuses particularly on the topics of good governance, the rule of law, municipal self-government, small and medium-sized business development, human and minority rights, regional development, the environment, trade unions, German–Turkish dialogue, gender issues, and freedom of speech and the press. These organizations received BMZ commitments in the amount of €48 million between 1990 and 2010 (BMZ 2011).

Perception analysis

Reactions to Erbakan's election to the office of prime minister in summer 1996 were initially restrained (*Frankfurter Rundschau* 1996a). His policies and rhetoric, however, soon became a matter of concern and gave rise to contradictory perceptions. On the one hand, the CDU-led government under chancellor Helmut Kohl signalled that 'one would have to watch out that the developments in Turkey would not catch them off guard like the Islamic revolution in the late 1970s in Iran had' (*Frankfurter Rundschau* 1996b). On the other hand, foreign minister Klaus Kinkel (FDP) saw no reason to mistrust Prime Minister Erbakan since he had suspended neither Turkey's NATO membership nor its participation in the customs union with the EU. Kinkel even regarded Turkey's 'normalization' of relations with its neighbours as a positive development for security in the entire region (*TAZ* 1997).

Yet, due to his anti-European and anti-German statements, Erbakan quickly became a burden to bilateral relations. Contrary to his promises during the electoral campaign, he did not make any serious efforts to address the 'Kurdish question' or human rights, which was not only an affront to German politicians but also paid no heed to the national interest in safeguarding domestic peace in Germany (*Die Welt* 1996).[6] Neither the 'soft coup' nor Erbakan's resignation drew official comment. Behind the scenes, however, both the German government and parliament were relieved over these outcomes because the RP's politicized Islam was on the verge of spreading to the Turkish diaspora in Germany via networks, business connections, and immigration (Schiffauer 2000).[7] Regarding the court case seeking to ban the RP, Germany released a joint statement with the EU that 'notes with regret' the party ban, while admonishing Turkey henceforth to respect democratic pluralism and freedom of speech (AA 1998).

Much like in 1996, the AKP's election victory in November 2002 was initially met with restraint in Berlin (*Berliner Morgenpost* 2002). However, the AKP government surprised Germany with its EU reform and democratization policies, which in the eyes of foreign minister Joschka Fischer (the Greens) served as a model for other Muslim countries (Fischer 2003). There was a similar shift in perception with regard to Kemalist state ideology. In its strategy statement on Turkey, the BMZ (which had been led by an SPD minister since 1998) explicitly identified it as a key obstacle to democratization and described it as being 'in need of reform', adding that the status of the Turkish military was 'not compatible with the European understanding of democracy' (BMZ 2000: 5).

The AKP was perceived in a much more positive light than the RP, especially thanks to its reform policies, and it enjoyed Germany's support in Turkey's domestic power struggle. For example, the Foreign Office criticized the coup threat against the AKP government (AA 2007c), and the AKP's election victory in the summer of 2007 as well as Gül's election to the office of president were welcomed by both chancellor Angela Merkel (CDU) and foreign minister Frank-Walter Steinmeier (SPD) (AA 2007a, 2007b; Bundeskanzleramt 2007a, 2007b), who, by contrast, described the proceedings to ban the party as 'incomprehensible' because the AKP had 'committed itself to the principles of democracy and the rule of law' (AA 2008c). The dismissal of the party ban process was welcomed by the German government as well as by the European Union (*FAZ* 2008).

Nevertheless, tensions arose in German–Turkish relations during the second half of 2007. Besides the AKP's increasing domestic authoritarianism referred to above, Prime Minister Erdoğan's public speech in Cologne in early 2008 was the subject of criticism when he recommended that migrants of Turkish origin should not let themselves be 'assimilated' by greater German society. Also the scandal involving the AKP-affiliated aid organization 'Deniz Feneri', which collected more than €40 million in donations from migrants of Turkish origin in Germany and is alleged to have misappropriated a large part of it, was noted with disapproval (*Frankfurter Rundschau* 2008).

The increased self-confidence evident in Turkey's foreign policy was described favourably by Foreign Minister Steinmeier, who stated that Turkey had 'gained considerable international respect and recognition for its balanced and constructive foreign policy' (AA 2009). The current CDU/CSU-FDP coalition government, by contrast, has characterized Turkey's foreign policy as 'Janus-faced'. The German government 'would rather see Turkey as a leader in the Middle East than Iran', but Erdoğan's 'attacks' on Israel as well as the joint opposition with Brazil to the sanctions against Iran are viewed critically.[8] At the same time, Foreign Minister Westerwelle (FDP) praised the constitutional reforms of September 2010, even if he noted cryptically that the 'concrete form of the power balance in the state has certainly not yet been finalized' (AA 2010).

Reaction analysis

The analysis of reactions in foreign and development policy cooperation shows that German ODA commitments to Turkey tripled from $101 million (1995) to $310 million (1997) during the RP government (OECD 2012). Even though Germany had demanded more democracy and human rights, it had not – unlike the United States – attached preconditions to ODA grants. In 1993, minister for development cooperation Carl-Dieter Spranger (CSU) had already favoured foregoing preconditions out of national interest, and did not see this as contradicting his own human rights postulate (*Frankfurter Rundschau* 1993). At the same time the BMZ increased its commitments for the Turkey-related projects of the political foundations: between 1990 and 1994 these amounted to approximately €3.7 million, and increased to €9.8 million between 1995 and 1998 (BMZ 2011).

Two further responses are evident during the RP period: first, the German domestic and justice policymakers were sensitized to the issue – with the support of secular Kemalist advocacy groups in Germany – and began legal proceedings against RP-affiliated and other (Turkish) Islamic organizations in Germany for fear of an 'Islamist indoctrination' of the diaspora.[9] Second, Turkey's 'compatibility with Europe' was called into question. In March 1997, several Christian Democratic European heads of government, including Chancellor Kohl, declared that as an 'Islamic country' Turkey was not considered a candidate for EU membership (*FAZ* 1997b).

Turkey's accession to the EU remained an important topic for German policy towards Turkey after the AKP's election victory. The SPD–Greens government as well as the opposition voiced their concern about the (re)emergence of political Islam – though with different implications: chancellor Gerhard Schröder (SPD) supported Turkey's accession out of 'national interest' and also so that 'Turkey does not drift into Islamic fundamentalism' (Schröder 2002). From the perspective of the CDU/CSU opposition (and some politicians from other parties), however, the accession negotiations were supposed to be conducted in an 'open-ended' fashion, and Turkey was to be offered a 'privileged partnership' for geographic, financial, and especially cultural reasons (see Karakaş 2006). The fact that the politicization of Turkey's accession runs counter to the EU's conditions-based policy while diminishing Germany's credibility, e.g. when calling for more democracy and human rights (including for the Christian minority in Anatolia) is a significant contradiction in Germany's policies towards Europe and Turkey, respectively (Andersen 2004).

What responses are evident with regard to German development cooperation during the AKP government? German ODA payments continued without interruption: between 2002 and 2010, approximately $1.1 billion were paid out to Turkey while Germany's development goals remained largely unchanged (OECD 2012). Apart from these direct payments, Turkey is also receiving roughly €4.8 billion in funding from Brussels under the Instrument for Pre-Accession Assistance for the period 2007 to 2013. As the biggest 'EU net contributor', Germany indirectly funds almost 20 per cent of EU pre-accession assistance (EU Commission 2011).

Another response was initiated by the BMZ and illustrates a new sensitivity to conflict: after the 9/11 attacks the ministry suggested a democracy-promoting discourse with the Islamic world (*FAZ* 2001). This exchange has been underway since late 2001, led by the Political Affairs Office of the German embassy in Ankara under the name 'Dialogue with the Islamic World'.[10] In addition, the Ernst Reuter Initiative was created in 2006 as part of the intercultural dialogue. It was the German–Turkish response to the 'Mohammed' caricatures and is supposed to foster basic values such as tolerance and freedom of religion through bilateral projects. The national 'Integration Summit' and the 'German Islam Conference' initiated by the minister for the interior Wolfgang Schäuble (CDU) as well as greater bilateral cooperation on matters of domestic security, such as the bilateral cooperation on arrests of German–Turkish terror suspects (e.g. that of the 'Sauerland Group') are also noteworthy in this context (German Embassy Ankara 2011).

A review of German ODA reveals that between 2005 and 2010 payments for projects in the area 'Government and Civil Society' amounted to around $27.1 million. At $15 million (55 per cent), the majority of German ODA focused on the 'public sector', while $8 million (29 per cent) benefited 'civil society' (OECD 2012; author's calculations). However, not only was the area 'Public Sector Policy and Administration Management' strengthened in recent years but increasingly also the political correctives, i.e. 'Democratic Participation and Civil Society', 'Judiciary Development', and 'Freedom of Speech and the Press' (OECD 2012; BMJ 2007; German Embassy Ankara 2009).

Three items stand out with regard to ODA. *First*, there was a process of adjustment to the AKP's needs by request of the GTZ, whose predominant mission is to provide technical support to the public sector. The GTZ praised the 'professional cooperation' with AKP administrations on the municipal level, although the topic of religion was not discussed.[11] *Second*, it is striking that the Foreign Office addressed democratic deficits in its human rights reports but did not mention the promotion of Muslim religious rights (e.g. with regard to headscarves) that the AKP and many Turkish Muslims in Germany had called for (AA 2008b, 2005). *Third*, the German government avoided applying pressure to the AKP government to lower the 10 per cent electoral threshold despite the fact that this has been a regular object of criticism by the Council of Europe and a few members of the opposition in the German parliament (Council of Europe 2008).[12]

Democracy assistance by Germany's political foundations led to irritations in bilateral relations in 2002/3. Acting on a nationalistic impulse, the Turkish judiciary brought proceedings against the foundations, accusing them of spying for the German state and of undermining the integrity of Turkish territory and society. While the case was dropped in late 2003 due to a lack of evidence, the bureaucratic requirements for the (not solely German) foundations nevertheless increased in its wake and have been complicating their work in the area of political education (*FAZ* 2003). All the same, the foundations continued their activities in Turkey unabated. BMZ funding to the foundations even increased: from 2002 to 2010, the political foundations together received more than €27.1 million, up from €18.7 million in the eight years between 1993 and 2001 (BMZ 2011).

A closer look at the work of the foundations shows some interesting differences. For example the Böll Foundation was 'unenthusiastic' about the RP's election victory because Erbakan's party was 'radical and extreme in its rhetoric'. HBS viewed the RP as a potential 'threat to women's rights' and responded with a targeted expansion of projects on the subject of equality of the sexes. The AKP, on the other hand, enjoyed a more positive perception. The Böll Foundation has since carried on a pragmatic relationship with the AKP, and on occasion has been working collaboratively with AKP-affiliated individuals or organizations.[13] The Ebert Foundation did not see the RP as an 'Islamist threat' but rather a pragmatic, flexible party whose more extreme inclinations were held in check by virtue of being in a coalition government. There was no direct collaboration with the RP and its organizations. However, FES has maintained a pragmatic relationship with the AKP that includes occasional collaborations with politicians and organizations.[14] The RP was judged much more critically by the Adenauer Foundation and the Naumann Foundation. While KAS supported a 'Dialogue with Islam' and noted that Muslim rights were circumscribed in Kemalist Turkey, it nevertheless refused direct collaboration with the RP – as did the FNS – and preferred cooperating with the Kemalist conservative parties, such as the DYP (the junior coalition partner in the Erbakan government) and ANAP. Interestingly, the two foundations differ in their perception and treatment of the AKP. The KAS has maintained – ever since the previous coalition partners DYP and ANAP first joined the ranks of the opposition before disbanding in mid-2000s – the closest contact with the AKP and its affiliated organizations due to the 'shared basis of religious, conservative values'. The relationship has chilled in recent years, however, particularly due to the Turkish government's harsh criticism of Israel. The FNS also has considered the AKP to be 'Islamic conservative', but this political and ideological orientation has meant that the foundation did not collaborate institutionally or structurally with the AKP – which does not, however, preclude individual contacts and invitations to AKP representatives. In general, the Naumann Foundation has supported strict separation of state and religion, and its work in Turkey is focused on working with secular groups and increasingly on projects related to the topic of 'secularism as integral part of a liberal democratic order'.[15]

The United States: between cooperation and confrontation

Profile of bilateral relations

The United States maintains close relations with Turkey, ties that are characterized primarily by geostrategic interests even after the end of the Cold War. The

United States regards its NATO ally Turkey as a 'pivotal state' due to its close proximity to 13 of the 16 'trouble spots' in which NATO sees the potential for conflict. This makes Turkey, in American eyes, the most important 'hinge' between the Balkans, the Caspian Basin and the Middle East (Makovsky 1999). A 'strategic partnership' was concluded in 1999, which provides for greater bilateral collaboration on matters of foreign policy, security, and the economy (US Embassy Ankara 2012).

Turkey's strategic importance is reflected in US military aid as well as the presence of various US military facilities: between 1990 and 2008, the United States provided military assistance amounting to $3.8 billion (US Overseas 2011), thus making Turkey the third-largest recipient after Israel and Egypt. The most important US military base in the Middle East is located in Incirlik in southeastern Anatolia. In 2007, approximately three-quarters of all US cargo flights into Iraq and Afghanistan were processed there, and between 50 and 90 US nuclear weapons are said to be stationed in Incirlik (Migdalovitz 2008: 13).

In the 1990s the United States pursued the following goals in its policy regarding Turkey: secure active and passive support from Ankara for the Iraq War to liberate Kuwait, as well as the subsequent surveillance of northern Iraqi air space; a diplomatic resolution of the squabbles between Greece and Turkey concerning border disputes in the Aegean and regarding Cyprus, with the goal of trouble-free NATO intra-operability; improvement of Turkish–Armenian relations after the Nagorno-Karabakh War; promotion of democracy and human rights; a peaceful settlement of the Turkish–Kurdish conflict; EU accession in order to strengthen Turkey's institutional ties to the West. Other US interests concerned the Turkish position vis-à-vis Iran, Syria and Libya – identified as 'rogue states' by the United States – as well as Turkey's partnership with Israel (Larrabee 2008; Lesser 2007). The latter had been agreed upon in 1996 and was hailed by president Bill Clinton as 'one of the most important political developments in the region since the 1991 Gulf War' (quoted in Gresh 1998: 203).

A new issue was added to bilateral relations in 1999 when the Clinton government embarked on an initiative that ended in an agreement to build an oil pipeline from Baku (Azerbaijan) via Tbilisi to Ceyhan on Turkey's Mediterranean coast. This pipeline satisfies not only US economic interests but also strengthens Turkey's strategic role as an energy hub (Boyer and Katulis 2008: 21).

The 9/11 terror attacks were followed by another adjustment. Since then, the United States has regarded Turkey as a 'model' or 'inspiration' for other Muslim countries (Taşpınar 2005: 9). Moreover, Ankara was not only supposed to play a role in the planned engagement in Iraq to topple Saddam Hussein's government but also support the United States in the fight against international terrorism, particularly in Afghanistan (International Security Assistance Force, ISAF). The latter is primarily of symbolic significance for the United States so that the ISAF campaign is not interpreted as a 'crusade' by Christian countries against the Islamic world.

Profile of US democracy promotion in Turkey

Turkey's importance for the United States is also reflected in the area of development cooperation: between 1990 and 2010, ODA disbursements amounted to $982 million (OECD 2012). The official reasons for US development aid to Turkey are cited as follows:

> Turkey is a vital strategic partner and NATO ally situated between Eastern Europe, the Middle East, and the former Soviet Union. In the aftermath of 9/11, Turkey has been a critical ally in the global war on terrorism. Turkey's policies and actions affect the resolution of a host of simmering regional conflicts, including Iraq, the Middle East, Cyprus, the Caucasus, and the Balkans.
>
> (USAID 2011)

In the 1990s, the USAID programme in the country envisaged the following measures: regional development; sustainable family planning, the political participation of women, the return of (Kurdish) refugees, and the treatment of torture victims. In the 2000s, the efforts focused on fighting regional poverty and unemployment as well as Turkey's socio-economic losses in the fight against international terrorism (USAID 2011).[16] Hence, democracy assistance was not a major issue for USAID.

During the period under study the State Department, by contrast, supported democratization projects by making individual grants, especially from the Human Rights and Democracy Fund (HRDF); these focused in particular on religious freedom, freedom of speech, human rights, and combating torture.[17]

The IMET programme for foreign military officers also entailed a certain element of democracy assistance. IMET is funded by the State Department and administered by the Defense Security Cooperation Agency (DSCA). Officers who participate in the programme learn not only how to improve interoperability between the US military and their own armed forces but are also told about the (subordinate) role of the military in a democracy.[18] Since 1990 Ankara has received IMET assistance worth almost $50 million (CBJ 2011; US Overseas 2011).

Promoting Turkish democracy is the brief of the NED. Between 1990 and 2010, the NED spent around $17 million on projects in Turkey (see NED various years). The main recipients of NED grants in Turkey have been the NDI and the IRI. In the 1990s, the NDI and the IRI used NED funds to promote good governance (separation of powers, anti-corruption, political participation), the rule of law (fair trials, ban of torture, judicial reform) and democratic norms (human and minority rights, freedom of speech). In the 2000s, NED-funded projects of the two institutes focused on women's rights, more effective parliamentary work, youth participation, and the strengthening of civil society (NED various years).

Perception analysis

The US government's response to Erbakan's election to the office of prime minister was muted (State Department 1996). While the United States welcomed an extension of air surveillance in Iraq, which was coordinated by Turkey, Erbakan's visits to Iran and Libya were criticized sharply as they undermined international sanctions as well as Western and NATO solidarity, respectively (cf. *New York Times* 1996; *FAZ* 1996). Official assessments of the RP's impact were equally contradictory. While the State Department highlighted the RP-DYP government's democratic legitimacy in a statement to Congress and dismissed an 'Iranization' of Turkey as unlikely (US Congress 1997a), it was ironically the US Defense Department – which supposedly wanted to imbue foreign military officers with democratic values via the IMET programme – that supported the 'soft coup': 'Ataturk, the founder of modern Turkey, put great emphasis on the importance of maintaining a secular government in order to create a Turkish democracy, a principle that the Turkish military is constitutionally-mandated and determined to uphold' (US Congress 1997b). While the United States advocated the military's civilian measures, it was opposed to a 'hard coup', as this would have risked destabilizing Turkey and isolating it internationally (State Department 1997). Moreover, the RP ban was viewed critically based on fears of further restrictions on freedom of speech and democratic pluralism in Turkey (State Department 1998).

The AKP's election victory initially also met with a muted reception in the United States (State Department 2002). One year after 9/11, however, the United States proved to be pragmatic and called Turkey *and* the AKP 'models' for the Muslim world (White House 2002). The positive perception of the AKP changed when in March 2003 the Turkish parliament, which was dominated by the AKP, voted against allowing US troops to invade northern Iraq from southeast Anatolian soil, granting only flyover rights instead. Deputy defense secretary Paul Wolfowitz openly regarded this as a breach of trust and revealed a peculiar understanding of democracy: 'I think we had a big disappointment.... I think particularly the military. I think for whatever reason they did not play the strong leadership role on that issue that we would have expected' (Wolfowitz 2003).

On the other hand, the administration of George W. Bush welcomed the AKP government's efforts regarding the reunification of Cyprus in spring 2004 as well as Turkey taking command of ISAF. In addition, President Bush was impressed by the Erdoğan government's democratization policies aimed at fulfilling the 'Copenhagen Criteria' that led – with support from the United States – to the commencement of EU accession negotiations in October 2005 (*Turkish Daily News* 2005). However, the United States observed the power struggle between the AKP government and the Turkish military with unease, as the struggle destabilized the country and because the coup threat resulted in early elections (2007) and the party ban proceedings (2008).

There are a number of interesting assessments of the situation. For example, the State Department reacted as follows to the coup threat: 'We have real confidence in Turkey's democracy and we have confidence in their constitutional processes.... We are encouraging *everybody* to participate in Turkey's democracy according to *their* constitution and laws' (State Department 2007c; emphasis added). With regard to the proceedings to ban the AKP, secretary of state Condoleezza Rice also hoped that a solution would be found that was in line with Turkey's semi-authoritarian constitution, which was written under the military's supervision after the 1980 *coup d'état*, and the Kemalist (rather than a liberal democratic) reasoning founded on national interest: 'We believe and hope that this will be decided *within Turkey's* democratic context and by its secular democratic principles' (State Department 2008; emphasis added). The State Department thus affirmed the superordinate role of the Turkish military as a political corrective as well as the principle of secularism as a counterweight to the AKP's policies and rhetoric. The preceding AKP election victory in the summer of 2007 and Gül's election as president had been met with restrained responses (State Department 2007a, 2007b).

A US perception of the AKP as a danger to the 'secular foundation of Turkey', however, was not only informed by the politicization of the headscarf issue and the power struggle within Turkey, but also resulted from its 'Islamic' foreign policy.[19] Prime Minister Erdoğan voiced criticism of Israel's Middle East policy with increasing frequency, expanded ties to Russia as well as with the 'rogue states' of Syria and Iran, and threatened to intervene in northern Iraq to fight the Kurdish PKK, without the blessing of the United States, if necessary (Barkey 2009).

The Obama Administration also takes a largely critical view of the AKP government. It was 'alarmed' at the Turkish government's 'hysterical' reaction to the Gaza flotilla raid and irritated about Brazil and Turkey's rejection of UN sanctions against Iran.[20] Defense Secretary Gates viewed the politicization of EU accession along cultural issues as an important reason for Turkey's new foreign policy. He thus indirectly put partial blame on Germany for Turkey's 'turning away from the West' (*BBC* 2010). With regard to the constitutional reforms of September 2010 the White House only made restrained statements in which President Obama praised, with diplomatic ambiguity, the 'vibrancy' of Turkish democracy (White House 2010).

Reaction analysis

An analysis of US foreign assistance during the time of the RP government underscores the fact that the United States was faced with the dilemma of balancing out the competing poles of geostrategic interest versus democracy and human rights. This, however, had nothing to do with the RP coming to power. To wit, the US Congress had shifted tack and introduced conditions-based allocation of foreign aid to Turkey in the mid-1990s due to serious human rights violations – that is, while aid was allocated its disbursement was contingent on progress in the areas of democratization and the opening of the Turkish–Armenian border (Callaway and Matthews 2008: 148–9). By contrast, for national security reasons Secretary of State Albright advocated foreign aid for

Turkey with no strings attached, regardless of the political affiliation of the government in Ankara (Albright 1997). In point of fact, tying US aid to conditions did sour bilateral relations with Turkey: almost all Turkish parties voiced criticism, claiming that Turkey's national security interests in its fight against the PKK were suffering as a result. Consequently, Turkey voluntarily relinquished some of the funds between 1996 and 1997 even though $220 million had been allocated by the United States for the period from 1995 to 1998 (see OECD 2012; Callaway and Matthews 2008).

It is also notable with regard to the RP that the shift to conditions-based ODA by the US Congress had no negative impact on NED funds; on the contrary: the democracy foundation, which only funds projects that support civil society, increased its annual aid to Turkey significantly while the RP was in power (i.e. between 1995 and 1998), reducing it again afterwards (see NED various years). NDI only started its Turkey-related work in early 1998 and thus no reaction was formulated; IRI, by contrast, has been operating in Turkey since 1993 and – unlike NED – classified the RP as 'Islamist' and saw it as corrosive to the principle of secularism in Turkey. Through its NED-funded projects in Turkey, IRI expanded its collaboration with secular Kemalist groups and parties and shared strategies for more professional electoral campaigns and advice for increasing political participation among women and youths (IRI 1995: 16; 1996: 16; 1997: 15; 1998: 15).

During the AKP's time in government it should be noted that the United States continued its ODA disbursements – despite mounting criticism voiced by the United States against the AKP government. Between 2002 and 2010 these amounted to $273 million (OECD 2012). This constitutes a noteworthy change, since US development aid for Turkey was scheduled to expire at the end of the 1990s due to Turkey's positive socio-economic development. The reasons provided for the new allocations were as follows:

> Turkey is a front-line state, a key ally in the war on terrorism.... Its success as a democratic, open-economy Muslim state rooted in the West is important to US efforts at political and economic reform in the Middle East and Eurasia.
>
> (CBJ 2007)

In addition to the regular foreign assistance, the United States also granted a special disbursement of $1 billion from the 'Economic Support Fund' to Turkey (CBJ 2003). President Bush thus wanted to 'buy' the AKP government's support for the upcoming war in Iraq (Kapsis 2006). US funds may not have been tied to conditions regarding democracy and human rights as they had been in the 1990s, but they were nevertheless not disbursed, since the Turkish parliament had refused to support the United States. All the same, in autumn 2003 the Bush Administration granted Turkey a low-interest credit in the amount of $8.5 billion to further stabilize the economy following significant turmoil in spring 2001, as well as to allow compliance with IMF conditions (Momani 2007).

It is also striking that agreement on the expansion of the 'strategic partnership', which had been inaugurated in 1999, was announced in a joint statement in summer 2006, despite the tense relations between the United States and the AKP government (US Embassy Ankara 2012). Just like administrations before them, the Obama and Bush governments also distanced themselves in autumn 2007 and spring 2010, respectively, from a Congressional resolution acknowledging the Turkish genocide of Armenians, an initiative that had been lobbied for by Armenian and Greek advocacy groups. The US government justified its disapproval in each instance by claiming that the resolution jeopardized geostrategic interests: Ankara had threatened to put military cooperation on hold, which would have had an adverse impact on supplying US troops in Afghanistan and Iraq (*New York Times* 2010).

The reaction analysis also shows that the United States had already raised its foreign aid in 2002 – independently of the AKP coming to power – and continued to provide it in subsequent years. In recent years the bulk of US foreign assistance has been devoted to the area of 'Peace and Security' with an emphasis on 'foreign military financing' (see CBJ 2002–10). The US displayed flexibility and pragmatism in order to protect geostrategic interests. The funds were disbursed to the AKP government so that, for example, logistics for US troops and the stabilization of post-war Iraq from the military base in Incirlik would remain in place and Turkey could fund and continue its ISAF deployment to Afghanistan. Moreover, US funding also supported Ankara's fight against Islamist and Kurdish terrorism *in* Turkey as well as an expansion of Turkish border control in the Caucasus and vis-à-vis Iran and Iraq, in order to support the non-proliferation of weapons of mass destruction and to contain the flow of refugees along the Iraqi border (see CBJ 2003–10).

There was also a new allocation of money from the 'Economic Support Fund' during the years from 2006 to 2008 in order to further the socio-economic development of Turkey's Kurdish southeast, where greater-than-average poverty and unemployment had promoted 'instability' (in other words, terrorism). US aid was supposed to contribute to the country's internal stability and speed up its accession to the EU (CBJ 2008). For the 2009 fiscal year, US aid was justified through Turkey's 'model function': 'Turkey can play a leadership role in the region and has served as a model for modernizing nations worldwide' (CBJ 2009).

Between 2002 and 2010, additional foreign assistance came from the State Department: funds for 'non-proliferation, anti-terrorism, refugee assistance' of more than $43 million as well as $32 million for the IMET training programme for foreign military officers. A significant funding increase in comparison to the reference period from 1993 to 2001 is evident in these areas as well (US Overseas 2011; CBJ 2011).

Closer attention should be paid to the increase in IMET funding. While this funding had been justified for the 2003 fiscal year by claiming that 'IMET training will ... teach fundamental democratic principles which help strengthen Turkey's commitment to democracy and human rights' (CBJ 2003), the rationale for the years 2004 to 2007 was that the United States merely had an interest in a 'well trained, *US-oriented* Turkish officer corps' – there was no longer any mention of democracy and human rights (CBJ 2004–2007; emphasis added). In subsequent years, the 'US orientation' of the Turkish military was also emphasized (CBJ 2008–10). The increase in IMET funding since 2002 reflects American fears of an Islamization or turning away of the pro-Western military from the United States, and means that the United States supported a Kemalist counterweight to the AKP.

The sector of the OECD database entitled 'Government and Civil Society' provides a precise overview of US disbursements for democratization projects. These amounted to $12.5 million between 2005 and 2010. Closer analysis reveals that this form of US aid was also supposed to benefit civil society especially, and thus meant to counterbalance the AKP. In concrete terms, out of the total of $12.5 million for the years 2005 to 2010 approximately $2.9 million, or 23 per cent, went to the 'public sector' (especially the focus area of 'Public Sector Policy and Administration Management') and $6.2 million, or around 49 per cent, to 'civil society', especially the areas 'Democratic Participation and Civil Society' and 'Elections' (OECD 2012; author's calculations).

Three items stand out with regard to US foreign aid. *First*, there was a process of adjustment on the part of the United States that on the one hand reflects the interests of the AKP government, and on the other hand demonstrates a more marked use of US aid to bolster political, military and civic organizations other than the AKP. *Second*, the State Department in its various democracy and human rights reports between 2005 and 2010 did not broach the issue of religious freedom for Sunni Muslims in Kemalist Turkey. *Third*, the 10 per cent electoral threshold was also not discussed (cf. State Department various years).

The following response patterns emerge with regard to democracy assistance by NED, NDI and IRI. NED increased its Turkey-related aid and, between 2002 and 2010, spent $12.4 million, more than twice the amount in the reference period 1993 to 2001 (see NED various years). Since the mid-2000s, IRI and NDI have made adjustments to their country programmes in Turkey – they now focus increasingly on promoting political participation and strengthening the legislature as a check on the executive (NED 2010). It is noticeable regarding the two party institutes that IRI has classified the AKP as 'Islamist' (IRI 2002: 15–16) – as had been the case with the RP. IRI declines institutionalized collaboration with Erdoğan's party, and has continued to prefer cooperating with secular parties and organizations. NDI, by contrast, has collaborated sporadically with AKP politicians and organizations, at least partially adopting a policy of influence through engagement.[21]

Results

German and US policies include elements of democracy promotion in the dimensions of foreign aid, diplomacy, and international cooperation. Democracy promotion through international observation of elections is not a relevant issue for

US or German policies towards Turkey. While US and German monitors participated in OSCE election monitoring missions, there were no complaints of election fraud (see ODIHR 2012).

In the area of development cooperation, both donors subordinated democracy promotion to regional socio-economic development (especially through the promotion of the economy, the environment, and infrastructure) in order to combat poverty, migration, and the appeal of extremist organizations. US and German democracy assistance aimed at the rule of law, inter-cultural dialogue, human and minority rights, civil society, good governance, party and parliamentary work, and political participation. In their diplomatic relations with Turkey, both donors broached issues of democracy publicly as well as in political dialogue and bilateral documents (e.g. in human rights reports). Bilateral cooperation (in the areas of politics, the economy, development policy, and the military) is tied to democracy standards.

There are, however, differences with regard to the use of incentives and sanctions. During the period under investigation (1995–2010), Germany neither made its development cooperation contingent on certain conditions nor used sanctions. US Congress, by contrast, tied foreign aid to democracy-related conditions, until the 'war on terror' after 9/11 changed priorities. There are also differences between the donors regarding Turkey's accession to the EU. The United States, out of geostrategic interests, called on the EU to admit Turkey to the EU. In Germany, by contrast, Turkey's accession is not a matter of national interest. While Berlin supported the commencement of accession talks with Turkey and thus helped bring about the EU's conditionality policies, the negotiations have also become an object exploited to pursue of party politics.

How did Germany and the United States deal with conflicting objectives? An *extrinsic conflict* ('democracy versus donor interests') occurred in Germany's case especially in dealing with the Welfare Party. The German government and parliament quietly accepted that the democratically elected RP government of Prime Minister Erbakan was systematically pressured by the military and was forced to resign by the threat of a *coup d'état*. This restraint can be explained by domestic interests: on the one hand, Erbakan had not taken Germany's interest in strengthening human rights seriously, and thus ignored concern about the prospect of a continued flow of Kurdish asylum seekers and migrants to Germany. On the other hand, there was the threat of a spill-over of the RP's politicized Islam to the Turkish diaspora and its mosques in Germany.

The United States also resolved the conflicting objectives in its dealings with the RP in favour of its own interests. 'Hard', i.e. non-negotiable, geostrategic interests dominated in this regard, such as the isolation of Iran and Libya and the fulfilment of obligations towards NATO allies, which in the view of the United States were being jeopardized by Erbakan.

There were contradictions in the donors' reactions to the AKP. These were the result of differing perceptions of the AKP and of Kemalist state ideology on the one hand, and of 9/11 on the other. On the whole, Germany classified the AKP – up until the emergence of its increasing authoritarianism and its criticism of Israel – more positively than the United States. Germany viewed the Erdoğan government as a 'guarantor of stability'; moreover, Kemalist ideology was seen as an impediment to democratization. The United States, by contrast, was openly critical of Turkey's rapprochement with Russia and especially with Iran, as it feared that this would strengthen semi-authoritarian regimes and a new strategic Moscow–Teheran–Ankara 'axis'. American concern that Turkey could subordinate its obligations as a NATO member to its newly articulated aspiration to take on the role of a leading nation in the Islamic world was not widespread on the German side. On the contrary: Germany, as a global exporting economy, placed its trust in the motto '(democratic) change through trade' and regards Turkey as a pro-Western stabilizing force that is bringing stability to a volatile region (i.e. the Middle East) through its mediation efforts and external trade. This positive stance had, incidentally, also been adopted vis-à-vis the Erbakan government. In addition, the AKP's successful economic policy launched positive socio-economic development that countered not only German fears of poverty-related Turkish–Kurdish immigration but also benefited Germany as an important foreign trade partner.

Both donors reacted in identical fashion to *intrinsic conflicts of objectives* ('democracy versus democracy'): in the case of the RP and Prime Minister Erbakan, they criticized the lack of progress on democracy and human rights issues as well as the politicization of religion; in the case of the AKP both donors praised the EU reform and democratization processes, but both also criticized Erdoğan's increasingly authoritarian tendencies. Yet on the part of Germany in particular there has been no turning away from Turkey. On the contrary: ODA disbursements continued without conditions and strengthened the public sector and thus also the AKP due to its government control both at the national level and in many municipalities. A decisive reason for the AKP government's support from Germany and its toleration by the United States is rooted in the party's political strength and democratic legitimacy within Turkey (recipient context). The AKP has won absolute majorities in several parliamentary elections, and a majority of the Turkish population supports its economic and foreign policies as well as the recent constitutional changes.

It is true that both donor countries also support counterweights to the one-party dominance of the AKP. However, the party's broad domestic support makes it difficult for critics in Germany and the United States to confront the AKP openly. It was also for those reasons that both donors made flexible, pragmatic and issue-oriented adjustments, following the view that 'while (foreign) governments may change, their own country's interests do not'. In the case of the United States, this adjustment can also be explained by a strategy of cooperative engagement to counter the possibility of the AKP government distancing itself from Washington even further. In any case, although the asymmetry of power was much higher in the US–Turkey dyad, the United States also refrained from actively infringing upon the Turkish government's right for self-determination.

It is also conspicuous that the concern felt by the United States that the principle of secularism might be undermined was largely not shared by Germany.

The donors did not actively resolve the conflict between the objectives 'democracy' and 'secularism', but rather waited to see the results of Turkey's constitutional reform. Although the German embassy is engaged in an inter-cultural dialogue with Ankara, it is noticeable that Berlin often fell back on ambivalence about the 'correct approach' for dealing with Islam and the headscarf issue respectively (AA 2008a). Germany's government avoided aggressively pursuing this delicate matter due to the interdependence of internal and external factors in bilateral relations and based on the fear of repercussions for Germany's domestic policies (e.g. a legal demand to wear the headscarf in the civil service).[22]

The issue of the 10 per cent electoral threshold was also not broached officially by the donors. This suggests that the donor countries do not regard the threshold as undemocratic a priori, and consider it to be potentially beneficial to stability and governability at the expense of broader democratic participation.

Analysis also showed that the United States has an instrumental understanding concerning Turkey's widely cited 'model' function with regard to other Muslim countries in terms of subordinating Islam and Islamic politicians to the Western-authoritarian Kemalist ideology for the sake of stability (i.e. secularism, pro-Western orientation). The German understanding of the 'model' function primarily adheres to the expectation that democratic elections and governmental responsibilities in Turkey's case can moderate Islamist parties both in political and ideological terms.

The two donors' rejection of a 'hard coup' is of little surprise. For the United States, however, the same perception and response patterns applied to both the RP and the AKP, i.e. Turkey was supposed to find a resolution within the framework of its secular constitution. Be that as it may, the Turkish constitution was written as part of the 1980 *coup d'état* and is undemocratic in many aspects because it limits civil rights and strengthens the role of political veto players such as the Kemalist military and judiciary. Here, the different contextual conditions outlined in the introductory chapter are of importance: if the United States had advocated a 'hard coup', Turkey would have been further destabilized and internationally isolated – not to mention the resulting suspension of EU accession negotiations. At the same time, US efforts at democratizing the 'broader Middle East', where the AKP is viewed in a largely favourable light, would have been reduced to absurdity. Furthermore, US support of a 'hard coup' would not only have served to intensify the anti-Americanism virulent in Turkey since the beginning of the Iraq War and thus have complicated the work of US organizations there; such support would also have prompted the AKP government to turn farther away from the United States. The specific recipient context in Turkey and the regional setting, which both have dramatically changed since the 1990s, thus significantly limited the political scope and the course of actions for the US government.

In Germany's case, the openly voiced criticism of the coup threat and of the party ban process against the AKP also aimed at alleviating the nationalistically motivated criticism of the work of the German foundations. Furthermore, the framework of EU conditionalities in which German policies towards Turkey are embedded (donor context) worked towards rejecting the anti-democratic measures of the Kemalist state elites.

To what extent can these response patterns be explained with the profiles (i.e. the respective configuration of determinants) that characterize both donors' bilateral relations with Turkey? As far as German policy is concerned, the result is contradictory: Germany fulfilled the theoretical expectations of a Civilian Power in the AKP's case, but not in dealing with the RP. At the beginning of the Erbakan Administration, the German government pursued an inclusion strategy; however, bilateral relations eventually grew more contested and ended in open confrontation and turning away from Prime Minister Erbakan. Germany was noticeably reserved with regard to both the threatened coup as well as Erbakan's forced resignation. His ouster was met with relief by German policy-makers.[23] Though the RP ban was denounced in a joint statement with the EU, it would be incorrect to speak of a 'values-oriented' foreign policy by Germany with regard to the RP. Apparently, Erbakan's policies and actions were regarded as a larger problem than the Kemalist authoritarian measures aimed at a change of policy and government.

Germany's approach differed in its dealings with the ideologically more moderate AKP, a fact that was also attributable to pro-AKP advocacy groups in the German diaspora. Berlin largely respected the AKP government's right to self-determination with regard to domestic, economic, and foreign policy. Germany, in its role as a Civilian Power, supported the democratically legitimized AKP government in Turkey's internal power struggle, while the increasing authoritarianism displayed by the latter did not result in exclusion or sanctions. One reason for this is probably that there was no classic competition between interests and norms, since no German national interests were under serious threat by the Erdoğan government. With regard to the close interdependence of bilateral relations – the most important determinant in German policy towards Turkey – the reaction analysis reveals a new sensitivity to conflict in Germany's domestic policy-making: the national interest of societal peace and security was provided for by inaugurating the national 'Integration Summit' and the 'German Islam Conference', as well as by deepening bilateral collaboration on domestic and justice policy issues.

However, Germany's handling of Turkey's EU membership aspirations has been inconsistent. While the SPD and the Green Party are in favour of Turkish membership, the CDU is (mainly for religious–cultural reasons) against it. Once again, the impact of contextual conditions comes into play. The case of Germany underlines the importance of domestic (donor) politics in foreign relations with Turkey. Although the EU has established a clear framework for accession talks with Turkey and conditions attached to accession, the changes in German government had an impact on the official attitude towards Turkey's possible EU membership and, ultimately, meant that the German government did not consistently make use of the EU conditionalities as an instrument of democracy promotion. In fact, the politicization of Turkey's EU membership aspirations by conservative parties in Germany led to Berlin undermining the international norms set by the EU vis-à-vis Turkey. The exploitation of cultural differences for party-political gain that shapes Germany's position on Turkey's EU accession runs counter to both the normative guidelines of a Civilian Power and to those domestic special interests constituted by the numerous Turkey-related advocacy groups (Kurdish and Alevi NGO, human rights organizations, churches, etc.) in Germany.

The United States, on the other hand, faced the classic tension between interests and norms much more strongly, and the response pattern does not match that of the Freedom Fighter in the case of either the RP or the AKP. The United States was confronted with Turkish governments that, although democratically legitimized, were often acting in an anti-Western and, in the case of the AKP, increasingly authoritarian manner. US policies have been trying to somehow strike a balance: to cooperate with the elected government in order to advance US national interests, while, at the same time, supporting the authoritarian Kemalist elites and counterweights to the AKP, which are secular but not liberal-democratic in their orientation. This, once again, demonstrates the restrictive impact of the recipient context: during the period considered in this study (1995–2010), the United States had no noteworthy pro-Western and liberal-secular political partners who could democratically take over the government.

Notes

1 The analysis will therefore neither deal with recent changes in Turkish foreign policy associated with the 'Arab Spring' and the civil war in Syria nor consider their implications for US and German relations with Turkey.
2 In this chapter, the terms *political Islam* and *Islamism* are used synonymously. They denote an ideology in which Islam is the central feature of a political identity in an attempt to legitimize claims to political and ethical dominance as a function of the Koran's 'universal validity'. In accordance with this, all of public life (e.g. the judiciary, culture, education) is supposed to be organized so that it adheres with religious imperatives and thus brings it in line with the Sharia. In contrast to the political term *Islamist*, *Islamic* designates primarily a socio-cultural and ritual dimension and describes thought and action based on the Koran (Esposito 2004).
3 The term *Kemalism* denotes the society and state doctrine formulated by state founder Mustafa Kemal (Atatürk) in 1931. Several state institutions are dedicated to safeguarding the Kemalist principles. Among these institutions, also referred to as the *Kemalist state elite*, are the Turkish military and the National Security Council, as well as parts of the judiciary, e.g. the Supreme Court and the Chief Prosecutor. These institutions have considerable authority and means for influencing politics that have thus far resulted in numerous *coups d'état* and the banning of individual political parties (Parla 1991).
4 See Kramer (2007, 2004); Pratt Ewing (2003); Weick (2000).
5 The HSS does not have a Turkey-related programme. The RLS has supported Turkey-related projects only sporadically since 2000, and is therefore not part of my analysis.
6 Interview with member of parliament Uta Zapf (SPD).
7 Interview with member of parliament Uta Zapf (SPD) and representatives of the German government.
8 Interview with representatives of the German government.
9 Interview with representatives of the Turkish Community in Germany ('Türkische Gemeinde in Deutschland').

10 As part of this dialogue, language courses are offered for Turkish imams who are about to be dispatched to Germany. These courses not only train participants in the German language but also share information on the subordinate role of religion in a democracy as well as on Islamism and integration issues in Germany. This initiative can also be regarded as an indirect form of democracy promotion and is attributable in particular to the interdependence of intrinsic and extrinsic factors in bilateral relations (interview with the German embassy in Ankara).

11 Interview with the GTZ in Ankara.

12 The members of parliament Uta Zapf (SPD), Claudia Roth (the Greens) and Ulla Jelpke (DIE LINKE) view the 10 per cent threshold as 'undemocratic' because its intention is to keep Kurdish parties in particular out of the Turkish parliament. Holger Haibach (CDU), by contrast, did not believe the threshold to be undemocratic a priori as it prevents 'the party system from splintering and promotes political stability'. He nevertheless regarded a 'moderate reduction' as 'useful'.

13 Interview at the HBS.

14 Interviews at the FES.

15 Interviews at KAS and FNS.

16 Interview with USAID.

17 Interview at the State Department.

18 Officially, the IMET programme aims at exposing 'foreign military and civilian personnel to the important roles democratic values and internationally recognized human rights can play in governance and military operations' (State Department 2011).

19 Interview with US official in Ankara.

20 Interview with US official in Ankara.

21 Interviews with IRI and NDI.

22 Interviews with representatives of the federal government and parliament.

23 Interview with member of parliament Uta Zapf (SPD).

References

AA (1998) *Erklärung der Europäischen Union zum Verbot der Refah-Partei in der Türkei*, 22 January, Bonn: Auswärtiges Amt.

AA (2005) *Siebter Bericht der Bundesregierung über ihre Menschenrechtspolitik in den auswärtigen Beziehungen und in anderen Politikbereichen*, Berlin: Auswärtiges Amt.

AA (2007a) 'Bundesminister Steinmeier gratuliert dem Präsidenten der Republik Türkei zu seiner Wahl', *Press Release*, 28 August, Berlin: Auswärtiges Amt.

AA (2007b) 'Bundesminister Steinmeier zum Ausgang der Wahlen in der Türkei', *Press Release*, 23 July, Berlin: Auswärtiges Amt.

AA (2007c) *Erklärung der Präsidentschaft der EU zur Wahl des Staatspräsidenten in der Türkei*, 28 April, Berlin: Auswärtiges Amt.

AA (2008a) *Wohin geht die Türkei. Rede von BM Steinmeier anlässlich der 11. Hannah-Arendt-Tage am 4.10.2008 in Hannover*, 6 October, Berlin: Auswärtiges Amt.

AA (2008b) *Achter Bericht der Bundesregierung über ihre Menschenrechtspolitik in den auswärtigen Beziehungen und in anderen Politikbereichen*, Berlin: Auswärtiges Amt.

AA (2008c) 'Bundesregierung kritisiert Verbotsverfahren gegen türkische Regierungspartei AKP', *Press Release*, 17 March, Berlin: Auswärtiges Amt.

AA (2009) 'Außenminister Steinmeier gratuliert seinem neuen türkischen Amtskollegen zur Ernennung', *Press Release*, 4 May, Berlin: Auswärtiges Amt.

AA (2010) 'Bundesaußenminister Westerwelle begrüßt Erfolg des Verfassungsreferendums in der Türkei', *Press Release*, 12 September, Berlin: Auswärtiges Amt.

Akıncı, U. (1999) 'The Welfare Party's Municipal Track Record: Evaluating Islamist Municipal Activism in Turkey', *Middle East Journal*, 53 (1): 75–94.

Albright, M. (1997) *Statement before the Subcommittee on Foreign Operations, Export Financing, and Related Programs*, 12 February. Online, available at: www.gpo.gov (accessed 21 December 2012).

Andersen, E. (2004) 'The Impact of Foreign Relations on Human Rights in Turkey', in L.G. Martin and D. Keridis (eds) *The Future of Turkish Foreign Policy*, Cambridge, MA: The MIT Press.

Barkey, H.J. (2009) *Preventing Conflict over Kurdistan*, Washington, DC: Carnegie Endowment for International Peace.

BBC (2010) 'US Defence Secretary Gates Blames EU for Turkey "Drift"', *BBC*, 9 June. Online, available at: www.bbc.co.uk/news/10275379 (accessed 15 May 2013).

Berliner Morgenpost (2002) 'Reaktionen nach politischer Wende in der Türkei bleiben zurückhaltend', *Berliner Morgenpost*, 5 November.

BMJ (Bundesministerium der Justiz) (2007) 'Deutschland und Türkei zeichnen Vereinbarung zur justiziellen Zusammenarbeit', *Press Release*, 21 February, Berlin: BMJ.

BMZ (1995) *Länderkonzept Türkei*, Bonn: BMZ.

BMZ (2000) *Länderkonzept Türkei*, Bonn: BMZ.

BMZ (2009) *Brückenschlag zwischen Europa und Asien. 50 Jahre Entwicklungszusammenarbeit Deutschland – Türkei*, Bonn: BMZ.

BMZ (2011) *Bewilligungen für die politischen Stiftungen und ihre Türkei-Arbeit*, Bonn: BMZ.

Boyer, S.P. and Katulis, B. (2008) *The Neglected Alliance: Restoring US–Turkish Relations to Meet 21st Century Challenges*, Washington, DC: Center for American Progress.

Bundeskanzleramt (2007a) *Merkel gratuliert Erdoğan zum Wahlsieg*, 23 July, Berlin: Bundeskanzleramt.

Bundeskanzleramt (2007b) *Glückwunschschreiben der Bundeskanzlerin an den türkischen Präsidenten*, 28 August, Berlin: Bundeskanzleramt.

Callaway, R.L. and Matthews, E.G. (2008) *Strategic US Foreign Assistance: The Battle between Human Rights and National Security*, Aldershot: Ashgate.

CBJ (various years) *Congressional Budget Justification on Foreign Operations*, several editions, Washington, DC: State Department.

Council of Europe (2008) *Protocol of the Parliamentary Assembly*, 23–27 June 2008, Strasbourg: Council of Europe.

Dağı, I. (2008) *Turkey between Democracy and Militarism*, Ankara: Orion.

Davutoğlu, A. (2005) *Stratejik Derinlik. Türkiye'nin Uluslararası Konumu*, Istanbul: Küre Yayınları.

Die Welt (1996) 'Schrille Töne aus Ankara – Erbakan verweigert Bonner Abgeordneten Dialog über Menschenrechte', *Die Welt*, 29 November.

DTR-IHK (German–Turkish Chamber of Commerce and Industry) (2011) *Homepage*. Online, available at: www.dtr-ihk.de (accessed 11 November 2011).

Esposito, J.L. (2004) *Islamic World. Past and Present*, Oxford: Oxford University Press.

EU Commission (2010) *Turkey 2010 Progress Report*, SEC(2010)1327, Brussels: EU Commission.

EU Commission (2011) *Turkey – Financial Assistance*. Online, available at: http://ec.europa.eu (accessed 11 November 2011).

FAZ (1996) 'Washington kritisiert Erbakans Libyen-Reise', *Frankfurter Allgemeine Zeitung*, 9 October.

FAZ (1997a) 'Die türkischen Militärs haben ein Machtwort gesprochen. Nationaler Sicherheitsrat bekräftigt Prinzipien Atatürks – Regierung ohne Islamisten?', *Frankfurter Allgemeine Zeitung*, 2 March.
FAZ (1997b) 'Ankara besteht auf Perspektive eines EU-Beitritts', *Frankfurter Allgemeine Zeitung*, 6 March.
FAZ (2001) 'Auf dem islamischen Auge blind – Deutsche Entwicklungspolitik muss umdenken', *Frankfurter Allgemeine Zeitung*, 17 November.
FAZ (2003) 'Kein Verfahren wegen deutscher Stiftungen', *Frankfurter Allgemeine Zeitung*, 31 December.
FAZ (2008) 'Die AKP wird nicht aufgelöst', *Frankfurter Allgemeine Zeitung*, 31 July.
Fischer, J. (2003) 'Rede, Deutscher Bundestag', in Bundestag (ed.) *Plenarprotokoll 15/78* (26 November), Berlin: Deutscher Bundestag, 6772.
Frankfurter Rundschau (1993) 'Ich halte am Kriterium Menschenrechte fest – Minister Carl-Dieter Spranger über die Bedingungen deutscher Entwicklungshilfe', *Frankfurter Rundschau*, 11 June.
Frankfurter Rundschau (1996a) 'Ganz gelassen wartet Bonn erst ein bisschen ab – Deutsche Politik will den neuen türkischen Regierungschef Erbakan nicht zuletzt am Verhältnis zu den Kurden messen', *Frankfurter Rundschau*, 9 July.
Frankfurter Rundschau (1996b) 'Der neue Mann in Ankara stört Bonns Gelassenheit nun doch ein wenig – Die Abkommen der türkischen Regierung mit ihren Nachbarn wecken Sorge deutscher Politiker', *Frankfurter Rundschau*, 16 August.
Frankfurter Rundschau (2008) 'Spendenbetrug für die islamische Sache', *Frankfurter Rundschau*, 18 September.
German Embassy Ankara (2009) 'Deutsche Justizministerin zu Besuch in der Türkei', *Press Release*, 23 February, Ankara: German Embassy.
German Embassy Ankara (2011) *Homepage*. Online, available at: www.ankara.diplo.de/Vertretung/ankara/de/Startseite.html (accessed 11 November 2011).
Gresh, A. (1998) 'Turkish–Israeli–Syrian Relations and their Impact on the Middle East', *Middle East Journal*, 52 (2): 188–203.
GTAI (Germany Trade and Invest) (2011) *Wirtschaftsdaten kompakt: Türkei*. Online, available at: www.gtai.de (accessed 11 November 2011).
Hofmann, S. and Reynolds C. (2007) 'Die EU-NATO-Beziehungen – Zeit für "Tauwetter"', *SWP-Aktuell*, 37, Berlin: SWP.
IRI (various years): *Annual Report*, several editions, Washington, DC: IRI.
Jenkins, G. (2009) *Between Fact and Fantasy: Turkey's Ergenekon Investigation*, Washington, DC: Central Asia-Caucasus Institute and Silk Road Studies Program.
Kapsis, J.E. (2006) 'The Failure of US–Turkish Pre-Iraq War Negotiations: An Overconfident United States, Political Mismanagement, and a Conflicted Military', *Middle East Review of International Affairs*, 10 (3): 33–45.
Karakaş, C. (2006) 'Gradual Integration: An Attractive Alternative Integration Process for Turkey and the EU', *European Foreign Affairs Review*, 11 (3): 311–31.
Karakaş, C. (2007) 'Turkey: Islam and Laicism Between the Interests of State, Politics, and Society', *PRIF Report*, 78, Frankfurt a.M.: Peace Research Institute Frankfurt.
Karakaş, C. (2008) 'Die AKP – Aufstieg, Wirken und Beinahe-Verbot einer türkischen Partei', *WeltTrends*, 62: 49–55.
Kramer, H. (2004) 'German Policy toward Turkey under the Red–Green Coalition Government (1998–2003)', in Ankara Foreign Policy Institute (ed.) *Contemporary Issues in International Politics*, Ankara: Foreign Policy Institute.

Kramer, H. (2007) 'Türkei', in S. Schmidt, G. Hellmann and R. Wolf (eds), *Handbuch zur deutschen Außenpolitik*, Wiesbaden: VS Verlag für Sozialwissenschaften.
Larrabee, F.S. (2008) *Turkey as a US Security Partner*, Washington, DC: RAND.
Leggewie, C. (ed.) (2004) *Die Türkei und Europa. Die Positionen*, Frankfurt a.M.: Suhrkamp.
Lesser, I.O. (2007) *Beyond Suspicion. Rethinking US–Turkish Relations*, Washington, DC: Woodrow Wilson International Center for Scholars.
Makovsky, A. (1999) 'Turkey', in R.S. Chase *et al.* (eds) *The Pivotal States: A New Framework for and US Policy in the Developing World*, New York, NY: W.W. Norton.
Migdalovitz, C. (2008) 'Turkey: Selected Foreign Policy Issues and US Views', *CRS Report for Congress*, no. RL34642, 29 August.
Momani, B. (2007) 'IMF Surveillance and America's Turkish Delight', *Perspectives*, 27: 5–24.
Müftüler-Baç, M. and Keyman, E.F. (2012) 'The Era of Dominant Party Politics', *Journal of Democracy*, 23 (1): 85–99.
NED (various years) *Annual Reports*, several editions, Washington, DC: NED.
New York Times (1996) 'Turkey's Troubling Deal with Iran', *New York Times*, 14 August.
New York Times (2010) 'Turkey Criticizes House Committee Vote on Armenian Killings', *New York Times*, 5 June.
ODIHR (Office for Democratic Institutions and Human Rights) (2012) *Turkey: Parliamentary Elections*. Online, available at: www.osce.org/odihr/elections/turkey (accessed 20 May 2012).
OECD (2012) *Query Wizard for International Development Statistics (QWIDS)*. Online, available at: http://stats.oecd.org/qwids (accessed 25 May 2012).
Özel, S. (2003) 'Turkey at the Polls: After the Tsunami', *Journal of Democracy*, 14 (2): 80–94.
Parla, T. (1991) 'Die Grundfunktionen des Staates in der Türkei 1920–1990', in R. Leveau and W. Ruf (eds) *Inner- und intergesellschaftliche Prozesse am Beispiel Algerien, Türkei, Deutschland und Frankreich*, Münster: LIT Verlag.
Pratt Ewing, K. (2003) 'Living Islam in the Diaspora: Between Turkey and Germany', *South Atlantic Quarterly*, 102 (2–3): 405–31.
Schiffauer, W. (2000) *Die Gottesmänner – Türkische Islamisten in Deutschland. Eine Studie zur Herstellung religiöser Evidenz*, Frankfurt a.M.: Suhrkamp.
Schröder, G. (2002) 'Rede, Deutscher Bundestag', in Bundestag (ed.) *Plenarprotokoll 15/13* (4 December), Berlin: Deutscher Bundestag, 88.
State Department (various years) *Country Reports on Human Rights Practices: Turkey*, several editions, Washington, DC: State Department.
State Department (1996) *Daily Press Briefing*, Briefer: Nicholas Burns, 1 July, Washington, DC: State Department.
State Department (1997) *Daily Press Briefing*; Briefer: Nicholas Burns, 16 June, Washington, DC: State Department.
State Department (1998) *Press Briefing by James P. Rubin*, 16 January, Washington, DC: State Department.
State Department (2002) *Press Briefing by Richard Boucher*, 4 November, Washington, DC: State Department.
State Department (2007a) *Press Briefing by Sean McCormack*, 15 August, Washington, DC: State Department.

State Department (2007b) *Press Briefing by Sean McCormack*, 27 July, Washington, DC: State Department.
State Department (2007c) *Press Briefing by Sean McCormack*, 30 April, Washington, DC: State Department.
State Department (2008) *Condoleezza Rice, Remarks at the American–Turkish Council Luncheon*, Washington, DC, 15 April, Washington, DC: State Department.
State Department (2011) *International Military Education and Training (IMET)*. Online, available at: www.state.gov (accessed 11 November 2011).
Steinbach, U. (1994) 'Die deutsch-türkischen Beziehungen – alte Freundschaft am Scheideweg?', *Südosteuropa Mitteilungen*, 34 (2): 79–84.
Taşpınar, Ö. (2005) *The Anatomy of Anti-Americanism*. Online, available at: www.brookings.edu (accessed 21 December 2012).
TAZ (1997) 'Kinkel: Keine Hysterie', *taz, die tageszeitung*, 17 August.
The Economist (2010) 'The Davutoglu Effect: All Change for Foreign Policy', *The Economist*, 23 October.
Turkish Daily News (2005) 'US Praises AKP Role in Turkey's Democratization', *Turkish Daily News*, 11 November.
USAID (2011) *Overview Turkey*. Online, available at: www.usaid.gov (accessed 11 November 2011).
US Congress (1997a) 'Questions for the Record Submitted by Mr. Frelinghuysen, Answer Submitted by State Department', in *House Committee on Appropriations: Foreign Operations, Export Financing, and Related Programs Appropriations for 1998, Part 2*. Online, available at: www.gpo.gov (accessed 21 December 2012).
US Congress (1997b) 'Questions for the Record Submitted by Ms. Pelosi, Answer Submitted by Department of Defense', in *House Committee on Appropriations: Foreign Operations, Export Financing, and Related Programs Appropriations for 1998, Part 2*. Online, available at: www.gpo.gov (accessed 21 December 2012).
US Embassy Ankara (2012) *Mission Statement*. Online, available at: http://turkey.usembassy.gov (accessed 11 May 2012).
US Overseas (2011) *US Overseas Loans and Grants, Obligations and Loan Authorizations*. Online, available at: http://gbk.eads.usaidallnet.gov (accessed 11 November 2011).
Weick, C.-T. (2000) *Die schwierige Balance. Kontinuitäten und Brüche deutscher Türkeipolitik*, Münster: LIT Verlag.
White House (2002) *Press Briefing by Ari Fleischer*, 10 December, Washington, DC: White House.
White House (2010) *Readout of the President's Call with Prime Minister Erdoğan of Turkey*, 12 October, Washington, DC: White House.
Wolfowitz, P. (2003) 'Interview with Cengiz Candar and Mehmet Ali Birand', *CNN Turk*, 6 May. Online, available at: www.defense.gov (accessed 21 December 2012).
Yavuz, H. (2003) *Islamic Political Identity in Turkey*, New York, NY: Oxford University Press.
Yürüsen, M. and Yayla, A. (1997) 'Die Türkische Wohlfahrtspartei', *Konrad-Adenauer-Stiftung (KAS) Interne Studien*, no. 134, Sankt Augustin: KAS.

7 Democracy promotion in Pakistan
The rise and fall of General Musharraf

Niels Graf and Iris Wurm

While Pakistan was already a close ally of 'the West' during the Cold War, the country reappeared on the radar screen of Western security policy around the turn of the millennium. The Pakistani nuclear tests in 1998 interfered with Western non-proliferation efforts, and the intervention in Afghanistan following 9/11 turned Pakistan into an important arena in the US-led 'war on terror'. Any Western military success in Afghanistan is hard to imagine without stability in its neighbouring country, which is the reason why since 9/11 the United States and, albeit to a lesser extent, Germany have regarded Pakistan as a strategically important security partner.

This strategic partner, however, has been a military regime for a fairly long time. In October 1999 Pervez Musharraf, at that time Chief of Army Staff of the Pakistani armed forces, took over power by means of a coup. He, thus, once again replaced a civilian government with a regime led by the army. Musharraf succeeded in expanding his power, which initially brought a certain degree of stability to the chronically unstable country. Yet, until his resignation in 2008, this also meant an end to democracy. Thus, the political project of the general was diametrically opposed to the declared normative preferences of the United States and Germany. Given Pakistan's strategic significance, both donor countries were therefore faced with serious conflicts of objectives in their foreign policy towards Pakistan.

This chapter analyses the way Germany and the United States dealt with these conflicting objectives. To this end, first, the political situation in Pakistan is summarized in order to identify the conflicts of objectives confronting the two donors. The chapter then examines German and US policies towards Pakistan and, in particular, analyses how the two donors reacted to the Musharraf regime.

Military rule and religious extremism as a conflict situation in Pakistan

The political history of Pakistan is characterized in particular by continuous fluctuation between democracy and autocracy (for an overview see Blood 1995; Cohen 2004). Elected civilian governments were forced to yield to military coups in 1958, 1977 and most recently in 1999. Especially under General

Mohammed Zia-ul-Haq, who ruled the country from 1977 to 1988, the army was able to expand its power base. As a result, Pakistan was then considered a 'state within the army' (Azfar 1991: 73). After Zia's death in 1988 elections were held again for the first time in ten years, and Pakistan formally returned to democracy. As with previous civilian governments, the new democratic regime remained chronically unstable throughout the 1990s: widespread corruption, economic mismanagement, the conflict with India over Kashmir as well as violent conflicts within Pakistan led to recurring government crises (see ul-Haq 2010).

In each of these crises it was ultimately the military that stepped in as the decisive power factor. The army traditionally sees itself as *the* supporting pillar of the country, putatively safeguarding Pakistan from the manifold domestic and external threats that endanger her survival – especially with regard to the ongoing conflict with India (see Wagner 2001: 288). Even when it is not directly ruling the country, the military plays a decisive role in many political and economic areas. At least behind the scenes, the military leadership pulls the strings (see Cohen 1998). With an active force of 650,000 personnel (Schetter and Mielke 2008: 20), the military accounts for about one-quarter of the annual state budget, has massive economic influence and is closely linked with the landed oligarchy (see Zingel 1989: 241). Attempts to establish civilian control over the armed forces thus come up against the vital interests of the military (see Siddiqa 2007).

After the 1988 elections the Pakistan People's Party (PPP) under the leadership of Benazir Bhutto, daughter of former prime minister Zulfikar Ali Bhutto, succeeded in forming a coalition government. However, accompanied by accusations of corruption, Bhutto was deposed as prime minister in 1990 – and, following her renewed election in 1993, forced to step down again in 1996. In both cases, Nawaz Sharif was elected as Bhutto's successor. Sharif's party, the Pakistan Muslim League (PML), and Bhutto's PPP have traditionally been the country's two main parties (see Bahadur 1998:147–63).

Among the most important events during Sharif's second term of office were the nuclear tests in 1998, which responded to India's nuclear tests (see Kerr and Nikitin 2010), as well as the lost Kargil War against India, which Pakistan provoked in 1999. The nuclear tests led to international sanctions (see below), and the defeat against India in the war on Kashmir intensified domestic criticism of Sharif, especially from within the army. The civilian government's meagre performance in terms of domestic and economic policy compounded the issues (see Wagner 2001: 288–9). Chief of army staff Pervez Musharraf took advantage of this situation. He took power by staging a bloodless coup in October 1999, thereby also avoiding his dismissal, which had been planned by Premier Sharif (see Follath and Stark 2007: 137–9). After suspending the constitution, Musharraf was sworn in as president and confirmed in office for another five-year term in April 2002.

In December 2003, Musharraf was able to push through a change to the constitution that further expanded his authority as president vis-à-vis government and parliament. This constitutional change was supported by a splinter group of the

PML, the 'Pakistan Muslim League-Quaid-e-Azam' (PML-Q), which after the elections in October 2002 formed a coalition government with a group of former PPP representatives and the Islamic party alliance 'Muttahida Majlis-i Amal' (MMA) (see Bearak 2000; Waseem 2006: 65; Rieck 2007: 24–6).

By contrast with his civilian predecessors, President Musharraf succeeded in systematically expanding his power. He was also able to achieve some kind of authoritarian political stabilization and even some economic success – thanks not least of all to massive financial support from the United States and other bi- and multilateral donors, which Pakistan received for its cooperation in the 'war on terror' (see below and Schetter and Mielke 2008: 44–8).[1] At the same time, even under Musharraf's rule, Pakistan's political system was regarded as relatively open in comparison with other military regimes. It was, therefore, frequently referred to as a 'liberal dictatorship' pursuing a modernization agenda (Schetter and Mielke 2008: 20).[2]

The impression of relative stability changed for the worse in 2007. On the one hand, there was an escalation of extremist militant Islamist violence. On the other, the suspension of chief justice Iftikhar Muhammad Chaudhry set off a domestic political crisis that ultimately led to Musharraf's resignation and Pakistan's return to at least formal democracy. Chaudhry's dismissal was met with widespread resistance in the media and opposition parties and led to mass protests, supported in particular by the country's lawyers' associations (see Buchsteiner 2007). Pakistan's Supreme Court withdrew its support of the president and reinstated Judge Chaudhry. Musharraf reacted by having himself re-elected as president in October 2007 – in accordance with the constitution by an assembly of national and provincial parliaments. In November 2007, he proclaimed a six-week state of emergency. Musharraf cited the worsening security situation in the country and, in particular, the threat posed by 'Islamist terrorists' as official reasons for this move. However, the measure was in fact primarily aimed at shutting out the increasingly independent judiciary and putting down protests (see Rohde 2007).

Not least due to intense international pressure, Musharraf finally backed down, announced parliamentary elections and resigned from his post as chief of army staff. The beginning of the election campaign was overshadowed by the assassination of Benazir Bhutto on 27 December 2007, who had just returned from exile in October of the same year. Bhutto's party, the PPP, won the most seats in the elections held in February 2008. United by the common goal of defeating Musharraf, the PPP was able to form a government coalition led by prime minister Yousuf Raza Gilani (PPP) that included, *inter alia*, the party of their old opponent Nawaz Sharif, the 'Pakistan Muslim League-Nawaz' (PML-N).[3] When Sharif and Bhutto's widower, Asif Zardari, announced impeachment proceedings against the president in August 2008, Musharraf decided to resign. Although the PPP/PML-N coalition failed over a disagreement on the reinstatement of the constitutional judges dismissed by Musharraf, PPP candidate Zardari won the presidential election in September 2008 by a comfortable margin (see Khalatbari 2008).

Zardari's taking of office marked the completion of Pakistan's return to a civilian-led democracy. However, for many observers this change just meant the 'return of a corrupt civilian government' (Stachoske 2009: 3). Indeed, the military continues to represent the most functional and influential institution in Pakistan's political system (see Stachoske 2009: 4–5). Furthermore, neither the conflict between the executive and the judiciary nor the increasingly violent confrontations between security forces and militant Islamists were resolved by President Zardari (see Enste 2008: 10; Stachoske 2009).

The violence by various Islamist groups in Pakistan has worsened since the turn of the century and is increasingly calling the integrity of the Pakistani state into question (for an overview see Weaver 2002; Schetter and Mielke 2008: 22–4). In addition to al-Qaeda fighters, the most important militant groups in Pakistan include the former Mujahideen as well as the Taliban and its different subgroups.[4] The Federally Administered Tribal Areas (FATA) along the northwest border with Afghanistan are the most important safe haven for these groupings.[5] Also, as a reaction to Musharraf's willingness to cooperate in the 'war on terror', starting in 2002 various militant Islamists opposed the Pakistani state with greater and greater violence. The storming of the Red Mosque in Islamabad by the Pakistani Army in July 2007 and the military action against Islamist rebels in the FATA provinces of North and South Waziristan as well as in the Swat region in 2009 represent the most intense phases of violence so far (see Schetter and Mielke 2008: 23; Stachoske 2009: 6). The situation is made more complicated by the double game being pursued by the Pakistani army and the country's main intelligence agency, Inter-Services Intelligence (ISI). While on the one hand fighting militant Islamists, the two on the other hand also support them financially as well as logistically (see Riedel 2008; Chawla 2009; Waldman 2010).[6]

In Pakistan, religiously justified violence is only supported by a radical minority of the population. Still, calls for a stronger political role for Islam enjoy widespread support within the population, thus representing a central challenge to Pakistani democracy. After all, the Islamic Republic of Pakistan was founded as an independent state for Muslims from the regions in the east and west of India with a Muslim majority. Both civilian and military governments were confronted with these demands but at the same time attempted to instrumentalize them in order to legitimize their own rule (see Haqqani 2004). For instance, in the 1990s two-time Prime Minister Sharif embraced an agenda of Islamization and strengthened the role of Islamic law on the basis of the Sharia (Rizvi 1999: 180). Musharraf at times also used Islam as a unifying element and temporarily relied on the support of Islamic parties. The two most important religious parties, the 'Jami'at-i Ulama-i Islami' (JUI) and the 'Jama'at-i Islami' (JI), have been in existence since the founding of Pakistan. They are considered to be rather moderate, even though they support Sharia and the Islamization of Pakistani society (Schetter and Mielke 2008: 19). Like the other Pakistani parties they do not directly oppose the armed forces and, as most recently under Musharraf, regularly enter into agreements with the military.

This political context in Pakistan obviously confronts external democracy promotion with numerous problems. These came to a head during the rule of President Musharraf (1999–2008) which therefore defines the core period investigated in this chapter. German and US democracy promotion was in particular confronted with the following extrinsic and intrinsic conflicts of objectives:

1   *Democracy versus donor interests (extrinsic).* With 9/11 and the beginning of the war in Afghanistan, Pakistan became a strategically indispensable partner in the region. This security interest was clearly inconsistent with actively pursuing democracy promotion. As president and chief of army staff, Musharraf was both the West's most important cooperation partner and also the central representative of the military regime created by him.
2   *Democracy versus democracy (intrinsic).* Musharraf's almost unchecked power as president and commander-in-chief of the army implied that democracy promotion would have to work towards his overthrow and a return to a civilian-led democratic government. At the same time, however, it was the chronic instability and the meagre performance of Pakistani democracy that had very much paved the way for the coup. Against the backdrop of this experience with democratic rule in the 1990s, President Musharraf could present himself as a bulwark against destabilization and Islamization, which would leave democracy little headway for gaining a foothold. Thus, the objective of a direct return to democracy competed with hopes of a gradual top-down process of 'controlled' democratization in the course of which political stabilization and social modernization would create the prerequisites for a functioning democracy in the country.

Germany: cooperative engagement with the Musharraf regime

Profile of bilateral relations

Officially, bilateral relations between Germany and Pakistan are 'traditionally friendly and good' (AA 2010). In the context of the 'war on terror' after 9/11 Pakistan took on greater importance in terms of security policy, which was also underscored by numerous visits to Pakistan by German government officials (see AA 2002: 9; Schetter and Mielke 2008: 39). However, Germany has devoted and continues to focus most of its attention in the region on Pakistan's neighbour, Afghanistan. In addition to worries that radical Islamist movements could come to power in Pakistan or assume control of its nuclear weapons, the primary concern is that destabilization in Pakistan might spill over to Afghanistan and the entire region, which gives the country 'strategic significance' (Schetter and Mielke 2008: 36).

Bilateral relations are concentrated on diplomacy and development cooperation. As a reaction to Pakistan's nuclear tests German development aid was shelved in 1998, but was gradually resumed starting in autumn 2000. Since

2000, Pakistan has been ranked a priority country of German development cooperation (see AA 2002: 12). Military cooperation, by contrast, did not play a major role (see Schetter and Mielke 2008: 38).[7] In economic terms, Pakistan has almost no relevance for Germany. There is little bilateral trade, and Pakistan is not considered very attractive for direct foreign investment (see GTAI 2012). The export of weapons to Pakistan, however, represents an 'important issue for German companies' (Schetter and Mielke 2008: 43).[8] German arms exports to the country have risen continuously since 2003 (see BICC 2009: 7–8). In 2010, the German government issued export permits worth €96.6 million, which meant that, after India, Pakistan became the most important recipient of German arms exports among developing countries (see BMWT 2011: 18).

Profile of German democracy promotion in Pakistan

Until 2009, Germany's foreign and development policy towards Pakistan scarcely involved any measures related to democracy promotion. Also, when German development aid significantly increased after 9/11, Germany concentrated on the priority areas already established in the 1990s: health, basic education and energy.[9] Projects that include the cross-cutting themes of good governance and human rights continued to be of minor significance (see Bundestag 1988: 101–2; Schetter and Mielke 2008: 40). It was not until 2009 that 'Good Governance' was established as a priority area (BMZ 2009).[10] Later, democracy-related issues also became a topic in the 'Strategic Political Dialogue' between the two countries (see below).

Correspondingly, the implementing agencies of German development cooperation have only recently begun to seriously engage in democracy promotion in Pakistan. The GTZ (later GIZ), which has had its own office in Islamabad since 1990, in 2005 adopted 'Good Governance – Democracy and Civil Society' as an objective of its work in Pakistan (see GTZ 2010). For Internationale Weiterbildung und Entwicklung gGmbH (InWEnt), which until its merger with GTZ and the DED operated only through its regional office in New Delhi, democracy promotion played no discernible role (see InWEnt 2008).[11] German financial cooperation as implemented by the KfW Development Bank also had no specific focus on democracy-related issues (see KfW 2011).

Only the political foundations have traditionally been engaged in promoting democracy in Pakistan. The FES has been represented in Islamabad by an office since 1980. Traditionally, FES mainly supported Pakistani trade unions, but since the mid-1990s it has also been active in democracy promotion in a narrower sense. In this area it has focused particularly on political education while also cooperating with civil society initiatives run by local NGOs. Since 1986, the FNS has pursued the goal of establishing a 'liberal democracy' in Pakistan. Cooperating with political and economic actors as well as civil society organizations from the liberal spectrum, FNS has focused its activities on human rights, civil liberties and economic liberalization (see FNS 2012). The HBS has had an office in Lahore since 1983 and has focused on democracy promotion since

2000, with particular emphasis on strengthening the political participation of women (see HBS 2012).

The HSS mainly organizes 'political dialogues', primarily with the involvement of academic institutions as well as party members from the entire political spectrum. Although the focus is on bilateral relations with Afghanistan, democracy-related issues are also discussed in these forums. In addition, the HSS is active in political education (see HSS 2012). The KAS, in Islamabad since 1978, ended its work in Pakistan in 1997, but resumed it in 2007. Its main focus is on strengthening the legislature and the judicial branch by advising members of parliament at the national and regional level and by carrying out training programmes for lawyers and judges (on the last point see KAS 2009).

Perception analysis

When General Musharraf assumed power in October 1999, the coup met with unanimous criticism in Germany. The German government called repeatedly and emphatically for respect for constitutional order and reinstating the overthrown government (see *Die Welt* 1999; *TAZ* 1999). All parties in the German parliament supported this stance. In May 2001, a motion jointly introduced by SPD, CDU/CSU, Bündnis 90/DIE GRÜNEN and FDP called upon the German government to persuade the Pakistani government to restore democracy 'by autumn 2002 at the latest' (SPD *et al.* 2001: 2). In the ensuing debate, however, a recurring theme was already evident that would soon become normal in the way Pakistan has been perceived after 9/11: despite all calls for the democratization of the country, its stability and its regional significance was not to be disregarded. In addition, the difficult history of Pakistan and its sobering experiences with democracy needed to be taken into account (see Bundestag 2001a: 16685–9, 16712–14).[12]

Once Musharraf had aligned himself with the West in the 'war on terror', the German government continued to take a critical view of violations of democratic principles. Now, however, the regime's stabilizing role and its willingness to cooperate were explicitly acknowledged. In this sense, Chancellor Schröder praised Musharraf's support against the Taliban despite substantial internal resistance and expressed his 'deep respect for the stabilizing role of Pakistan' (*AFP* 2001). Foreign Minister Fischer characterized Musharraf as a 'social democratic general' who continued to be a problem in terms of democracy and human rights to be sure, but who still strove to improve the well-being of his own people (*Frankfurter Rundschau* 2003). Musharraf was said to have the potential to develop Pakistan into a 'moderate centre in the Islamic world' (*Die Welt* 2001).

Only when the clashes between the president and the judiciary escalated and Musharraf declared a state of emergency in November 2007, did Germany return to explicitly calling upon him to implement democratic reforms. In a series of speeches in parliament Foreign Minister Steinmeier demanded 'that the emergency be ended as quickly as possible and a constitutional order restored', including 'immediate preparation of genuinely free and fair elections'. In this crisis anyone who wanted to achieve 'sustainable stability' was 'compelled to follow the path of rule of law and democracy. Like his predecessor, however, Steinmeier also emphasized Musharraf's achievements, stating that the president had done everything possible to present himself as an 'important ally of the entire West' (Steinmeier 2007).[13]

Against this background, the German government welcomed the resignation of Musharraf as chief of army staff and the results of the parliamentary elections in 2008 (AA 2007, 2008). However, it also emphasized the importance of a Pakistani government 'which would contribute to the stabilization of the country' (AA 2008). In this sense, the governing parties in the German parliament welcomed the 'return to democracy' under the new government of Prime Minister Gilani and President Zardari 'after nine years of military dictatorship' (Bundestag 2009a: 1), but at the same time drew attention to the fact that further efforts and reforms to stabilize Pakistan were urgently needed (see Bundestag 2009a: 314, 2009b: 22260–5; *Berliner Morgenpost* 2011; BMZ 2011b). Germany remained quite sceptical as to whether the new civilian government would be in a position to achieve this (see Bundestag 2009b: 22260–5; BMZ 2011a: 4, 9).[14]

Reaction analysis

At the time Musharraf seized power in a coup, Germany had already cancelled development cooperation with Pakistan in reaction to the 1998 nuclear tests (Schetter and Mielke 2008: 39). However, Pakistan was already identified as a priority country of German development cooperation in May 2000, and in autumn 2000 the sanctions were lifted completely (see Bundestag 2001b: 97).[15] The official rejection of the abolition of democracy thus had no lasting consequences for Musharraf. After 9/11, Germany significantly expanded its development aid to Pakistan. During a visit to Pakistan in October 2001, Chancellor Schröder and Minister for Development Wieczoreck-Zeul announced a substantial increase in funds. In addition, the German government helped the country to cut its debts by cancelling about DM50 million in bilateral debts and rescheduling a further DM500 million (see *TAZ* 2001). Increases in arms exports to Pakistan have already been mentioned above.

After 9/11 the question of democracy played no discernible role in German foreign and development policy towards Musharraf. Although the South Asia concept issued by the Foreign Office in 2002 stated the intention 'to engage more strongly in democracy promotion' in Pakistan (AA 2002: 12), this proved to be no more than lip service. Contrary to the cross-party motion in the Federal Parliament in May 2001 (SPD *et al.* 2001), the Musharraf government was not encouraged to pursue democratic reforms.[16] Development cooperation primarily focused on the strengthening of public education, with the explicit aim of combating terrorism (see Bundestag 2002: 22328).

Data on bilateral ODA to Pakistan clearly reflects this subordinate role of democracy assistance. According to OECD data from 2002 to 2004, average annual ODA in the 'Government and Civil Society' sector amounted to only $500,000. Though these payments increased to $3.6 million annually between 2005 and 2008, democracy-related measures remained marginal with a relative share of, on average, 5.4 per cent of total ODA (OECD 2012; own calculations). In addition, the projects in this sector carried out by GTZ primarily aimed at the capacity building of state institutions and therefore were conducted in close cooperation with the regime. For instance, GTZ supported the Federal Bureau of Statistics (between 2005 and 2008) and the Ministry for Women (between 2006 and 2009) (Schetter and Mielke 2008: 41).[17] A closer look at the ODA data confirms this focus on cooperative engagement: between 2005 and 2008, just short of 90 per cent of German aid in the 'Government and Civil Society' sector was channelled through the public sector, with only a small fraction targeting civil society (OECD 2012; own calculations).[18]

It was the political foundations alone that cooperated directly with independent forces within society. In doing so, however, they barely went beyond their focus on inclusive dialogue and workshops and generally stuck to the profiles described above. In no instance did their work include explicit cooperation with the Pakistani opposition. FES responded to the military coup by expanding its activities to include civil society actors, and as of 2000 it began cooperating with Pakistani NGOs to support the local population in articulating their needs to Pakistani politicians (see FES 2011). FNS continued to focus on liberal politicians and businessmen as well as on like-minded civil society organizations such as the Liberal Forum Pakistan (LFP) and the Economic Freedom Network Pakistan (ENF) (see FNS 2012). Both LFP and ENF regard themselves as independent, 'neutral' think tanks committed to promoting civil and economic freedom; however, under Musharraf they did not adopt any explicit stance opposing the regime. In addition to its rule of law program, KAS concentrated on the legislature. Yet, this work, which was aimed at members of parliament from across the entire political spectrum, began only after Musharraf's resignation.[19] The cooperation of HBS with Pakistani women's organizations has already been discussed.

The German government only began to more vigorously call for a return to democratic order by applying political pressure on the regime after Musharraf had proclaimed the state of emergency. At the end of 2007, Berlin declared that it was considering limiting development aid to Pakistan, particularly in the priority area of energy (see *AFP* 2007). Foreign Minister Steinmeier stated before parliament that 'for the time being we will only provide development aid for projects which help the people directly'. In bilateral relations Germany would not continue with business as usual, in addition, Germany's 'already restrictive arms export policy toward Pakistan' would have to be 'examined in the light of recent events' (Steinmeier 2007).[20] In addition to democracy-related questions, the fact that Musharraf was no longer in a position to guarantee political stability in Pakistan obviously played a role in these considerations. Speaking for the SPD, Walter Kolbow, for example, declared that it made 'little sense to support a dictator who opposes the democrats and cannot defeat the Islamists' (*DDP* 2007).[21]

After Musharraf had resigned, these considerations were no longer relevant. In addition to German commitment in the international group Friends of Democratic Pakistan, which Foreign Minister Steinmeier helped found in the United Nations in September 2008,[22] German development cooperation was 'nearly doubled' in intergovernmental negotiations in 2008 (Bundestag 2009a: 1–2).[23] This growing commitment certainly responded to Pakistan's increasing importance for the war in Afghanistan, but it was also a direct reaction to the formation of a 'democratically legitimized government' (Bundestag 2009a: 1). Under these new circumstances, the two governments also agreed on establishing 'Good Governance' as a priority area of German development cooperation with Pakistan (BMZ 2009). Initially intended as a temporary activity only, the BMZ declared in 2011 that there was now a 'consensus with the partner' on continuing and further expanding the new priority area (BMZ 2011a: 3).

German support in the area of good governance was explicitly conditional upon further reforms being implemented by the Pakistani government (BMZ 2011a: 9).[24] Actual activities, however, did not touch on democracy in a narrow sense, but instead focused on administrative quality and state performance: the measures carried out by GTZ/GIZ in this area were aimed at generally improving the administration, strengthening state services and reforming the tax system in particular. In addition, there is support for those state institutions that fight against gender-specific violence (see BMZ 2011a: 10; GIZ 2012).[25] German development cooperation thus continued to centre 'on less visible interventions' and still 'hardly any projects' were directly concerned with the major areas of conflict in the country (Schetter and Mielke 2008: 41).[26]

Since the political crisis in 2007/8, however, German policies have been guided by the assumption that political stability in Pakistan requires a government that is democratically legitimized, but above all capable of functioning reasonably well. The 'internal stability of Pakistan' is seen not only as the core problem of the country itself but also as an 'important prerequisite for stabilising the region' (BMZ 2011a: 4; see Steinmeier 2007; Westerwelle 2010; BMZ 2011b). From the German perspective, given limited resources and little opportunity to exert influence, the most appropriate way to contribute to political stability in the long term was to indirectly and cooperatively promote democracy by strengthening the capacity of state institutions. At the same time, the political foundations continued their activities orientated towards civil society, parties and dialogue.[27]

On the occasion of Prime Minister Gilani's visit to Germany at the end of 2009 and the signing of a new investment protection treaty, the two governments also agreed on the framework of a 'strategic political dialogue'. Initially, the aim of this dialogue was to deepen cooperation in economic, energy and security policy, with democracy-related issues playing no role at all (see Bundesregierung 2009; *Deutsche Welle* 2009). Later, however, issues of governance, the rule of law and human rights were also included as topics (see BMZ 2011a: 11).

The United States: promoting autocracy, not democracy

Profile of bilateral relations

The history of US relations with Pakistan is characterized by striking fluctuations. Over time, security and military cooperation have been the focal issues in bilateral relations (see Cohen 1997; Kux 2001). During the Cold War, Pakistan was an important ally of the United States and a cornerstone of the US alliance system in southwest Asia. In the wake of the Soviet War in Afghanistan (1979–88/89), Pakistan became a 'frontline ally' in the region, received massive military and foreign aid and served as the operational base for the US clandestine war in Afghanistan (Kronstadt 2009: 32; see Hilali 2005: 67–70).

With the withdrawal of the Soviet Union from Afghanistan and the end of the Cold War, however, Pakistan lost geostrategic significance from a US standpoint. The ongoing Pakistani nuclear programme, which had already cast a shadow over bilateral relations with the United States since the 1970s, now led to sanctions: in 1990 the US suspended almost all economic and military aid to Pakistan.[28] These sanctions were relaxed in 1995, but comprehensive punitive measures permitting only humanitarian and food aid were reintroduced following the Pakistani nuclear tests in 1998 (see Rennack 2001: 2).

This period of alienation was further reinforced by Musharraf's coup but brought to an immediate end by 9/11 and the subsequent 'war on terror', which once again led to close bilateral cooperation. In line with US preferences, this meant in particular cooperation in the fight against terrorism and the war in Afghanistan.[29] Through apparently massive threats Washington coerced Musharraf into entering the 'coalition against terror'.[30] After Pakistan agreed to support the United States in the fight against the Taliban and al-Qaeda in Afghanistan (see Rudolf et al. 2008), the US president repeatedly waived the sanctions, which remained in place in principle. As a result, Pakistan once again received very substantial US foreign assistance (see Hussain 2005: 5; Kronstadt 2009: 49).

Compared with security and military cooperation, the United States has no significant economic interest in Pakistan. Bilateral trade mainly involves cotton and textiles; Pakistan figures prominently as a sales market for US arms manufacturers only. FDI in Pakistan comes mainly from US companies. From the US perspective, however, the amount of US investment is marginal, primarily because of the difficult security situation in the country (see Kronstadt 2009: 81–4; US Chamber of Commerce/US–Pakistan Business Council 2009: 5–6).

Profile of US democracy promotion in Pakistan

In the 1990s, bilateral relations were largely at a standstill. This situation offered no appreciable opportunity for US democracy promotion in Pakistan to gain a footing. Development aid was almost completely suspended and the sanctions, which had already been imposed on Pakistan during the period of democratic rule, also limited the scope available for promoting democracy through political conditionality. As a consequence, the punitive measures adopted by the Clinton Administration in response to Musharraf's coup were only of symbolic importance (see Hussain 2005: 14; Wurm 2011: 275). After 9/11, democracy promotion was officially declared a goal of US Pakistan policy (see Kronstadt 2009: 76–7). However, in the framework of the 'war on terror' democracy promotion played a minor role, if at all.

US foreign assistance to Pakistan directly reflects these priorities. Of the total of almost $22 billion in US aid to Pakistan in fiscal years 2002 to 2011, two-thirds were directed at military and security-related measures and one-third at socioeconomic programmes (see CRS 2011). As demonstrated below, the share of democracy assistance as part of overall US aid during this period was marginal.

Due to the above-mentioned sanctions, USAID had left Pakistan in 1995, but resumed operations in 2002. As shown in more detail below, measures by the US development agency were initially focused on education, but were extended to include 'Democracy and Governance' as a priority area in 2003. In general, democracy assistance by USAID has been focused on strengthening state institutions (see USAID et al. 2010: 22; US Department of State 2010a).

The NED started supporting projects in Pakistan in 2000. NED-funded activities initially focused on educational measures for democracy and human rights as well as on strengthening political parties (see Joseph 2004). During the period under investigation, the CIPE, the IRI and the American Center for International Labor Solidarity (Solidarity Center) were the primary recipients of NED funding. Whereas CIPE and the Solidarity Center primarily supported economic associations and trade unions, IRI, which has been active in Pakistan since 2002, offered training programmes for political parties (see IRI 2011).

The NDI, which opened an office in Pakistan in 2002, also implemented an NED-funded programme to support political parties (see Joseph 2004) and, in addition, conducted election monitoring (see NDI 2012).[31] NDI's cooperation with political parties included parties across the entire political spectrum. These activities were supported not only by NED and USAID, but also by the US State Department as well as European donors.

Perception analysis

The Musharraf coup was sharply criticized by the US government. President Bill Clinton and secretary of state Madeleine Albright repeatedly condemned the coup and demanded a return to democracy.[32] However, similarly to the German case, the criticism voiced by the Clinton Administration was tempered by its emphasizing the fragility and instability of Pakistani democracy before the coup.[33] The US government thus also identified positive aspects of the new ruler – especially considering his potentially stabilizing role (Clinton 1999c; see Wurm 2011: 70–1). This latter way of looking at Musharraf clearly became dominant after 9/11 and the country's rapid entry into the 'coalition against terror'.

In this context, the Bush Administration saw Musharraf as a crucial anchor of stability, and as a result the US government refrained from discussing the undemocratic nature of the military regime. Instead, US policy was now explicitly aimed at supporting the Musharraf regime as 'a stable presence in that part of the world' (Bush 2001a). As a consequence, President Bush described Musharraf as a 'strong leader' to whom the United States was 'deeply appreciative for his leadership' (Bush 2001b; see Powell 2001). Carrying this rationale even further, the Pakistani military government was now referred to as the country's main hope for modernization and democratization. President Musharraf was said to be striving for a 'modern' Pakistan in which democracy and Islam could be reconciled with each other (see Bush 2003, 2004; Powell 2003).[34]

From 2005 on, however, the political situation in Pakistan grew increasingly unstable, while Musharraf continued to refuse to make way for a civilian government. As a response, Washington again voiced increasingly critical tones, and calls for a return to democracy re-intensified (see Bush 2006; Rice 2005, 2006). Yet the criticism remained restrained as long as the Bush Administration was convinced that it needed Musharraf in the struggle against 'extremist' forces. According to the dominant line of reasoning in Washington, only the military could keep the Islamist movements under control and thereby prevent Pakistan from collapsing (see Cohen and Chollet 2007: 8; Markey 2007: 89; Rudolf et al. 2008: 10, 13). Even when Musharraf came under mounting domestic pressure in 2007 – and, in this context, resorted to increasingly undemocratic tactics –, the US government still regarded him as an important anchor of stability.

This perception did not change until the end of 2007 when Musharraf declared the state of emergency. This move was sharply condemned by the US government (see Bush 2007; Rice 2007). However, the assassination of Bhutto meant the Bush Administration lost its favourite candidate for the forthcoming elections (see Wurm 2011: 75–6). Against this background, in February 2008 Secretary of State Rice welcomed the elections as contributing to the establishment of a 'democratic civilian government' and emphasized that the building of a coalition was indeed a 'Pakistani affair', but at the same time signalled the desire to continue cooperation with President Musharraf (Rice 2008).

The Obama Administration's attitude to the new coalition government in Pakistan was no less sceptical. From the very beginning, the US president made it clear that he expected progress in the 'war on terror' from the 'democratically elected' government (Obama 2008). Further cooperation would depend on appropriate measures being taken by the new Pakistani government (*BBC* 2009). At the same time, doubts were expressed about whether the 'very fragile' civilian government was in a position to do this (*CNN* 2009). Responding to the actions by the Pakistani Army against Islamist units in the Swat Valley, Secretary of State Clinton acknowledged Pakistan's efforts to achieve stability; yet she also emphasized the lingering distrust and the 'significant challenges' that continued to hamper bilateral relations (Clinton 2011). The US crackdown on and killing of Osama bin Laden in Pakistan in May 2011 further increased mutual distrust (see *New York Times* 2011).

Reaction analysis

The initial US reaction to the 1999 coup was entirely in line with democracy promotion. Because of the existing sanctions, however, the available means for reacting with tangible measures were limited. Nonetheless, the US administration initially held much more strictly to the principle of imposing democratic conditions on cooperation than the German government did, which had already begun to resume development cooperation in 2000. This changed, however, after 9/11, which – once more – led to a comprehensive change in US foreign policy towards Pakistan.

Immediately after Musharraf's entry into the 'coalition against terror', concerns about the military regime in Pakistan faded completely into the background. The Bush Administration continued to emphasize its interest in a democratic Pakistan.[35] However, observers agree that US policy was now almost entirely shaped by security considerations, which meant sacrificing democracy promotion in favour of cooperation with President Musharraf and the Pakistani military (Kronstadt 2009: 76–7; see also Carothers 2003: 85–6; Fair et al. 2010: 142). As compensation for Pakistani support in the 'war on terror', the sanctions were waived, the regime was showered with extensive aid, and in 2004 the country was declared a 'major non-NATO ally' (see Schaffer 2002: 179; Rudolf et al. 2008: 9; Fair et al. 2010: 150). Most US foreign assistance served security-related purposes and went directly to the Pakistani government or the military.

Between 2002 and 2011, Pakistan received approximately $14.6 billion in US military and security assistance. Of this, $8.8 billion came from the Coalition Support Funds (CSF). The CSF were controlled by the Pentagon and served to fund the Pakistani government's activities in the 'war on terror'. In the same period, US development aid to Pakistan, which also included some democracy assistance, totalled $286 million; an additional $17 million were spent on specific human rights and democracy funds (see CRS 2011). Calculations show that compensation for Pakistan's contribution to the 'war on terror', budget support for the government as well as the funding of substantial sales of US arms and training programs for the military accounted for 90 per cent of US financial support for Pakistan in fiscal years 2002 to 2007 (see Cohen 2007: 25–42; Cohen and Chollet 2007: 12–15).[36]

The prime beneficiaries of this close security cooperation were the Pakistani military and the Musharraf government. As shown above, the US administration at the time considered both as indispensable anchors of stability and crucial partners in the 'war on terror'. The United States somehow framed this policy as a kind of long-term promotion of democracy, since only the effective combating of terrorism would create conditions for a free and modern Pakistan. In actual fact, however, the military regime led by Musharraf 'was for more than five years given a "free pass" on issues of representative government' (Kronstadt 2009: 77). The massive influx of funds, the use of which was barely controlled or which from the outset could be used at the discretion of a non-democratic military regime (see Schetter and Mielke 2008: 46; Tellis 2008: 44; Fair 2009:

153), amounted to a de facto US policy of autocracy promotion vis-à-vis Pakistan.

It was only when the political crisis in Pakistan escalated in 2007 that US support for Musharraf wavered. Washington grew increasingly doubtful that the military regime was actually using the aid to fight insurgency and terrorism. Now, the Bush Administration started to call upon the Pakistani side to pursue more decisive measures (see Ibrahim 2009: 8; Kronstadt 2009: 18; Zaidi 2011: 10–11).[37] In addition, the US government responded to the military regime's loss of domestic support by more openly addressing issues of democracy and by calling upon Musharraf to lift the state of emergency, resign as army chief and hold elections. Musharraf's presidency, however, was not initially questioned; instead, Washington even sought to consolidate his political role through elections and an alliance with Benazir Bhutto (see Cohen 2007: 14; Fair et al. 2010: 141–2). The Bush Administration abandoned Musharraf only when Bhutto's assassination and Musharraf's loss in the January 2008 elections left no other option.[38] Afterwards, the US government presented itself as an unwavering supporter of the return to civilian government and greeted Zardari's election as the end of Pakistan's political crisis. In response to the relatively democratic elections in April 2008, the United States finally decided to permanently lift the sanctions announced after the coup (see Kronstadt 2009: 41–2, 90).

During the crisis of the Musharraf regime, US cooperation with Pakistan was subjected to conditions for the first time since 9/11. However, these conditions initially relied solely on Pakistan's cooperation in the 'war on terror': to the dismay of the Bush Administration, the new Democratic majority in Congress in 2007 pushed through the Implementing Recommendations of the 9/11 Commission Act, making military support and further arms transfers for fiscal year 2008 conditional upon comprehensive efforts by the Pakistani government in the fight against terrorist activities. In response to Musharraf's emergency legislation, the Consolidated Appropriations Act of December 2007 also imposed democracy-related conditions. Military aid totalling $50 million would be held back until the implementation of democratic reforms, and the use of further military aid limited to anti-terrorism measures.[39]

This stronger conditioning and monitoring of US funds as well as an increasing frustration over the lack of success in the Pakistani fight against terrorist groups continued to shape US policy under the Obama Administration. In keeping with warnings from the new US administration, the Enhanced Partnership with Pakistan Act that came into force in October 2009 confirmed that further military aid was contingent upon progress being made by the Pakistani government in the fight against terrorism. As a democracy-related condition, the act added that the Pakistani military would also have to refrain from intervening in the political process (see GAO 2011: 4; Zaidi 2011: 8–9).[40]

The new US strategy for Afghanistan and Pakistan declared the defeat of terrorist groups on Pakistani territory and the stabilization of Pakistan as core purposes of US policy (White House 2009: 1; see Fair et al. 2010: 141; White House 2010). In order to achieve this, the Obama Administration, on the one hand, aimed at expanding and better focussing military activities.[41] On the other hand, civilian aid was also increased: for fiscal years 2010 to 2014, the Enhanced Partnership Act allocated $7.5 billion for development projects that would benefit infrastructure projects in particular, but that should also be used for stabilizing fragile democratic institutions at the local and national level (see US Department of State 2009: 5–9). In accordance with the US interest in Pakistan's stability, US assistance was thus focused on improving Pakistani government capacity (see US Department of State 2009: 5–9; Kronstadt 2010: 59–60; US Department of State 2010c: 25–8).

The expansion and diversification of US assistance to Pakistan is reflected in the activities of USAID. When the development agency resumed its work in 2002 with a very small staff, its aim was 'to build support for Pakistan's decision to join the international war on terrorism and thwart further terrorist recruiting' (USAID 2003: 2). USAID initially concentrated solely on the area of education. The reasoning behind these activities, which continued throughout the period under investigation, is that, especially in the FATA, better education is necessary to combat religious extremism (cf. USAID 2003: 7; 2011a: 1). In 2003, USAID extended its programme in Pakistan and, among other things, established 'Democracy and Governance' as an additional priority area. Initially, work in this area concentrated on strengthening legislative and governmental capacity at the local level (see USAID 2003: 10–13). Politically sensitive issues and potentially conflict-ridden interventions were thus avoided, and education was given clear priority over the promotion of democracy (see USAID 2003: 23; Fair and Chalk 2006: 58, 63).

However, when the Musharraf regime was swept up in crisis, US democracy assistance in 2007 and 2008 briefly focused on supporting the announced elections (see Cohen and Chollet 2007: 15). To this end, USAID assisted the National Electoral Commission with voter registration and trained Pakistani election officials and observers. In addition, in 2008 USAID supported an election monitoring mission led by the US-based consultancy firm Democracy International (see Democracy International 2008: 1; USAID 2009). After the elections, however, USAID abandoned democracy assistance as a priority area, promoting democracy only as a cross-cutting theme (cf. USAID 2011b). Strengthening the legislature and improving government capacity once again took precedence (see USAID *et al.* 2010: 22–7; US Department of State 2010a).

By contrast, NED concentrated from the beginning on the support of civil society actors and strengthening political parties in Pakistan. Since 2000, NED's Pakistan programme has been continuously and massively expanded. Whereas in 2000 only one organization was supported with $130,000, in 2009 NED distributed nearly $4.2 million to 27 organizations (see NED *various years*).

Since 2005, IRI has regularly been one of the largest recipients of NED grants. As part of its support for political parties, IRI offered training and workshops for parties across the political spectrum. At regular intervals, it also carried out surveys of political development in Pakistan in order to increase awareness of public opinion among the parties (see IRI 2011). Before the 2008 elections, the White House reportedly tried to prevent the publication of such a survey. The results pointed to a defeat for Musharraf's party and, by exerting pressure on IRI and NED, the US government was obviously eager to prevent further weakening of Musharraf's position in Pakistan.[42]

As in the 1980s and 1990s, NDI was active both in strengthening political parties and in monitoring elections. With a view to the 2002 elections, NDI trained local election observers, and in May and October 2007 NDI itself carried out an election monitoring mission. The institute also monitored the organization of the 2008 elections and, on this occasion, voiced considerable criticism (see NDI 2007). Furthermore, since 2007, the NDI has been implementing a FATA programme that offers workshops for tribal representatives as well as leaders of political parties and civil society organizations in these provinces (see NDI 2009).

Results

Promoting democracy was not an important goal of either German or US policy towards Pakistan. After Musharraf joined the US-led 'war on terror', both donors refrained from advancing Pakistan's return to democracy. On the contrary, they supported the military regime more or less openly. Only when Musharraf came under increasing domestic pressure and was forced to initiate a transition to civilian rule did both donors return to more actively committing themselves to democracy promotion. Their activities in this regard, however, remained limited in terms of objectives and size.

A comparative look at the dimensions of democracy promotion confirms its subordinate role. In their development cooperation, both donors established a democracy-related priority area that complemented the parastatal support of the German foundations and the US party institutes for Pakistani political parties and civil society. In German development cooperation, however, this priority area was only introduced after Musharraf left office. In both cases, democracy assistance played a marginal role – even when compared only to the other areas of development cooperation. International observation in the form of election monitoring temporarily grew in importance, especially with the announcement of elections in 2007. Germany was indirectly active in this area through the EU.[43] The United States was involved in election monitoring both through its own activities as well as through the support of Pakistani actors.

Diplomatic appeals played a role immediately after the 1999 military coup and with the declaration of the state of emergency in late 2007. On both occasions, Germany and the United States were relatively explicit in calling for a return to a democratic order. In the years between these two events, however, neither government commented at all on the issue of democracy. On the contrary, they reverted to the position that on closer inspection support of Musharraf would ultimately help democracy in Pakistan. Democracy-related issues were certainly mentioned in the political dialogue between the United States and Pakistan. In the case of Germany, such a dialogue forum was established only in 2009 and began dealing with governance and human rights issues even later.

In the case of the United States, bilateral cooperation was and is officially linked to standards of democracy, even if sanctions in response to the coup tended to have a symbolic meaning only. After 9/11, by annually waiving existing sanctions, the US government essentially abandoned this policy of conditionality. It was only partially re-established by Congress after the state of emergency was declared. In the case of Germany, the coup had no recognizable impact on development cooperation, which is the focus of bilateral cooperation between Germany and Pakistan. In response to the state of emergency, the German government hinted at democratic conditions attached to its support by considering a partial suspension of specific projects.

How did Germany and the United States deal with conflicting objectives in their Pakistan policy? Following 9/11, both governments were confronted with the question to what extent they should insist on democratic standards in dealing with a military regime whose security cooperation was considered vital for military success in the war in Afghanistan. The United States consistently decided this *extrinsic conflict of objectives* in favour of its overriding security interests. The United States provided some low-profile democracy assistance, but this was clearly outweighed by massive security and military assistance that supported Musharraf's regime directly. The German government, on its part, refrained from actively promoting democracy through its development cooperation with the military regime, and in essence left it up to the United States to look after 'Western' security interests in Pakistan. However, Germany also provided direct support for the Musharraf government by means of development assistance, arms exports and diplomatic recognition.

Dominant security-related interests also shaped both donors' reactions to the *intrinsic conflict of objectives*, in which the desire for a stable Pakistan had to be balanced against the potentially destabilizing effects of democratization. Here, Germany and the United States consistently prioritized. In view of the sobering experiences with democracy in Pakistan, an increasing fear of Islamization after 9/11 and the perceived need for an effective government, both Germany and the United States saw the Musharraf government as a bulwark and a stabilizing force against Islamist tendencies. In the tradition of modernization theory, both governments also argued that the conditions for successful democratization in Pakistan would first have to be created, and to this extent honoured Musharraf's promise to modernize the country. In this way, the intrinsic conflict of objectives was clearly resolved in favour of stability. Actively promoting a return to democracy, thus, became a task for a potentially distant future. As long as Germany and the United States saw their preference for stability and their security interests preserved by Musharraf, both countries ultimately accepted the open breach of democratic order in Pakistan.

This interpretation is supported by the observation that the United States and Germany discussed – and in the case of the United States also imposed – democracy-related sanctions only when the ability of the Musharraf regime to stabilize Pakistan was openly called into question and doubts about the effectiveness of Pakistan's fight against terrorism increased. At any rate, the two donors did not adopt somewhat more serious measures of democracy promotion until Pakistan's transition to an elected civilian government – that is, at a time when the preference for stability and the interest in security no longer clashed with democracy promotion.

These reaction patterns largely correspond to theoretical expectations deriving from the respective configuration of factors that were hypothesized to determine German and US policy towards Pakistan. The preference for stability and the security interests heavily reinforced by the war in Afghanistan clearly shaped German policy and, most of the time, displaced the instrumental and normative goal of democratization. At the same time, the policy of cooperatively engaging Pakistan, which Germany had already adopted before 9/11, corresponds with the normative dispositions of a Civilian Power. In this case, however, the recourse to modernization theory meant that almost no room was left for active democracy promotion. This only changed in the course of the transition to a civilian government, but even then German democracy assistance continued to be focused on cooperating with the Pakistani government and on strengthening public-sector capacity. From the German point of view, competent state institutions represent the basic prerequisite for functioning democracy in Pakistan – a perspective that is well in line with the preference for stability, security interests as well as the assumptions about modernization and democratization typical for a Civilian Power.

US foreign policy towards Pakistan was clearly dominated by security interests. This left no scope for actively promoting democracy in Musharraf's Pakistan. US Pakistan policy thus did not correspond to the behaviour of a Freedom Fighter. On the contrary: as a result of the overwhelming interest in security cooperation with Pakistan after 9/11, the sanctions adopted in response to the 1999 coup no longer played a role, and the Bush Administration actually provided autocracy assistance to the Musharraf regime. During Pakistan's domestic political crisis, the Bush Administration called for new elections and Congress imposed some democracy-related conditions on US cooperation. At the same time, however, the US government worked towards a controlled, top-down transition led by President Musharraf. Although democracy promotion has since taken on more importance, the primary goal has continued to be strengthening existing state institutions, as in the German case. It is donor interests that explain this policy: the United States promotes democracy only if and when this serves – or, at least, does not threaten – US security interests in Pakistan. Hence, the immediate objective is stability, not democracy.

Finally, it is striking that changes of government in the donor countries did not cause significant modifications of either German or US policy towards Pakistan. This applies without restrictions for the German case. In the case of the United States, the Obama Administration has increasingly emphasized imposing stronger conditions on military cooperation as well as complementary civilian aid. This, however, does not represent a substantial change from the policies of the Bush Administration either. Rather, it continues a trend that had already started under President Bush.

Notes

1 The Musharraf Administration initially managed to contain the excessive debt and to lower the rate of inflation. At the beginning of Musharraf's rule, investment increased significantly. In terms of political reforms, Musharraf's agenda included strengthening local government and reforming the education sector. He also sought to reduce the power of the 'Madrasas', Pakistan's religious schools (see Reetz 2003).
2 As a result, Freedom House gave Pakistan a 'partly free' rating for most of Musharraf's rule. Only at the end of his presidency in 2007/8, was the country given a 'not free' rating (see Freedom House various years). Since 2002, the Polity IV index has also classified Pakistan not as an 'autocracy' but as an 'anocracy'.
3 Despite state aid for the election campaign of the governing PML-Q, Mucharraf's party was handed a clear electoral defeat (see Enste 2008: 8–9).
4 The Mujahideen were originally supported by the Pakistani intelligence agency and trained to fight India in Kashmir. Parts of these groups have close connections with al-Qaeda and the Taliban and are now opposing the Pakistani state (see Stachoske 2009: 3).
5 The former North-West Frontier Province was renamed 'Khyber Pachtunkwa' in 2010. Pakistan exercises only nominal control over this area. Such control is particularly tenuous in the case of the FATA where state organizations are scarcely present. The province of Baluchistan and the rebels of the independence movement there are a further focal point of political violence (see Schetter and Mielke 2008: 13–14, 22; Stachoske 2009: 5–6).
6 Parts of the army and the ISI are closely linked to militant Islamists. From the 1980s, these ties allowed the army and the intelligence agency to build up resistance in Kashmir and opposition to the Russian occupation forces in Afghanistan. Continuous support of the Taliban since the 1990s has also been designed to keep India from exerting influence on the political situation in Afghanistan.
7 Nevertheless, longstanding relations exist between the German and Pakistani military, and representatives of the Pakistani Army are regularly invited to Germany (see AA 2002: 9).
8 In order to deepen economic ties, German companies founded a Pakistan Working Group (see AA 2002: 11). In recent years, bilateral trade has been growing and in 2011 amounted to just under €1.7 billion (see GTAI 2012).
9 Since the mid-1990s, 'Renewable Energies and Energy Efficiency' has formed a key topic in the area of energy cooperation. No new grants are planned in the area of basic education. Measures already in progress will continue through 2015 (see BMZ 2011a: 2).
10 According to the German embassy in Islamabad, the 'Governance Sector' represents an innovation in German development policy efforts (Deutsche Botschaft Islamabad 2010).
11 The Integrated Experts of the CIM also did not support democracy projects, and the DED had no operations in Pakistan.
12 For example, Christian Ruck (CDU/CSU) emphasized that, as a democrat, one could not welcome 'the military coup in Pakistan', but that it was equally impossible to be satisfied 'with the political conditions brought about by democratic elections'. As a result, 'the choice was to either stick to the principle of democracy, or to conditionally support the government of General Musharraf in its announced efforts to bring about urgently needed reforms'. With the motion 'a decision was made for both' (Bundestag 2001: 16685). Johannes Pflug (SPD) added that one should not ignore 'the history and the conditions in Pakistan' and apply 'inappropriate standards' (Bundestag 2001: 16686–7). Werner Hoyer (FDP) referred to 'not decking the Musharraf Regime with laurel wreaths in advance and demanding the rapid and complete restoration of a functioning democratic state system in Pakistan', but still emphasized the necessity of 'measures to promote political stability in Pakistan' (Bundestag 2001: 16713–14).

13 This attitude was supported by all parties, if most strongly within Steinmeier's SPD party (see Bundestag 2007: 12761–75). For instance, Uta Zapf (SPD) commented that, despite all the criticism, it had to be asked who in Pakistan would be worth considering as a partner at all:

> The various political parties are not as we would like them to be.... None of the parties, neither Musharraf's party nor the other two major parties, has any political idea of how to stabilize this country. They only have power-related ideas about how to plunder or dominate this country.
>
> (Bundestag 2007: 12772)

14 Holger Haibach (CDU/CSU), for example, pointed out that Musharraf had indeed

> been replaced by a government legitimized in elections, but I venture to voice doubt whether this should give rise to the slightly romantic idea that as a result, so to speak, the victory march of democracy had begun in Pakistan. Even democratic elections in this and many other countries are too frequently decided along ethnic lines and not through the competition of ideas; the situation is too unstable; the rule of law, which is the indispensable prerequisite for a functioning democracy, is still insufficiently developed.
>
> (Bundestag 2009b: 22260–1)

15 For 2001, Pakistan was offered €36 million in German development assistance. According to a representative of the BMZ, this was a response to 'unequivocal signals' by India and Pakistan that they would sign the nuclear test ban treaty. The German Foreign Office termed the decision 'a political signal' (*Berliner Zeitung* 2000).

16 German parliament did not concern itself with Pakistan or its political order any more either. This did not change until a planned submarine delivery to Pakistan in May 2007 and the proclamation of the state of emergency in November 2007.

17 Generally, and in accordance with the preferences of the Pakistani government, the GTZ concentrated on gender-related issues. From 2005 to the beginning of 2010 the GTZ implemented four projects that were aimed at stronger political participation of women and at raising awareness of violence against women (see Schetter and Mielke 2008: 41; GTZ 2010).

18 In a parliamentary motion in 2008, the Green Party critically summarized German policy towards Musharraf:

> Instead of supporting democratic and civil society forces, in recent years the West has aligned itself with the authoritarian rule of President Pervez Musharraf. In accordance with this, the Pakistani Army and the intelligence agency were actively supported with arms deliveries.
>
> (Bundestag 2008: 1)

19 The KAS partner in this programme was the Pakistan Institute for Parliamentary Services (PIPS), a research service institution of the Pakistani parliament founded after Musharraf's resignation.

20 Starting in 2005, the number of applications to export armaments to Pakistan rejected by the German government has increased: whereas in each of the years 2001 to 2004 only one to four applications was rejected, from 2005 to 2010 the figure was six to ten per year (see Bundesregierung various years).

21 In a similar way, in a debate in the Federal Parliament on the state of emergency, Eckart von Klaeden (CDU/CSU) complained that the 'tragic and especially wrong thing about Musharraf's behaviour' was

> that ... by declaring the state of emergency he was opposing precisely those whom he so desperately needed to combat radical Islam, and in doing so created the

conditions for failure of the project ... which is so enormously important for our own security.

(Bundestag 2007: 12764)

Similar statements are also found in Holger Haibach's speech (CDU/CSU) (Bundestag 2007: 12771).

22 The 'Friends of Democratic Pakistan' pursued the primary objective of supporting Pakistan in overcoming its difficult financial problems. In addition to Germany, 23 other countries participate in this group, including the United States and the United Kingdom (see *FAZ* 2008).
23 German ODA has been continuously increasing since 2003: after an initial peak in 2002 ($76.6 million), German ODA to Pakistan totalled $36.3 million in 2003, $46.2 million in 2005, and $71 million in 2007, $110.8 million in 2009, and $156.6 million in 2010 (see OECD 2012).
24 The most recent BMZ Pakistan strategy (BMZ 2011a: 9) generally emphasizes that development cooperation should concentrate on areas 'in which there is substantial Pakistani ownership and willingness to change'. In cases of 'lack of progress in reforms', the paper provides for 'the option of re-assessing cooperation in the area in question'.
25 As of 2012, the GIZ was carrying out three programmes in the area of 'Good Governance' (on gender, taxation and administrative reform), which were to run until 2020. The fourth programme in this area (support to the Federal Bureau of Statistics) expired in 2011 (see GIZ 2012).
26 The following observation holds true for European Pakistan policy in general: Europe 'excludes highly charged security problems and awkward questions relating to political reform and focuses strongly on development aid in the education and finance sectors' (Rudolf *et al.* 2008: 26).
27 At the initiative of the military attaché of the German embassy in Islamabad, KAS has recently started a programme to improve civil–military relations. In the framework of this programme, high ranking Pakistani generals and members of parliament are invited to Germany.
28 With these sanctions, the Pressler Amendment was applied for the first time. This amendment, passed by the US Congress in 1985, linked aid to Pakistan to the condition that the country possess no nuclear warheads and stipulated that US assistance should contribute to reducing the risk of nuclear armament by Pakistan (see Rennack 2001: 2; Rudolf *et al.* 2008: 8; Kronstadt 2009: 32).
29 Furthermore, the nuclear power Pakistan is also a 'critical partner' of the United States in the area of nuclear proliferation (Rudolf *et al.* 2008: 10).
30 Specifically, the United States demanded that Pakistan adopt seven measures, among them the handover of intelligence information, flyover and landing rights for US military aircraft and access to Pakistani military facilities (see National Commission on Terrorist Attacks 2004: 331). The US government is reported to have openly threatened Pakistan with military action if it refused to cooperate (see Musharraf 2006: 201; Rudolf *et al.* 2008: 9).
31 NDI had already carried out election observation missions in Pakistan in the 1980s and 1990s.
32 'We don't like it when military leaders forcibly displace elected governments, and we made that clear.... I would hope that the military government will soon transition to a civilian one' (Clinton 1999a; see also Albright 1999; 2000; Clinton 1999b, 2000).
33 By referring to the 'events in Pakistan' as 'another setback to Pakistani democracy' (Clinton 1999b), Clinton explicitly qualified the coup as just one instance of a series of blows to democracy. For an earlier US assessment of Pakistani democracy, see Christopher (1993).
34 The report of a bipartisan commission, established by the US Congress to review the

9/11 terror attacks, also identified Musharraf as 'the best hope for stability' and recommended that the US government should support Musharraf in his course of 'enlightened moderation' (National Commission on Terrorist Attacks 2004: 369).
35 This was evident, for example, in the 'strategic dialogue' to which the governments of the United States and Pakistan agreed in March 2006. This strategic dialogue envisaged, among other things, increased cooperation on democracy-related issues (see White House 2006). During the 2010 meeting of the strategic dialogue, however, democracy was no longer among the areas on which increased cooperation had been agreed (see US Department of State 2010b).
36 A detailed list of US arms shipments to Pakistan has been published by the US Government Accountability Office (GAO 2011: 14). In addition to the above measures, the US–Pakistan Defense Consultative Group (DCG), inactive between 1997 and 2001, was reinstated. The DCG coordinates military cooperation and specifically counterterrorism measures. Furthermore, economic cooperation with Pakistan was also expanded (see Hussain 2005: 6; Kronstadt 2009: 33, 57, 84; Fair *et al.* 2010: 151–4).
37 At the end of 2007, a US Department of Defense audit concluded that previous payments had not served their purpose, and a greater focus on counterinsurgency was needed. A 2008 report by the GAO supported this conclusion, noting that the Taliban would have a safe haven in the FATA in particular, and that US foreign policy had no recognizable strategy for changing this. At the same time, the GAO called for more intensive monitoring of the use of funds (see GAO 2008: 27–8; Ibrahim 2009: 8; Kronstadt 2009: 51).
38 For example, John Negroponte, Secretary of State Rice's deputy, pointed out in the spring of 2008 that the future role of Musharraf must be a result of 'the internal Pakistani political process' (cited in Kronstadt 2009: 42).
39 See the detailed discussions in Rudolf *et al.* (2008: 19–20); Tellis (2008: 38–9) and Kronstadt (2009: 91–2).
40 In reality, these conditions only applied to military aid distributed as FMF. Other forms of military assistance, such as payments from the CSF, or the Pakistan Counterinsurgency Capability Fund (PCCF), were not affected by these regulations (see GAO 2011: 6).
41 See Ahmad (2010: 200); Kronstadt (2010: 33, 57–8) and Rudolf (2010: 27–9). Specifically, military aid tailored to counterinsurgency measures was extended. This is reflected for example in the terms of the PCCF. This fund was established by the Supplemental Appropriations Act in early 2009 and aimed at making counterinsurgency efforts by the Pakistani military more effective. At the same time, US drone strikes in Pakistan's tribal areas have steadily intensified since 2009 (see Ahmad 2010: 195; Rudolf 2010: 27–8; GAO 2011: 3).
42 This incident was reported in different interviews conducted in Washington, DC. Meanwhile, however, such surveys are also officially supported by USAID (see USAID *et al.* 2010: 22).
43 The EU dispatched an election monitoring mission with German participation during the 2008 elections (see EU 2008).

References

AA (2002) *Aufgaben der deutschen Außenpolitik. Südasien am Beginn des 21. Jahrhunderts*, Berlin: Auswärtiges Amt.

AA (2007) 'Bundesminister Steinmeier: Pakistan muss zur verfassungsmäßigen Ordnung zurückkehren', *Press Release*, 4 November, Berlin. Online, available at: www.auswaertiges-amt.de (accessed 15 October 2010).

AA (2008) *Nach den Parlamentswahlen in Pakistan*, 20 February, Berlin. Online, available at: www.auswaertiges-amt.de (accessed 15 October 2010).
AA (2010) 'Pakistan', *Countries A to Z*, May. Online, available at: www.auswaertiges-amt.de (accessed 29 July 2010).
AFP (2001) 'Der Zwischenstopp in Pakistan wurde doppelt so lange wie geplant. Schröder sagt Bürgschaften und Hilfe bei Schuldenabbau zu', *AFP*, 28 October.
AFP (2007) 'Berlin erwägt Einschränkung der Entwicklungshilfe für Pakistan', *AFP*, 5 November.
Ahmad, I. (2010) 'The US Af-Pak Strategy: Challenges and Opportunities for Pakistan', *Asian Affairs. An American Review*, 37: 191–209.
Albright, M. (1999) *Interview on CNN's 'Late Edition' with Wolf Blitzer*, 17 October, Washington, DC.
Albright, M. (2000) 'Op-Ed on the President's Trip to South Asia', *Diario las Americas*, 2 April, Miami, FL.
Azfar, K. (1991) 'Constitutional Dilemmas in Pakistan', in S.J. Burki and C. Baxter (eds) *Pakistan Under the Military: Eleven Years of Zia-ul-Haq*, Boulder, CO: Westview Press.
Bahadur, K. (1998) *Democracy in Pakistan: Crises and Conflicts*, New Delhi: Har-Anand Publications.
BBC (2009) 'Pentagon Chief in Taleban Warning', *BBC*, 23 April. Online, available at: http://news.bbc.co.uk (accessed 4 January 2012).
Bearak, B. (2000) 'Pakistan Court Upholds Coup but Orders Reforms', *New York Times*, 13 May. Online, available at: www.nytimes.com (accessed 8 March 2012).
Berliner Morgenpost (2011) 'Reise mit Hindernissen', *Berliner Morgenpost*, 9 January, 2.
Berliner Zeitung (2000) 'Sanktionen "Eindeutige Signale"', *Berliner Zeitung*, 6 October.
BICC (Bonn International Center for Conversion) (2009) *Informationsdienst Sicherheit, Rüstung und Entwicklung in Empfängerländern deutscher Rüstungsexporte. Länderportrait Pakistan*. Online, available at: www.bicc.de (accessed 20 October 2011).
Blood, P.R. (1995) *Pakistan: A Country Study*, Washington, DC: US Government Printing Office.
BMWT (Bundesministerium für Wirtschaft und Technologie) (2011) *Bericht der Bundesregierung über ihre Exportpolitik für konventionelle Rüstungsgüter im Jahre 2010*, Berlin: BMWT.
BMZ (2009) 'Pakistan', December. Online, available at: www.bmz.de (accessed 30 July 2010).
BMZ (2011a) *Länderkonzept Pakistan*, Bonn: BMZ.
BMZ (2011b) 'Dirk Niebel mahnt Reformen in Pakistan an', *Press Release*, 17 June. Online, available at: www.bmz.de (accessed 24 November 2011).
Buchsteiner J. (2007) 'Demonstranten stützen "unbeugsamen" Richter', *Frankfurter Allgemeine Zeitung*, 16 March. Online, available at: www.faz.net (accessed 15 October 2011).
Bundesregierung (various years) *Bericht der Bundesregierung über ihre Exportpolitik für konventionelle Rüstungsgüter*, several editions, Berlin: Bundesministerium für Wirtschaft und Technologie.
Bundesregierung (2009) *Pressestatements der Bundeskanzlerin und des pakistanischen Premierministers Syed Yousuf Raza Gilani*, 1 December. Online, available at: www.bundesregierung.de (accessed 20 October 2011).
Bundestag (1988) *Siebenter Bericht zur Entwicklungspolitik der Bundesregierung.*

Unterrichtung durch die Bundesregierung (BT-Drs. 11/2020, 16 March), Bonn: Deutscher Bundestag.
Bundestag (2001a) *Stenographischer Bericht, 170. Sitzung* (Plenarprotokoll 14/170, 17 May), Berlin: Deutscher Bundestag.
Bundestag (2001b) *Elfter Bericht zur Entwicklungspolitik der Bundesregierung. Unterrichtung durch die Bundesregierung* (BT-Drs. 14/6456, 7 June), Berlin: Deutscher Bundestag.
Bundestag (2002) *Stenographischer Bericht, 225. Sitzung* (Plenarprotokoll 14/225, 15 March), Berlin: Deutscher Bundestag.
Bundestag (2007) *Stenografischer Bericht, 123. Sitzung* (Plenarprotokoll 16/123, 8 November), Berlin: Deutscher Bundestag.
Bundestag (2008) *Antrag der Fraktion Bündnis 90/Die Grünen. Für eine umfassende Strategie zur demokratieverträglichen und zivilgesellschaftlichen Stabilisierung Pakistans* (BT-Drs. 16/8752), Berlin: Deutscher Bundestag.
Bundestag (2009a) *Antrag der Fraktionen der CDU/CSU und SPD. Pakistan stabilisieren und seine demokratische Entwicklung vorantreiben* (BT-Drs. 16/12432), Berlin: Deutscher Bundestag.
Bundestag (2009b) *Stenografischer Bericht, 205. Sitzung* (Plenarprotokoll 16/205, 12 February), Berlin: Deutscher Bundestag.
Bush, G.W. (2001a) 'Remarks on United States Financial Sanctions Against Terrorists and Their Supporters and an Exchange With Reporters', *Public Papers of the President*, 24 September, Washington, DC, 1149–54.
Bush, G.W. (2001b) 'Remarks Following Discussions with President Pervez Musharraf of Pakistan and an Exchange with Reporters in New York City', *Public Papers of the President*, 10 November, Washington, DC, 1181–3.
Bush, G.W. (2003) 'The President's News Conference with President Pervez Musharraf of Pakistan at Camp David, Maryland', *Public Papers of the President*, 24 June, Washington, DC, 681–5.
Bush, G.W. (2004) 'Remarks Following Discussions with President Pervez Musharraf of Pakistan and an Exchange with Reporters', *Public Papers of the President*, 4 December, Washington, DC, 3041–4.
Bush, G.W. (2006) 'Remarks to the Asia Society', *Public Papers of the President*, 22 February, Washington, DC, 314–21.
Bush, G.W. (2007) 'The President's News Conference with President Nicolas Sarkozy of France in Mount Vernon, Virginia', *Public Papers of the President*, 7 November, Washington, DC. Online, available at: www.presidency.ucsb.edu (accessed 13 October 2011).
Carothers, T. (2003) 'Promoting Democracy and Fighting Terror', *Foreign Affairs*, 81 (1): 84–97.
Chawla, S. (2009) *Pakistan's Military and Its Strategy*, New Delhi: KW Publishers/Centre for Air Power Studies.
Christopher, W. (1993) *Statement at Senate Confirmation Hearing*, 13 January, Washington, DC.
Clinton, B. (1999a) 'The President's News Conference', *Public Papers of the President*, 14 October, Washington, DC, 1777–90.
Clinton, B. (1999b) 'Statement on the Military Coup d'Etat in Pakistan', *Public Papers of the President*, 13 October, Washington, DC, 1767.
Clinton, B. (1999c) 'Remarks on Budget Negotiations and an Exchange with Reporters', *Public Papers of the President*, 18 October, Washington, DC, 1808–11.

Clinton, B. (2000) 'Television Address to the People of Pakistan From Islamabad', 25 March, *Weekly Compilation of Presidential Documents* 36 (13): 635.
Clinton, H.R. (2011) *Remarks at the Launch of the Asia's Society's Series of Richard C. Holbrooke Memorial Address*, 18 February, New York, NY. Online, available at: www.state.gov (accessed 4 January 2011).
CNN (2009) 'Obama Transcript: First 100 days', *CNN*, 29 April. Online, available at: www.cnn.com (accessed 4 January 2012).
Cohen, C. (2007) 'A Perilous Course. US Strategy and Assistance to Pakistan', *CSIS Report*, Washington, DC: Center for Strategic and International Studies.
Cohen, C. and Chollet, D. (2007) 'When $10 Billion Is Not Enough: Rethinking US Strategy toward Pakistan', *Washington Quarterly*, 30 (2): 7–19.
Cohen, S.P. (1997) 'The United States, India, and Pakistan. Retrospect and Prospect', *ACDIS Occasional Paper*, University of Illinois: Program in Arms Control, Disarmament, and International Security.
Cohen, S.P. (1998) *The Pakistan Army*, Oxford: Oxford University Press.
Cohen, S.P. (2004) *The Idea of Pakistan*, Washington, DC: Brookings Institution Press.
CRS (Congressional Research Service) (2011) *Direct Overt US Aid Appropriations and Military Reimbursements to Pakistan. FY 2002–2012*, 9 August, Washington, DC. Online, available at: www.fas.org (accessed 10 October 2011).
DDP (2007) 'Bundestag verurteilt Ausnahmezustand in Pakistan', *DDP*, 8 November.
Democracy International (2008) *US Election Observation Mission to Pakistan. General Elections 2008. Final Report*, Bethesda, MD: Democracy International.
Deutsche Botschaft Islamabad (2010) *Development Cooperation with Pakistan*. Online, available at: www.islamabad.diplo.de (accessed 30 July 2010).
Deutsche Welle (2009) 'Deutschland und Pakistan rücken zusammen', *Deutsche Welle*, 1 December. Online, available at: www.dw-world.de (accessed 20 October 2011).
Die Welt (1999) 'Pakistan: Islamisten könnten durch Putsch Einfluss gewinnen', *Die Welt*, 13 October.
Die Welt (2001) 'Fischer in Pakistan: "Die Deutschen müssen das durchstehen"', *Die Welt*, 20 October, 5.
Enste, G. (2008) *Politischer Jahresbericht Pakistan/Afghanistan 2007/2008*, Heinrich Böll Stiftung Pakistan. Online, available at: www.boell.de (accessed 18 August 2010).
EU (2008) *EU Election Observation Mission to Pakistan 2008*. Online, available at: www.eueompakistan.org (accessed 15 October 2011).
Fair, C.C. (2009) 'Time for Sober Realism: Renegotiating US Relations with Pakistan', *Washington Quarterly*, 32 (2): 149–72.
Fair, C.C. and Chalk, P. (2006) *Fortifying Pakistan: The Role of US Internal Security Assistance*, Washington, DC: US Institute of Peace Press.
Fair, C.C., Crane, K., Chivvis, C.S., Puri, S. and Spirtas, M. (2010) *Pakistan: Can the United States Secure an Insecure State?*, Santa Monica, CA: RAND.
FAZ (2008) 'Die Freunde eines demokratischen Pakistans', *Frankfurter Allgemeine Zeitung*, 27 October. Online, available at: www.faz.net (accessed 5 January 2012).
FES (2011) *FES Pakistan – Project History*. Online, available at: www.fes.org (accessed 5 February 2012).
FNS (2012) *Our Work in Pakistan*. Online, available at: http://southasia.fnst.org (accessed 5 February 2012).
Follath, E. and Stark, H. (2007) 'Wo der Terror wohnt', *Der Spiegel*, 38, September, 134–52.
Frankfurter Rundschau (2003) 'Besuch eines Geschäftspartners: In Berlin sucht Pakistans

Präsident Musharraf vor allem internationale Anerkennung', *Frankfurter Rundschau*, 30 June, 6.

Freedom House (various years) *Freedom in the World: Pakistan*, several editions, Washington, DC: Freedom House.

GAO (2008) *Combating Terrorism: Increased Oversight and Accountability Needed over Pakistan Reimbursement Claims for Coalition Support Funds*, Washington, DC. Online, available at: www.gao.gov (accessed 4 January 2012).

GAO (2011) *Pakistan Assistance: Relatively Little of the $3 Billion in Requested Assistance Is Subject to State's Certification of Pakistan's Progress on Nonproliferation and Counterterrorism Issues*, 19 July, Washington, DC. Online, available at: www.gao.gov (accessed 4 January 2012)

GIZ (2012) *Programme und Projekte in Pakistan*. Online, available at: www.gtz.de (accessed 5 February 2012).

GTAI (Germany Trade and Invest) (2012) *Aktuelle Trends aus Pakistan*, 24 February. Online, available at: www.gtai.de (accessed 26 February 2012).

GTZ (2010) *Die GTZ in Pakistan*. Online, available at: www.gtz.de (accessed 30 July 2010).

Haqqani, H. (2004) 'The Role of Islam in Pakistan's Future', *Washington Quarterly*, 28 (1): 85–96.

HBS (2012) *Heinrich-Böll-Stiftung Pakistan*. Online, available at: www.boell-pakistan.org (accessed 5 February 2012).

Hilali, A.Z. (2005) *US–Pakistan Relationship: Soviet Invasion of Afghanistan*, Aldershot: Ashgate Publishing.

HSS (2012) *Pakistan/Afghanistan Office*. Online, available at: www.hsf-pak-afghan.org (accessed 5 February 2012).

Hussain, T. (2005) 'US–Pakistan Engagement, the War on Terrorism and Beyond', *USIP Special Report* no. 145, Washington, DC: United States Institute of Peace.

Ibrahim, A. (2009) 'US Aid to Pakistan – US Taxpayers Have Funded Pakistani Corruption', *Belfer Center Discussion Paper* #2009–06, Cambridge, MA: Belfer Center for Science and International Affairs.

InWEnt (2008) 'InWEnt-Vertretung in New Delhi eröffnet', *Press Release*, 27 February. Online, available at: www.openpr.de (accessed 30 July 2010).

IRI (2011) *Pakistan Overview*, July. Online, available at: www.iri.org (accessed 4 January 2012).

Joseph, B. (2004) *Pakistan: A Human Rights Update*, 13 May, Washington, DC. Online, available at: www.ned.org (accessed 4 January 2012).

KAS (2009) *Pakistan-Broschüre, KAS Pakistan Office*. Online, available at: www.kas.de (accessed 30 July 2010).

Kerr, P. and Nikitin, M.B. (2010) 'Pakistan's Nuclear Weapons: Proliferation and Security Issues', *CRS Report for Congress*, no. RL 34248, 2/2010, Washington, DC: Congressional Research Service.

KfW (2011) *Pakistan*. Online, available at: www.kfw-entwicklungsbank.de (accessed 20 October 2011).

Khalatbari, B. (2008) 'Vom Witwer zum Präsidenten. Asif Ali Zardari ist Pakistans neues Staatsoberhaupt', *Konrad Adenauer Stiftung Länderbericht*, 7 September. Online, available at: www.kas.de (accessed 30 July 2010).

Kronstadt, K.A. (2009) 'Pakistan–US Relations', *CRS Report for Congress*, no. RL 33498, February, Washington, DC: Congressional Research Service.

Kronstadt, K.A. (2010) 'Pakistan: Key Current Issues and Developments', *CRS Report for Congress*, no. R41307, June, Washington, DC: Congressional Research Service.

Kux, D. (2001) *The United States and Pakistan, 1947–2000. Disenchanted Allies*, Baltimore, MD: The Johns Hopkins University Press.

Markey, D. (2007) 'A False Choice in Pakistan', *Foreign Affairs*, 86 (4): 85–102.

Musharraf, P. (2006) *In the Line of Fire. A Memoir*, New York, NY: Free Press.

National Commission on Terrorist Attacks (2004) *The 9/11 Commission Report*, Washington, DC. Online, available at: www.gpo.gov (accessed 30 July 2010).

NDI (2007) *Statement of the NDI Pre-Election Delegation to Pakistan*, 21 October, Pakistan. Online, available at: www.ndi.org (accessed 5 February 2012).

NDI (2009) *New Report Details Urgent Need for Democratic Rule in Pakistan's Tribal Areas to Stem Unrest*, 26 February. Online, available at: www.ndi.org (accessed 5 February 2012).

NDI (2012) *Pakistan*, Washington, DC. Online, available at: www.ndi.org (accessed 4 January 2012).

NED (various years) *Annual Report*, several editions, Washington, DC. Online, available at: www.ned.org (accessed 4 January 2012).

New York Times (2011) 'Obama Warns Pakistanis on Militants', *New York Times*, 7 October, A4.

Obama, B. (2008) *Meet the Press Transcript*, 7 December. Online, available at: www.msnbc.msn.com (accessed 4 January 2012).

OECD (2012) *Development Database on Aid Activities: CRS online*. Online, available at: http://stats.oecd.org (accessed 20 February 2012).

Powell, C. (2001) *Interview on Meet the Press*, 23 September, Washington, DC. Online, available at: http://2001-2009.state.gov/secretary/former/powell (accessed 4 January 2012).

Powell, C. (2003) *Interview by Robin Wright of the Washington Post*, 29 December, Washington, DC. Online, available at: http://2001-2009.state.gov/secretary/former/powell (accessed 4 January 2012).

Reetz, D. (2003) 'Pakistan. Internationaler Partner oder Problemfall?', *FES-Analyse*, Bonn: Friedrich-Ebert-Stiftung.

Rennack, D.E. (2001) 'India and Pakistan: Current US Economic Sanctions', *CRS Report for Congress*, no. RS 20995, updated 12 October, Washington, DC: Congressional Research Service.

Rice, C. (2005) *Interview with Reuters News Agency*, 11 March, Washington, DC. Online, available at: http://2001-2009.state.gov/secretary (accessed 4 January 2012).

Rice, C. (2006) *Briefing En Route to Islamabad*, 26 June, Pakistan. Online, available at: http://2001-2009.state.gov/secretary (accessed 4 January 2012).

Rice, C. (2007) *Interview with Zain Verjee of CNN*, 3 November, Istanbul, Turkey. Online, available at: http://2001-2009.state.gov/secretary (accessed 4 January 2012).

Rice, C. (2008) *Briefing on Recent Africa Trip and Upcoming Asia Trip*, 22 February, Washington, DC. Online, available at: http://2001-2009.state.gov/secretary (accessed 4 January 2012).

Rieck, A. (2007) 'Pakistan zwischen Demokratisierung und "Talibanisierung"', *Aus Politik und Zeitgeschehen*, 39, 24–32.

Riedel, B. (2008) 'Pakistan and Terror: The Eye of the Storm', *Annals of the Academy of Political and Social Science*, 618 (1): 31–45.

Rizvi, H.-A. (1999) 'Pakistan in 1998: The Polity under Pressure', *Asian Survey* 39 (1): 177–84.

Rohde, D. (2007) *Pakistani Sets Emergency Rule, Defying the US*, 4 November, Islamabad. Online, available at: www.nytimes.com (accessed 10 October 2011).

Rudolf, P. (2010) 'Barack Obamas Afghanistan/Pakistan-Strategie. Analyse und Bewertung', *SWP-Studie*, Berlin: Stiftung Wissenschaft und Politik.

Rudolf, P., Wagner, C. and Fröhlich, C. (2008) 'Die USA und Pakistan. Probleme einer Partnerschaft', *SWP-Studie*, Berlin: Stiftung Wissenschaft und Politik.

Schaffer, T.C. (2002) 'US Influence on Pakistan: Can Partners Have Divergent Priorities?', *Washington Quarterly*, 26 (1): 169–83.

Schetter, C. and Mielke, K. (2008) 'Entwicklungszusammenarbeit mit Pakistan – eine Analyse aus der Ankerlandperspektive', *DIE Discussion Paper*, Bonn: Deutsches Institut für Entwicklungspolitik

Siddiqa, A. (2007) *Military Inc. Inside Pakistan's Military Economy*, London: Pluto Press.

SPD/CDU/CSU/BÜNDNIS 90/DIE GRÜNEN/FDP (2001) *Für die demokratische Erneuerung Pakistans, Antrag der Fraktionen SPD, CDU/CSU, BÜNDNIS 90/DIE GRÜNEN und FDP* (BT-Drs. 14/5684), Berlin: Deutscher Bundestag.

Stachoske, B. (2009) 'Das politische System Pakistans zwei Jahre nach dem Wechsel: Die Zementierung eines kritischen Zustandes?', *GIGA Focus*, no. 12, Hamburg: German Institute of Global and Area Studies.

Steinmeier, F.-W. (2007) *Rede von Bundesaußenminister Frank-Walter Steinmeier im Deutschen Bundestag in der aktuellen Stunde zu den jüngsten Entwicklungen in Pakistan*, 8 November, Berlin. Online, available at: www.auswaertigesamt.de (accessed 15 August 2011).

TAZ (1999) 'Schelte für Putschisten', *taz, die tageszeitung*, 14 October, 1.

TAZ (2001) 'Mehr Entwicklungshilfe für Pakistan', *taz, die tageszeitung*, 30 October, 2.

Tellis, A.J. (2008) *Pakistan and the War on Terror: Conflicted Goals, Compromised Performance*, Washington, DC: Carnegie Endowment for International Peace.

ul-Haq, N. (2010) 'Governance and Democracy in Pakistan', *IPRI Journal*, X (1): 1–21.

USAID/Department of State/Department of Defense (2010) *Quarterly Progress and Oversight Report on the Civilian Assistance Program in Pakistan*, 31 December, Washington, DC. Online, available at: http://oig.usaid.gov (accessed 19 February 2012).

USAID (2003) *USAID/Pakistan: Interim Strategic Plan May 2003–September 2006*, 5/2003, Islamabad. Online, available at: http://pdf.usaid.gov (accessed 4 January 2012).

USAID (2009) *Partnership for Democracy and Governance. Fact Sheet*, July, Washington, DC. Online, available at: www.usaid.gov (accessed 5 February 2012).

USAID (2011a) *Education in Pakistan Working Paper*, April. Online, available at: www.usaid.gov (accessed 5 February 2012).

USAID (2011b) *Pakistan: Country Profile*, September. Online, available at: www.usaid.gov (accessed 5 February 2012).

US Chamber of Commerce/US–Pakistan Business Council (2009) *Strengthening the US–Pakistan Economic Partnership: Policy Recommendations to the Obama Administration and Members of Congress*, Washington, DC. Online, available at: www.uschamber.com (accessed 5 February 2012).

US Department of State (2009) *Pakistan Assistance Strategy Report*, 14 December, Washington, DC. Online, available at: www.state.gov (accessed 4 January 2012).

US Department of State (2010a) *Pakistan: Advancing Freedom and Democracy Reports*, May, Washington, DC. Online, available at: www.state.gov (accessed 4 January 2012).

US Department of State (2010b) *US–Pakistan Strategic Dialogue at the Ministerial Level*, 25 March, Washington DC. Online, available at: www.state.gov (accessed 14 October 2010).

US Department of State (2010c) *Afghanistan and Pakistan Regional Stabilization Strategy*, February, Washington, DC. Online, available at: www.state.gov (accessed 4 January 2012).

Wagner, C. (2001) 'Parteien, Staat und Demokratie in Pakistan' in U. Eith, and G. Mielke (eds) *Gesellschaftliche Konflikte und Parteiensysteme. Länder- und Regionalstudien*, Wiesbaden: Westdeutscher Verlag.

Waldman, M. (2010) 'The Sun in the Sky: The Relationship between Pakistan's ISI and Afghan Insurgents', *Crisis States Discussion Papers*, no. 18, London: London School of Economics.

Waseem, M. (2006) *Democratization in Pakistan: a Study of the 2002 Elections*, Oxford: Oxford University Press.

Weaver, M.A. (2002) *Pakistan: in the Shadow of Jihad and Afghanistan*, New York, NY: Farrar, Straus & Giroux.

Westerwelle, G. (2010) *Grundsatzrede von Bundesaußenminister Westerwelle bei der Deutschen Gesellschaft für Auswärtige Politik*, 21 October, Berlin. Online, available at: www.auswaertiges-amt.de (accessed 15 November 2011).

White House (2006) *Joint Statement on United States-Pakistan Strategic Partnership*, Washington, DC, 4 March. Online, available at: http://merln.ndu.edu (15 October 2010).

White House (2009) *White Paper of the Interagency Policy Group's Report on US Policy toward Afghanistan and Pakistan*, Washington, DC. Online, available at: www.whitehouse.gov (accessed 4 January 2012).

White House (2010) *Overview of the Afghanistan and Pakistan Annual Review*, 16 December, Washington, DC. Online, available at: www.whitehouse.gov (accessed 4 January 2012).

Wurm, I. (2011) 'Fremde oder Freunde? Die Kooperationspolitik des demokratischen Hegemons USA gegenüber seinen autokratischen Partnern Saudi-Arabien und Pakistan', unpublished doctoral thesis, Goethe University Frankfurt a.M.

Zaidi, S.A. (2011) 'Who Benefits from US Aid to Pakistan?', *Carnegie Policy Outlook*, 21 September, Washington, DC: Carnegie Endowment for International Peace.

Zingel, W.-P. (1989) 'Das Militär in Pakistan: Garant oder Bedrohung nationaler Einheit und wirtschaftlicher Entwicklung?' in R. Steinweg (ed.) *Militärregime und Entwicklungspolitik*, Frankfurt a.M.: Suhrkamp.

8 Democracy promotion in Belarus
Dealing with 'Europe's last dictatorship'

Azar Babayev

Not least due to its geographic proximity to the European Union and NATO, Belarus presents a political challenge to Western democracies.[1] The pro-Soviet Alexander Lukashenko succeeded in quickly establishing a post-Soviet autocracy after his accession to power in 1994, which drew international attention to the East European nation in transition. He consolidated his regime by undertaking extensive (re-)integration efforts with Russia over the course of years.

In the West, President Lukashenko's rapid autocratization gave rise to serious concern, particularly since in the 1990s political transition in the former Eastern bloc was expected to unfold only towards democracy – according to the democracy euphoria prevalent at that time. An undemocratic constitutional amendment in 1996 finally led the European Union and the United States to break with the Lukashenko government. From a Western perspective, ever since the second half of the 1990s Belarus is to be considered Europe's most troubling 'problem child' with regard to democracy and human rights.

It is generally of vital importance to the West that Belarus not only preserves its independence and sovereignty but also integrates into the transatlantic community of democracies. Its geographic location in Eastern Europe between the EU and the NATO member states on the one hand and Russia on the other has raised its importance in international politics.

Today Belarus is seen as a typical example of failed democratization. The post-Soviet country has developed into a 'sad exception' in a Europe consisting of 'democratic and open' societies (Council of the European Union 2006a). This state of affairs has confronted Western democracy promoters especially with a long-term dilemma of whether they should pragmatically accept or ideologically reject this exception. The present study analyses the extent to which 'the exceptional case' of Belarus has led to conflicting objectives in German and US policies, and how both states dealt with such conflicts.

Authoritarian development and the conflict situation in Belarus[2]

Lacking its own independence movement, Belarus is among those countries in Eastern Europe that received their national sovereignty merely as a gift following the collapse of the Communist bloc, whereas other countries had to fight for their national-democratic rebirth. Thus, Belarus's path to independence did not lead to a change of the political elite or institutions. Yet, an important transitional turning point was the adoption in 1994 of a new constitution creating a presidential system. Based on this, the first presidential and parliamentary elections were held in the same year, with the intention of taking the first step in the 'young democracy's' formal institutionalization. But Lukashenko's surprising victory raised early doubts about whether the ensuing consolidation of the new political system was going to be successful.[3]

Indeed, the new ruler introduced a policy of re-Sovietization. Steeped in Soviet nostalgia, Lukashenko initially paid homage to the allegedly better past both rhetorically and symbolically. The Soviet Union's 'achievements' had passed the 'challenges of time'. He glorified the Soviet past and again flew the Soviet-Belarusian flag over the seat of government as well as reviving the Soviet anthem (*Der Spiegel* 1996). Moreover, a referendum in 1995 introduced Russian as the second official language, a new state flag and a new state coat-of-arms, both clearly based on Soviet symbolism. By stopping the early 1990s liberalization and privatization process, Lukashenko reinforced the dominant role of the state in the country's economy.

With regard to foreign policy, Lukashenko oriented himself exclusively toward Russia. He first used the referendum in 1995 to obtain the Belarusian people's approval for his integration policy with Russia. Subsequently, Belarus signed a Treaty on Union with Russia in 1996, envisaging a common constitution, shared economic planning and a common currency.[4] In addition to political and cultural affinity, there were also economic reasons why Lukashenko preferred a close relationship with Moscow. He hoped for lower energy prices and other benefits. Furthermore, the special relations with Russia allowed the new ruler to ignore Western criticism of his increasingly authoritarian rule (Sahm 2008: 52).

In institutional terms, the first step of Lukashenko's reautocratization policy was the above-mentioned referendum in 1995, granting him the right to dissolve parliament. Another constitutional referendum in 1996 gave the president far-reaching powers, violating the principle of the separation of powers. The referendum introduced extensive legislative rights and allowed presidential decrees, orders and directives with binding force that were de facto superior to laws. Subsequent political practice turned out to be even more explosive: first, Lukashenko extended his term of office until 2001, dissolved the Supreme Soviet, and convened a national assembly without holding elections. Having disempowered the parliament as a political counterweight, he also tried to put the opposition, civil society and the independent media under pressure.

In 2000, the first parliamentary election after the controversial constitutional referendum took place. In the run-up to the vote, the OSCE was keen to provide the necessary prerequisites for democratic elections. When these efforts failed, most parties decided to boycott the election, especially because the regime had increased its repression of the opposition, *inter alia*, making some prominent regime opponents 'disappear'. However, the opposition took part in the 2001 presidential election. Mediated by the OSCE mission in Minsk, they also succeeded in agreeing on a common candidate. But Lukashenko was able to win the elections by a large majority of the votes cast. The OSCE evaluated both elections as undemocratic.[5]

On 17 October 2004, the next parliamentary election was held. All opposition candidates failed to gain seats in parliament. OSCE observers again criticized severe violations of democratic norms. Along with the parliamentary election, another referendum on a constitutional amendment was passed with the aim of eliminating presidential terms and thus allowing Lukashenko to run for office without restriction. According to official figures, a large majority of voters agreed to this – a 'successful' beginning to preparations for the next presidential election on 19 March 2006. Officially, Lukashenko also won this election with 82.6 per cent of the vote, while his major opponent Alexander Milinkievich received only 6 per cent. The election was followed by a protest rally of approximately 10,000 persons in Minsk. Opposition leader Milinkievich refused to accept the official results, and demanded an election re-run. The Orange Revolution in Ukraine served as inspiration for the Belarusian opposition. However, unlike protest in the neighbouring country, protest in Belarus did not develop into a mass movement in the following days.

The parliamentary elections on 28 September 2008 took place in an international context that had primarily been changed by deterioration in the relationship with Russia. In the course of its foreign policy 'economization', Moscow started to charge Belarus higher prices for energy in 2007. In addition, Russia entered a war with Georgia in August 2008, and subsequently recognized its breakaway regions, Abkhazia and South Ossetia, as independent states. However, contrary to expectations, Minsk refused to follow Russia in recognizing these regions. The notion of Belarus as an actor independent (of Russia) took concrete shape, opening up new spaces for geostrategic considerations in Western policy towards Belarus.

Lukashenko on his part hoped that Western governments would reassess their stance towards his regime as well as their financial aid policy. After the release of all political prisoners, he also promised a free election as a positive signal (*Der Spiegel* 2008).[6] Actually, there was reason for hope that the new election would be held with less control and manipulation than earlier ones, since there had been some progress in the work of electoral commissions, and permission granted to opposition candidates to run for office including running election campaigns (cf. Sahm 2008: 54). Although no opposition candidate succeeded in winning a seat in parliament, the OSCE made a relatively lenient judgment (OSCE/ODIHR 2008: 1). However, the opposition criticized the election, calling it a 'farce' and an 'election staging' for the West (*SZ* 2008).

On 19 December 2010, the last presidential election to date was held in Belarus. A further deterioration in relations between Belarus and Russia, marked by controversy over energy supplies, placed the focus of the election campaign on regional issues. In the run-up to the election, by accusing the Russian leadership of plotting to bring down his government Lukashenko caused a political crisis to break out between Minsk and Moscow (Russland-Aktuell 2010).[7] President Medvedev reacted with surprisingly strong criticism of Lukashenko, blaming him for stirring up hostility between the two countries (Kremlin 2010). However, the tide turned in early December when the two presidents agreed in a one-to-one meeting in Moscow that Russian oil exports to Belarus would be exempted from export duties from 2011, if Minsk ratified the customs union agreements with Russia and Kazakhstan.

Officially, Lukashenko won the election with an overwhelming majority of almost 80 per cent of the vote, while none of the rival candidates received more than 3 per cent.[8] The OSCE observation mission stressed that the election had not met OCSE standards (OSCE/ODIHR 2010: 1). The election was again followed by post-electoral riots in Minsk, when several thousand regime opponents – according to official accounts 3,000 protesters, but according to independent media about 15,000 to 25,000 – demonstrated against electoral fraud. The protest rally was violently dispersed by security forces, and more than 600 persons were arrested, among them almost all presidential candidates. Further arrests and house searches as well as seizures affected not only participants in the protest rally but also the opposition in general. Several opposition activists including some former presidential candidates were later charged with inciting riots and sentenced to multi-year prison terms. Responding to the sharp criticism by the OSCE and the West, the Belarusian leadership also shut down the OSCE office in Minsk.

The time period of the present study coincides with Lukashenko's term in office, starting from the beginning of his presidency in 1994 to the 2010 presidential election and ensuing repression in early 2011. A special focus are the national elections and referendums in Belarus, in particular the parliamentary and presidential elections in 2008 and 2010 respectively. Since Lukashenko 'successfully' held his first parliamentary and presidential elections (in 2000 and 2001) and was thus able to consolidate his power, Belarus has come to be considered an authoritarian regime.[9] Since then, no opposition parties have been represented in the Belarusian parliament. In addition, the government refused the weakened opposition access to relevant national media.

On the other hand, the increasingly repressive political system in Belarus has further isolated the country from the West. Western organizations, particularly the US agencies, face an adverse or even hostile situation in Belarus due to anti-Western attitudes dominated by the image of the United States (and NATO) cast in hostile terms. Many organizations were not allowed to open their offices in Belarus, or were refused entry visas for staff members. As a result these organizations are forced to run their Belarus programmes from neighbouring countries (cf. Jarábik and Rabagilati 2010: 4–5).

For external democracy promoters, two conflicting objectives result from this undemocratic situation:

1. *Democracy versus donor interests (extrinsic).* According to its transatlantic self-conception, the open autocratization of a European country is intolerable.

External democracy promoters, therefore, have to actively fight the Belarusian regime through sanctions and direct support of democratic forces. In contrast to this, there are, however, geostrategic interests of Western democracy promoters that manifest themselves in two opposing directions: on the one hand, Russia may regard active democracy promotion in Belarus as a threat to its own 'privileged' interests in the country. This results in a (geostrategic) stance of not confronting Russia in its 'back yard'. On the other hand, it is in the interest of Western policy that Belarus maintains not only its sovereignty and independence (from Russia), but also orients itself primarily towards the West. However, taking a hard line in the matter of democracy and a corresponding policy of isolating Lukashenko could drive the country into the arms of Russia, making it economically and politically dependent on its eastern neighbour, and thus jeopardizing Belarus's independence.

2   *Democracy versus democracy (intrinsic).* The people of Belarus – as in most post-Soviet states – have generally negative recollections of the democracy-like conditions in the early 1990s, which were characterized by economic and political instability. People thus harbour fears about the unpredictability associated with change. In addition, the early post-Soviet authoritarian consolidation in Belarus went hand in hand with increasing political and economic stability. It was Lukashenko who saved Belarus – e.g. in stark contrast to Russia – from post-Soviet 'early capitalism' and its dire consequences. This permitted a (tacit) understanding between society and government based on which the people gain a certain amount of stability and welfare in exchange for their political abstinence, an arrangement similarly attributed to Putin and Russia.[10] From an external democracy promoter's perspective, this can result in a conflict of objectives, as a rapid regime change may not count on direct support from large sections of the population and can also bring about increased risks to stability (such as economic deterioration). Sanctions may then only strengthen the legitimacy of the regime within Belarus.

Germany: more confrontation than cooperation

Profile of bilateral relations

Following the end of the Soviet Union in 1991, German–Belarusian relations initially developed positively. Until the mid-1990s, intensive visits at the ministerial level took place in both countries. However, after Lukashenko took office in Belarus, his domestic policy increasingly strained relations with Germany.[11] In 1997, the EU decided 'to restrict political relations with Belarus' (AA 2011a). Nevertheless, Germany initiated an expansion of the 'Wider Europe' concept underlying the EU Neighbourhood Policy (ENP) to include Belarus as well. Previously, the country had already been identified as a potential partner for the ENP at an early stage (Lindner 2004: 202).[12]

Moreover, Belarus became relevant for the specific security interests of Germany, especially after the EU's eastward enlargement in 2004. Since then, it has been more important not only as a transit country between East and West for movements of goods and persons (especially for Europe's energy supply),[13] but also because of illegal transports. From a German perspective, the struggle against smuggling is – although not overly so – relevant in terms of security policy.

Against the background of the German occupation during the Second World War – Belarus was one of the countries that were most affected by the war – Germany's historical responsibility to Belarus plays a role. There are many civil-society connections between the two countries related to dealing with the past (*Vergangenheitsbewältigung*) and reconciliation. In addition, the Chernobyl catastrophe is a factor in bilateral relations concerning a wide range of German Chernobyl initiatives.

Due to political restrictions, German policy towards Belarus is focused on promoting civil society and on economic relations in particular. Despite the difficult basic conditions, currently 360 German companies are operating in Belarus. The German economy has had a representative office in Minsk since 2001. Furthermore, Germany is one of Belarus's most important trade partners. In 2009, German exports to Belarus amounted to €2.29 billion, and imports from Belarus totalled €650 million (Statistisches Bundesamt 2011).

Profile of German democracy promotion in Belarus

Germany's political elite regards Belarus as a 'European country with a European tradition'. Therefore, it is in their interest that this country becomes 'a valuable and respected part' of Europe (Bundestag 2006b: 1694). The lack of democracy in Belarus is contrasted rhetorically with its geographic proximity as the country is only one-and-a-half hours by air away from Berlin. In this regard, it is a matter of interest for Germany whether or not fundamental democratic rights are respected (Bundestag 2006d: 2270).

Germany has focused more and more strongly on democracy promotion in its transition policy towards Belarus. In the context of the TRANSFORM programme for advanced East European nations in transition, between 1993 and 2003 the German government provided €40 million for government advisory services on legal questions, promotion of private entrepreneurship, education and qualification of experts and management-level staff, the agricultural sector as well as civil society and independent media (Deutsche Botschaft Minsk 2011). However, democracy promotion in the strict sense was only secondary. ODA data for recent years from the OECD shows that in keeping with generally increasing development assistance for Belarus (from $13.9 million in 2005 to $21.6 million in 2009), disbursements in the sector 'Government and Civil Society', which is relevant for democracy promotion, have grown as well: from $2.0 million in 2005 to $3.3 million in 2009. The sectors promoting democratic participation and civil society (from $30,000 to $1.3 million) together with promotion of media (from $60,000 to $1.04 million) grew the most (OECD 2011; own calculation).[14]

Apart from the Foreign Office, the main players in German democracy promotion in Belarus are the Ministry for Economic Cooperation and Development (BMZ), the GTZ and the German political foundations. Furthermore, the KfW Development Bank has been running the TRANSFORM succession programme in Russia, the Ukraine and Belarus since 2005. Due to the political situation, activities concentrate on the private sector and on cooperating with NGOs (BMZ 2011). Since there is no intergovernmental agreement with Belarus, cooperation agreements are signed directly with civil society actors. Thus, the GTZ has been promoting civil-society and free-market structures at a grassroots level (GTZ 2010).

In this context, the Belarus Promotion Programme ('Förderprogramm Belarus') is to be highlighted as a key element of German development policy, focussing on support for civil society and sustainable economic development (GTZ 2010). Introduced in 2002 after extended lobbying by German NGOs concerned with Chernobyl aid, the programme is coordinated by the International Education and Exchange (IBB, 'Internationales Bildungs- und Begegnungswerk') in Dortmund and its sister IBB organization in Minsk. By largely supporting smaller projects of German–Belarusian initiatives in areas not directly related to democracy such as social policy, environment, education and economy, it seems to be attempting rather unobtrusive action. For example, cooperation mostly relies on informal arrangements instead of intergovernmental agreements, and it is administered centrally by the GTZ but consists of many smaller initiatives (Kunter 2009:2). The programme thus takes into account long-term trends in Belarus and demonstrates the willingness to adapt, carry on dialogue and continue cooperation.[15]

Of the German political foundations, only the FES has an office in Minsk (with just one local employee working there). FES was the first German foundation since the early 1990s to take up its activities in the country and has emphasized strengthening civil society and Belarusian–European cooperation (FES 2011). Since 2004, the KAS has also maintained a Belarus country programme operated by a Belarus office in exile located in Vilnius, Lithuania, with the objective of consolidating and strengthening democratic forces, supporting structural reform of the country's economy towards social market economy and raising the population's awareness of a European integration perspective (KAS 2011).

Similarly, the Kiev Office of the FNS has been responsible for Belarus since March 2009. Through cooperation with NGOs and political representatives, it is seeking to support liberal and democratic actors in Belarus (FNS 2011). Furthermore, the Minsk Forum of the private 'German–Belarusian Society' (dbg, deutsch–belarussische Gesellschaft) is an important initiative, which has been holding an international annual conference on policy, economy and society in Belarus since 1997.[16]

Overall, German–Belarusian relations are part of the EU framework and initially focussed on negative consequences for the Lukashenko regime in that context. Germany later became a driving force behind a critical-constructive EU policy on Belarus, remaining mostly sceptical about sanctions (Timmermann 2008: 411). Moreover, Berlin worked actively to ensure that Minsk was not released from its OSCE commitments, namely the resumption of the OSCE mission in Belarus beyond 2003 (Lindner 2004: 200). On the other hand, Germany provided substantial assistance in support of Belarusian transformation beginning in the early 1990s. At the same time, Germany gave priority to promoting civil society, whereas support of political parties was avoided.

Perception analysis

From both a European and German perspective, the controversial constitutional referendum in 1996 was generally classified as a constitutional coup. In this regard, Germany considered the new constitution 'a serious setback' for democratic development in Belarus (Bundestag 1996: 13046). From a German perspective, developments in the country became even worse due to the Belarusian regime being an 'authoritarian presidential system' that 'largely' abolished the separation of powers (Bundestag 1997a: 1). Even before the parliamentary election in 2000, Germany therefore described the government as a 'dictatorial regime averse to democracy' (Bundestag 2000: 11966).

Furthermore, Berlin critically observed the ongoing and increasing repression of democratic institutions after Lukashenko's re-election in 2001. A main point of concern was the free media and the opposition being 'muzzled', while violations of human rights accumulated (Bundestag 2006d: 2281). For example, in the run-up to the parliamentary election in 2004 the 'intensified political repression' characterized by massive hampering of the opposition, repression of the civil society, prohibition of various NGOs and increased harassment of free media was criticized (Bundestag 2004: 1–2).

Especially with regard to the presidential election in 2006, the evaluation of the political situation by the German Bundestag was in clearly negative terms. Prior to the elections, representatives commented on the greater restrictions of parties, the lack of separation of powers, the judiciary's increasing dependency on the government, and intensification of media harassment from one election to the next (Bundestag 2006a: 1). In the relevant debate, Manfred Grund (CDU/CSU) noted for example that Belarus is a 'well-functioning dictatorship', Michael Link (FDP) characterized Belarus as 'the last existing dictatorship on European soil', and Uta Zapf (SPD) called Lukashenko 'the so-called last dictator in Europe' (Bundestag 2006b: 1693, 1695 and 1697). This intensified in the aftermath of the election when the 'reactionary' and 'inhuman' Lukaschenko regime was even compared to the socialist regime in the former GDR: the 'die-hard dictator' was said to have established a 'repression regime in the middle of Europe' (Bundestag 2006d: 2270 and 2275). Furthermore, German politicians saw Russia as a key factor for solving the problem (Bundestag 2006d: 2270–1).

In the following period there were also cautiously positive appraisals among the general public who saw some progress in Belarus, e.g. by Rainer Lindner, then expert on Belarus at the German Institute for International and Security

Affairs (SWP, Stiftung Wissenschaft und Politik), who discussed the situation before the parliamentary election in 2008. He noted positively that there were no political prisoners in Belarus for the first time in the last 11 years, and that Minsk even allowed an OSCE team to observe the electoral process (Kahlweit 2008).[17]

However, during the 2010 presidential election, the negative image of Belarus re-emerged. The German Bundestag expressed the fear that the election would again neither be free nor fair, but just a staging of the 'pseudo-democratic legitimacy' for an 'autocratic leader' to be confirmed in office (Bundestag 2010a: 1). Bundestag members criticized systematic violations of human rights, restrictions on the free press as well as on freedom of assembly and speech, stronger *obstacles to* NGO registration, further harassment of registered groups and the arbitrary nature of the judicial system as a means of applying pressure (Bundestag 2010b: 9144–5).[18]

Berlin's interest in the presidential election was matched by its condemnation of the outcome and especially of the subsequent repression. Together with his Polish colleague, Foreign Minister Westerwelle classified the election as a 'severe setback' and harshly condemned the post-electoral violence (AA 2010b). The events in Minsk were 'shocking' to Germany, especially as the Lukashenko regime was accused of dismantling the opposition 'ruthlessly and systematically' and thus revealing its 'true colours' (AA 2011b). The outcome of the election and in particular the violence that followed it, unleashed a storm of outrage in Berlin. All political parties condemned this. German Foreign Minister Westerwelle concluded that the government in Minsk had failed the 'test of democracy'. According to him, Belarus was definitely disqualified as a 'partner in value-based cooperation' and the prospects of rapprochement with the EU had become extremely remote (AA 2011c). In February 2011, the German Bundestag also evaluated the elections as 'neither free nor fair', and welcomed the new EU sanctions, because 'European values and norms' had been severely violated by 'the brutal actions' of the Lukashenko government against opposition and civil society (Bundestag 2011b: 2).

Reaction analysis

From the beginning, the German reactions to Lukashenko's turning away from liberal-democratic principles were clearly negative and focussed on appropriate consequences for bilateral relations. In particular, the controversial constitutional referendum in 1996 marked a turning point in bilateral relations with Belarus, leading finally – not least on Germany's initiative – to the first EU sanctions against the Lukashenko regime in September 1997 (cf. Bundestag 1997b: 8–9 and 11). As a result, the partnership and cooperation agreement of 1995 was suspended, a contact ban at ministerial level imposed, and all technical assistance of the EU and its member states (except for democracy promotion or humanitarian aid) was stopped. This so-called 'selective restrictions' approach of the EU has since constituted the political framework for German policy on Belarus (cf. Timmermann 2008: 415).

For a long time, Germany was among those EU countries that favoured wide-ranging cooperation with Belarusian society but also envisaged a limited engagement with the state at lower levels in order to avoid cutting the country off from the EU (Rontoyanni 2005: 56). Germany's basic attitude is generally reflected in a statement of its ambassador in Minsk 2007–10, Gebhardt Weiss: 'patience often is much more effective than pressure' (Weiss 2008).

Germany's interest was mainly focused on elections in Belarus. With regard to the 2004 parliamentary elections, the German Bundestag called upon the German government to continue to pressure Belarus to adopt a 'process of disavowing authoritarian and repressive practices and initiating a return to democracy and the rule of law'. At the same time, the German government was urged to support forces in the country welcoming reforms (Bundestag 2004: 3). When the election and the referendum did not meet German/European expectations, a reaction not by the German government but at EU level followed. In November 2004, the EU council imposed a travel ban on those responsible for the electoral fraud and for the crackdown on peaceful demonstrators. This intensified isolation policy of Brussels towards the Belarusian regime was initiated not by Germany but by the two neighbouring EU members Poland and Lithuania, which until then had aimed at officially engaging with Belarus (cf. Sahm 2005: 84).

In 2006, German foreign policy again focused on Belarus. In the run-up to the 2006 presidential elections, the Bundestag called on the German government to work internationally for Belarus to meet its assumed commitment to free elections, and to continue supporting reform-minded forces as well as to develop a common EU policy towards Belarus (Bundestag 2006a: 3).[19] In addition to this, Chancellor Merkel welcomed the opposition candidate Milinkievich in Berlin in order to demonstrate Germany's solidarity with the Belarusian opposition (Wittrock 2006).

Following the presidential election Berlin endorsed the OSCE judgment evaluating it as not in line with European standards. As a result, the German Bundestag demanded concrete steps for the release of prisoners, the sustainable support of civil society and for a common EU policy towards Belarus, including sanctions (Bundestag 2006c: 3). It is remarkable that the Bundestag again demanded an ongoing dialogue with Russia on the situation in Belarus. Regarding a policy of further isolation, however, the German government initially responded hesitantly, and turned against a 'containment policy demanded by some, advocated by many' at EU level because this would not help the people in Belarus (Bundesregierung 2006a: 48). But Lukashenko's harsh measures against the opposition in the aftermath of the election led the German government to abandon its stance against sanctions (cf. Bundesregierung 2006b: 59).[20]

Thus, in 2006 the EU council passed a resolution – in accordance with the demands of the Bundestag – to ban visas and freeze the assets of all members of the Belarusian government who had been directly responsible for violating international election standards and for the harsh measures against the opposition (Council of the European Union 2006b). The new EU sanctions had great symbolic power, in particular because Lukashenko was personally affected. Thus, the isolation policy against Minsk intensified on the occasion of the 2004 parliamentary election and assumed a highly political dimension. At the same time, with this decision the EU reinforced its commitment to increased support of civil society in Belarus (European External Action Service 2011b: 1).[21]

For German policy towards Belarus, the year 2008 was very important, even though the parliamentary election that year did not draw much political attention. Shortly after the war between Russia and Georgia, in October 2008, the EU council opened the door for a rapprochement with Belarus that ended the post-electoral isolation policy of 2004 and 2006. The contact ban at ministerial level since 1997 and the visa ban since 2006 were suspended for six months, with just a few exceptions. In addition to – Russia-related – geostrategic motives, the EU wanted to demonstrate to the Lukashenko regime its firm will to react positively to the fulfilment of one of its core demands, namely the release of political prisoners. At the same time, it declared stronger support for civil society. The German government for its part strongly supported reinstating the previously suspended EU relations with Minsk, a proposal that was not uncontested within the EU. This was based on the conviction that further improvement of the situation could only be achieved through political dialogue (Steinmeier 2008).

The EU policy of rapprochement became most apparent in Belarus's accession to the Eastern Partnership in May 2009. With this the EU ceased its policy of isolation, in place since 1997, for the time being. The 'thaw' in the EU–Belarusian relationship had a positive effect on German–Belarusian bilateral relations. In February 2009, Foreign Minister Steinmeier welcomed his Belarusian colleague Martynov in Berlin. In addition, the Belarusian Minister of Foreign Affairs was invited to the Munich Security Conference in February 2010, where he also met Foreign Minister Westerwelle.

During this time, the German government also supported Belarusian security forces, above all with training and material support. Between 2008 and 2011, the German Ministry of the Interior trained members of the Belarusian police and border guards, and provided them with equipment and vehicles. This has been justified not only in terms of Germany's specific security interests (such as fighting organized crime, above all drug and human trafficking, cybercrime, terrorism as well as illegal migration) but also of the 'recognizable liberalization trends since 2008' in Belarus (Bundestag 2012:3).[22]

As a logical step in the rapprochement policy, in October 2010 – just before the 2010 presidential election – the EU extended the suspension of sanctions against Belarus for a further year for a 'critical engagement', and underlined its willingness to continue intensifying bilateral relations, contingent upon democratic developments (Council of the European Union 2010). The European engagement culminated in a visit by German Foreign Minister Westerwelle – the first visit by a German minister in 15 years – and his Polish colleague Sikorski in Minsk on 2 November 2010. The combination of diplomatic pressure and positive incentives was designed to deliver 'a clear message for free and fair elections' to the government in Minsk (AA 2010a). On behalf of the EU, both ministers offered Minsk €3 billion in financial aid for coping with the acute economic crisis on the condition of free elections (*Spiegel Online* 2010). The following day, the chief of the German chancellery, Roland Pofalla, declared at the Minsk Forum that the upcoming election was a 'touchstone' for measuring progress in the democratic principles that were demanded by the EU (Pofalla 2010: 5). In addition, the German Bundestag demanded that pressure be applied on Minsk in order to secure fundamental democratic rights and ensure the necessary conditions for free elections (Bundestag 2010a: 3).

In response to the controversial election and the violence that followed, the German government immediately threatened Minsk with 'consequences', because respect for democracy, human rights and the rule of law was a prerequisite for closer cooperation with the EU (AA 2010b). Shortly afterwards, the German government advocated new sanctions against Minsk due to continued repression of the opposition. In light of the situation in Belarus, Chancellor Merkel stated that imposing the suspended sanctions again 'needed to be considered' (Bundesregierung 2011). The German Bundestag also argued for tough sanctions against Minsk and called for an end to the repression (cf. Bundestag 2011a: 9452–62).

Germany, together with Poland, took the lead at European level, encouraging the EU to formulate a clear reaction to Minsk's unacceptable electoral practices. Berlin made clear that Germany would not accept the 'hindrance of elections' and 'oppression of freedom' and would urge the EU to formulate a 'categorical response' (*FAZ* 2011). Germany (along with Poland, Sweden and Great Britain) has argued in favour of adopting a harder line against Minsk since the first EU meetings in January 2011.

As demanded by Germany, the EU ultimately came up with a 'clear response' by deciding in favour of strong sanctions against Belarus on 31 January 2011. Entry bans were imposed on Lukashenko and 157 representatives of his regime, and their assets were frozen. The EU also decided on more tightly focused support for civil society. At a donor conference in February 2010 the German government therefore announced that it would promote Belarusian civil society with €6.6 million in the current year,[23] and would waive national visa fees for Belarusian students and academics as well as backing the waiver of Schengen visa fees for members of civil society (AA 2011d).[24]

Given the ongoing repression in Belarus (e.g. sentencing of several opposition members to long prison terms), the EU later decided to tighten sanctions against Minsk. It extended the list of Belarusian officials subject to targeted sanctions, enforced an arms embargo, and froze the assets of three Belarusian companies closely linked to the regime – and thus imposed the first economic sanction against Belarus. Moreover, the German Ministry of the Interior, in consultation with the Foreign Office, reduced its support measures for the Belarusian police and later abandoned the programme entirely in view of the 'further intensification' of Lukashenko's repression in 2011 (Bundestag 2012: 8).[25]

Not necessarily closely in line with the official political pronouncements, the programmes of official German development cooperation (GTZ/IBB and KfW) mentioned above avoided the politically sensitive issues of democracy and political rule, and remained without significant changes during the period under study. Similarly, the activities of the German political foundations covered a broad spectrum. The FES, the only foundation running an office in Belarus, pursued – possibly for this reason – a balanced approach of cooperating both with civil society and state institutions as part of a long-term strategy. By contrast, the KAS, running an office in Lithuania, adopted an openly political approach.[26] In 2010, its newly elected president, Hans-Gert Pöttering, used his first trip to Minsk to clearly demonstrate support of the democratic movement in Belarus.

All in all, Germany's response to the Lukashenko regime, which has turned away from democracy since the mid-1990s, showed an unusual readiness to impose political sanctions. Facing intensified repression in the 2000s, Berlin became even more willing to forcefully impose sanctions on the Belarusian regime, for instance in the aftermath of the presidential election in 2006. However, pursuant to the 2008 parliamentary election, Germany strongly encouraged the EU's engagement policy in order to respond to the few positive developments in the election year and to the geostrategic opportunities opened up by the increasing tensions between Minsk and Moscow. In that respect, Germany showed – even if temporarily – cooperative behaviour towards Belarus. This ended with the 2010 presidential election and its fraudulent practices and violence, which Berlin considered a 'slap in the face of the rapprochement policy' (Bundestag 2011a: 9454). As a result, Berlin's way of dealing with the Lukashenko regime again became clearly confrontational.

The United States: consistent democratic conditionality

Profile of bilateral relations

In the early 1990s, US–Belarusian relations were promising. This was marked, above all, by official visits at the highest level. Belarus's acceptance of disarmament obligations from START I in the Lisbon Protocol and its accession to the Treaty on the Non-Proliferation of Nuclear Weapons in 1993 were of particular importance for the United States, which had a strong interest in preventing more former Soviet republics becoming nuclear powers.[27] On the other hand, the Clinton Administration had difficulty in approaching a Belarusian leadership that seemed to be dominated by the Soviet nomenclature and shaped by political conservatism. Clinton's arrival and departure within one day during his visit to Minsk in 1994 shows the country's 'relative unimportance' from the perspective of the US government (Legvold 1999: 133).

Lukashenko's arrival in power in 1994 led to a remarkable cooling of bilateral relations. The mounting anti-Western rhetoric of the new ruler disconcerted the US government. From the US point of view, Lukashenko's rhetoric sounded like the nationalist forces in Russia – the major difference was that they were not in power there (Legvold 1999: 138). Additionally, Washington had the impression that Belarus under Lukashenko was moving in the wrong direction both economically and politically. This in turn led to the growing alienation of the Clinton Administration from Minsk. High-level visits and meetings were correspondingly rare (Legvold 1999: 138).

The downward spiral in US–Belarusian relations was also due to Minsk's foreign policy. Though Washington did not object to Lukashenko's reintegration with Russia in principle, these particular efforts seemed from the US perspective too close to the Soviet model on the one hand, and to foster anti-Western tendencies (above all related to NATO enlargement) in the foreign policy of both states (Legvold 1999: 141).

Overall, American–Belarusian political relations remained at a very low level from the late 1990s. The same applies to business. Trade relations between the two countries are marginal. In 2009, US exports to Belarus amounted to $137 million, while imports from Belarus reached $573 million (US Census Bureau 2011). The United States does not even appear on the list of Belarus's 15 most important trading partners, while Russia and the EU are the two most important partners (EXPORT.BY 2010).

Profile of US democracy promotion in Belarus

Due to the fact that the US government has regarded the Belarusian regime as a full-blown dictatorship since the early 2000s, its Belarus policy was meant to be a 'robust' democracy promotion policy, with the aim of contributing to an 'empowering' of the Belarusian population to overcome this dictatorship (US Department of State 2009). In concrete terms, it was about 'to build NGO capacity, to increase public participation, bolster the capacity of democratic political parties to unify, strategize, organize and connect with constituents and strengthen independent media and expand access to objective information' (Helsinki Commission 2008a). In order to improve relations with Minsk, compliance with OSCE commitments to democracy and human rights was of central importance for the United States. The declared US policy was put in a nutshell by president George W. Bush: 'We will ... assist those seeking to return Belarus to its rightful place among the Euro–Atlantic community of democracies' (White House 2004).

The worsening of political relations since the mid-1990s is reflected in US governmental assistance to Belarus. Reaching a peak in 1993 at $134 million, aid declined sharply after Lukashenko came to power. In 2008, US assistance to Belarus amounted to $17 million. At the same time, the proportion of assistance accounted for by the Freedom Support Act (FSA) and thus specifically devoted to democracy promotion, rose steadily from $4.4 million in 1993 to $10.2 million in 2008, i.e. from 3 per cent to almost 60 per cent of total aid (US Department of State 2009).

In spring 2008, bilateral relations reached another diplomatic low point after the 'Drozdy affair' in 1998.[28] Reacting to the first economic sanctions by the United States, Minsk drastically reduced its diplomatic personnel in Washington and claimed a similar step by the US government. Thereupon, based on reciprocity, nearly 30 US diplomats had to leave the country, including the ambassador.

Since then, only five employees have been left in the US embassy in Minsk, with a chargé d'affaires (*ad interim*). The US embassy was a major instrument for US democracy promotion on the ground, protected by diplomatic immunity. Due to the drastic reduction of staff, US activities are more limited than previously.

The central actors in US democracy promotion in Belarus are the State Department, USAID, the IRI, the NDI and the NED. The Belarus programme, which has been funded by USAID since 1992, has two focal points: engaging citizens in political and social decision-making and supporting social and health care (USAID 2009). The emphases of IRI's Belarus programme (active in the country since 1997) financed by USAID and the State Department are strengthening political parties and candidates, empowering women and youth leadership (IRI 2011). NDI has been conducting democracy promotion programmes since 2000, with a special focus on support for political parties and civil society, financed primarily by NED, USAID and the State Department (NDI 2011). NED, on its part, finances Belarus projects in the areas of independent media, NGOs, civil society, politics/elections and human rights (NED 2010).

The US government consistently inserted democracy-related demands in the country's relation with Belarus. At the same time, support for democratic forces was at the top of the political agenda in order to promote democratization by challenging the government (cf. US Department of State 2010a).

Perception analysis

Like Germany, the US administration classified the constitutional amendment of 1996 as well as the new parliament as illegitimate, because they were introduced 'in an unconstitutional manner' by violating 'fundamental democratic principles'. Washington critically observed how Lukashenko was leading the country back to 'Soviet-era authoritarian practices' (US Department of State 1998). By the turn of the century, the United States described the Belarusian government as an 'authoritarian' regime (USAID 1999).

The US picture of Belarus continued to deteriorate in the early 2000s. The US government saw the political developments surrounding the parliamentary election in 2004 in terms of the logic of those repressions against civil society that Lukashenko undertook in order to systematically suppress democratic forces in the aftermath of his 2001 re-election: the White House specifically criticized the Belarusian government for reacting with violence and arrests to the 'peaceful expression' of opposition. The parliamentary election itself was strongly condemned by President Bush due to a 'climate of abuse and fear' and a victory achieved 'by fraudulent means'. Since the Lukashenko government was turning the country into 'a regime of repression in the heart of Europe', Bush showed zero tolerance: 'There is no place in a Europe whole and free for a regime of this kind' (White House 2004).

In the following period the United States castigated Lukashenko's regime even further. At her Confirmation Hearing in January 2005, the nominee for secretary of state, Condoleezza Rice, declared Belarus an 'outpost of tyranny' that needed to be opposed.[29] Furthermore, in April 2005 she spoke of Belarus as 'the last real dictatorship in the heart of Europe and the time for change has truly come' (*Spiegel Online* 2005).

Before the 2006 presidential election, the US Helsinki Commission[30] referred to the 'more dictatorial' regime of Lukashenko as 'a stark anomaly in an increasingly democratic Europe' (Helsinki Commission 2006), while a US governmental report of March 2006 suspected Belarus of supporting international terrorism.[31] In addition, Vice President Cheney also classified Belarus as 'the last dictatorship in Europe' at a summit of leaders from the Baltic and Black Sea states in Vilnius in May 2006 (Thomas 2006b). And the 2006 presidential election once again provoked prominent official criticism from Washington: President Bush strongly condemned the election as well as the subsequent repression by the Belarusian government (White House 2006).

Yet in the context of the parliamentary elections in 2008, the US evaluation of the political situation in Belarus was rather ambivalent. In particular, the fulfilment of a key US demand – the release of all political prisoners – seemed to create 'a glimmer of hope for the beginning of long-awaited change' (Helsinki Commission 2008a). Shortly before the election, a Belarus Hearing of the Helsinki Commission took place and positively highlighted 'Minsk's reluctance to endorse the Russian aggression in Georgia' (Helsinki Commission 2008a). For Washington this was another 'glimmer of possibility for an improvement in Belarus's ties with the United States'. However, there was no indication that these elections would differ significantly from previous ones (Helsinki Commission 2008b and 2008c).

The US government responded hesitantly to the election's outcome, expressing its disappointment that the elections fell short of international standards. Nevertheless, it took into account that 'a demonstration was held after the elections in a peaceful and orderly manner' (US Department of State 2008a).

As in the German and European case the 2010 presidential election and particularly the post-electoral repression made the situation in Belarus even worse in Washington's eyes. In an immediate reaction the White House declared the election to be illegitimate, and condemned the violent actions of the government (White House 2010). The Helsinki Commission also strongly condemned the violence and wave of arrests. Despite some procedural improvements in the election, the crackdown by the government was seen as a sign that there was still a 'long road ahead for democratic progress' in Belarus (Helsinki Commission 2010). Washington interpreted both the electoral fraud and the subsequent crackdown on opposition protests as an 'unfortunate step backwards in the development of democratic governance and respect for human rights' (US Department of State 2010c) and a 'clear step backwards on issues central to our relationship with Belarus' (White House 2010). The US government was especially 'troubled' by the fact that such a 'crackdown occurred in the heart of Europe in the twenty-first century' (US Senate 2011a).

Reaction analysis

US reactions to Lukashenko's dictatorial consolidation of power can be described as a consistent policy of isolation and confrontation. At first, in February 1997 the United States answered the obvious autocratic tendencies – reaching a peak in the so-called 'constitutional coup' in 1996 and the following dissolution of the elected parliament – with a policy of 'selective engagement'. Official contacts with Belarus were downgraded to the level of assistant secretary and below. US foreign aid to the Belarusian government as well as government consulting activities were restricted, with some exceptions including humanitarian aid and educational exchange programmes. Hence, Washington cut back its political and economic relations with the Belarusian state and focused on supporting the non-state sector.

In the following period, Washington reacted in particular to the ongoing undemocratic electoral practices. Only a few days after the 2004 parliamentary election President Bush signed the 'Belarus Democracy Act', intended as confrontational democracy promotion. The act announced explicit support for democratic forces (political parties, NGOs and independent media) and forbade the US government from providing Belarus with bilateral or multilateral loans and investments except humanitarian aid.

Subsequently, the United States sought to act as a strong voice against the Belarusian regime. It sponsored an anti-Lukashenko resolution of the UN Human Rights Commission, and initiated a series of donor coordination meetings with European partners. In addition, the US government implemented the travel restrictions announced in 2004 on Belarusian officials responsible for the disappearances of opposition members and election fraud (Helsinki Commission 2006), and promised focused democracy promotion in the following areas: 'promoting independent news media, supporting political initiatives toward democracy, encouraging a national movement for free government and unifying the opposition around a common candidate to challenge President Alexander Lukashenko in 2006' (Kessler 2005). Generally, as seen above, US foreign aid to Belarus was mainly focused on the promotion of democracy. In 2005 and 2006 President Bush and Secretary Rice met repeatedly with Belarusian democratic activists – symbolic demonstrations of confrontational US policy towards Minsk.

Given the colour electoral revolutions of 2003–5 in the CIS region, the focus of US policy towards Belarus was directed at the 2006 presidential election especially. During the election campaign the United States provided large amounts of financial aid amounting to several million dollars, mostly to opposition parties to support the rival candidate Milinkievich (Kunter 2007: 37–8). US organizations, coordinated by USAID and supplemented by smaller European donations, dominated external aid during this period (Kunter 2009: 2).[32]

The 2006 presidential election itself provoked strong US reactions. Following Lukashenko's 'pervasive election fraud, corruption and human rights abuses', a US travel ban was imposed on him and other leading officials in May 2006

(Thomas 2006c). In June 2006, the Bush Administration endorsed targeted sanctions by freezing all US assets held by Lukashenko and other members of government, and prohibited US citizens from entering into business relations with them (US Department of State 2006).[33] US Congress on its part passed a new Belarus law in July 2006 'to provide assistance for democracy-building efforts, fund radio and television broadcasting to the people of Belarus and introduce additional sanctions against the regime of the Belarusian dictator' (Thomas 2006a).

Thus, in both 2007 and 2008 respectively, $20 million was earmarked for democracy promotion activities such as support for NGOs and international exchanges, as well as $7.5 million for radio and television broadcasting to the Belarusian people.[34] Sanctions ranged from a ban on US entry for Belarusian government members to a variety of targeted financial sanctions, including a 'request' to the US government to vote against non-humanitarian financial aids to Minsk at the international level (Thomas 2006a).

In the following period, the release of political prisoners was the central issue in US policies. Washington responded to the Belarusian salami tactics for the first time with economic sanctions.[35] In November 2007, accounts of the oil company Belneftechim, the biggest Belarusian exporter to the United States, were frozen, and sanctions expanded to encompass two subsidiary companies in March 2008. Five months later, Minsk finally released all political prisoners, which Washington welcomed as a step in the right direction (Helsinki Commission 2008a: 4). To Washington, especially the economic sanctions seemed to have caused Minsk to back down to a US political demand for the first time.[36] At this juncture, assistant secretary David Merkel travelled to Belarus to explore the possibility of dialogue. Following this, the US government suspended sanctions against both Belneftechim and its subsidiary companies for six months.[37]

According to the 'thaw' between the West (especially the EU) and Belarus, the United States did not announce additional sanctions as a reaction to the 2008 parliamentary election, but declared its intention 'to maintain our dialogue with the government and people of Belarus' (US Department of State 2008a). The incoming Obama Administration also held out the prospect of improvements in bilateral relations. However, a rapprochement did not take place. This was due to the lack of further 'significant steps' towards improving the political situation after the limited reforms in 2008 (Secretary of State 2009). Consequently, political sanctions were kept in place and diplomatic relations virtually frozen. The *ad interim* representation with a chargé d'affaires at the US embassy became a permanent condition, while all in all US attention to Belarus declined. As a result, Washington's handling of Minsk was consistently tied to political conditions: 'The status quo on reform in Belarus should be met by status quo on our sanctions' (Secretary of State 2009).

In the run-up to the 2010 presidential election, US engagement was significantly lower than in the 2006 election.[38] In addition to massive criticism of the election outcome and the repression, Washington urged the Belarusian authorities to immediately release all those arrested and to protect citizens' right to free media (White House 2010). On 23 December 2010, secretary of state Hillary Clinton condemned the regime in a joint statement with EU high representative Catherine Ashton, and demanded that Minsk comply with the OSCE commitment to democratic reforms. She once again stressed the explicit conditionality of US relations with Belarus (US Department of State 2010c). In a US Senate hearing dealing with the 'crackdown in Belarus' in January 2011, responses to the Lukashenko regime were discussed, in particular the question of how to ensure that Minsk finally lived up to its democratic commitments (US Senate 2011b).

At the end of January 2011, the State Department announced the US response to the controversial presidential election in Belarus and the ensuing crackdown. This included three specific 'sets of actions': tightening of sanctions against the government,[39] increased support for democratic forces,[40] as well as close cooperation with the EU aimed at demonstrating determination and unity through a coordinated transatlantic Belarus policy (cf. US Department of State 2011). It was no coincidence that the State Department announced new sanctions against Belarus on 31 January 2011 – at the same time as the Council of Europe did. In February, a US delegation attended an international donor conference in Warsaw in order to announce increased assistance to Belarusian democratic forces and encourage others to take similar steps.[41]

The increased US support for democratic counterweights (especially civil society, independent media and political parties) is also evident at the level of democracy aid. This applies to USAID, IRI and NDI (see above). IRI, for example, expanded its promotion of opposition and pro-democratic forces in the last two years, especially in connection with their election preparations and participations (IRI 2011). In addition to the above-mentioned FSA aid, the NED increased its grants for Belarus projects significantly: from $1.8 million in 2005 to $2.8 million in 2009. In particular the spending dedicated to the promotion of freedom of information (from $0.6 million in 2005 to $0.8 million in 2009) and civil society (from $0.6 million in 2005 to $1.1 million in 2009) was increased.[42] In addition, NED introduced a new border-crossing funding area 'to support the activities of Central European organizations which are carrying out democracy-building programs and sharing their experiences, skills and programme models with counterparts in Belarus' (NED 2010).

In sum, the US reaction – like Germany's – to Lukashenko's autocratic course since the mid-1990s has been to impose political sanctions that in the middle of the 2000s ultimately led to an openly confrontational strategy towards Minsk. Accordingly, the US government used stigmatizing rhetoric against the regime and sanctioned its leading representatives directly. This, in turn, was supplemented in the 2006 presidential election by directly supporting the opposition in order to build up political counterweights and, later, by the first economic sanctions. The intensity of the confrontational strategy can be traced back on the one hand to the strong ideological bias of US foreign policy (under Bush's Freedom Agenda, cf. Poppe 2010), and on the other hand to the euphoria triggered by the colour revolutions. In the following period, the United States coordinated its

Belarus policy more closely with the EU, remaining generally – apart from a brief phase of partial easing of sanctions – faithful to its policy of conditionality. Under Obama, however, the highly ideological Belarus rhetoric has been downgraded.

Results

The established authoritarian conditions in Belarus, together with a complicated geostrategic context, have impeded not only a change in power and regime, but also a successful democracy promotion policy by Germany and the United States. On the one hand, the recipient context in Belarus restricts the possibilities of external democracy promotion: so far, the Lukashenko regime has not been willing to react to Western demands for democratic reforms, and key players from the political opposition and civil society have not succeeded in establishing noteworthy political counterweights. On the other hand, Russia's dominant position shapes the regional context for Western policy towards Belarus. The year 2004, with its Orange Revolution in Ukraine, marks a watershed in the direction of 'authoritarian backlash' and resolute resistance to Western democratization attempts within the CIS. At the same time, Russia as a (disturbing) factor was increasingly taken into consideration in Western policy towards Belarus. After Putin took office in 2000, Western perception of Russia increasingly changed for the worse.

At the same time, German and US policies towards Belarus indicate an orientation to democracy promotion – except for military intervention – across all dimensions: international observation, development policy, diplomacy and international cooperation. Both states regularly participated in the OSCE electoral observation missions in Belarus and condemned the government for instances of election frauds that occurred. With regard to development policy, both focused on promoting civil society. However, Germany avoided – apart from some activities of the political foundations – supporting opposition groups and political parties, while the United States was very active in the (direct) support of the opposition. At the same time, both governments condemned – with the United States doing so more explicitly – the undermining of democratic institutions (e.g. through referendums) as well as the repression of the opposition and in general of civil society.

As part of the common EU policy, Germany conditioned its political cooperation with Belarus consistently on democratic norms. In response to violations of liberal-democratic principles Germany imposed political sanctions, stopped carrying on advisory activities for the government and severed political contacts at the highest level. However, most of the time the German government remained sceptical about a comprehensive strategy for isolating Lukashenko and generally about tightened sanctions. This only changed recently under the conservative-liberal government of Angela Merkel and Guido Westerwelle. In a similar way, the United States consistently made democracy-related demands in its policy towards Belarus. In response to Lukashenko's rapid autocratization, the United States also imposed political sanctions at an early stage. Over time, the United States demonstrated greater willingness to impose sanctions than Germany or the EU. In addition to targeted sanctions against the political leadership, the first economic sanctions were imposed on Belarus in 2007/8. Although the change of government from Bush to Obama was followed by a moderation of the stigmatizing rhetoric, the overall US policy towards Belarus continued to be marked by continuity.

How did Germany and the United States deal with conflicting objectives? Germany was initially confronted with the *extrinsic conflict of objectives* between democracy and national interests, less due to Belarus itself than to (geostrategic) respect for Russia. Berlin was sceptical about the dominant position of Russia in Belarus, accompanied by Lukashenko's dictatorial rise, but did not initially consider it a serious problem, and was willing to take Russian interests into account. Consequently, Germany's democracy promotion did not challenge the 'privileged' interests of Russia too directly. In the following period, Putin's Russia was, however, identified not only as a disturbing factor for the democratization of Belarus, but also as possible danger for its independence. For Berlin, this became apparent in the 'economization' of Russian foreign policy in 2007, and came to a head in the Russo-Georgian war in 2008. Not least for this reason, German policy was partially and temporarily shaped by an oscillation between cooperation and confrontation. Pursuing the EU's engagement policy, Germany subordinated the objective of regime change to the postulate of Belarusian independence and its orientation towards the West, although Lukashenko's post-electoral repression in 2010/11 caused this to remain short-lived.

For the United States, the regional context – that is the geostrategic competition with Russia – gained in importance comparatively early. However, it barely gave rise to an extrinsic conflict of objectives that would have significantly challenged the confrontational US policy towards Belarus. From a US perspective, a policy of regime change served to promote democracy as well as a Western orientation and the independence of the country. Hence, from the beginning the United States pursued a proactive policy of democracy promotion directed against the political influence of Russia in Belarus. Accordingly, the temporary rapprochement of the United States in response to concessions by the Lukashenko regime in 2008–10 remained more limited than in the case of the EU/Germany, but also coincided with a period of declining interest and increasing disengagement on the part of Washington.

For Germany, the *intrinsic conflict of objectives* (democracy versus democracy) was only very indirect. When a regime change in Belarus came to be more and more strongly desirable in the early 2000s due to the dictatorial power consolidation and political repression, no fear was expressed on the German side that a rapid change might also give rise to considerable instability or run counter to the will of the majority. Such a conflict was not a matter of discussion concerning the (robust) sanctions against the regime. In response to Lukashenko's 'constitutional coup' in 1996, as well as to the controversial presidential elections in 2006 and 2010, with the repressions that followed, Berlin chose (with the EU) a course of comprehensive political and at least limited economic sanctions. The temporary rapprochement between 2008 and 2010 was less due to an intrinsic conflict of objectives in democracy promotion than to the strategic consideration that an (institutional) bonding of the country might facilitate a Western orientation as well as – albeit in the medium to long term – a democratization of Belarus.

US policy on Belarus was confronted even less with intrinsic conflicts of objectives. In the second half of the 1990s, the US government reacted to Lukashenko turning away from democracy by extensively restricting bilateral political and economic relations. Accompanied by political sanctions, in the 2000s Washington delegitimized the Belarusian regime as the 'last dictatorship in Europe' and aimed at rapid change in Belarus. Especially during the presidential election in 2006, the US government was strongly committed to helping the Belarusian opposition achieve a change in government. At the same time, the United States relied on direct support of the opposition and later even on economic sanctions.

To what extent can these reaction patterns be explained by the profiles – i.e. the respective configuration of determinants (see Chapter 3) – that characterize the bilateral relations of the two democracy promoters with Belarus? In the German case, economic and security interests as well as domestic special interests have only a limited effect. However, this effect is contradictory: material interests favour a preference for cooperation, while there are democracy-orientated NGOs (such as the dbg) in the area of special interests. Particular importance is to be attached to international democracy norms insofar as Germany committed itself primarily in the EU context to the democratization of Belarus. The importance of the EU for German democracy promotion towards Belarus became even more pronounced when three neighbouring countries – Lithuania, Latvia and Poland – joined the EU. Since 2004, these new member states have set the tone for a more active EU neighbourhood policy towards Belarus.

Additionally, German democracy promotion is shaped by a shared identity that leads to Belarus being perceived as a European country. In normative terms Germany is therefore highly demanding towards Belarus, in contrast to other CIS countries. Furthermore, the different traditions of Germany's political parties are also relevant for the strategy chosen towards Belarus. While for the SPD, Willy Brandt's eastern policy principle of 'change through rapprochement' still plays a major role, the CDU supports this idea to a lesser extent. In the absence of German economic and security interests in Belarus, the Christian Democrats traditionally emphasize calls for democracy.

Regarding the case of the United States, neither economic and security nor domestic special interests make a significant difference, especially as bilateral relations are marked by a simple lack of relevant interests. The perception of Belarus as a European country also constitutes an important identity reference point for the United States – if not as decisive as in the case of Germany – while the international democracy norm – in terms of common OSCE membership –

has a limited effect that becomes manifest particularly in OSCE election observation activities. Except for the Bush Administration's more offensive rhetoric, which exacerbated confrontation with Lukashenko, the repeated change of government between Democrats and Republicans did not bring about any significant policy changes.

In addition, Germany and the United States have a high to very high power position vis-à-vis Belarus. This generally had the effect of supporting confrontational democracy promotion. In this respect, Belarus differs markedly from Russia, which meets Germany and even the United States at eye level.

In the case of Belarus, Germany deviates from theoretical expectations. This has been evident especially in the – if temporarily suspended – policy of imposing sanctions against the Lukashenko regime since 1997. Along with the EU, German policy oscillated, contrary to the ideal-type Civilian Power, from political sanctioning of the Belarusian regime (1997 and 2006) to a rapprochement policy (2008–10) and back to a now proactively pursued sanctions policy. However, the second side of the two-track approach – the support of civil society – corresponds to the expectations for a Civilian Power insofar as it was of a non-confrontational nature. Generally, the behaviour of Berlin 'deviating' from the norm can indeed be confirmed. Possibly, increased sensitivity for the lack of democratic developments in the immediate European neighbourhood led the German government to become more 'freedom-fighting' in nature.

In line with theoretical expectations, the United States acted as a protagonist of the ideal-type Freedom Fighter. Washington's approach to dealing with the 'last dictatorship of Europe' remained consistent in tying policy to conditionality. Shaped by the absence of relevant economic and security interests on the one hand and by ideological predispositions on the other, US democracy promotion in Belarus consequently developed into a clear dual strategy following the 'selective engagement' policy of 1997: political and economic sanctions against the regime as well as direct support of democratic forces in the country. The period when sanctions were eased in 2008 remained not only brief but also limited.

Notes

1 This became even more relevant when both the EU and NATO approached Belarusian borders in 2004. With the Eastern Enlargement of the EU in May 2004 three Belarusian neighbours – Poland, Lithuania and Latvia – concurrently joined the Union; equally, in March 2004, Lithuania and Latvia became members of NATO. Poland has been a member country of NATO since 1999.
2 On transformation in Belarus cf. Förster (1998), Lorenz (2001), Korosteleva et al. (2003), Sahm (2002), Timmermann (2008).
3 The German news magazine *Der Spiegel* called the then unknown Lukashenko a 'charlatan', whose election meant an escapade on the part of Belarus. Lukashenko – in former times instructor for KGB border troops, Kolkhoz chairman and the only Belarusian delegate to vote against the dissolution of the Soviet Union in 1991 – linked his candidacy with the populist promise to expel all the 'rogues' and 'corrupt clerks' from the government. Lukashenko had already acquired the reputation of a

fighter against corruption prior to the election, being the head of a parliamentary anti-corruption commission. His foreign policy strategy amounted to the following: 'We cannot just separate from Russia. We are born to be connected.' (*Der Spiegel* 1994).

4 However, this Union, conceived as a remake of the Soviet Union, did not have any consequences. Instead it resembled a 'simulated integration' with Russia (Sahm 2008: 52). Only the Defence and Customs Unions were implemented at a later date.

5 Lukashenko responded by calling the mandate of the OSCE mission into question, accusing them of interference in internal affairs. The mission was terminated at the end of 2002 and replaced only by a monitoring office.

6 The Belarusian leadership also seemed to reach out to the EU. In November 2008 they delivered a non-paper to the EU, confirming their willingness to discuss the new media law and the electoral code. Concrete steps taken included allowing some independent newspapers to have access to state-controlled presses and distribution networks (Sahm 2008: 57–8).

7 Earlier, a television documentary about Lukashenko broadcast on the Kremlin-controlled NTV channel, accused him among other things of abuse of authority, contacts with criminal elements as well as being responsible for the disappearance of political opponents.

8 In contrast, only 51.1 per cent of the voters supported Lukashenko in independent exit polls. Here also, no opposition candidate had notable success (RFE/RL 2011).

9 Already since 1996 Freedom House has rated Belarus as 'not free' (cf. Freedom House no date). Polity IV attributes a constant value of '−7' to the country, which on a scale from '−10' to '+10' depicts it as an autocracy (Systemic Peace no date).

10 From spring 2011, given the worst economic crisis in Belarus since independence, this understanding, however, has been facing a crucial test the outcome of which is still uncertain.

11 However, Lukashenko's first working visit led him to Germany in 1996, followed by attendance at the Hannover Fair in 1998, where he was also officially welcomed by then prime minister of Lower Saxony and later German chancellor Gerhard Schröder.

12 Indeed the EU did not arrange an action plan for their neighbourhood policy, but released an outline in a non-paper 'What the European Union could bring to Belarus'. It offered eased travel conditions to the EU for Belarusian citizens, support to the Belarusian economy and development cooperation in various areas, provided that the Belarusian government respected democratic rules and allowed free and fair elections, freedom of opinion and assembly, and that it released all political prisoners as well as resolved the cases of opposition members who had disappeared (European External Action Service 2011a).

13 Russia supplies 8 per cent of the gas and 12 per cent of the oil needs of the EU via Belarus (Ulrich 2010:113).

14 According to ODA criteria, Belarus was not included in international development aid until 2005. Thus, the country has been an ODA recipient for only a few years.

15 I owe this suggestion to Astrid Sahm and also thank her for commentary on an earlier version of this chapter.

16 During this conference German and European representatives meet regularly with official representatives of Belarus in an open dialogue. The conference also provides an important platform for Belarusian civil society and the government.

17 In the run-up to the election, the EU also showed a positive attitude to Belarus. On 15 September 2008, it welcomed the latest developments and announced a possible change of policy in the context of the parliamentary election, while linking such a change with the demand for progress (Council of the European Union 2008).

18 But it also referred to slight improvements in the human rights situation for the opposition, compared with the local elections in early 2010 and the presidential election in 2006 (Bundestag 2010a: 1–3).

19 Although the evaluation by the Leftist parliamentary group ('Die Linke') of political

conditions in Belarus was similarly critically, it rejected Western interference as ideologically motivated and thus as undermining the national sovereignty and political self-determination of the Belarusian population (cf. Bundestag 2006b: 1698–9).

20 The German government noted post-electoral events in Belarus 'with great concern'. It insistently urged the Belarusian leaders to allow freedom of speech and assembly to their citizens and made them responsible for the personal safety of demonstrators (AA 2006a). When Belarusian security forces adopted drastic measures against demonstrators in Minsk, Steinmeier even formulated the German claims more succinctly, condemning 'the unjust use of violence' and the 'inappropriate action' against detained activists of the democracy movement, and urged the release of all those imprisoned. At the same time, he underlined continued support for the opposition as well as the talks with his Russian colleague Lavrov on this issue (AA 2006b).

21 As a symbolic act of support for the Belarusian opposition, the presidential candidate Milinkievich was honoured with the Sakharov Award of the European Parliament in 2006. It was also not surprising that Angela Merkel again welcomed the opposition candidate in Berlin after his electoral defeat (*Die Welt* 2006).

22 As late as summer 2012 these activities became public and prompted harsh criticism in Germany.

23 These funds are intended to finance scholarships, training for journalists, and projects to promote democracy and the rule of law.

24 According to a resolution of the Bundestag in February 2011, the German government was supposed to campaign for a review of international credits for Belarus as well. Furthermore, complimentary visas should be provided especially for those Belarusian citizens at risk of 'political prosecution'. At the same time, the parliamentarians called upon the EU to discuss developments in Belarus with Russia in order to establish a joint approach towards the Lukashenko government (Bundestag 2011b: 2). It is remarkable, however, that there was no consensus among the parties concerning the entry of Belarusian citizens into the Schengen area. While the SPD required the possibility for 'principally all' Belarusians to enter the EU on a no-charge basis (Bundestag 2011c: 2), the Greens went even further and called for complete abolition of visas (Bundestag 2011d: 2).

25 The dramatic aggravation of the situation concerning democracy and human rights in Belarus subsequent to the presidential election even prompted the dbg, an organization mostly engaged in dialogue between the two countries, to cancel its upcoming Minsk Forum in autumn 2011.

26 After the opening of the Bureau for Belarusian Affairs in Lithuania in 2007 the KAS tried to improve their relationship of mutual trust to democratic opposition in Minsk, and started an EU financed project to promote independent media (KAS 2008: 85). Furthermore, ahead of the parliamentary election in 2008, leaders of the Belarusian opposition were brought together with international experts for a meeting under the slogan of 'A chance for democracy' (KAS 2009: 77).

27 The Soviet Union's nuclear stockpile was sited in Russia, Belarus, Ukraine and Kazakhstan. Belarus was the first former Soviet Republic to (unconditionally) abandon nuclear weapons.

28 Lukashenko's seizure of several Western embassy buildings in 1998, including the residence of the US ambassador, was responded to with the recall of Western ambassadors and a visa ban for members of the Belarusian parliament. Political relations consequently reached a temporary deadlock. Only in 1999 and after protracted negotiations did the Western ambassadors return and move out of their disputed residences, whereas Minsk had to pay compensation.

29 At global level, she placed Belarus in the same category with Cuba, Burma, North Korea, Iran and Zimbabwe (US Senate 2005: 4).

30 This is an independent agency of the US government, founded in 1976, to monitor and promote compliance with the Helsinki Final Act and other OSCE commitments in its member states.

31 These were 'numerous reports of Belarusian sales or delivery of weapons or weapons-related technologies to states of concern, including state sponsors of terrorism.' (Thomas 2006a).
32 This dominance led to a strong influence of US democracy promoters in developing the strategies of the opposition forces in the country (Kunter 2007: 38).
33 The US treasury expanded these sanctions in February 2007 to six other Belarusian government representatives as a result of their involvement in political oppression (Kaufman 2007).
34 However, these Congressional budget requests were not fully implemented. The actual US foreign assistance to Belarus in 2007 and 2008 amounted to $16 million and $17 million respectively (US Department of State 2009).
35 Previously the United States has avoided this kind of sanctions in order to prevent negative consequences for the population.
36 However, assistant secretary David Kramer drew attention to the geostrategic context as well: 'the Russian attack against Georgia also contributed to Belarus' decision to take this step.... The repercussions of that move on all of Russia's neighbours have forced them to rethink some of their policies and approaches' (Helsinki Commission 2008a: 8).
37 This was again extended for three months in March 2009 and for six months in June 2009.
38 In the context of an OSCE summit US Secretary of State Clinton only declared in a joint statement with her Belarusian colleague Martynov on 1 December 2010 that 'enhanced respect for democracy and human rights in Belarus remains central to improving bilateral relations' (US Department of State 2010b). The main focus of the statement was, however, the Belarusian contribution to nuclear security.
39 The sanctions included: the revocation of the general license authorizing US persons to cooperate with the two subsidiaries of Belneftekhim, a significant expansion of the list of Belarusian officials subject to the travel ban, and imposition of additional financial sanctions against Belarusian individuals and/or entities that were blamed for repression and human rights violations.
40 Therefore, expansion of US assistance to the Belarusian civil society, independent media and democratic parties by at least 30 per cent was announced for 2011 (in 2010 the United States provided $11 million in assistance).
41 Some 40 countries including EU members, the United States, Japan and Turkey as well as many NGOs participated in the conference 'Solidarity with Belarus'. Altogether, €87 million in aid was promised for Belarus (AA 2011a).
42 Sponsored partners were primarily the opposition coalition 'United Democratic Forces' as well as youth groups, labour unions, regional NGO Resource Centres and independent/alternative media (US Department of State 2008b: 882).

References

AA (2006a) 'Bundesminister Steinmeier zur Situation in Weißrussland', *Press Release*, 23 March. Online, available at: www.auswaertiges-amt.de (accessed 2 May 2011).

AA (2006b) 'Weißrussland', *Press Release*, 26 March. Online, available at: www.auswaertiges-amt.de (accessed 3 May 2011).

AA (2010a) *Europa endet nicht an der Ostgrenze Polens. Die Außenminister Westerwelle und Sikorski im Interview mit dem Tagesspiegel*, 5 November. Online, available at: www.auswaertiges-amt.de (accessed 3 May 2011).

AA (2010b) 'Westerwelle und Sikorski: Wahlen in Belarus ein herber Rückschlag', *Press Release*, 20 December. Online, available at: www.auswaertiges-amt.de (accessed 5 May 2011).

AA (2011a) 'Belarus', *Countries A to Z*, March. Online, available at: www.auswaertiges-amt.de (accessed 5 May 2011).
AA (2011b) *Gemeinsam gegen das weißrussische Regime. Von William Hague und Guido Westerwelle*, 28 January. Online, available at: www.auswaertiges-amt.de (accessed 5 May 2011).
AA (2011c) *Klare politische Antwort an Belarus*, 7 January. Online, available at: www.auswaertiges-amt.de (accessed 6 May 2011).
AA (2011d) *Solidarität mit Belarus*, 2 February. Online, available at: www.auswaertiges-amt.de (accessed 24 May 2011).
BMZ (2011) *TRANSFORM-Programm*, 6 October 2009. Online, available at: www.bmz.de (accessed 16 June 2011).
Bundesregierung (2006a) 'Deutschland, die Europäische Union und Russland. Partnerschaft für die Zukunft', *Bulletin*, no. 30–3, 21 March. Online, available at: www.bundesregierung.de (accessed 26 June 2011).
Bundesregierung (2006b) 'Rede des Bundesministers des Auswärtigen, Dr. Frank-Walter Steinmeier, in der Debatte zum Haushaltsgesetz 2006 vor dem Deutschen Bundestag am 29. März 2006 in Berlin', *Bulletin*, no. 34–2, 29 March. Online, available at: www.bundesregierung.de (accessed 26 June 2011).
Bundesregierung (2011) *Pressekonferenz zu den 28. deutsch-italienischen Regierungskonsultationen von Bundeskanzlerin Merkel und Ministerpräsident Silvio Berlusconi*, 12 January. Online, available at: www.bundesregierung.de (accessed 26 June 2011).
Bundestag (1996) *Stenografischer Bericht. 144 Sitzung* (Plenarprotokoll 13/144, 4 December), Bonn: Deutscher Bundestag.
Bundestag (1997a) *Belarus muß zu Demokratie und Rechtsstaatlichkeit zurückkehren* (BT-Drs. 13/8659), Bonn: Deutscher Bundestag.
Bundestag (1997b) *Die politische Lage in der Republik Belarus* (BT-Drs. 13/7942), Bonn: Deutscher Bundestag.
Bundestag (2000) *Stenografischer Bericht. 124. Sitzung* (Plenarprotokoll 14/124, 12 October), Berlin: Deutscher Bundestag.
Bundestag (2004) *Belarus vor den Parlamentswahlen und dem Referendum* (BT-Drs. 15/3811), Berlin: Deutscher Bundestag.
Bundestag (2006a) *Belarus vor den Präsidentschaftswahlen 2006* (BT-Drs. 16/816), Berlin: Deutscher Bundestag.
Bundestag (2006b) *Stenografischer Bericht. 22. Sitzung* (Plenarprotokoll 16/22), Berlin: Deutscher Bundestag.
Bundestag (2006c) *Belarus nach den Präsidentschaftswahlen* (BT-Drs. 16/1077), Berlin: Deutscher Bundestag.
Bundestag (2006d) *Stenografischer Bericht. 28. Sitzung* (Plenarprotokoll 16/28), Berlin: Deutscher Bundestag.
Bundestag (2010a) *Freie und gleiche Wahlen in Belarus einfordern – Menschenrechtslage verbessern* (BT-Drs. 17/4194), Berlin: Deutscher Bundestag.
Bundestag (2010b) *Stenografischer Bericht. 81. Sitzung* (Plenarprotokoll 17/81), Berlin: Deutscher Bundestag.
Bundestag (2011a) *Stenografischer Bericht. 84. Sitzung* (Plenarprotokoll 17/84), Berlin: Deutscher Bundestag.
Bundestag (2011b) *Belarus – Repressionen beenden, Menschenrechtsverletzungen sanktionieren, Zivilgesellschaft stärken* (BT-Drs. 17/4685), Berlin: Deutscher Bundestag.
Bundestag (2011c) *Belarus – Repressionen beenden, Menschenrechtsverletzungen sanktionieren, Zivilgesellschaft stärken* (BT-Drs. 17/4667), Berlin: Deutscher Bundestag.

Bundestag (2011d) *Belarus – Repressionen beenden, Menschenrechtsverletzungen sanktionieren, Zivilgesellschaft stärken* (BT-Drs. 17/4686), Berlin: Deutscher Bundestag.

Bundestag (2012) *Zusammenarbeit der Bundesregierung mit Polizei und Grenzsicherungstruppenin Belarus* (BT-Drs. 17/10603), Berlin: Deutscher Bundestag.

Council of the European Union (2006a) *Presidency Conclusions (7775/06): Declaration on Belarus*, 23–4 March 2006. Online, available at: www.consilium.europa.eu (accessed 28 June 2011).

Council of the European Union (2006b) *Press Release 7939/06 (Presse 95)*, 10–11 April. Online, available at: www.consilium.europa.eu (accessed 28 June 2011).

Council of the European Union (2008) *Press Release 13030/08 (Presse 255)*, 15–16 September. Online, available at: www.consilium.europa.eu (accessed 28 June 2011).

Council of the European Union (2010) *Conclusions on Belarus. 3041st Foreign Affairs Council Meeting*, 25 October. Online, available at: www.consilium.europa.eu (accessed 28 June 2011).

Der Spiegel (1994) 'Belorußland: Schüsse in der Nacht', *Der Spiegel*, 27 June, 126–7.

Der Spiegel (1996) 'Belorußland: Führer der Slawen', *Der Spiegel*, 23 September, 162.

Der Spiegel (2008) 'Weissrussland: Der Spieler von Minsk', *Der Spiegel*, 22 September, 113.

Deutsche Botschaft Minsk (2011) *Germano-belorusskie dvustoronnie otnošenija* [German–Belarusian Bilateral Relations]. Online, available at: www.minsk.diplo.de (accessed 6 June 2011).

Die Welt (2006) 'Merkel empfängt Milinkewitsch', *Die Welt*, 7 April. Online, available at: www.welt.de (accessed 15 May 2013).

European External Action Service (2011a) *Non-Paper. What the European Union could bring to Belarus*. Online, available at: http://eeas.europa.eu (accessed 6 July 2011).

European External Action Service (2011b) *EU–Belarus Relations*. Online, available at: http://eeas.europa.eu (accessed 6 July 2011).

EXPORT.BY (2010) *External Trade*. Online, available at: http://export.by (2 July 2011).

FAZ (2011) 'Bundesregierung kritisiert Lukaschenka scharf', *Frankfurter Allgemeine Zeitung*, 1 January. Online, available at: www.faz.net (accessed 15 May 2013).

FES (2011) *Die Arbeitsschwerpunkte der FES in Belarus*. Online, available at: www.fes.kiev.ua (accessed 6 July 2011).

FNS (2011) *Unsere Projektarbeit in der Ukraine und Belarus*. Online, available at: www.freiheit.org (accessed 1 July 2011).

Förster, H.L. (1998) *Von der Diktatur zur Demokratie – und zurück? Eine Auseinandersetzung mit der Problematik der Systemtransformation am Beispiel der ehemaligen Sowjetrepublik Belarusland*, Hamburg: Dr. Kovač.

Freedom House (no date) *Belarus*. Online, available at: www.freedomhouse.org/country/belarus (accessed 15 May 2013).

GTZ (2010) *Die GTZ in Belarus: Förderprogramm Belarus*. Online, available at: www.gtz.de (accessed 10 November 2010).

Helsinki Commission (2006) *Freedom Denied: Belarus on the Eve of the Election*, Hearing, 9 March. Online, available at: www.csce.gov (accessed 4 April 2011).

Helsinki Commission (2008a) *Business as Usual? Belarus on the Eve of Elections*, Hearing, 16 September. Online, available at: www.csce.gov (accessed 4 April 2011).

Helsinki Commission (2008b) 'Helsinki Commission to Hold Hearing on Upcoming Elections in Belarus', *Press Release*, 9 September. Online, available at: www.csce.gov (accessed 4 April 2011).

Helsinki Commission (2008c) 'Belarus still Lacking Progress in Human Rights and

Democracy in Run Up to Election', *Press Release*, 24 September. Online, available at: www.csce.gov (accessed 5 April 2011).
Helsinki Commission (2010) 'Helsinki Commission Condemns Violence amid Elections in Belarus', *Press Release*, 21 December. Online, available at: www.csce.gov (accessed 5 April 2011).
IRI (2011) *Belarus Overview· Belarus Program Summary*. Online, available at: www.iri.org (accessed 5 April 2011).
Jarábik, B. and Rabagilati, A. (2010) 'Assessing Democracy Assistance: Belarus', *FRIDE Report*, May 2010. Online, available at: www.frice.org/publication/772/belarus (accessed 9 May 2011).
Kahlweit, C. (2008) *Wahl-Werbung. Weißrussland und die EU*, 19 September. Online, available at: www.sueddeutsche.de (accessed 7 June 2011).
KAS (2008) *Jahresbericht 2007*. Online, available at: www.kas.de (accessed 2 June 2011).
KAS (2009) *Jahresbericht 2008*. Online, available at: www.kas.de (accessed 2 June 2011).
KAS (2011) *Auslandsbüro Belarus: über uns*. Online, available at: www.kas.de (accessed 2 July 2011).
Kaufman, S. (2007) *Six More Belarusian Officials Sanctioned by United States*, 28 February. Online, available at: www.america.gov (accessed 5 April 2011).
Kessler, G. (2005) 'Rice Encourages Belarus Opposition. Russia Criticizes Secretary's Actions', *Washington Post*, 22 April, A-12.
Korosteleva, E.A., Lawson, C.W. and Marsh, A.J. (eds) (2003) *Contemporary Belarus. Between Democracy and Dictatorship*, London: Routledge.
Kremlin (2010) *Bessmyslennaja polosa naprjaženija v otnošenijach s Belorussiej objazatel'no zakončitsja* [The Senseless Period of Tension in Relations with Belarus is certain to Come to an End]', video blog of the Russian President, 3 October. Online, available at: www.kremlin.ru (accessed 2 April 2011).
Kunter, B. (2007) 'Belarus: Do No Harm. Forderungen an externe Demokratieförderung', *Osteuropa*, 57 (1): 35–48.
Kunter, B. (2009) 'Förderung der Zivilgesellschaft in Belarus nach dem 11. September 2001', *Newsletter Wegweiser Bürgergesellschaft* 18, 11 September. Online, available at: www.buergergesellschaft.de (accessed 16 June 2011).
Legvold, R. (1999) 'Belarus in US Foreign Policy', in S.W. Garnett and R. Legvold (eds) *Belarus at the Crossroads*, Washington, DC: Carnegie Endowment for International Peace.
Lindner, R. (2004) 'Am Ende des Lateins? Belarus, die EU und das europäische Erbe', *Osteuropa*, 54 (2): 195–205.
Lorenz, A. (2001) *Vorwärts in die Vergangenheit? Der Wandel der politischen Institutionen in der Republik Belarus seit 1991*, Berlin: Humboldt-Universität.
NDI (2011) *Belarus*. Online, available at: www.ndi.org/Belarus (accessed 2 May 2011).
NED (2010) *Annual Yearbook 2010*. Online, available at: www.ned.org (accessed 2 May 2011).
OECD (2011) *Datenbank Qwids*. Online, available at: www.oecd.org (accessed 7 July 2011).
OSCE/ODIHR (2008) *OSCE Election Observation Mission Statement of Preliminary Findings and Conclusions: Belarus – Parliamentary Elections, 28 September 2008*, 29 September. Online, available at: www.osce.org/ (accessed 12 September 2011).
OSCE/ODIHR (2010) *International Election Observation Statement of Preliminary*

Findings and Conclusions: Belarus – Presidential Election, 19 December 2010, 20 December. Online, available at: www.osce.org/odihr/74638 (accessed 12 September 2011).

Pofalla, R. (2010) *Rede des Chefs des Bundeskanzleramtes, Bundesminister Ronald Pofalla, MdB anlässlich der Eröffnung des 13. Minsk-Forums am 3. November 2010, Minsk. EU und Belarus am Vorabend der Präsidentschaftswahlen*. Online, available at: www.ibb-d.de (accessed 2 July 2011).

Poppe, A.E. (2010) 'Whither to, Obama? US Democracy Promotion after the Cold War', *PRIF Report*, no. 96, Frankfurt a.M.: Peace Research Institute Frankfurt.

RFE/RL (Radio Free Europe/Radio Liberty's Belarus Service) (2011) *НІСЭПД: за Лукашэнку – 51,1%* [NISEPD: for Lukashenko – 51.1%], 19 January. Online, available at: www.svaboda.org (accessed 4 March 2011).

Rontoyanni, C. (2005) 'Belarusian Foreign Policy' in L. Dov (ed.) *Changing Belarus*, Paris: Institute for Security Studies (Chaillot Paper, no. 85).

Russland-Aktuell (2010) *Lukaschenko sieht sich als Leidensgenosse von Luschkow*, 1 October. Online, available at: www.aktuell.ru (accessed 21 March 2011).

Sahm, A. (2002) 'Isolationärer Autoritarismus. Die innere Entwicklung in der Republik Belarus', in D. Bingen and K. Woycicki (eds) *Deutschland – Polen – Osteuropa. Deutsche und polnische Vorüberlegungen zu einer gemeinsamen Ostpolitik der erweiterten Europäischen Union*, Wiesbaden: Harrassowitz.

Sahm, A. (2005) 'Nach der Wahl ist vor der Wahl. Belarus weiter auf Isolationskurs?', *Osteuropa*, 55 (1): 77–90.

Sahm, A. (2008) 'Simulierter Wandel? Belarus '08', *Osteuropa*, 58 (12): 51–8.

Secretary of State (2009) *Belarus: Demarche to EU Members on Sanctions*, Cable 09STATE112644, 2 November. Online, available at: http://wikileaks.ch (accessed 4 May 2011).

Spiegel Online (2005) 'Rice unterstützt Opposition gegen Lukaschenko', *Spiegel Online*, 21 April. Online, available at: www.spiegel.de (accessed 15 May 2013).

Spiegel Online (2010) 'Lukaschenko kritisiert Westerwelles "Belehrungen"', *Spiegel Online*, 2 November. Online, available at: www.spiegel.de (accessed 14 April 2011).

Statistisches Bundesamt (2011) *Genesis-Online Datenbank*. Online, available at: www-genesis.destatis.de (accessed 7 June 2011).

Steinmeier, F.-W. (2008) *Grußwort des Bundesministers des Auswärtigen, Dr. Frank-Walter Steinmeier, zur Eröffnung des XI. Minsk-Forums am 13. November 2008*, 13 November, Berlin.

Systemic Peace (no date) *Polity IV Country Report 2010: Belarus*. Online, available at: www.systemicpeace.org/polity/Belarus2010.pdf (accessed 15 May 2013).

SZ (2008) 'Opposition spricht von Farce', *Süddeutsche Zeitung*, 29 September. Online, available at: www.sueddeutsche.de (accessed 15 June 2012).

Thomas, J. (2006a) *New Congressional Measure Aims to Promote Democracy in Belarus*, 1 August. Online, available at: www.america.gov (accessed 8 February 2011).

Thomas, J. (2006b) *Cheney at Summit in Lithuania Says Russia Has "Choice to Make"*, 4 May. Online, available at: www.america.gov (accessed 8 February 2011).

Thomas, J. (2006c) *Bush Bans Travel to US by Belarusian Dictator*, 16 May. Online, available at: www.america.gov (accessed 8 February 2011).

Timmermann, H. (2008) 'Die Republik Belarus', in W. Schneider-Deters, P.W. Schulze and H. Timmermann (eds) *Die Europäische Union, Russland und Eurasien. Die Rückkehr der Geopolitik*, Berlin: Berliner Wissenschafts-Verlag.

Ulrich, R. (2010) 'Die Politik der EU gegenüber Belarus', doctoral thesis, Universität Wien. Online, available at: http://othes.univie.ac.at (accessed 7 June 2011).

USAID (1999) US*AID Assistance Strategy for Belarus, 1999–2002*. Online, available at: http://pdf.usaid.gov (accessed 10 July 2011).
USAID (2009) *Belarus. Country Profile*. Online, available at: www.usaid.gov (accessed 10 July 2011).
US Census Bureau (2011) *Trade in Goods with Belarus*. Online, available at: www.census.gov (accessed 9 July 2011).
US Department of State (1998) *Belarus Country Report on Human Rights Practices for 1997*, 30 January. Online, available at: www.state.gov (accessed 3 May 2011).
US Department of State (2006) *Bush Imposes Financial Sanctions on Top Belarusian Officials*, 20 May. Online, available at: www.america.gov (accessed 3 May 2011).
US Department of State (2008a) *Statement on Parliamentary Elections in Belarus. Statement by Sean McCormack*, 29 September. Online, available at: www.america.gov (accessed 3 May 2011).
US Department of State (2008b) *Congressional Budget Justification, FY 2009*. Online, available at: www.state.gov (accessed 3 May 2011).
US Department of State (2009) *Foreign Operations Appropriated Assistance: Belarus. Factsheet*, 1 December. Online, available at: www.state.gov (accessed 3 May 2011).
US Department of State (2010a) *Background Note: Belarus*, 27 August. Online, available at: www.state.gov (accessed 3 May 2011).
US Department of State (2010b) *US–Belarus Joint Statement on Nuclear Security, Human Rights*, 1 December. Online, available at: www.state.gov (accessed 3 May 2011).
US Department of State (2010c) 'Joint US–EU Statement on Post-Presidential Elections' Situation in Belarus', *Media Note*, 23 December. Online, available at: www.state.gov (accessed 4 May 2011).
US Department of State (2011) 'Belarus Sanctions', *Press Statement*, 13 January. Online, available at: www.state.gov (accessed 4 May 2011).
US Senate (US Senate Committee on Foreign Relations) (2005) *Opening Statement by Dr. Condoleezza Rice*, 18 January. Online, available at: http://foreign.senate.gov (accessed 9 July 2011).
US Senate (2011a) *Crackdown in Belarus: Responding to the Lukashenka Regime. Testimony of Philip H. Gordon*, 27 January. Online, available at: http://foreign.senate.gov (9 July 2011).
US Senate (2011b) *Crackdown in Belarus: Responding to the Lukashenka Regime. Hearing*, 27 January. Online, available at: http://foreign.senate.gov (accessed 9 July 2011).
Weiss, G. (2008) *Vybory sdelali Belarus' unikal'noj stranoj* [Elections turned Belarus into a Unique Country], 6 October. Online, available at: http://naviny.by (accessed 6 March 2011).
White House (2004) 'Statement on the Belarus Democracy Act of 2004', *Press Release*, 20 October. Online, available at: http://georgewbush-whitehouse.archives.gov (accessed 9 July 2011).
White House (2006) 'Presidential Message on Belarus', *Press Release*, 24 March. Online, available at: http://georgewbush-whitehouse.archives.gov (accessed 9 July 2011).
White House (2010) 'Statement by the Press Secretary on Belarusian Elections and Political Violence', *Press Release*, 20 December. Online, available at: www.whitehouse.gov (9 June 2011).
Wittrock, P. (2006) *Milinkewitsch in Deutschland. Lukaschenko ist geschockt*, 7 April. Online, available at: www.spiegel.de (accessed 4 June 2011).

9 Democracy promotion in Russia
The ambivalent challenge posed by Putinism

Hans-Joachim Spanger

The Russian Federation poses a special challenge to democracy promotion for a number of reasons. For decades, as the former Soviet Union, it represented the ultimate antithesis to Western democracies. It was the systemic antagonism between East and West that forged and emphasized the collective self-conception and self-awareness of the West as a democratic community. Conversely, it was necessary for the Soviet Union to disappear for democracy promotion to gain a prominent place in the canon of Western policy it had previously been denied under the auspices of Cold War era power politics.

In addition, the democratic transformation of the Russian Federation, in line with the other republics of the former Soviet Union, proved far more difficult than in the Central and East European countries. From the beginning, purpose and direction had remained nebulous and it was on the territory of what used to be the USSR in the middle of the last decade that the much cited 'backlash' against democracy promotion first took form.

Furthermore, Russia – despite its territorial meltdown to a size not seen since Peter the Great and despite the loss of its once paramount importance in world politics – is anything but a negligible quantity: geographically the largest country in the world, the most populous in Europe, the most potent military power next to the United States and economically endowed with natural resources unparalleled in the world. Despite its secular decline the Russian Federation has as a result been, and still is, such an important player that relations with it can hardly be reduced to a single dimension, in particular not to that of democracy promotion.

The fact that Russia's decline after ten years of self-destructive transformation – comparable to a modern-era *smuta*, the early seventeenth-century 'Time of Troubles' that brought Russia to the brink of disintegration – finally came to an end, and that Russia and the Russians became increasingly aware of their country's importance, is associated with the name of one man: Vladimir Vladimirovich Putin. However, he also stands for the price to be paid for stabilization: the destruction of nascent Russian democracy. His person and the policy agenda of Putinism he embodies together place in very sharp relief the conflicting objectives of Western policy.

Putin's authoritarian stabilization and the conflict situation in Russia

The Russian Federation was able to emerge on the political stage as an independent state on 1 January 1992 because of a bold promise: without the ailing machinery of the Soviet Party apparatus and without the burden of Asian benefactors and European free riders, not only would Russia be in a position to benefit exclusively from its wealth but it would also collectively generate that wealth provided that political participation and economic market forces achieved their full potential. Yet this promise soon proved illusory. In reality Russia was plunged into a ten-year continuous and deep crisis. The crisis played out in four dimensions: the emergence of a political system somewhere between democracy and autocracy, the uncertain survival of the no longer centrally managed economy, the search for a new international role for a country that had lost its former magnitude and – above all – status, and not least coming to grips with the socio-cultural traces that 70 years of state socialism had left behind within the population.

These four dimensions of crisis were not only inextricably intertwined, they also reinforced each other in such a way that the 1990s amounted to another low point in Russia's twentieth century of catastrophes. There was thus relatively widespread approval when Putin stopped ennobling the end of the USSR as a prelude to Russia's 'return to civilization' and instead castigated it as 'the greatest geopolitical catastrophe' of the last century (*BBC* 2005). Putting an end to that catastrophe and initiating the return to its former pre-eminence became the core mission of his presidency after 2000. He implemented this plan with impressive consistency and enduring consequences in all four dimensions of the crisis.

First and foremost, during his rule oligarchic power came to an end. In Yeltsin's 1990s, these 'new Russians' had not only snapped up Russia's choicest economic assets, but had also 'piratized' the state itself. This, however, was accompanied by the demise of freedom of the press as well as of the freedom of association that followed shortly thereafter. A similar fate befell the presidents and governors of Russia's at times up to 89 constituent entities. It is true that these political leaders had regarded – and abused – their local constituencies as fiefdoms and were gradually incorporated into the 'vertical power' machine cultivated by Putin; however, this took place at the expense of democratic participation.

Economic policy proved similarly contradictory. Having started with courageous reforms – an example is the introduction of a flat tax on income of 13 per cent – and dedicated to an orthodox culture of macroeconomic stability, at the same time Putin paved the way for a thoroughly corrupt bureaucracy to make good on their losses and defeats in the previous decade. Nevertheless: thanks to steadily rising energy prices for the first time in decades the country experienced annual economic growth of 7 per cent on average – until the world economic crisis of 2008/9 briefly interrupted this economic upswing.

The same disparate picture is to be found in foreign policy. Here Putin succeeded in lending substance to Yeltsin's hollow superpower fantasies, and thus ensured that Russia was again taken seriously, at least to some extent. This, however, did not mean that the country had finally found its place and role, still vacillating as it was between multilateralism and multipolarism, between cooperative and confrontational overtures.

In the middle of the last decade, a new system developed, which – labelled 'Putinism' – relies on the trinity of authoritarian control, state capitalism and great power status. This system persisted beyond 2008, when during an interlude of four years Putin continued his political career as prime minister. His handpicked successor as president, Dmitry Medvedev, in the final analysis represented only the friendly persona of Putinism. Medvedev was partially and temporarily successful in emancipating himself from his mentor, but this was limited to attempts to achieve intellectual hegemony based on the rhetoric he used to portray himself as a self-styled guarantor of Russia's future, which also implied that Putin was a man of the past. However, it remains to be seen whether the old authoritarian state-centred pattern of Putinism has really lost momentum, as the depth of the 2009 economic crisis, the slow pace of economic modernization and diversification away from the resource-based economy and the obvious depression in many parts of the urban elites would appear to suggest. Putin's return to the presidency and the concurrent rise of the familiar autocratic tide among the ruling class signify the opposite.

The time frame of the case study is set by Vladimir Putin, starting with his takeover of the presidency on 1 January 2000 and ending with his return to the Kremlin on 7 May 2012. Key milestones and observation points are (*a*) the arrest of Mikhail Khodorkovsky in October 2003, followed by the dismissals of the last officials of the Yeltsin era – the head of the Kremlin administration Aleksandr Voloshin in the same month and of prime minister Mikhail Kasyanov in February 2004; (*b*) the attack on the school in Beslan in September 2004, used to justify the abolition of direct elections of governors; (*c*) the Orange Revolution in Ukraine in November 2004; (*d*) Putin's legendary and widely noted speech at the Munich Security Conference in February 2007; (*e*) the war in Georgia in August 2008; and (*f*) the apparent drifting apart of the political tandem in the years 2010/11 which came to a sudden and revelatory end on 24 September 2011 when the swapping of offices was announced.

Putin and his system of governance perfectly reflect the three fundamental dilemmas of democratization. *First*, there is the contradiction between democracy and stability. Neither Putin nor Medvedev have ever left any doubt that they were striving for a democracy in the liberal European tradition. But achieving this objective is said to be subject to preconditions and in the context of 'sovereign democracy' Russia feels no need for Western lecturing of any kind. Yet it reflects Putin's dialectic that stability and welfare are declared to be preconditions of democracy, but can only be achieved through undemocratic means. Consequently, under his reign theory and practice have been drifting further and further apart. Rising from its knees and shaking off the humiliation that Russia suffered in the name of democracy in the 1990s, constituted the rhetorical backdrop for Putinism as much as the claim to have placed the country on a path of stable development did.

The *second* contradiction – the one between democracy and governability – is directly linked to the point above. Putin's concept of rule – not least shaped by his own experience as a Soviet intelligence agent – is based on two pillars: 'manual control', as Putin's inclination to monopolize decision-making has been labelled in Moscow, and the 'power vertical' combined with the 'dictatorship of law'. The latter, however, was not so much intended to hold power in check as it was to serve as a source of legitimacy. Certainly, even in the less than favourable conditions of Putinism the rule of law could make some progress and not all elements of a democratic system have been dismantled. Nevertheless, the regime has left no doubt that it feels Russia needs a firm hand that cannot be answerable to democratic control. So far the Putin government has held fast to this approach, although the loss of democratic transparency and control is already laying bare the dysfunctional and debilitating downside of bureaucratic routines.

The *third* contradiction – that of democratic procedures versus democratic majority – can also be found in Russia, because it is one of the peculiarities of Putinism that for most of Putin's tenure he relied on fairly broad popular support. Opinion polls, even those conducted by independent institutes, and electoral successes of the Kremlin's party 'United Russia' in 2003 and 2007 – albeit won with the support of quite a few 'administrative resources' and other shady means – present such a clear picture that the results would probably not have turned out radically different in a less constrained competition. Apparently, electoral support was predicated on a social contract in which the population exchanged its political rights for stability and welfare. In the serious economic and social crisis of 2009 that contract was subjected to considerable strain; and the voting results in the 2011/12 elections not only resulted in large demonstrations not seen since the demise of the Soviet Union, but also made clear that this contract would not last forever.

Democracy promoters can identify two conflicting goals from this conflict situation:

1 *Democracy versus donor interests (extrinsic).* There is a yawning gap separating the values of the Russia of Vladimir Putin and Western democracies. None of the conventional standards allow Russia's political system to be placed on a democratic development path. Since 2005, confronting the political leadership in Moscow with this diagnosis and urging corrections has regularly triggered fervent defensive reflexes – and thus endangered cooperation and as a result economic and security interests as well.

   On the other hand, Putinism can point to a record of success that corresponds less with Western values though certainly with Western interests. The stabilization of the country has reined in the potential for chaos of the 1990s; economically, Russia has mutated from being the sick man on the Moskva River to being a market of boundless opportunities; and in foreign policy, it has become a predictable partner after all. The 'Partnership for Modernization', first launched by Germany's Foreign Minister Steinmeier in spring 2008, certainly attempts to gradually reconcile values and interests, but nevertheless the relationship between Russia and the West still displays reservations on both sides due to the gaping divide in values – and it is no accident that talk about 'modernization partnership' has all but disappeared in the course of 2012.

2   *Democracy versus democracy (intrinsic)*. Taking stock of democratization in the 1990s is devastating from the perspective of most Russians: the decade led to the rule of the oligarchy and of the provincial governors and their cronies, with the twin consequences of privatizing the state and pauperizing the population. This has erected a serious barrier to democratization. Putin can take credit for having ended that, but at a price that created barriers that were no less serious. However, the promotion of political forces that handed the country over to capitalist pirates and brought it to the brink of collapse in the 1990s – a pattern also observed after the Orange Revolution in Ukraine – could jeopardize achievements without necessarily overcoming the barriers that Putin has erected.

Germany: the 'trading state' preserves its interests

The profile of bilateral relations

For Germany, Russia is one of the most important countries, immediately after the United States as the leader of NATO and France as its foremost EU partner. The German attitude towards Russia can be summarized as follows: because of its size, its population and its historic role, Russia remains a great power and deserves appropriate treatment. It still has impressive military potential and vital natural resources while offering virtually unlimited market opportunities. At the same time Russia undoubtedly forms a part of Europe geographically, historically and culturally, although to a lesser extent when judged against (Western) European political standards. And its historical role has proved no less ambivalent than that played by Germany, as Russia has suffered the most in Germany's racist war of extermination and the citadel of the world's proletariat still exerts a measure of influence all the way into the eastern part of Germany proper today.

Economic relations are – neither side leaves any doubt over this – the foundation and driving force behind German–Russian relations. This is true not only for the first half of the last decade, during which Gerhard Schröder as 'chief salesman' of the resource- and energy-dependent German trading state and Vladimir Putin as Russian modernizer in the Petrinite statist tradition complemented each other ideally. The ideal pairing has been seamlessly continued by Merkel and Medvedev joining hands in an explicit 'modernization partnership'. This was not always the case as in the 1990s the economic relationship was marked by continual crisis management, and only the ascent of Putin (and the concurrent rise in world energy prices) resulted in sustained growth – until the economic crisis of 2009 left deep scars.¹ In 2008, Russia was among the ten largest trading partners of Germany: at €37.1 billion (2009: €25.2 billion) it was eighth among German imports and at €33.1 billion (in 2009 only €20.6 billion) was twelfth in German exports, whereas Germany at that time was still the biggest trading partner of Russia, although in the meantime and in spite of strong recovery after the slump in 2009 it has fallen behind China (cf. Statistisches Bundesamt 2010).²

Against this background, German–Russian relations gained an importance of their own and are recognized and cultivated as a value in their own right. This is also reflected in policy documents such as the German coalition agreements that show, regardless of party composition, an astonishing continuity along the lines of a 'strategic partnership' with Russia, either referred to explicitly or in substance (Spanger 2010).

This does not mean, however, that German–Russian relations have not been affected by crises. Yet such phases were almost exclusively induced externally: mostly as a consequence of drastic changes in the global political climate and the importance of showing solidarity vis-à-vis one's allies. The brief war between Russia and Georgia in 2008 marked the most serious crisis in German–Russian relations since the war in Kosovo in 1999. However, the energy crises, in which Russia cut off the gas supply to Ukraine in January 2006 and again in January 2009 and stopped supplying oil to Belarus in January 2007, had a similarly detrimental effect on the perception of Russia. The same happened with the infamous speech by Putin in February 2007 at the Munich Security Conference, which was widely perceived as a return to the Cold War era. All this meant that between 2007 and 2009 Germany's Russia policy was largely confined to damage control, sandwiched between Russia's ostentatious self-assertion and an American unilateralism that garnished its ignorance of Russian interests with an increasingly confrontational attitude.

The profile of German democracy promotion in Russia

In the very last years of the Soviet Union and the early years of the Russian Federation, German democracy promotion operated under a basic premise: to secure the political survival of those supposed guarantors of Russia's transformation to whom the German political class felt especially indebted – not least with respect to German unification. This initially applied to Mikhail Gorbachev and later to Boris Yeltsin, who was in close touch with German chancellor Helmut Kohl through a much-touted and equally maligned 'sauna friendship'. This goal shaped most official activities such as the provision of 1,000 training positions annually for young Soviet business people by the chancellor in 1988, the extensive compensation payments for the withdrawal of the Western Group of Soviet forces or the untied credit of DM3 billion, which Helmut Kohl granted Boris Yeltsin in support of his re-election in January 1996. This cosy relation continued under Gerhard Schröder and Vladimir Putin – yet with a short break since the rapprochement between the two ultimate 'buddies' was not free of conflict.

Yet, since the middle of the last decade, the view has dominated in Germany's political class that democracy in Russia must be established not so much in cooperation with but rather in spite of the political leadership in Russia. Although this view prevailed much earlier – in the turbulent 1990s – among the relevant German organizations of democracy promotion in Russia – the political foundations –, it originally had little impact on decision-makers in Berlin.

Russia does not fit into the classical institutional framework of democracy promotion. The country is not a recipient of ODA. Instead, it participated in TRANSFORM, the official programme to support the transition in the CIS, which was originally administered by the Federal Ministry of Economics and Technology and later by the Federal Ministry of Development (BMZ). But this can only to some extent be considered democracy promotion. The state-run KfW Development Bank currently responsible for implementing the successor to TRANSFORM has an office in Moscow. Its focus is on the 'promotion of the private corporate sector', the banking and financial sector and the training of managers in the private and public sector (KfW 2010). The GTZ/GIZ 'International Services' also runs its own office. Its main client is the European Commission, with activities 'in the areas of economic reform and legal and institutional advice' (GTZ 2010).[3] Until the merger with GTZ to form GIZ the same was true for InWEnt, which emphasized 'foreign trade promotion, the expansion of international education systems and the promotion of good governance', yet without an office of its own (InWEnt 2010).

Governmental organizations that are not officially pursuing democracy promotion but may have an impact in the long term are worthy of note as well: the German Academic Exchange Service (DAAD, Deutscher Akademischer Austauschdienst), the German Research Foundation (DFG, Deutsche Forschungsgemeinschaft) promoting scientific cooperation and exchange as well as the Goethe Institute responsible for external cultural policy. For many years they have been represented with their own offices in Moscow, and the Goethe Institute also maintains offices in St Petersburg and Novosibirsk.

Russia is one of the few countries where all political foundations have their own offices headed by German staff in the capital city Moscow. The first and largest foundation has been the FES, whose office was opened in April 1989, followed by branches in St Petersburg and more recently in Novosibirsk.[4] It was followed in 1993 by the KAS, which also maintains a branch office in St Petersburg, the FNS in 1993 and shortly thereafter by the Bavarian HSS. In 1999, they were joined by the HBS, which is aligned with the Greens, and in May 2003 finally by the RLS of the Left (Linke) party.[5] They are the key players in German democracy promotion in Russia.

Significant differences are not evident in the basic policy documents of these foundations. The foundations are all devoted to establishing a democratic order and the rule of law, a pluralist society and an open market economy, and have an interest in aligning Russia more closely with the European Union. All the foundations support federalism and local self-government, promote freedom of the media, an independent judiciary and promising junior elites, and all are committed to peace and conflict prevention. Additional subjects are contemporary history and German–Russian relations. In their practical work all foundations collaborate with a fairly wide range of NGOs, political parties, citizens' initiatives, human rights organizations and academic institutions. Exclusive partnerships, as was the case in the early phase of the FES in Russia, no longer exist today (Spanger and Reddies 2011). The instruments are predominantly traditional: political education, policy advice and 'policy dialogue' in particular, implemented through conferences, seminars and study tours.

Beyond this declaratory homogeneity of the foundations, however, there are a number of differences in day-to-day practice that partly reflect their party affiliations, and partly the preferences of individual representatives. Thus only the FES interacts with Russian trade unions and only the KAS concerns itself with the Russian Orthodox Church; the HBS has a specific interest in social initiatives and advocacy groups, including 'Memorial' as its most important partner. The FNS is devoted to a virtually invisible phenomenon – Russian liberalism – and the HSS focuses on the visit and contact requests of compatriots from Bavaria. It is also in line with respective general preferences that the HBS places an emphasis on gender, ecological sustainability and nonviolence, whereas the RLS has a strong interest in critically addressing neoliberal globalization and assisting marginalized groups in Russian society.

Officially, the preferred addressee of the foundations is the 'democratic' or 'liberal' spectrum in Russia, which has fairly limited visibility and has more or less fundamentally opposed Putin since he took office. Therefore, there is some pushing and shoving among the foundations for their partners of choice. But even more pointedly than the German government, they must cope with the dilemma of finding a middle ground between political irrelevance and bad compromise. Forging a broad political dialogue has been the answer to this, a path being pursued by all the foundations.

Perception analysis

Since the end of the Soviet Union, Germany has clearly grasped that Russia's political order corresponded only to a very limited degree to liberal democratic standards. However, whereas during the 1990s a secular change for the better was suggested, since 2000 a negative trend has dominated the picture. Surprisingly, the 'candid words' called for every now and then, gradually died away. The 1990s were characterized by extensive demands on the Russian leadership, typical for the patronizing nature of the asymmetrical East–West discourse of that period. These demands included the improvement of regulatory conditions for German business in Russia, the classical set of liberal political norms, foreign policy demands such as a departure from traditional thinking in spheres of influence, and also suggestions on how to appropriately deal with Russia's history (see, for example, Huterer and Krumrei 2001). There was a consensus that its defeat in the Cold War would be followed by unilateral Russian adaptation.

Russia was called upon to recognize 'the democracy-promoting goals of the EU' as 'the basis for partnership' (Ischinger 2000: 12).

With the advent of Putin the balance of power gradually changed, and to Germany this made Russia simultaneously more attractive as well as more problematic. While German business interests called for strong links and German security interests at least suggested cooperation, because Russia's consolidation as a state and rise as an economic power clearly corresponded with a decline in democratic standards, emphasizing democratic values became an impediment. This triggered some irritation in German politics and society and somehow even impaired the definition and pursuit of German interests. Although in Germany no human rights and democratization industry of US proportions exists, policy towards Russia must always assert itself against latent misgiving rooted in more than 200 years of history. Although democracy did not play any role at that time, human and civil rights and their implementation have become the linchpin in the current debate. This regularly proves problematic when pursuing a purely interest-based policy. And it has led to peculiar shifts in political perception.

This is especially true for Gerhard Schröder. At the beginning of his tenure he also subscribed to the established language and in line with the democracy provisions of the EU partnership agreements called upon Russia to bear in mind that: 'The community of values is the first prerequisite for the further integration of Europe' (Schröder 2001). At the end of his term he saw this as already achieved – at least in bilateral relations: 'We have launched a future-oriented partnership that is founded on the commitment to common values and interests' (Schröder 2005). This demonstrates a fairly unique interpretation of Russia's democratic evolution, which he also presented on other occasions, culminating in his characterization of Putin as an 'impeccable democrat' in 2004.[6]

Indeed the CDU/CSU opposition publicly criticized these extravagant judgments and, after taking over government in 2005, stated that it would place the relationship on a new basis, emphasizing its own liberal norms.[7] However, apart from a few skirmishes driven by purely domestic considerations not much remained of that announcement. Continuity has also been the hallmark of the current coalition of CDU/CSU and FDP. Hence Foreign Minister Westerwelle declared in 2010 that 'democracy and human rights' are always a topic of his Russian visits, but that it was not possible to 'measure [in] centimetres or metres,' how far Russia deviates from the rule of law (cf. AA 2010).

Only the German business community accompanied the Putin era without any critical overtones. Its most prominent representative, Klaus Mangold, long-time chairman of the Eastern Committee of German Business, boldly stated that Putin had not only implemented 'the most radical reforms' that 'Russia ever experienced' (*Handelsblatt* 2003), it was also a 'stroke of luck' that he had chosen Medvedev as his successor (Mangold 2008). By contrast, in the German Bundestag critical voices predominated that professed to view Russia first of all through democratic lenses, irrespective of partisan leanings. To the business community such an attitude appeared entirely inappropriate. As important as Russia is in German policy, its image in Germany remains contradictory.

Reaction analysis

The basic pattern of German–Russian relations can be summed up in one word: continuity. That is the result of very pronounced – namely economic – interests in Russia. And continuity moderates the reactions of Germany's political leadership to extraordinary events – whether it concerns the various stages of the Khodorkovsky trial, the carefully managed Russian elections, or the intermittent suppression of rallies by the opposition (such as the regular gatherings of the *nesoglasnyje*, the dissenters, until 2011). At the same time, Germany's political leadership frequently used the continuity argument to contain latent mistrust against Russia and dampen a sometimes widespread critical view taken by the German public. The German government benefited in part from the fact that Putin's authoritarianism did not come about in a forcefully programmatic manner, but only fully manifested itself around 2005/6 after gradually unfolding behind the veil of strict rule of law and democratic respectability. And even this proved temporary insofar as between 2008 and 2011 optimistic expectations of democratic tendencies were revived by Medvedev's declared support for necessary and rigorous reform. In the wake of Medvedev's exit in 2011/12 these expectations focused on the rebellion of the 'new' Russian middle class, which – in the dialectical twist of modernization – seems to be not only the offspring of Putinism but also its adversary – and has since provoked ever more Putin-style authoritarian retaliation.

Continuity has been the rule even given that changes in government originally aroused different expectations – yet another peculiar aspect of German–Russian relations (cf. Spanger 2005). This has to do with the structural dilemma that in German Russia policy the *entente cordiale* that regularly emerged at the very top contrasts with a marked distance at the social and political base. Only the German business community can be considered a reliable and articulate lobby for Russia, whereas each dissonance immediately mobilizes anti-Russian reflexes in society and the media. This usually finds a political outlet in the parliamentary opposition, irrespective of the party involved. And these voices tend to survive for a while in official pronouncements and partially also in the government's actions after a change of power.

Gerhard Schröder's government is a case in point. He began his term with a firm criticism of the *tête-à-tête* and the 'sauna friendship' between Helmut Kohl and Boris Yeltsin, and promised a 'new realism'. This entailed not only a 'diversification of political contacts' in favour of democratic forces – compulsory for all newly appointed Western officials – but also 'restraint on new financial assistance programmes' (Erler 1998). Seven years later, he sounded very different: 'Today, Germans and Russians are joined together more closely than ever before. We are united by a strategic partnership for a peaceful, prosperous Europe and a stable world order'. For Schröder this summary of his policy achievements regarding Russia was 'one of the wonders of European history, considering the horrors of the past' (Schröder 2005).

This pattern was essentially repeated by Angela Merkel, although not quite so enthusiastically. Her preference for a value-based policy towards Russia referred to above was qualified by the CDU/CSU foreign policy spokesperson Friedbert Pflüger even before the general election in 2005 by assuring that there would be 'a lot of continuity in German–Russian relations' under a CDU/CSU-led government. Moreover, Angela Merkel was said to have 'a good and close trusting relationship with the Putin Administration and Putin himself,' because Russia is 'a huge country with vast energy resources' and a 'booming country' which is also crucial for peace and security in Europe (Pflüger 2005). However, in spite of the pragmatic tone, the subjective factor also played a noticeable role for Merkel. The end of German–Russian 'cronyism' – Schröder's equivalent to Kohl's 'sauna friendship' – contrary to Pflüger's expectations manifested itself in a distance to Vladimir Putin that even extended to the body language of Angela Merkel (and vice versa). By contrast, her relationship with Dmitry Medvedev proved almost intimate from the beginning. It was no coincidence and of deliberate symbolic importance, that even before his inauguration she was the first to pay a courtesy visit to the newly elected president on Women's Day, i.e. on 8 March 2008.[8]

This visit may have been inspired by competition within the coalition government, because foreign minister Frank-Walter Steinmeier had had a close relationship with the new president since his days as head of the chancellery, a position in which Medvedev had served as Steinmeier's counterpart in the Kremlin. In terms of competition, a whole range of activities and counter-activities of the chancellor and the foreign minister can be noted. The fact that Steinmeier strove to act independently in shaping relations with Russia inevitably resulted in mutual demarcation and occasional tensions. Thus the chancellor's office responded with some restraint when in 2007 the planning staff of the foreign ministry produced a strategy paper entitled 'Rapprochement through Interlinking', with which, in the tradition of the Social Democratic *Ostpolitik*, it wanted to forge a new beginning for democratic change in Russia by incorporating it into pan-European structures. The opposite happened in the case of the 'candid words' used in public statements by Chancellor Merkel intended to highlight the gap in values between Germany and the Putin regime. Steinmeier was far more restrained than Merkel in this regard.

Finally, in spring 2008 Steinmeier seized the opportunity offered by the new ostensibly reformist Russian president to find a common denominator for democracy promotion and German interests in cooperation with Russia – in the shape of a 'modernization partnership'. Just a few months later the explicit 'confidence,' however, that 'the time for a substantial refinement and deepening of the EU–Russian, but especially the German–Russian relationship, has finally come,' faded away in the wake of the Caucasus war – and with it the 'great opportunity' that we must not 'miss under any circumstances' (Steinmeier 2008). Thus the 'modernization partnership' enjoyed only a brief career, although its rationale, perceiving Russia as 'indispensable partner' for the 'political ordering of the world of tomorrow' lived on (Steinmeier 2009). In addition, since 2009 the 'modernization partnership' has made a surprise comeback, this time via Brussels. Thus it was Foreign Minister Westerwelle who described German–Russian relations as 'strategic' and as a 'modernization partnership' based on a 'solid and broad foundation' and carried out in 'a close and trusting' way. More specifically this refers to the 'so far unmatched intensity' of economic interdependence, cultural exchange, political dialogue and the numerous contacts between the civil societies of both countries (Westerwelle and Lavrov 2010).[9] Yet Putin's return to the Kremlin in 2012 has apparently again silenced talk about this kind of German–Russian partnership.

German–Russian relations under the conditions of Putinism are therefore a classical example of the research finding that 'hard' interests invariably prevail over 'soft' values. But this diagnosis is not quite as straightforward as it seems, and needs qualification. For instance, German references to historical responsibility and the need for German–Russian reconciliation, i.e. appeals to values, justify the imperative of cooperation to an equal degree. In addition, the much avowed 'value gap' represents a critical element insofar as political decision-making cannot be separated from the suspicions harboured by the public regarding all things Russian. Therefore values are a nuisance to be reckoned with, but they are far from decisive for cooperation with Russia, as is the case with Belarus. Nevertheless, clashing values have repeatedly provoked official criticism.

This criticism concerns, for instance, Russian elections, which since 2003/4 can no longer be deemed fair and only partly free (if in fact they ever were). Here the German government has endorsed the judgment of the official observers from the OSCE and the Council of Europe.[10] But this was ultimately of no avail, because no consequences followed. For instance, after the State Duma elections in 2007, the German deputy government spokesman Thomas Steg declared that there was no doubt that the election had not been democratic, but that it had to be acknowledged that for Russia 'the road to democracy is not behind it but still lies ahead'. This too was said to underline the alleged need for a 'strategic partnership' (*Spiegel Online* 2007). The German government also criticized other actions by the Russian leadership. This applied in particular to the 'law to regulate the activities of non-commercial organizations,' introduced in autumn 2005 in the State Duma, which also affected the activities of the German political foundations by subjecting them to restrictive admission procedures and complex reporting requirements. Compared with the virtually unlimited opportunities in the 1990s, their scope of action became increasingly narrower during this period, for reasons that were both political and bureaucratic. However, thanks to the close German–Russian relations the German foundations received relatively favourable treatment, unlike foundations from, for instance, the United Kingdom and the United States.[11] And with the establishment of the civil society-oriented Petersburg Dialogue and of a German–Russian Youth Exchange Office they even expanded their activities, with official Russian blessing, into the realm of civil society. Moreover, under the premise that the work of the foundations had been aiming at initiating state–society dialogues, there was no immediate need for adaptation on their part – as long as this dialogue could include representatives from the opposition, which is still the case.

Another peculiarity of German–Russian relations should not be overlooked: continuity was threatened less by Russia than by the multilateral framework in which German policy operates. Since their admission to NATO and the EU the parameters of this framework have been determined to a great extent by Germany's eastern neighbours and their inclination to keep Russia at a distance – by the delay of negotiations on a new Partnership Agreement with the EU, by the speedy inclusion of Ukraine and Georgia in NATO, or by the resuscitation of political associations such as GUAM,[12] whose democracy postulates are directly aimed at Russia, Putin's and Yeltsin's alike. These activities took place predominantly in close coordination with the second country in this study, the United States of America.

The United States: balancing out interests and values

The profile of bilateral relations

In contrast to Germany, in the United States the importance of Russia has declined steadily since the end of the Cold War, and reached a low point during the Bush Administration (cf. Spanger 2008). The reason: Russia no longer serves as a partner in US global politics, highlighted by the withdrawal of the United States from arms control, once the most important bilateral instrument to that effect. The 'New START' (Strategic Arms Reduction Treaty) has changed little, although under Obama the once popular self-confidence of the indispensable hyperpower with a universal mission, which existed at Bush's time, has given way to a preference for multilateralism. Since the Bush era, if not earlier, Russia is perceived only through the 'prism of other problems'.[13] Here the 'global war on terror' as well as Iran and Afghanistan function as incentives for cooperation, while the US inclination to overcome nuclear deterrence by means of missile defence and its democratization agenda hold considerable potential for conflict.

A further complicating factor is that – also in contrast to Germany – the US economy does not provide much leverage with regard to Russia – economic relations are simply too weak. Thus, US exports to Russia amounted to $9.3 billion in its best year to date, in 2008 (in 2009 it fell to only $5.4 billion), while imports were significantly higher, standing at $26.8 billion (2009: $18.2 billion).[14] Overall, foreign trade with Russia is comparable to that with countries such as Hong Kong, Thailand, Nigeria and Colombia, amounting to less than one-tenth of US trade with China. However, in the interim there has been considerable dynamism; consequently, the Bush Administration made some efforts to emphasize the 'great untold story' of economic relations with Russia (Congressional Record 2007: 4747).[15]

Between the poles of cooperation and rejection, US policy towards Russia has proved anything but coherent under the conditions of Putinism. Nothing has become symbolically more charged than Bush's legendary look into Putin's eyes at their first meeting in June 2001, which gave him 'a sense of his soul' (Bush 2001b). With that he departed from the twofold change in course that his presidency originally professed: rejecting Clinton's 'alliance with Russian reforms,' and distancing itself from Clinton's 'happy talk,' with which he had allegedly courted the Russian leadership. By contrast, Bush originally preferred a 'tough realism'.[16] This realism explicitly refrained from democratizing interventions, because Western reform strategy in Russia had failed anyway as the rouble crisis of 1998 aptly demonstrated. Moreover, the creation of a 'democratic world' had to been seen as a 'second-order effect' that would come about by itself in the course of consistently pursuing American interests, as Condoleezza Rice noted (Rice 2000: 50). The emerging harmony at the top was deepened considerably by 9/11 because Russia immediately chose the right side in the war on terrorism and in the 'black and white world' proclaimed by Bush. However, the harmony was gradually and continuously lost over the years that followed, and at the end of his administration Bush left a wrecked relationship that, according to general opinion, had reached its lowest point since the end of the Cold War. Thus, Obama's 'reset' of US policy towards Russia was the logical consequence.

This development was also the result of an unfortunate coincidence, because Russia's importance for the United States diminished to the same extent as democracy promotion in US foreign policy and rhetoric increased in importance; 9/11 was a defining moment in this respect. The combination of these two factors led straight to the alienation caused by the clash between Bush's freedom and Putin's authoritarian mission. But even if at first glance the convergence of interests inspired by the realism of the initial phase of George W. Bush's presidency gave way to the subsequent divergence of values inspired by the idealism, we are actually confronted with a fluid and partly contradictory amalgam of values and interests in US policy towards Russia.

The profile of US democracy promotion in Russia

The daily business of US democracy promotion in Russia reflects Bush's freedom agenda much less than the rhetorical design would lead one to expect – at least as far as the resources that were provided by USAID for this purpose are concerned (Table 9.1).

The figures show a continuous increase in expenditures on democracy promotion until the middle of the last decade, from when they have remained by and

Table 9.1 USAID Russia programme 'Democratic Development'

	2000	2001	2002	2003	2004	2005	2006	2007	2008	2009	2010	2011	2012
Req.	16.45	15.03	17.37	20.56	15.83	19.48	17.40	28.18	26.20	30.33	35.90	35.20	35.40
Real	14.53	16.10	21.90	20.21	19.04	29.22	43.43	34.17	40.13	33.85	37.00	37.20	34.60

Sources: budget justifications USAID/Russia, online, available at: www.USAID.gov.

Note
In US$ millions. 'Req.' stands for 'requested', meaning the budget as proposed by the US administration. 'Real' stands for actual expenditures.

large at the same level until today. In 2012, democracy promotion comprised four programmes: 'Rule of Law and Human Rights', 'Good Governance', 'Political Competition and Consensus-Building' and 'Civil Society'. At the same time, the data also shows that during the Bush era it was the Congress which made the increases happen – despite Bush's ostentatious freedom agenda: especially between 2005 and 2008, appropriations for the promotion of democracy were considerably higher than the requests of the administration.[17] These rose significantly under Obama, who incidentally places much less emphasis on democracy promotion. Conversely, the generosity of Congress must come as a surprise in view of the scepticism of the Republican majority about granting such soft money and in light of the fundamental criticism they had levelled against Clinton's promotion of democracy in Russia.[18]

Another donor is the NED, which much like German political foundations operates in the institutional grey area between state and society and is endowed with its own Congress-approved budget. In 2009, the NED financed projects in Russia to the tune of just under $4 million, a decrease from $5.3 million in the previous year. Originally intended to provide the politically controversial funding of the two party foundations NDI and IRI, as well as the politically uncontroversial funding of the business and trade union organizations, the CIPE and American Center for International Labor Solidarity (Solidarity Center), the NED today also provides considerable funding to Russian organizations directly.[19]

In comparison with the German political foundations, the permanent presence of US democracy promoters in Russia is weak, because most offices were forced to close. The last to suffer this fate was USAID, which was forced by the Russian government to close its office by 30 September 2012; with 13 American and 60 Russian nationals, its level of staffing was remarkable.[20] This state of affairs results in a different profile in several respects. While the German foundations, mainly in cooperation with Russian partners, carry out their own activities and have ceased to provide direct financial support, it is quite the opposite with the US players. And while all German foundations pursue programmes that promote a broad-based dialogue, the efforts of the US foundations in democracy promotion have traditionally focused on 'empowerment' through training, technical equipment and financial aid. With the active assistance of NDI and IRI, the original intention was to support political parties in Russia, but the focus has progressively been shifted to civil society organizations, because hopes for the evolution of a viable democratic party system have all but disappeared. USAID-funded legal advice in the shape of programmes on the 'Rule of Law' and on 'Local Government' are the only area in which US democracy promotion – on a very limited scale – still maintains cooperative relations with Russian authorities.

Finally, several organizations primarily engaged in academic activities operate in Russia. Unlike their German counterparts these are privately financed and engage in democracy promotion to different degrees. The John D. and Catherine T. MacArthur Foundation and the Ford Foundation, for example, are represented with their own offices and special programmes in Russia; a few years ago the Open Society Foundation, called into life by George Soros, closed its office in Moscow and discontinued its work in Russia. In contrast, the Carnegie Endowment for International Peace maintains a large office, which employs mostly (well-known) Russian scholars and has achieved high visibility in the political discourse in Russia's capital.

Perception analysis

The political regime in Putin's Russia is viewed with great scepticism on both sides of the Atlantic; it is equally true for both that this scepticism is articulated much more loudly in the public arena and in parliament than by the respective governments. The consequences, however, have been very different in Berlin and Washington, where contrary to German continuity remarkable swings in policy have occurred. This was not primarily caused by Russia, but by the fact that over the last decade realism and ideological neo-conservatism had a very different weight in American politics and implied equally different views of Russia. At least under Bush Jr. the United States was really 'exceptional' in this regard.

Two programmatic statements by Condoleezza Rice in 2000 as Bush's campaign advisor and in 2005 as his secretary of state show the range of opinion. In 2000, she was still very committed to traditional realism, which at the time was much en vogue among the Republicans, and stressed the paramount importance of 'great powers' for peace, stability and prosperity. This, however, ignored 'the role of values, particularly human rights and democracy promotion,' as critics stressed. In her justification she pointed to the time needed to create a 'balance of power' internationally and nationally that permitted the ultimate 'triumph' of universal American values: 'And in the meantime, it is simply not possible to ignore and isolate other powerful states that do not share those values.'[21]

Since in January 2005 Bush had presented each nation with the 'moral choice' of choosing 'between oppression, which is always wrong, and freedom, which is eternally right' (Bush 2005), and since the Iraq war with its sovereign disregard of external and internal balances of power, this restraint no longer applied. In the changed conditions Rice proclaimed the exact opposite – pretty much in line with the notorious neo-conservatives:

> Our experience of this new world leads us to conclude that the fundamental character of regimes matters more today than the international distribution of power. Insisting otherwise is imprudent and impractical. The goal of our statecraft is to help create a world of democratic, well-governed states that can meet the needs of their citizens and conduct themselves responsibly in the international system.
>
> (Rice 2005a)

Obama, for his part, prefers the careful consideration of power-related factors, which means that his latent basic missionary disposition is of significantly lower operational relevance.

From this, however, it does not follow that Rice I demanded cooperation and Rice II demanded confrontation in Washington's dealings with Russia, even if from 2005 onwards her views on Russia increasingly focused on democracy and became correspondingly more critical. Rather, benign neglect was the starting point and malign neglect the terminating point of the reign of George W. Bush. Only Obama's 'reset' gave US policy towards Russia a basically consensus-based orientation. But even this has not taken place without any conditions.

Reaction analysis

While in the case of Germany continuity was the dominant pattern of relations with Russia, the opposite is true for the United States, although the respective ruling party in Washington did not consist of a coalition as it did in Berlin. However, the growing rift between Moscow's 'sovereign' and Washington's 'liberal' democracy illustrates only one defining element, especially since until the end of his two terms Bush showed some restraint in this regard, despite criticism in the United States and from a number of allies. Ignorance of Russian interests concerning missile defence, NATO expansion or the support of 'electoral revolutions' in the CIS proved more important, and since 2006 have provoked growing Russian resistance – and corresponding levels of escalation. Starting in 2007, ideological demarcation and the less than cooperative attitude of the United States have provided the background for the re-emergence of 'Cold War' images, leading relations between the two countries to the lowest point since the end of the Cold War.

This happened in several stages: after a bumpy start, up until the 2003/4 Russian election cycle the Bush Administration continued the 'happy talk' of the Clinton Administration, initially with Bush's peering into Putin's soul, and did not shy away from giving testimonials about Russia's democratic progress. Neither Chechnya nor the rapidly imposed limitations on freedom of the press in Russia provoked officially articulated concerns beyond the commitment to jointly advocate 'human rights, tolerance, religious freedom, the protection and promotion of free speech and independent media' (Bush 2001a).

Even the differences on Iraq could not call into question the 'trusting relationship' with Putin initiated in Ljubljana in 2001. Instead, immediately after the Iraq War the two 'allies in the war on terror' tried to pick up the thread where they had left off. On 27 September 2003 at Camp David and at the peak of its unrestrained statements of affection, Bush coined the oft-quoted words to that effect:

> Our goal is to bring the US–Russian relationship to a new level of partnership. I respect President Putin's vision for Russia: a country at peace within its borders, with its neighbors, and with the world, a country in which democracy and freedom and rule of law thrive.
>
> (Bush 2003b)

This rosy picture of the political situation in Russia came about in spite of Bush's turning to the idealistic interventionism that held global expansion of democracy high as a 'pillar' of peace and security of free nations.[22] But on 26 January 2004, just a few months after Camp David, the change in course finally began to affect relations with Moscow, when the first high-ranking member of the Bush Administration, secretary of state Colin Powell, fired an official shot across the bows over authoritarian tendencies in an article published in the Russian newspaper *Izvestiya*. This was preceded by elections to the State Duma in December 2003 and the arrest of Mikhail Khodorkovsky on 25 October 2003, with which the dismantling of the largest private oil company Yukos commenced.

In 2005, criticism of Putin's political course was voiced even more clearly. The criticism was delivered at a higher level, too, because for the first time the 'D' question was given prominence when Bush and Putin met in Bratislava in February 2005. This followed Bush's democracy euphoria in his second inaugural speech, which was to a large extent inspired by the colour revolutions in the CIS. In light of these apparent success stories Russia appeared to many in Washington's political class to be just another domino, which could be knocked over by means of consistent support for the electoral-revolutionary democratic movements. Although the administration shared these sympathies, it preferred to base its Russia policy on two more pillars: a continuous dialogue with the Kremlin on the rule of law and on democracy and keeping the country in organizations promoting economic liberalization and democratic development – such as the G8 (see Rice 2005c).

The practical consequences thus remained limited as the US administration refused to tie democracy-related conditions to the 'strategic partnership'. Instead it demonstratively expressed understanding for the difficult conditions in Russia and expressed its trust in the gradually democratizing impact of economic modernization. Accordingly, in 2005 Condoleezza Rice reiterated the 'vital importance' for the United States of 'the protection of democracy in Russia,'[23] but shifted this notion into the future, because 'for US–Russian relationships to really deepen, and for Russia to gain its full potential, there needs to be democratic development' (Rice 2005b). The geostrategic rationale was revealed even more clearly by the widely publicized speech Vice President Cheney delivered on 4 May 2006 in Vilnius. There he lashed out at Putin's authoritarian course, only to express his admiration for the economic and democratic achievements in Kazakhstan just a few days later.[24]

From that juncture until the end of his second term Bush was solely preoccupied with damage control in the 'complicated relationship' aimed at preserving the 'common ground for solving problems'.[25] The dual strategy of articulating 'strong differences' and pursuing 'mutual interests,' however, did not become more coherent because of the cordial relations between the presidents. This is all the more true as the agreement in the much-vaunted fields of international cooperation remained no less vague. There were only two issues where the interests of both 'quite nicely intersect,' as Nicholas Burns remarked on behalf of the administration: terrorism and non-proliferation.[26] In all other cases differences prevailed, making it necessary 'to push back' (Kramer 2007).

Not least with regard to Washington's own interests there were therefore plenty of reasons for a 'reset' of relations with Russia, which vice president Joseph Biden finally announced in February 2009. But it took some time to repair a relationship that his successor, William J. Burns, again on behalf of the administration, characterized as 'badly broken' one year later; therefore progress still appeared 'tentative and fragile' (Burns 2010: 3, 8) to him. The basic rationale of the new approach was not to allow differences to prevent opportunities for cooperation: 'We ought to be able to build on shared interests while not pulling our punches on differences.' This included granting Russia appreciably more sizeable political heft by approaching the country with 'respect' and acknowledging its 'due role as a great power' (Burns 2010: 2).

The confrontational element of 'pushing back,' however, did not disappear completely; in fact it still provokes reciprocal irritation from time to time. Thus Burns emphasized that the United States is not willing to accept 'nineteenth century views about spheres of influence' in the space of the former Soviet Union as well as the intention of being 'plainspoken and unapologetic about our interest in universal human rights' (Burns 2010: 5, 7). This, however, did not extend beyond a moderate expression of regret when the Russian authorities condemned US interference and thus terminated USAID's presence in the country.[27]

Yet for the ideological wing of the former Bush Administration this approach does not go far enough. In their criticism of Obama's Russia policy conservatives insist that a stable relationship was simply not possible without a fundamental change in Moscow. David Kramer, the former deputy assistant secretary of state for European and Eurasian Affairs and later assistant secretary of state for democracy and human rights, summarized this in the following statement: 'Until there is real change in Russian behavior and policy, both internally and in its foreign policy, the Obama Administration's efforts to reset relations are not likely to be reciprocated'. Hardly coming as a surprise, Kramer also explicitly sought to reinvigorate his dual strategy, quoted above, that had already led to the impasse under Bush: 'working with Russia wherever possible, while pushing back on Russian misbehavior whenever necessary' (Kramer 2010: 75).

Such attitudes still resonate strongly in the US Congress – across all party lines. As early as 2002 Congress adopted a 'Russian Democracy Act,' in which more than $50 million was earmarked for US democracy promotion in Russia.[28] After the arrest of Mikhail Khodorkovsky, congressmen even founded a 'Congressional Russia Democracy Caucus,' not as a lobby for Russia – which still does not exist–, but in order to focus political attention on undemocratic tendencies in Russia.

In the past, two longstanding Russia bashers played a particularly prominent role: Tom Lantos, who for a time served as Democratic chairman of the House Committee on Foreign Affairs, and John McCain, Republican senator and in 2008 presidential candidate. McCain, along with the former Democrat and later independent senator Joseph Lieberman, initiated a resolution in November 2003 that would have made the observance of democratic standards a prerequisite for Russia's participation in the G8 – an initiative that was pursued with growing insistence in the years that followed.[29] McCain and Liebermann also attempted to promote Bush's freedom agenda as the mandatory guideline for American foreign policy against latent reservations from within the administration by introducing the 'ADVANCE Democracy Act' in both houses of Congress in March 2005.[30]

In keeping with this, even after the admittance of Russia into the WTO in August 2012, Congress needed five more months to finally repeal the Jackson–Vanik Amendment.[31] For years Congress resisted moves by various administrations, because it sought to maintain this completely outdated legislation so that it could apply 'some modicum of real political pressure' to encourage democratic reforms in Moscow (US Senate 2005: 1). After passing Congress, the law repealing the Jackson–Vanik Amendment was signed by President Obama on 14 December 2012, yet only in conjunction with the so-called Magnitsky Act, which again primarily targets Russian officials.[32]

Numerous analyses and reports, regularly published by a plethora of think tanks and their task forces in Washington indicate that these attitudes do not represent isolated cases, particularly the demand to expel Russia from the G8. The most prominent example of the last decade is the extensive report 'Russia's Wrong Direction' of the Council on Foreign Relations published in March 2006. It was compiled under the joint chairmanship of the former Democratic presidential candidate John Edwards and the Republican Jack Kemp together with Madeleine Albright's former Russia expert, Stephen Sestanovich, as project director and co-editor.[33] The report – to which, among others, Obama's official adviser on Russia and since January 2012 ambassador to Moscow, Michael McFaul, contributed – manifested above all the considerable overlaps between the 'liberal interventionists' of the Clinton Administration and the 'neo-conservatives' of the Bush Administration. However, McFaul's resolutely pursued 'reset' policy in the Obama Administration also shows how readily democratic values are crushed in the mills of *realpolitik*.

Results

A focus on democracy promotion is reflected in German and US policy towards Russia in all relevant dimensions: political relations, electoral observation and promotion of democracy in the narrow 'positive' sense, directed at both civil society and the government. However, with the exception of election monitoring, mainly carried out by international organizations, the picture is not uniform, neither over time nor between the two actors.

Democracy promotion by US organizations is predominantly aimed at civil society. In contrast to the 1990s, support of political parties and government advice only take place on a very limited scale, due to the lack of adequate addressees. On the part of the German actors, the distinction between state and society is far less pronounced. The dominant aim of facilitating broad dialogue, shared by everybody, precludes strict separation. By contrast, US organizations still pursue the goal of 'empowering' relevant organizations, which by definition entails choosing sides politically.

Bilateral relations with Russia – in the areas of politics, economics and security – have been officially associated in both cases with the aim of universal democratic standards. However, there is no democratic conditionality: unlike the case of Belarus, to date there have been no sanctions, which would have been justified by violations of democratic standards by Russia's leadership, although calls for such action have been heard in both societies, namely the suspension of Russian membership in the G8, which was advocated in the United States more prominently than in Germany.

At the same time a more or less intense, and a more or less regular, exchange with the Russian leadership on the observation of these democratic standards has taken place. At the lowest level this involves the fairly ritualized repetition behind closed doors of the complaints addressed against Russia in Western public discourse; on a slightly higher level it involves sometimes equally ritualistic meetings with representatives of the opposition; and at the highest level it involves official criticism and demands to reverse specific actions. The latter, for instance, applied to the NGO law or the rulings handed down against the Russian oligarch Khodorkovsky.

How have Germany and the United States managed the conflicting goals? The *extrinsic conflict* between democracy promotion and interests: Germany has emphatically resolved this conflict in favour of its – economic – interests and thus in favour of the categorical imperative of cooperation. There is no case in which Germany would have postponed economic projects in Russia or would have denied its usual support because of conflicts with its democracy promotion goals. On the contrary, both Gerhard Schröder – openly – and Angela Merkel – in a more concealed manner – have admitted that in the specific Russian circumstances the current stable and prosperous conditions are clearly to be preferred over the uncertain prospects of a democratic renewal. Ideally, the economic and the transformational interests have been merged in a harmonious way as in the case of the 'modernization partnership' initiated in 2008.

In the United States we can observe a different pattern, because the extrinsic conflict appeared much less pronounced. For Washington, policy on Russia is less about genuine interest in Russia, and more about the importance of Russia in the enforcement of broader American interests, specifically in the fight against terrorism and nuclear non-proliferation. Against this background, differences in political values could much more easily allow the two countries to drift apart. The fact that during the Bush Administration benign neglect gradually turned into malign neglect corresponds with increasingly sharper criticism of the authoritarian forms of Putinism. Likewise, Obama's 'reset' policy primarily reflected the changed coordinates of American foreign policy, a change made atmospherically more palatable by the friendly face of Putinism, Dmitry Medvedev. Hence the United States has not sacrificed its interest in support of

Russian democracy; rather it has perceived its interests with regard to Russia as of such secondary importance that their definition could be substantially affected by the differences in values.

The *intrinsic conflict* between democracy promotion and stability, governability and majority occurs in a particularly sharp form against the backdrop of Russia's history of post-Communist transition and the *raison d'être* of Putin as a stabilizer. There was much to learn from the Russia of the 1990s regarding the collateral damage of democratization. The response to this was particularly blistering in Germany, resulting in political control and transformational gradualism becoming the policies of choice. The conflict was thus settled emphatically in favour of stability and governability. The obviously high approval ratings for Putin and his government during most of his tenure made this preference even more plausible.

The same applies to some extent to the United States, where similar propositions by Bush and even more clearly by Obama that emphasize the positive effects of gradual modernization and functional integration can be found, even if these will be realized in the long-term only. As a result they also expressed a preference for stability. However, in the United States the voices within society and the expert community are much more inspired by democratic fundamentalism than in Germany, which makes more urgent the need for the political leadership to justify its pragmatic largesse. And the practice of promoting democracy at the grassroots level is – in marked contrast to Germany – overwhelmingly dedicated to the unmitigated promulgation of liberal democratic principles.

To what extent are these patterns of response in line with the profiles – i.e. with the respective configurations of determining factors that are relevant for the bilateral relations of the two actors with Russia? Looking at the relevant determinants one after another, in the German case economic interests clearly dominate, closely followed by security interests which, however, point in the same cooperative direction – in marked contrast to the countries along Germany's eastern border. As far as the role of pressure groups is concerned, the picture is more varied. First, there is a partly articulate, but in any case influential pro-Russian business lobby; second, there are critical advocacy groups that are more articulate, but confined to the public sphere; and finally, there is a diverse emigrant community, as yet without missionary zeal concerning their country of origin – unlike for instance the Cuban exiles in Florida. The institutional pluralism of democracy promotion is especially pronounced in the Russian case, because every political foundation is present and they are the only significant actors. But despite the pluralism of respective party allegiances and relatively broad autonomy, they subscribe to a fairly broad common operational denominator.

In the case of the United States, security interests are most important, albeit with varying political weight, whereas economic interests hardly matter. Pressure groups are less relevant: a Russia lobby does not exist in American society, and in the political arena, including established think tanks, a critical distance predominates, calling Cold War enmities to mind that are shared by corresponding circles in Moscow. As democracy promoters carry out their operations on the short leash of the State Department and the US embassy, their pluralism is less pronounced than in the German case.

Considering the determining factors in their respective configurations, there is in both cases evidence that fits with theoretical expectations. German policy towards Russia complies with an extraordinarily high degree of continuity to the ideal type of Civilian Power, which is surprising because Russia for its part is not compatible at all with such a mode of behaviour. There is a broad consensus in Germany that calls for strategic patience vis-à-vis Russia and for gradual piecemeal changes. In addition, Germany has frequently taken steps to promote a pragmatic and functional integration of Russia – following the logic of its own principled multilateralism, but being constrained by it at the same time. And after the very ambivalent experience with the fairly patronizing democracy and market promotion of the 1990s, promotion of democracy has since avoided too much of an educational attitude. All this combines nicely with the logic of the 'trading state' where the driving force of German policy towards Russia can really be found.

Whereas Germany clearly decides the classical clash between norms and interest in favour of the latter, this conflict plays a much less important role in the case of the United States. This has given the two poles a different weight depending on circumstances. Admittedly, in US rhetoric on Russia almost every sound bite of the ideal type of Freedom Fighter is present – particularly at the time of George W. Bush – including the essential importance of universal democratic values, the enthusiasm for (colour) electoral revolutions, the rejection of Putin's authoritarianism on principle, and the unimpeded propagation of its own democratic model. Yet this only provides the background music for significant shifts in political strategies pursued, flip-flopping argumentation and a considerable degree of general incoherence and disorientation. Incidentally, with regard to Russia the US leadership never really decided what objective to pursue in the classic conflict between norms and interests.

Notes

1 However, the roots of German–Russian economic relations go back much further, in the case of energy relations to the early 1970s when the basic pattern was set by the gas-pipeline deal that led to the conclusion of long-term contracts.
2 But trade recovered rapidly: 2010 exports grew to €26.4 billion and in 2011 to €34.4 billion, imports to €31.8 billion in 2010 and €40.6 billion in 2011.
3 Currently, this comprises a programme on 'Environmental Monitoring Systems', 'Support to the implementation of instruments of estate and property policies' and the 'transfer of former military facilities to civilian use'.
4 In the autumn of 2012, in their drive against 'foreign agents', the Russian authorities started questioning the legal base of these branch offices.
5 The smaller foundations (FNS, HSS, HBS, RLS) are, in different formats, also responsible for other CIS countries.
6 It is often overlooked that in his much broader remarks in this interview with Reinhold Beckmann on 23 November 2004 on German TV he mentioned all the critical

issues to be found in the debate about Russia's democratic shortcomings: the historical legacy, the socio-economic conditions, shortcomings, and the primacy of stability.
7 The deputy chairman of the CDU/CSU parliamentary group in the Bundestag and coordinator for German–Russian inter-societal cooperation, Andreas Schockenhoff, declared that with the advent of Angela Merkel 'clear changes of emphasis' in relations with Russia would take effect that also included openly addressing 'deficiencies in democracy and the rule of law' (Schockenhoff 2006).
8 And on the occasion of the Petersburg Dialogue in Hannover in July 2011 Merkel publicly declared her barely concealed preference for Medvedev as presidential candidate – referring to the Russian term for an academic doctoral degree: *kandidat nauk*.
9 A no less classical example is the agenda prepared by Chancellor Merkel for intergovernmental consultations in Yekaterinburg in 2010:

> The aim is to intensify relations and – different from international conferences, where there is a lot of talk about problems in foreign policy – we will of course look at where the German–Russian cooperation can lead to better economic cooperation, a modernization. We will also talk about domestic issues, about the various issues that also have to do with human rights, but no less also about research, education and health, that is about issues to which we, Germany, can contribute, I believe, something to Russia's development.
> (Bundesregierung 2010)

10 This criticism also extended to the decision of the Russian Election Commission and the Ministry of Foreign Affairs to reduce the number of election observers from the OSCE for the State Duma elections in 2007 from 450 to 70, and to no longer permit long-term monitoring, which led to the cancellation of the mission. This was not repeated in the same way in 2011.
11 This was also true for the HBS and their work, which is mainly oriented towards oppositional NGOs. However, on more than one occasion the German foundations too suffered from bureaucratic disruptions requiring the German embassy and even the German government to intervene. For example, in late summer 2012 the Russian authorities, in clear violation of a 2006 status agreement, suddenly requested work permits from the foreign staff of the various offices and forced the FES to close down its branch offices in St Petersburg and Novosibirsk, officially for purely bureaucratic reasons. A typical Russian paradox is presented by the fact that the KAS, which for years has cultivated a particularly close relationship to Moscow's leadership, had at times the most serious problems with Russian bureaucracy, notably between 2010 and 2011.
12 This is an abbreviation for 'Georgia, Ukraine, Azerbaijan and Moldova', initially – as GUUAM – encompassing Uzbekistan as well. Founded in 1997 with the support of the United States, the organization was supposed to serve as a counterweight to Russian influence in the CIS, but never really became a viable force.
13 As stated by the former holder of the Russia Desk at the National Security Council, Thomas Graham (2001).
14 In the US case the recovery was slower than in the German case: 2010 exports amounted to $6.0 billion and 2011 to $8.3 billion, whereas imports in 2010 grew to $25.7 billion and in 2011 to $34.6 billion.
15 For comparison: 2002, US exports totalled only $2.4 billion and imports $6.8 billion.
16 Bush as quoted from Goldgeier and McFaul (2003: 306).
17 This also applies in principle to the NED, the budget of which has also risen massively since 2005, from an original $18 million to $40 million in 2005 and to some $100 million in 2008. Here it was Bush who initiated a doubling of the budget in his 'State of the Union Address' in 2004. Nevertheless, here too it was ultimately Congress which pushed for the increase – with a regional focus on the Middle East.
18 In 2000, the Republicans criticized Clinton's 'Bolshevik' approach to the implementation of 'reforms' in Russia in a major report published by the House of Representatives

entitled 'Russia's Road to Corruption'. Allegedly, in 2000 Russia was 'more corrupt, more lawless, less democratic, poorer and less stable' than at the beginning of Clinton's term and that of his vice president Al Gore. These men were also held responsible for the fact that US–Russian relations were 'shattered' and that Russian foreign policy had fallen back into Cold War mode (US House of Representatives 2000: 5, 11).
19 In 2009 neither NDI nor IRI received funds for their work in Russia by the NED, while in 2008 each received $1 million in funding respectively.
20 In 2002 the same thing had happened to the US Peace Corps. And in November 2012 NDI voluntarily followed USAID and moved most of its US staff to Lithuania, leaving only a small number of Russian employees in Moscow.
21 Against this background it is only logical that democratization – which was only mentioned in passing – was understood by her in the spirit of classical modernization theory: 'The growth of entrepreneurial classes throughout the world is an asset in the promotion of human rights and individual liberty, and it should be understood and used as such' (Rice 2000: 50).
22 See his programmatic policy speech given in London (Bush 2003a).
23 As quoted by Nichol (2006: 29).
24 As stated at the joint press conference during his visit to Astana (Cheney 2006).
25 As stated in his first reaction to Putin's Munich speech (Bush 2007).
26 Nicholas Burns on 21 February 2007 (Burns 2007). At the time he was undersecretary of state for political affairs and thus third-ranking official in the State Department.
27 See on this US State Department spokeswoman Victoria Nuland's remarks at the daily press conference on 18 September 2012 and the criticism levelled against it by the current president of Freedom House, David J. Kramer (2012).
28 The Russian Democracy Act also notes that US democracy promotion in Russia should focus on civil society and independent media (see Nichol 2006: 33–4).
29 See the concurrent resolutions adopted by the US Senate (2003) and the US House of Representatives (2003).
30 Among other things, this entailed its own democracy office and an advisory committee in the State Department as well as the provision of an additional $250 million for democracy promotion (see McCain 2005). Tom Lantos and Frank Wolf proposed the initiative in the House of Representatives.
31 The Jackson–Vanik Amendment of 1974 prohibited the United States from pursuing normal economic relations with countries that restrict the freedom of emigration of their citizens and was originally intended to encourage emigration of Jews from the Soviet Union.
32 Replacing the Jackson–Vanik Amendment by a 'Magnitsky Act' in memory of the death of a Russian lawyer in Russian custody in 2009 was proposed in Congress in autumn 2011. The law consists of a visa ban and seizure of financial holdings of people implicated in similar gross human rights violations, notably some 60 Russian civil servants thought to be responsible for Magnitsky's death.
33 See Council on Foreign Relations (2006). Apparently it was conceived as a tit-for-tat response to the report by the Republican majority in Congress in 2000 critical of Clinton and thus intended as a formally bipartisan attempt by the Democrats to attack the Republican administration's Russia policy.

References

AA (2010) 'Außenminister Westerwelle zu seiner Reise nach Russland, Belarus und Litauen', *Süddeutsche Zeitung*, 30 October. Online, available at: www.auswaertiges-amt.de (accessed 27 November 2010).
BBC (2005) 'Putin Deplores Collapse of USSR', *BBC*, 25 April. Online, available at: http://news.bbc.co.uk/2/hi/4480745.stm (accessed 15 May 2013).

Bundesregierung (2010) 'Bundeskanzlerin Merkel in Jekaterinburg', *Press Statement*, 14 July. Online, available at: www.bundesregierung.de (accessed 27 November 2010).

Burns, N. (2007) *The Atlantic Council of the United States*, 21 February, Washington DC. Online, available at: www.acus.org (accessed 20 December 2011).

Burns, W.J. (2010) *The United States and Russia in a New Era: One Year After 'Reset'*, Speech at the Center for American Progress, 14 April. Online, available at: www.state.gov (accessed 7 January 2013).

Bush, G.W. (2001a) *A New Relationship between the United States and Russia: Joint Statement by President Bush and President Putin*, 13 November, Washington, DC. Online, available at: www.state.gov (accessed 24 June 2007).

Bush, G.W. (2001b) *Press Conference by President Bush and Russian Federation President Putin, Brdo Pri Kranju, Slowenia*, 16 June. Online, available at: http://georgewbush-whitehouse.archives.gov (accessed 20 December 2011).

Bush, G.W. (2003a) *President Bush Discusses Iraq Policy at Whitehall Palace in London*, 19 November. Online, available at: www.whitehouse.gov (accessed 16 July 2007).

Bush, G.W. (2003b) *The President's News Conference with President Vladimir Putin of Russia at Camp David, Maryland*, 27 September. Online, available at: www.gpo.gov (accessed 23 July 2007).

Bush, G.W. (2005) *President Sworn-in to Second Term*. Online, available at: http://georgewbush-whitehouse.archives.gov (accessed 20 December 2011).

Bush, G.W. (2007) *Press Conference by the President*, 14 February. Online, available at: http://georgewbush-whitehouse.archives.gov (accessed 20 December 2011).

Cheney, D. (2006) *Vice President's Remarks at the 2005 Vilnius Conference*, 4 May. Online, available at: www.whitehouse.gov (accessed 15 May 2006).

Congressional Record (2007) 'US–Russian Economic Relationship', in *Congressional Record – Senate*, 19 April. Online, available at: www.gpoaccess.gov (accessed 11 May 2007).

Council on Foreign Relations (2006) *Russia's Wrong Direction: What the United States Can and Should Do: Report of an Independent Task Force*, New York, NY: Brookings Institution Press.

Erler, G. (1998) *Der 'Neue Realismus' zwischen Bonn und Moskau. Presseerklärung des Stellvertretenden Fraktionsvorsitzenden der SPD-Bundestagsfraktion*, 18 November. Online, available at: www.spdfraktion.de (accessed 7 January 2013).

Goldgeier, J.M. and McFaul, M. (2003) *Power and Purpose: US Policy toward Russia after the Cold War*, Washington, DC: The Brookings Institution.

Graham, T. (2001) 'US–Russian Relations', *ICAS Special Contribution*, no. 2001-0315-TEG, 15 March. Online, available at: www.icasinc.org (accessed 22 June 2007).

GTZ (2010) *GTZ International Services in der Russischer Föderation*. Online, available at: www.gtz.de (accessed 20 July 2010).

Handelsblatt (2003) 'Berlin und Moskau bauen Kooperation aus. Energieprojekte stehen im Mittelpunkt', *Handelsblatt*, 10 October.

Huterer, M. and Krumrei, C. (2001) 'Russland und der Westen. Eine schwierige Integrationsaufgabe', *Internationale Politik*, 56 (10): 27–34.

InWEnt (2010) *Zusammenarbeit mit Europa*. Online, available at: www.inwent.org (accessed 31 July 2010).

Ischinger, W. (2000) 'Die Zukunft Russlands liegt in Europa', in *Frankfurter Allgemeine Zeitung*, 11 July: 12.

KfW (2010) *Förderschwerpunkte. Russland – zurück zu wirtschaftlicher Stärke*. Online, available at: www.kfw-entwicklungsbank.de (accessed 31 July 2010).

Kramer, D.J. (2007) *Deputy Assistant Secretary for European and Eurasian Affairs: The US and Russia: Remarks to the Baltimore Council on Foreign Affairs*, 31 May. Online, available at: http://merln.ndu.edu (accessed 20 December 2011).

Kramer, D.J. (2010) 'Resetting US–Russian Relations: It Takes Two', *Washington Quarterly*, 33 (1): 61–79.

Kramer, D.J. (2012) 'Will Obama stand up against Putin's abuses?', *Washington Post*, 19 September.

McCain, J. (2005) *McCain and Lieberman Introduce 'Advance Democracy Act'*. Online, available at: http://mccain.senate.gov (accessed 20 December 2011).

Mangold, K. (2008) 'Glücksfall Medwedjew', *Frankfurter Allgemeine Zeitung*, 6 May. Online, available at: http://fazarchiv.faz.net (accessed 7 January 2013).

Nichol, J. (2006) 'Democracy in Russia: Trends and Implications for US Interests', *CRS Report for Congress*, no. RL 32662, August, Washington, DC: Congressional Research Service.

Pflüger, F. (2005) *Interview mit Deutschlandradio Kultur*, 8 September. Online, available at: www.dradio.de (accessed 7 May 2010).

Rice, C. (2000) 'Campaign 2000: Promoting the National Interest', *Foreign Affairs*, 79 (1): 45–62.

Rice, C. (2005a) 'The Promise of Democratic Peace', *Washington Post*, 11 December. Online, available at: www.state.gov (accessed 27 May 2007).

Rice, C. (2005b) *Interview with Aleksey Venediktov of Ekho Moskvy Radio*, 20 April. Online, available at: www.state.gov (accessed 6 June 2007).

Rice, C. (2005c) *Remarks to the Press en Route Ankara*, 6 February. Online, available at: http://merln.ndu.edu (accessed 20 December 2011).

Schockenhoff, A. (2006) *Deutsche Außenpolitik unter der Regierung Merkel. Rede in der Internationalen Abteilung des ZK der KPCh*, 19 April, Beijing. Online, available at: www.kas.de (accessed 28 November 2010).

Schröder, G. (2001) 'Partner Russland. Gegen Stereotype, für Partnerschaft und Offenheit – eine Positionsbestimmung', *Die Zeit*, no. 15, 5 April: 10–11.

Schröder, G. (2005) 'Eine neue Qualität der deutsch-russischen Beziehungen', *Handelsblatt*, 8 September: 9.

Spanger, H.-J. (2005) 'Paradoxe Kontinuitäten. Die deutsche Russlandpolitik und die koalitionären Farbenlehren', *HSFK-Report*, no. 12, Frankfurt a.M.: Peace Research Institute Frankfurt.

Spanger, H.-J. (2008) 'Between Ground Zero and Square One: How George W. Bush Failed on Russia', *PRIF Report*, no. 82, Frankfurt a.M.: Peace Research Institute Frankfurt.

Spanger, H.-J. (2010) 'Die deutsche Russlandpolitik', in T. Jäger, A. Höse and K. Oppermann (eds), *Deutsche Außenpolitik*, Wiesbaden: Verlag für Sozialwissenschaften (second updated and expanded edition).

Spanger, H.-J. and Reddies, B. (2011) *Die Arbeit der Friedrich-Ebert-Stiftung in der UdSSR/Russland und in der Volksrepublik China – Geschichte der internationalen Arbeit der Friedrich-Ebert-Stiftung*, Bonn: Verlag J.H.W. Dietz Nachf.

Spiegel Online (2007) 'Bundesregierung kritisiert Duma-Wahl als undemokratisch', *Spiegel Online*, 3 December. Online, available at: www.spiegel.de (accessed 27 November 2010).

Statistisches Bundesamt (2010) *Atlas der Außenhandelsstatistik*. Online, available at: http://ims.destatis.de (accessed 20 December 2011).

Steinmeier, F.-W. (2008) *Globale Herausforderungen gemeinsam gestalten –*

Perspektiven der deutsch-russischen Modernisierungspartnerschaft Rede von Bundesaußenminister Frank-Walter Steinmeier anlässlich des Treffens des bilateralen Lenkungsausschusses des Petersburger Dialogs, 3 July. Online, available at: www.petersburger-dialog.de (accessed 7 January 2013).

Steinmeier, F.-W. (2009) *Rede des Bundesministers für Auswärtiges, Dr. Frank-Walter Steinmeier, bei der Russischen Akademie der Wissenschaften*, 10 June, Moscow. Online, available at: www.auswaertiges-amt.de (accessed 7 May 2010).

US House of Representatives (2000) *106th Congress, Members of the Speaker's Advisory Group on Russia, Russia's Road to Corruption: How the Clinton Administration Exported Government Instead of Free Enterprise and Failed the Russian People*, September. Online, available at: www.fas.org (accessed 12 September 2007).

US House of Representatives (2003) *H.Con.Res.336 – 108th Congress (2003-2004)*. Online, available at: http://beta.congress.gov/bill/108th-congress/house-concurrent-resolution/336 (accessed 15 May 2013).

US Senate (2003) *S.Con.Res.85 – 108th Congress (2003-2004)*. Online, available at: http://beta.congress.gov/bill/108th-congress/senate-concurrent-resolution/85 (accessed 15 May 2013).

US Senate (2005) *Republican Policy Committee, Conditioning Russia's Graduation from Jackson–Vanik: A Congressional Message for President Putin*, 17 February. Online, available at: http://rpc.senate.gov (accessed 20 December 2011).

Westerwelle, G. and Lavrov, S. (2010) 'Die deutsch-russische Modernisierungspartnerschaft', *Frankfurter Allgemeine Zeitung*, 30 May. Online, available at: www.faz.net (accessed 7 January 2013).

Part III
Results and conclusions

10 Democracy promotion as international politics

Comparative analysis, theoretical and practical implications

Jonas Wolff

Promoting democracy is a complicated business. It encompasses a variety of policy areas and involves a broad spectrum of actors, who make use of very different instruments. The common denominator is their stated goal. This may include a politically motivated free trade agreement, a military intervention aimed at overthrowing a regime, a diplomatic appeal to show respect for democracy and human rights, or a development project for the strengthening of democratic institutions. Whether these different activities really serve the cause of democracy in the target country cannot be stated categorically – and even in specific cases mostly remains a matter of debate. However, the measures just mentioned are part of the business of international democracy promotion to the extent that they explicitly strive to have a direct and positive effect on democracy. But even if the actual impact is ignored, the goal remains complex. Democracy, and consequently democracy promotion, potentially concerns all aspects of the political system as well as the diverse forms of interaction between state and society.

For this reason, democracy promotion as an object of academic research cannot be dealt with through straightforward questions and answers. The case studies whose results are discussed and compared here demonstrate this clearly. As a result, the forms that democracy promotion policies take in the 12 cases examined cannot be represented as dichotomous (democracy promotion: yes/no) or linear (greater or less promotion of democracy) scales. What is much more necessary is a broad overview of the different dimensions of democracy promotion. Consequently, in discussing the findings on how democracy promoters deal with conflicting objectives, the question is not whether a given donor chooses goal A or goal B; instead, we observe significantly more complex patterns of reactions. These empirical patterns are summarized in the first, descriptive–comparative section of the concluding chapter, which discusses the dimensions of democracy promotion and donor reactions to conflicting objectives.

The second, causal–analytic section explains the observed patterns of reaction. In discussing the factors identified as driving donor behaviour, the eclectic perspective developed in the introduction proves useful. The causal strategy is, thus, not to seek to isolate the causal effect of individual determinants of democracy promotion but to identify the general logic according to which configurations of causal factors interact in specific contexts. A third section draws more general theoretical conclusions and argues that democracy promotion can be regarded as de facto reflexive and characterized by alternatively conditioned double standards. The final sections discuss the practical implications and future prospects for democracy promotion in the twenty-first century.

Empirical patterns

Dimensions of democracy promotion

The case studies reveal significantly different profiles of democracy promotion across the 12 pairs of states. The following section assesses these profiles by examining the five dimensions of democracy promotion identified in the introduction.

The dimension of *international observation* concerns electoral observation in particular. In this regard, Germany contributed to multilateral missions (EU, OECD, Council of Europe) in all six cases. Except for this indirect involvement, elections did not play any decisive role in German foreign or development policy. Even in countries in which clear infringements of the principle of free and fair elections were observed, Germany did not take any measures (Pakistan, Russia).[1] Belarus was an exception: here the German government made specific demands prior to the elections, and reacted to irregularities or fraud observed. However, it was not the electoral fraud alone that provoked a sharp reaction, but rather the political repression that ensued.

For the United States, elections were a significantly more important topic and area of activity. In addition to contributions to bilateral and multilateral election observation missions, the United States employed instruments that clearly went beyond pure observation. For instance, support for local election observation encompassed technical and financial assistance to state agencies and NGOs. In addition, the US government regularly voiced its opinion on the elections in the countries under observation. In some cases the government made use of diplomatic statements and/or foreign aid in order to influence the electoral process – to the advantage or disadvantage of a particular candidate. This was especially the case with Belarus, but was also apparent in Bolivia in 2002 and in Pakistan in 2008.[2]

The *promotion of democracy through foreign aid* (democracy assistance) varies according to the character of the recipient state. In the case of democratic developing countries such as Bolivia and Ecuador, democracy assistance formed the core of the explicitly democracy-related activities of Germany and the United States. Even if it did not constitute the most important area of developmental aid in any of the pairs of states, there were democracy programmes in all four cases. These programmes supported state and non-state partners in order to build capacity and/or empower specific actors (political parties, interest groups, NGOs).

At the other end of the spectrum, in the case of relatively wealthy recipient states (Russia, Turkey), provision of democracy aid was mainly limited to parastatal organizations such as Germany's political foundations and the NED, the NDI, or the IRI on the part of the United States.³ The same is true for the non-democratic but allied developing country Pakistan (under Musharraf, after 9/11). In addition to parastatal activities, the official German development cooperation here was 'non-political', whereas the United States de facto promoted autocracy – by providing budgetary support for the military regime, which clearly outweighed the limited democracy assistance measures (with a focus on elections and the legislature).

In the cases that were investigated, partisan approaches to democracy assistance were the exception. Only in the case of US policy toward Belarus was civil society support explicitly aimed at empowering the opposition to Lukashenko, who was regarded by the United States as both a dictator and a political opponent. Although the German government shared this opinion and also adopted a fairly confrontational stance, support for Belarusian civil society by the GTZ and political foundations did not go beyond the traditional, cooperative and politically non-partisan profile of German democracy promotion. US foreign aid for Bolivia tended to support counterweights to President Morales. Overall, however, assistance remained fairly ambivalent in nature. Striving to continue cooperation with the Bolivian government, the United States and specifically USAID showed themselves to be remarkably flexible in adapting democracy assistance to Bolivian preferences.

In the area of *diplomacy*, bilateral dialogues between donor and recipient governments regularly dealt with democracy and related topics such as human rights, the rule of law, and good governance. In their official public statements and democracy-related appeals, however, there was substantial difference between the German and the US governments.

Washington almost always made a clear judgement on particular political developments and events in the recipient countries, regularly evaluated the state of democracy and human rights, and made corresponding demands. This involved public statements during visits of official delegations as well as official assessments in US government reports (e.g. in the Human Rights Reports of the US Department of State). However, a closer look at the diplomatic statements relating to varying recipients reveals striking inconsistencies. In the case of Turkey, the traditional close relationship with the Kemalist elite and a sceptical view of the Islamic parties kept the US government from unequivocally criticizing even obviously undemocratic developments (such as the partly successful, partly unsuccessful attempts to bring down elected governments or to prohibit 'undesirable' political parties).

As regards Pakistan, the Clinton government publicly condemned Musharraf's seizure of power. But with the passage of time – and especially after 9/11 – US rhetoric became more restrained, even to the point of supporting Musharraf. Only when internal protests against Musharraf escalated did the United States revert to voicing pro-democracy appeals and reprimands.⁴ With reference to

Putin's Russia, a significant change was identified in official rhetoric: from astonishingly positive statements about Putin's vision of a democratic and free country during the first George W. Bush Administration to much more critical comments during his second term.

The general pattern is that officially the United States paid less attention to democratic 'deficits' as soon as bilateral relationships improved (e.g. in relation to Pakistan and Russia after 9/11) or when US interest in improved bilateral relationships increased (e.g. in relation to Bolivia and Ecuador during the second Bush Administration as well as, generally, after the Obama Administration came into office).

Berlin, by contrast, only occasionally made public statements on matters of democracy and human rights in the various recipient countries. Only with regard to Belarus did the German government regularly resort to diplomatic appeals and critical commentary. In its relationship with Turkey it remained silent on the 'soft coup' against Prime Minister Erbakan in the 1990s, but in the following decade it publicly supported the Erdoğan government against similar threats. With regard to Russia, the (semi-)official complaints about deficits in democracy and the rule of law, a common practice in the 1990s, gradually disappeared in the following decade; public criticism of the state of Russian democracy came mostly from opposition parties (regardless of political hue).

The German government reacted to Musharraf's coup in 1999 and the declaration of a state of emergency in late 2007 with calls for a return to constitutional order, but largely remained silent in the eight intervening years. Only after Musharraf had resigned did Germany's government, in negotiations with Pakistan, emphasize the necessity of making progress in advancing democracy. There were few official reactions by Germany to events in Bolivia and Ecuador, which tended to be general calls for dialogue and compromise.

With regard to the *conditioning of international cooperation*, both Germany and the United States officially made their cooperation with recipient countries contingent upon democracy-related requirements. In a number of cases the US government responded with sanctions (or the threat of sanctions) to disruptions of democratic order (Belarus 1996, Pakistan 1999, Ecuador 2000) and to electoral fraud followed by political repression (Belarus 2006, 2010). In the case of Turkey in 1997, however, when the premature dissolution of the elected government corresponded to US interests and was supported by US allies within the country, there was no sign of democratic conditions being imposed.

As regards Putin's Russia, the US perception of political developments became increasingly critical (including in official statements). But US interest in ongoing cooperation with the Russian government led the Bush Administration to refrain from adopting the kind of penalties demanded by members of Congress. When after 9/11 massive 'national interests' called for cooperation with Pakistan, the US suspended sanctions without demanding democracy-related concessions from the military regime. Conversely, the threat of sanctions against Bolivia in 2002 and the 'decertification' and cancellation of US trade preferences in 2008 did not primarily result from democracy-related considerations.

These measures were instead motivated by foreign policy interests, especially related to the 'war on drugs'. The suspension of Bolivia's participation in the MCA was justified by the country's worsening rating on international governance indices, even though this was not really the cause of the suspension.

Regardless of official pronouncements, Germany reacted in a significantly more restrained manner when it came to imposing democracy-related sanctions. The German government made use of this 'negative' form of democracy promotion only in the case of Belarus – and even here it did not involve German but, instead, joint EU sanctions. Within the EU, Germany most of the time advocated restraint and showed a preference for engaging Lukashenko (decisive exceptions were the reactions to the 1996 referendum and to the repression after the 2010 elections). In German relations with Turkey, the process of accession to the EU represented – and still represents – a framework of far-reaching political conditionality. Despite its support for the conditions laid down by the EU, the German government nonetheless undermined the entire scheme of conditionality: since the CDU/CSU parties came to power in 2005, Germany clearly has been signalling to Turkey that it would reject its entry to the EU regardless of any possible compliance with the accession criteria.

In the case of Pakistan, at the time of the coup Germany had already suspended its development cooperation (in response to the 1998 nuclear test). Therefore, the question of how to react to Musharraf's coup was not raised. It is, however, remarkable that Germany resumed its development cooperation with Pakistan already in 2000, without demanding any democracy-related concessions from the Musharraf government.

The present study concentrates on democracy promotion in countries that after 1990 had established basic forms of democratic government at least temporarily and whose stance towards the North-West was not generally confrontational. The promotion of democracy through *military intervention*, therefore, did not play a significant role The use of direct (physical) force was seen only in exceptional cases and then always in cooperation with – or at the least tolerated by – the particular recipient government. This was the case with military and paramilitary US activities in Pakistan (in the framework of the so-called 'war on terror') as well as in Bolivia and Ecuador (in the framework of the so-called 'war on drugs').[5]

Dealing with conflicting objectives

The conflict situations in the recipient countries investigated pose very different challenges to democracy – and thus to its external promoters. At the same time, the profiles of the two donors' interests in relation to the six recipient countries differ significantly. As a result, there was a correspondingly wide variance in the conflicts of objectives Germany and the United States were confronted with in their democracy promotion policies.

German policy toward Bolivia, Ecuador, Turkey and Belarus was scarcely confronted with extrinsic conflicts of objectives (democracy versus self-interest).

With regard to Bolivia and Ecuador conflicting objectives were of low intensity: respect for self-determination versus measures against rejection of 'neoliberalism' and orientation to Venezuela.[6] In the case of Turkey, Germany certainly had substantial security and economic interests, and the Turkish diaspora in Germany implies that Turkey also has an immediate relevance for German domestic politics. However, this scarcely led to tangible conflicts of objectives.[7]

In the case of Belarus, relations between the Lukashenko regime and Russia meant that Germany had certain strategic interests in Belarus that concerned the regional context (in the sense of either limiting Russian influence or refraining from provoking Russia). In the final analysis, however, neither German nor US Belarus policy was confronted with extrinsic conflicts of objectives worth mentioning. As the overthrow of Lukashenko was generally regarded as contributing to the reduction of Russian influence in Belarus, 'the West's' regional strategic interests only reinforced the impulse for active democracy promotion.

The remaining seven pairs of states were characterized by acute extrinsic conflicts of objectives. In the case of the United States, security and broader strategic interests took precedence. Toward Bolivia, drug-related security issues and strategic considerations (rejection of 'neoliberalism', anti-US provocations, and an orientation to Venezuela) competed with respect for Bolivian self-determination. Much the same was true for Ecuador, although security and strategic interests were less seriously endangered there; nevertheless, economic interests (protection of US companies) also came into play. In the case of US policy toward Turkey, the goal of 'respect for self-determination' collided with the security interest in a NATO partner anchored in 'the West' which was endangered by the anti-Kemalism of the Welfare Party (RP) and the Justice and Development Party (AKP). In addition, the democratic reforms of the AKP government reduced the political role of the Turkish military, an important security partner for the United States.

With respect to Pakistan, extrinsic conflicts became strikingly apparent when, after 9/11, the war in Afghanistan made the military ruler Musharraf a vital partner of the United States in the 'war on terror': democracy promotion, then, openly clashed with the security-related aim to cooperate with an autocratic regime. In the case of Russia too, US interests in security cooperation stood in the way of vigorous promotion of democracy; however, this was predominantly oriented towards third countries and related issues (e.g. 'war on terror', Afghanistan, Iran). Similar to the United States, an extrinsic conflict of goals also emerged for German Pakistan policy with the military intervention in Afghanistan in 2001. In the case of the Russian government, German interest in cooperation was significantly higher than that of the United States – and was directly oriented towards Russia: massive economic and tangible security interests in cooperating with a stable and friendly government in Russia acted as a disincentive for actively promoting democracy vis-à-vis an increasingly authoritarian regime.

The way extrinsic conflicts of objectives were handled in the case studies confirms the finding that democracy-related goals recede into the background when they clash with foreign policy interests (cf. Carothers 1999: 16; Schraeder 2003: 41; Spanger and Wolff 2007: 264). This was clearly seen regarding US policy towards Pakistan and Turkey as well as in the case of German (and US) policy towards Russia.[8] Conversely, the democracy promotion policies of both donor countries with respect to Belarus also support this finding: the confrontational attitude to 'Europe's last dictatorship' was in the context of a very low level of foreign policy interests.

This prioritization of 'national interests', however, cannot be understood as the simple implementation of *realpolitik* motivated by donor interests. *First*, both donors were at pains to depict their policy as normatively appropriate, even when they clearly favoured material interests over the goal of promoting democracy. In order to relativize doubts about Russian democracy, the German government emphasized the (early) phase of democratic development and the difficult socio-economic conditions in the country. Modernization was the rationale used to explain Germany's strategy of engaging Russia. Germany and the United States justified their support for Musharraf in a similar way: in view of Pakistan's history as an unstable democracy and the threat of Islamic terrorism, stabilizing the country was presented as necessary for readying the country for democracy.

In the case of Turkey, the US government justified its refusal to support the AKP government against threats of an internal coup by referring to the country's constitution and the 'secular democratic principles' anchored therein.[9] Bolivia's exclusion from the US MCA was officially in accordance with prescribed political stipulations. The focus on counternarcotics that characterized US policy with regard to the Andean countries was presented as not only a matter of pure self-interest, but as also indispensable in stabilizing threatened democracies.

This is, *second*, consistent with the observation that it was obviously impossible to ignore the topic of democracy (promotion) completely. Here the domestic politics of international democracy promotion come into play: in parliament and in public, donor governments are confronted with their own rhetorical commitments and the normative expectations of society. For example, opposition parties, NGOs, and the media openly challenged the relatively sympathetic attitude of the German government to Putin's Russia again and again. As a result, democracy and human rights remained part of the bilateral agenda – albeit at a relatively low-level intensity and embedded in an agenda of 'modernization', which blended interests and values into a single concept. The same was true of close US cooperation with Pakistan after 9/11, until domestic political resistance to Musharraf made it increasingly difficult for the US administration to remain supportive of the Pakistan ruler.

Third, the supposedly 'realistic', interest-driven policies were implemented in strikingly inconsistent ways when they met with democratically elected recipient governments. Unlike during the Cold War, even the powerful United States was not in a position – or not willing – to push through its own foreign policy interests if this required active and open measures against a democratically elected government in a recipient state. Apart from a few negative reactions, the Bush

Administration recognized the new governments in Bolivia and Ecuador as democratically legitimate – although both openly contravened vital US interests. In its relations with Turkey, the United States stood by its traditional allies in the Kemalist elite and especially in the military. But it also relied on cooperation with the AKP government and assumed a relatively neutral stance regarding Turkish internal conflicts.

In these three cases, US reactions were probably marked less by genuine respect for the norm of democratic self-determination than by pragmatic acceptance of the power relationships within the particular recipient country. Still, it can be concluded that the governments in Bolivia, Ecuador and Turkey were, to a certain extent, protected against overt US countermeasures by their democratic legitimation. This protection permitted actions running counter to US security interests that would have been difficult to imagine in earlier times. Generally, this restraint in US power politics draws attention to the vital importance of the recipient's context for the way democracy promotion is carried out – a condition that is even more obvious for the middle-ranking, Civilian Power Germany (see below).

In contrast to the collision of 'interests' and 'norms', intrinsic conflicts of objectives are characterized by a clash of different dimensions and sub-goals of democracy promotion. Conflicts of this kind are evident throughout the case studies. The only exception is Belarus, where Germany and the United States perceived the Lukashenko government as indisputably autocratic and anticipated no risks (of destabilization or ungovernability) arising from democratization. Most of the time, however, extrinsic conflicts were closely interlinked with intrinsic ones.

After taking office, Putin did not simply set about systematically dismantling Russian democracy but initially established stability, governability and the relative autonomy of the state – a quite plausible response to the Yeltsin era, which was not particularly democratic and was essentially teetering on the edge of collapse. Whether Putin would have a positive, neutral, or negative net effect on Russian democracy in the medium term could not be determined during his first years in power.[10] The 1999 coup in Pakistan, without a doubt, violated basic democratic rules. But here, too, the problems of Pakistani democracy in the 1990s and the difficult domestic and regional context gave some plausibility to Musharraf's official claim to be seeking a path of controlled modernization as the best long-term strategy for democratization.[11]

The consequences of the policies of Morales (Bolivia), Correa (Ecuador), and Erdoğan (Turkey) for democracy were also ambivalent, if – in comparison with Pakistan and Russia – with far more democratic credentials. All three presidents were, on the one hand, undoubtedly democratically legitimated and committed to democratic reforms. But, on the other, their political projects contained elements that – from the point of view of external democracy promoters – implied threats to liberal democracy. These perceived threats concerned (*a*) plebiscitary, majoritarian support for the respective governments that could lead to one-party dominance and to the concentration of power in the executive, thus undermining pluralism and checks and balances; and (*b*) local conceptions of political order – based on indigenous, socialist, or Islamic values – which collided with liberal-democratic standards.[12]

In dealing with these intrinsically conflicting objectives, both Germany and the United States evaluated the situation according to their particular – liberal, representative, 'Western', capitalist – conceptions of what constitutes good political order. As a result, they were generally sceptical about pro-Islamic parties in Turkey and feared an agenda of 'Islamization'; and they were interested in retaining, as far as possible, the liberal-democratic (and market-economy) character of the emerging political regimes in Bolivia and Ecuador. In accordance with its own democratic tradition, the United States tended to give significantly greater emphasis to checks and balances or political counterweights. In contrast, Germany focused on the rule of law and governance.

In the final analysis, however, neither the United States nor Germany insisted on dogmatically imposing their own particular image of democracy. Both were relatively flexible and pragmatic in their willingness to adapt their policy to local conditions. This was particularly apparent when processes of political change in the recipient country were undisputedly legitimized democratically and supported by a broad majority of the population – as in the case of the AKP in Turkey and the governments of Morales as well as Correa in South America. In addition, a relatively good performance in terms of stability, peace, and governability led donors to judge other democracy-related problems in a less critical light. This was seen, for example, in the case of the achievements of the Turkish AKP government and the Correa government in Ecuador, which were perceived as performing relatively well. The same applies to Musharraf and Putin, whose (perceived) successes in terms of stability and governability mitigated the critical assessment carried out by donors.

In dealing with intrinsic conflicts of objectives, donors officially showed respect for sovereign decisions and country ownership. Where intrinsic conflicts were perceived as such, typical donor statements called on 'all parties' to respect the constitution and to support democracy, stability, and peace.[13] Overall, the case studies show that neither Germany nor the United States, after at best brief periods of criticism, consistently opposed internally driven transformations or regime changes – even when they were regarded as turning away from or breaking with democracy. The only exception is Belarus, where there were neither significant extrinsic nor relevant intrinsic conflicts of objectives. As has been shown, the donors, in the end, even tolerated the *coup d'état* regime in Pakistan. When political protests against Musharraf increased in Pakistan, Germany and the United States placed stronger emphasis on democracy; but, still, neither of the two openly pressed President Musharraf to surrender power.

In the case of Turkey, donors accepted both the successful overthrow of the elected Erbakan government in the 1990s as well as the failure of similar strategies directed against the AKP a decade later.[14] Likewise, donors recognized that in the foreseeable future there was no viable alternative to the governments of Morales (Bolivia) and Correa (Ecuador). And even with regard to Belarus, the episode around 2008, when the EU and Germany as well as the United States sought a rapprochement, suggests that – in the absence of any realistic alternative – the donors would even have accepted a still authoritarian but less violent and repressive Lukashenko regime.[15]

Ultimately, the donors accepted whatever 'solution' of intrinsic conflicts of objectives established itself in the recipient country.[16] At the same time, however, both the United States and Germany attempted to influence this local 'solution'. 'Technical' support, measures for capacity-building and promotion of dialogue and participation served the donors as instruments for disseminating their conceptions of democracy and development, promoting pluralistic debate and strengthening 'moderate' (democratic, liberal, pro-Western) voices. In addition, donors signalled their preferences through public statements and in governmental negotiations.

Causal dynamics

With a view to explaining the behaviour of democracy promoters, the introduction to this volume identified six determinants. In the following section, the causal relevance of these factors will be examined, at first individually and then in their configurational and context-specific interaction.

Determinants of democracy promotion

The determinant *relative power position* is based on the idea that democracy promotion – especially in conflict situations – is only rational when a substantial difference in power between donor and recipient offers adequate opportunities for influence. More specifically, as power asymmetry increases, the degree to which democracy promoters are active and willing to take risks should increase. Confirming this expectation, German policy proved to be far more driven by the goal of promoting democracy in the cases of Belarus, Bolivia and Ecuador than it was toward Pakistan and Russia. At first glance, German policy on Turkey deviates from this pattern, insofar as the relatively small power differential in favour of Germany contrasts with the broad range of democracy-related conditions. The latter, however, concerns EU – not German – conditionality, and the power asymmetry between the EU and Turkey is significantly higher. Furthermore, German bilateral democracy assistance to Turkey, which has mainly been delegated to political foundations, does reflect the relatively low level of power asymmetry.[17]

A similar pattern is evident with the United States: in the case of extreme power asymmetry (Belarus, Bolivia, Ecuador) democracy promotion was emphasized more strongly than in the other cases (Pakistan, Russia, Turkey). Nonetheless, as was seen above, even in the case of 'small' countries the United States was only capable of influencing local actors and events to a very limited degree. In the case of Bolivia, for example, the United States acquiesced to suspending the democracy assistance programme as demanded by the Bolivian government. In conclusion, the case studies show that small (or even negative) power asymmetries directly limit the scope of democracy promotion by reducing potential influence (and, as a rule, go hand in hand with relatively strong donor interests). A large difference in power does not, however, necessarily lead to a high level of influence and, therefore, does not reliably cause an active and comprehensive policy of democracy promotion.

German and US reactions to conflicting objectives were shaped in particular by the *security and economic interests* of the donors. More specifically, German policy was shaped less by security issues than US policy was. Even in regard to Russia, whose significance for German security is obvious, security issues were overshadowed by dominant – but all the same closely aligned – economic interests. Given Germany's military involvement in Afghanistan, Germany had, and still has, significant security interests in Pakistan. The impact of these interests on German policy remained, however, limited, insofar as Germany's security interests there were de facto taken care of by the United States. In the case of Turkey, German security interests in cooperation and integration played a recognizable role – but in contrast to the United States this was due less to its NATO partner's international role than to Turkey's significance for Germany's internal security.

Security and economic interests had a direct effect on democracy promotion when they implied cooperation with the recipient government. Under these conditions Germany, like the United States, refrained from openly challenging even those governments that they regarded as unequivocally autocratic (Pakistan) or as increasingly authoritarian (Russia). As a result, critical democracy-related appeals were toned down, democratic conditionalities ignored, and democracy assistance organized in such a way that the governments in office were not directly provoked.[18]

When donor interests were threatened by a democratically elected government, the consequences were less clear-cut. Morales was able to expel the US ambassador and the US DEA from Bolivia; the Ecuadorian government was able to shut down the US military base in Manta; and the Turkish parliament did not allow US troops to invade Iraq from Turkish soil. In all cases, the US administration continued cooperation with these governments and refrained from openly confrontational measures.

The determinant of *domestic special interests* was related specifically to the strength of interest groups within the respective donor country, which lobbied for or engaged in advocacy work on behalf of a recipient country (the broad spectrum of various domestic special interests is discussed below as part of the 'donor context'). The comparative survey in Chapter 3 showed that such interest groups and NGOs could only be expected to have a significant political influence on German policy toward Turkey, and to a lesser degree toward Russia.

In fact, the relations between Germany and Turkey were shaped by a complex interaction between domestic and foreign policy. Through migration processes and the various Turkey-specific interest groups in Germany, intra-Turkish conflicts and crises produce spill-over effects to Germany. This, in turn, constitutes a direct interest on the part of the German government in democracy, peace, and above all stability in Turkey as well as in ongoing cooperation with a Western-oriented Turkish government. Yet, the implications of this pattern of interests for German democracy promotion in Turkey are contradictory. Especially in the 1990s there was a collision between, for instance, the promotion of human rights for Turkish Kurds and interest in cooperation with the Turkish government. Traditionally, Germany (like the United States) regarded the Kemalists as the guarantors of Turkey's Western orientation. More recently, however, the achievements of the AKP in terms of democratization, stabilization, and economic growth added to Germany's general interest in cooperation and suggested support of the democratic government against domestic challenges from the old Kemalist elite.

In relations with Russia, special interests within Germany pointed in different directions. German business successfully lobbied for a cooperative attitude to the Russian government and downplayed troubling 'deficits' in the area of democracy and human rights. Critical advocacy groups, by contrast, emphasized cases where human rights were not sufficiently respected in Russia. Yet, while highly visible in the public domain, they had only limited influence on government policy.

In regard to *political culture* as a determinant, Chapter 2 analysed the official outlines of German and US democracy promotion. It was shown that the two donors are characterized by differing culturally embedded conceptions of democracy promotion, which should lead to diverging policies. Basically, both German and US democracy promotion profiles and their approach to conflicting objectives confirm this expectation of differing approaches. With the exception of Belarus, the German government avoided open interference in the internal affairs of all recipient countries. It reacted in a tolerant manner when governments departed from German notions of liberal democracy. In accordance with the ideal-type conception of a Civilian Power, Germany had a tendency to follow strategies of inclusion and engagement (even with regard to Musharraf and well before 9/11). As a rule, it refrained from challenging ruling governments. German democracy assistance, in all cases, was politically cautious and non-confrontational: official democracy assistance tended to focus on governance issues, the public sector and cooperation with the state; German political foundations relied on broad dialogue and long-term capacity-building. The rhetoric of German democracy promotion was marked by a low degree of explicitness: strategy papers as well as democracy-related pronouncements on individual recipient countries preferred vague statements, did not formulate direct political demands, and avoided dichotomous or linear thinking.

The rhetoric of the United States as a democracy promoter proved to be significantly more explicit. In accordance with the ideal-type conception of a Freedom Fighter, US administrations emphasized specific normative standards and openly criticized decisions by recipient governments that they saw as violations of such standards. As seen above, in a number of cases the United States reacted to breaches of the democratic order with (the threat of) sanctions. With regard to the only country officially labelled a dictatorship (Belarus), Manichean rhetoric and a strategy of isolation prevailed. In cases that were seen as more ambivalent (such as Bolivia and Ecuador), examples of polarized thinking and cultivating an enemy image as well as demands for confrontation and exclusion were also observed, even if less on the part of the US administration than within the larger US discourse, specifically in the US Congress.[19]

As in the German case, the spectrum of US democracy assistance included many cooperative, government-oriented, and long-term strategies. But, in contrast to Germany, it *also* involved explicit support to opposition (civil-society) groups and political counterweights as well as instruments for short-term interventions (such as the USAID OTI). Under certain circumstances, the United States even tried to directly influence internal democratic processes: the return to democracy in Pakistan in 2007/8, the Bolivian elections in 2002, and various elections in Belarus.

However, there is also evidence that runs counter to the expectation of a conceptual difference between the Civilian Power Germany and the US Freedom Fighter. With regard to Germany, this refers to Belarus and Turkey in particular. In the case of Belarus, both German rhetoric and actual policy proved to be unusually confrontational. While the German government did commit itself to the EU attempt to engage Lukashenko in 2007/8, after 2010 it very much adopted the Freedom Fighter-like discourse and practice of the United States.

With regard to Germany's Turkey policy, the growing scepticism of the German government about Turkish accession to the EU – and specifically the rejection by the CDU/CSU of possible accession – directly contradict the expectations for a Civilian Power. The EU enlargement process, which aims at promoting democracy and human rights through non-violent multilateral cooperation, international law and supranational institutions, corresponds to the normative guidelines of a Civilian Power (cf. Kirste and Maull 1996: 300–1) in a way no other strategy of democracy promotion does. The opposite is true for the 'culturalist' argument that is advanced to defend the rejection of Turkey's future EU membership: that a Muslim country would threaten the identity of the EU. This clearly contradicts the appeal to universal norms and change through inclusion that is at the core of the self-image of a Civilian Power. This draws attention to a very specific donor context that characterizes German–Turkish relations and is only approximately covered by the determinant 'domestic special interests' (see below).

The pattern of US democracy promotion deviated even more substantially from the ideal type of the Freedom Fighter. For instance, the US government ignored clear breaches of democratic standards when its 'national interests' required cooperating with the government in question. Pakistan and, to a certain degree, also Russia after 9/11 are typical examples of this. With regard to Bolivia, Ecuador and Turkey, the United States behaved in a relatively cooperative way, although the governments of Morales, Correa and Erdoğan were regarded as posing threats to liberal-democratic principles. As seen in this volume, individual confrontational reactions by the US government in these cases did not respond to democracy-related concerns but to developments running counter to US economic or security interests. In general, in discourse and practice, US democracy promotion shows itself to be guided by a particular understanding of democracy and democratization, but there is scarcely any evidence in the case studies that the United States dogmatically insisted on imposing its own liberal-democratic standards.

Finally, the case studies found only little evidence for the effects of *international democracy norms* that bind both donor and recipient in a given bilateral relationship. In none of the pairs of states did such democracy-related norms as established by international organizations have any recognizable influence on democracy promotion.

Undisputedly, the EU, and specifically the accession process, plays a central role as an instrument of democracy promotion. But the strong (precise, comprehensive and binding) democracy norms that are institutionalized in this framework made Germany's bilateral democracy promotion in Turkey no more proactive and/or consistent than in Bolivia or Ecuador, where no comparable normative framework exists. Nor does Germany's Russia policy reflect the relatively strict democratic obligations it shares with Russia through the membership of both countries in the Council of Europe. The international democracy norms that link Germany and Belarus via the OSCE, by contrast, are weaker. But this did not stop the German government from treating Belarus as a European country that is bound to such norms by virtue of its geography (different from, for instance, remote Pakistan). In the case of US policy, the relatively strong democracy norms of the OAS, which link the United States with Bolivia and Ecuador, did not make US democracy promotion in the Andean countries remarkably different from US policy toward Belarus or Turkey.

This finding can be interpreted as indicating that international norms shape democracy promotion more in the general sense of limiting the range of policy options. Thus, the international democracy norms established in Europe and the Americas mean that a US or German government would probably have to reckon with substantial resistance (domestically and in the region) if it were to openly support a *coup d'état* in Latin America or Europe. By contrast, the fact that most of the time both donors neglected to voice misgivings about democracy in working with Musharraf did not arouse much attention at all.[20] At the same time, the normative consensus on at least minimal conditions of representative democracy within the Western hemisphere makes it relatively difficult for the US to openly oppose an unwanted but elected government in Latin America.

Finally, the example of Belarus suggests that it is not so much the formal establishment of democracy-related norms in a joint international organization that matters. At least in this case, the embedding of democratic norms in an (imagined) common identity seems more important for giving democracy promotion high standing in bilateral relationships. In this sense, it would be the perception of Belarus as a European country – and more precisely as 'Europe's last dictatorship' – that made explicit and confrontational measures for democracy promotion normatively appropriate in dealing with Lukashenko but not, for instance, with Musharraf.

Configurations and contexts of democracy promotion

The discussion of the causal impact of the individual determinants already suggests that the observed patterns of democracy promotion can only be understood by looking at the respective configuration of factors. This interaction takes place in historically and geographically specific constellations of actors and structures, which draws attention to the significance of the contexts discussed in the introduction to this volume. Figure 10.1 depicts the resulting – configurational and context-sensitive – analytic framework.

The basic pattern that characterizes *German handling of conflicting objectives in Bolivia* corresponds with the expectation that derives from the configuration of determinants. A strong relative power position and the absence of 'disruptive factors' based on German material interests made it possible for the Civilian Power disposition to fully exert itself. The specific contextual factors supported this. The political leadership in Bolivia was based on clear democratic legitimation, and no political alternative to the Morales government seemed available (recipient context). The various German development agencies in Bolivia had an interest in continued cooperation. This was supported by the German Federal Ministry for Economic Cooperation and Development (BMZ), which is relatively

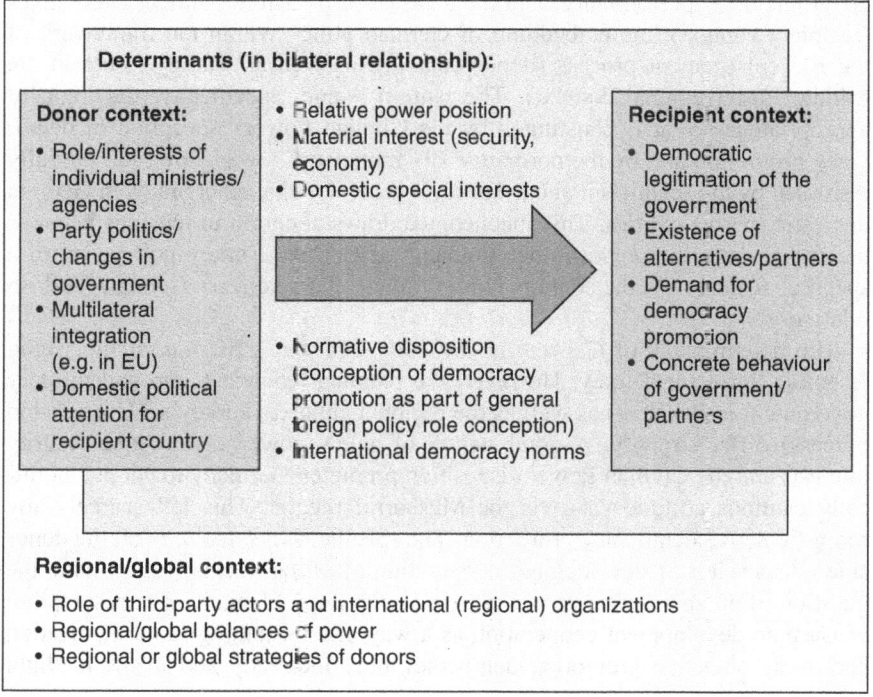

Figure 10.1 Democracy promotion in configurations and contexts (source: author's own illustration).

strong in German policy toward Bolivia (compared to the Foreign Office) and whose social-democratic leadership, at the time when Morales came to power, was relatively close programmatically to the new government (donor context). Finally, Latin America's 'leftist turn' provided additional motivation for a strategy of engaging Bolivia: in order to prevent a radicalization of the Morales government and limit Bolivia's rapprochement with Hugo Chávez (regional context).

Germany's policy in regard to Ecuador matches this pattern: here too, the Civilian Power disposition came to fruition almost without limitation – in view of the absence of 'disruptive factors' and a high relative power position supported by specific contextual factors similar to the Germany/Bolivia dyad.

In the case of *Germany's Turkey policy*, the configuration of determinants combined a small relative power position, substantial economic and security interests, organized domestic special interests, the Civilian Power disposition, and the democracy norms laid down by the EU accession process. This led to a way of dealing with conflicting objectives that was generally committed to democratic norms but relied primarily on multilateral (EU) strategies for promoting democracy; bilateral democracy assistance was non-confrontational, politically cautious and implemented through indirect measures.

This pattern was reinforced by the clear democratic legitimation of the AKP government, its performance, and the absence of plausible political alternatives (recipient context); the embedding of German policy within the framework of the EU enlargement process (donor context); as well as Turkey's role in the Middle East (regional context). The pattern – and, specifically, the logic of appropriateness that is constituted by the Civilian Power conception of democracy promotion and by the normative EU framework – was, however, partially disrupted by the scepticism about Turkey's accession that emerged from German domestic (party) politics. This incoherence draws attention to tensions between the *foreign* and the *domestic* determinants of German Turkey policy, i.e. to a specific feature of the donor context that characterizes German–Turkish relations.[21]

The determinants of *German policy with regard to Pakistan*, at first sight, resemble those for Turkey. However, the recipient context (coup and military government in Pakistan) as well as the regional context (Turkey's EU accession process) differ strongly. A combination of a low power asymmetry, security interests and the Civilian Power disposition prompted Germany to adopt a politically cautious attitude vis-à-vis the Musharraf regime. This left scarcely any room for active democracy promotion. The specific *status quo ante* on the donor side (suspension of development cooperation after the nuclear tests) made the question of an appropriate response to the coup unproblematic. The resumption of German development cooperation as a way of contributing to modernization had as its objective promoting democracy only indirectly and in the medium term.

A limited scope of action, relevant donor interests and the Civilian Power disposition thus led to a policy that generally stuck to a democratization agenda but refrained from any activities that would have a direct effect on the regime in power. Dispensing with active democracy promotion was supported by the sobering experiences with Pakistani democracy in the 1990s and the perception of Musharraf as a guarantor against destabilization and 'Islamization' (recipient context) as well as by the changed regional context after 9/11. Active democracy promotion – in rhetoric and development assistance – only came about when changes on the recipient side explicitly called for it: after the resignation of Musharraf, the external demand for democracy became unproblematic and support for 'good governance' was even requested by the new Pakistani government.

The unusually pronounced Freedom Fighter features that characterize *German Belarus policy* can be traced back to a very specific combination of factors: a clear case of autocratic consolidation; strong power asymmetry (intensified by the EU context); absence of material interests; and the informally strengthened normative framework (democracy as part of a shared European identity). German policies, however, also adhered to the overall Civilian Power conception of democracy promotion to the extent that – in contrast to the United States – there was no proactive support of the opposition. Development cooperation remained largely 'neutral' and, in the case of assistance to the Belarusian police and border patrol, even included direct support to the government. Germany also operated within the multilateral EU framework (donor context) and, in doing so, temporarily advocated strategies of rapprochement and non-isolation. In addition, the intensified sanctions were not a response to a 'mere' infringement of liberal-democratic norms, but in particular to gross violations of basic principles of 'civilian' coexistence constituted by post-electoral repression.

At the same time, the tendency to a Freedom Fighter-like approach to democracy promotion, which has been observable since 2010, corresponds to the entry into office of the conservative–liberal coalition and the change at the top of Germany's Foreign Office from an SPD to an FDP foreign minister. The new government's rhetoric and its proactively applying pressure for sanctions within the EU are indeed unusual for German foreign policy. Within the range of the cases studied in this book, German–Belarusian relations present the only pair of states in which a changing constellation of actors on the donor side has been linked to a perceptible change of policy. This policy change on the German side, however, also corresponds with changes in the regional context: the European (and general 'Western') attempt at rapprochement with Lukashenko, which was supported by Germany, was not least a reaction to tensions in Russian–Belarusian relations.

In *German–Russian relations*, the configuration of determinants in turn yields clear expectations, which were confirmed in practice: the power asymmetry in favour of Russia and the strong German economic and security interest in cooperation with Russia led to a high degree of continuity in Germany's Russia policy. Changes in the German government and the increasingly authoritarian face of 'Putinism' disturbed this continuity only in terms of atmosphere. On the donor side, this pattern is embedded in what might be called the *raison d'état* for cooperation with Russia: a notion of historical responsibility, the Civilian Power disposition, and Germany's material interests unite – and are backed by the business lobby.

The work of the political foundations and multilateral efforts within the framework of the Council of Europe round this out: these activities explicitly promote democracy but in ways that do not strain intergovernmental relations.[22] On the recipient side, experience with the 'chaotic' democracy under Yeltsin, the (initial) performance and domestic approval of Putin, as well as the transition to the ostensibly more liberal Medvedev, made it possible to present this governmental cooperation in accordance with the Civilian Power as a long-term 'modernization partnership' – at least temporarily.

In the case of *US policy toward Bolivia*, the extreme power asymmetry and the clear 'national interests' of the United States that the Morales government did not adhere to could well have translated into a policy of confrontation in accordance with the Freedom Fighter ideal type: an assertive strategy of democracy promotion directed against 'radical-populist' forces involved in illegal drug trafficking. It is the specific context conditions that make it understandable why this did not happen. In Bolivia, there was no plausible alternative to Morales at the national level, while open support of the regional opposition (with secessionist tendencies) against the incontestably democratically legitimated government was difficult to justify as democracy promotion.

Additionally, within Latin America, there was relatively strong sympathy for Morales ('leftist turn'), broad support of elected governments, and rejection of an interventionist US policy. The regional context, therefore, further reduced the prospects of success for a strategy of confrontation and increased its (potential) costs – as the tentative US support for the failed coup against Chávez in 2002 had shown. At the same time, however, an explicitly cooperative Bolivia policy was prohibited by determinants such as security interests and the Freedom Fighter disposition, as well as, on the recipient side, by Morales's openly critical stance towards the United States. This resulted in the ambivalent and incoherent policy that was observed.

Although in many regards similar to the US–Bolivia dyad, *US–Ecuador policy* was clearly less contradictory. This was especially the result of the fact that, from the US point of view, Correa proved significantly more cooperative in the area of counternarcotics than Morales. Consequently, with a view to US security interests, negative developments (closing of the military base) were partially offset by positive ones. Correa was also more ambivalent in diplomatic relations with the United States and in his position vis-à-vis the Venezuelan-led Bolivarian Alliance for the Peoples of Our America (ALBA). As a result, the effects of the specific features of the recipient and regional contexts, which contributed towards making US policy more cooperative and politically restrained (democratic legitimation, lack of an alternative, regional support for the government), were stronger in the case of Ecuador.

The ambivalence evident in *US policy on Turkey*, embedded in a general framework of cooperation between the governments and non-confrontational democracy assistance, corresponds to the expectation arising from the configuration of determinants. Given the ambivalent position of the AKP government, as discussed above, security and economic interests as well as the Freedom Fighter disposition suggested a kind of reluctant cooperation with Erdoğan's Turkey. As the AKP succeeded in forcing the Kemalist, secular camp into the defensive, this changed recipient context made alternative US strategies particularly difficult.

However, the traditional importance of cooperation with the Turkish military (recipient context) as well as the important role of the Pentagon and the US military for US Turkey policy (donor context) precluded unequivocal support of the AKP government. The combination of US concern about 'tendencies toward Islamization' in connection with the idea of presenting Turkey as an example of an Islamic, but pro-Western democracy in the Middle East (regional context) also had an ambivalent effect.

The way the *United States* dealt with conflicting objectives *in Pakistan* shows how security interests can completely suspend the normative Freedom Fighter disposition. The United States reacted to the coup with sanctions, albeit without significant activities to actually promote a return to democratic rule. After 9/11, security interest in cooperation exerted itself directly. Also later, as the 'war on terror' shifted more and more to Pakistan, democracy-related concerns played no recognizable role. It is no coincidence that the post-9/11 US–Pakistan dyad, which in some ways resembles the strategic US cooperation with allied dictatorships during the Cold War, is the only one among the cases analysed here that involves open support of an autocracy. Analogous to Germany, in US policy, too, it was only changes within Pakistan (escalation of protests against Musharraf) that put democracy promotion back on the agenda – even if it continued to be substantially tempered by security-related concerns.

Similarly unambiguous – if in the opposite direction – is the pattern of *US policy toward Belarus*. In view of the power asymmetry and lack of interest in cooperation, the Freedom Fighter disposition consistently exerted itself vis-à-vis a regime that was unequivocally regarded as a dictatorship. The regional context supported this: a potential overthrow of Lukashenko seemed both functional (in terms of US–Russian competition over spheres of influence) and possible (given the example offered by the 'colour revolutions'). This harmony between security interests and the Freedom Fighter disposition was, in the end, reinforced by the short phase in which a rapprochement with Lukashenko against Russia seemed possible. In keeping with this, the sobering experiences with confrontational democracy promotion in Belarus and the change from Bush to Obama did not lead to a change of strategy, but merely to generally waning and rhetorically less aggressive efforts.

In *US–Russian relations*, a combination of factors impeded a vigorous policy of democracy promotion that would have explicitly challenged 'Putinism'. A relatively small power asymmetry and lack of political alternatives on the recipient side limited the possibilities for exerting influence. At the same time, the US government was interested in securing cooperation with Russia in matters of global security policy ('war on terror', Afghanistan, Iran). The result was low-intensity cooperation marked by scepticism on both sides. In the area of democracy assistance, this was reflected in reduced US commitment and activities that in the last decade have been aimed less at genuine (party) political forces than at civil society groups. This is in accord with a recipient context in which no promising partners are available for explicitly political support. The strong wording used by George W. Bush in his democracy rhetoric during his second term of office had no notable operational consequences. Still, it reflects the strong democracy-related criticism of Russia in the United States (donor context), and can thus be understood as a compensatory concession to the Freedom Fighter disposition.

Theoretical conclusions

The analysis shows that we can understand the basic causal dynamics behind the observed patterns of democracy promotion by looking at the configurational and context-sensitive interaction of determinants as summarized in Figure 10.1. When approaching our findings from a rationalist perspective, relative power position and donor interests do explain an important part of our observations. Comprehensive and coherent patterns of democracy promotion 'survive' conflict situations in the recipient countries only when large power asymmetries combine with limited donor interests. In such a situation, scarcely any extrinsic conflicts of objectives arise.[23] Conversely, little remains of the proclaimed goal of democracy promotion when it clashes with tangible material interests.[24]

However, there are several pairs of states between these two poles in which the parsimonious focus on objectively defined power relations and interests falls short of making the overall pattern of democracy promotion comprehensible.[25] This corresponds to the normative expectations of democratic peace theory, as identified in the introduction to this volume. In this sense, the possibility of and/or will to interest-driven confrontation is limited as soon as the recipient government is democratically legitimated. In general, the added value of the configurational perspective is that it helps us understand donor policies that, from a rationalist perspective, seem to be too cooperative or too strongly oriented to democracy promotion but which, from an idealistic point of view, are too confrontational or too restrained.[26] However, just as 'material interests' must first be perceived as such, normative expectations of democratic peace can be understood in very different ways – hence the relevance of diverging conceptions of democracy promotion.

In view of the contextual factors that shape the interaction of the determinants in concrete constellations, the 'recipient context' in particular runs through the analysis as a common thread. Normatively, this refers to the question of democratic legitimation of recipient governments. Pragmatically, it clearly matters whether donors identify political alternatives and potential partners for democracy promotion in the recipient country. Even where democracy promotion corresponds to the constellation of material power and interests as well as to the donor's normative disposition, its implementation still depends on whether such a strategy seems possible and promising in view of the situation 'on the ground'. Democracy promotion, as it requires continuous interaction with actors on the recipient side, is therefore particularly recipient driven (see 'Outlook'). The regional context can either restrict these possibilities for external influence[27] or expand them,[28] just as it can provide additional incentives for or against active democracy promotion.[29] Finally, it is worth noting that in the case studies specific events and political changes within the 'donor context' have scarcely any observable effect on bilateral democracy promotion policies.

Drawing on these empirical results, the following sections will summarize the most important theoretical conclusions of the study in three steps. Prior to this, however, I will deal with the basic question of how far our analytic focus on states as democracy promoters has proven to make sense at all.

The actor question: democracy promotion as state policy

The present volume has analysed 'Germany' and 'the United States' as democracy promoters in order to identify the factors that shape the foreign behaviour of these two collective actors. The analysis of German and US democracy promotion generally supports the argument of Peter Burnell (2000: 34) that the diversity of actors and organizations participating in democracy promotion makes it difficult to identify 'the real agenda behind international democracy promotion' and to work out a 'valid and comprehensive general theory' of democracy promotion. This problem affects democracy promotion in particular. Here, in contrast to 'traditional' foreign policy areas, the level of implementation in the recipient country is added.[30] And, unlike in 'normal' development cooperation, democracy promotion also includes the broad field of diplomatic and also trade or security policy. The theoretical framework presented above takes this into account. It therefore includes not only the general determinants but also the specific contextual factors identified with both the donor and recipient as relevant – if also frequently idiosyncratic – elements of the explanatory model.

At the same time, the study shows that an analysis of 'German' and 'US' democracy promotion policy is clearly fruitful. Although the case studies confirm that the broad field of democracy-related foreign and development policy is characterized by a pluralism of actors, overall patterns, dynamics and determinants of democracy promotion can nonetheless be identified: empirical patterns and causal dynamics that make the analytic and political constructs 'Germany' and 'United States' plausible as approximations of a certainly much more complex reality.[31] Notably, these overall patterns are also not disturbed by changes of government on the donor side. This is the case despite the fact that during the period of investigation there were highly significant (party) political shifts in both donor countries: from Bush to Obama or from the 'red–green' coalition (SPD and the Green Party) via the Grand Coalition (CDU/CSU and SPD) to a centre-right government (CDU/CSU and FDP).

The German political foundations, the NED, and the US party institutions are, of course, not simply instruments of governmental democracy promotion. Their strategies and reactions do not directly follow the prescriptions of 'their' governments. Nonetheless, these organizations are not only financially dependent on the state and subject to control by the government. More generally, their political role and orientation are the result of official political decisions. They reflect a deliberate division of labour in foreign policy as much as the general pattern of political culture of the respective donor country. In fact, the case studies show that it is precisely the relative autonomy of the foundations and institutes that makes them functional from the governmental point of view: in sensitive areas of democracy promotion, their nongovernmental status enables activities and partnerships that would be impossible for official state agencies.

Across the cases, the strategies of the parastatal foundations and institutes were generally not at odds with the overall pattern of the respective donor's democracy promotion, but instead fitted relatively well into the picture. This is not to say that the particular logics and self-interests of these sub-actors proved to be irrelevant. As a rule, however, they rounded out the general pattern of foreign policy rather than thwarting it – even when they focused on opposition forces in the recipient country. Both observations, the relevance of self-interest and the tendency to complement official foreign policy, also apply to the governmental agencies implementing official development cooperation such as GTZ/GIZ and USAID.

Having said this, the constellation of (implementing) actors in the two donor countries is, of course, not identical. Rather, the differences between the two correspond with the general patterns of democracy promotion. USAID as part of the State Department corresponds to the stronger foreign policy orientation of US democracy assistance; the more pronounced differentiation on the German side is consistent with a broad and inclusive strategy of democracy promotion (see below).[32] An in-depth study of the 'inter- and intra-bureaucratic politics of democracy promotion' (Burnell 2011: 304) would certainly be rewarding, but was not possible within the confines of this study.

For Germany, the role of the EU raises additional questions concerning the status of different actors. As was emphasized in the introduction, scholars working on democracy promotion beyond the United States largely focus on the EU, while German policies in this field are scarcely investigated. The case studies show that the relevance of the EU in framing and shaping German democracy promotion varies enormously: it is high in the cases of Belarus and Turkey, limited in the case of Russia, and marginal in the cases of Bolivia, Ecuador and Pakistan. But in all cases, Germany has its own bilateral policies of democracy promotion. At the same time, the EU – also and specifically in cases such as Turkey and Belarus – not only provides a framework for, but is also an instrument of German foreign policy. With the exception of those countries in which there is a clearly defined common EU policy, it is much more plausible to speak of 'a German' policy of democracy promotion that is partly embedded in an EU framework than of 'a European' policy that also encompasses a specific German component.

Alternatively conditioned double standards

The scholarly finding that, in the case of conflicting objectives, foreign policy interests prevail over the 'normative' aim of democracy promotion is consistent with much-heard political criticism of double standards in the foreign policies of democratic states. This consensus view has to be differentiated both empirically and theoretically. The results of the present study point to a pattern that can be called *alternatively conditioned double standards*. It can neither be observed that interests always prevail over norms, nor can this be explained in terms of an unequivocal dominance of interests. Rather, double standards apply to power-, interest- and norm-based determinants – and are reinforced by their interactions.

In view of the relative power position – measured in terms of material capabilities –, small power asymmetries clearly limit the possibilities for democracy promotion. The expected effect here is plausibly low, the potential costs high. The result is restraint in actual democracy promotion policies. Conversely, however, even extreme material power asymmetries do not consistently lead to active democracy promotion. High power asymmetry between states does not automatically mean that the (perceived) possibilities for exerting influence in the recipient country are correspondingly high. Influence depends to a large extent on specific conditions in the recipient country, and specifically on existing alternatives to the incumbent government as well as potential entry points and partners for democracy promotion. This differentiation – a general constraining effect of low power asymmetry, a conditional enabling effect of high power asymmetry – can thus be explained in terms of power. However, this requires a broader understanding of relative power than was conceptualized in the introduction. If 'relative power' in the area of democracy promotion is to encompass possibilities of influence in a given recipient country, it is not enough to look at the relative distribution of material power capabilities between donor and recipient. The entry points for exercising power in the recipient country must also be taken into account.

Security and/or economic interests have a direct effect when they call for cooperation with a recipient government. Under these circumstances, donors will only engage in democracy promotion within the narrow constraints defined by their interests. Where a clear 'national interest' exists in cooperating with a government in power and thus in supporting the status quo on the recipient side, possible normative misgivings play a subordinate role. However, when interests are opposed to a recipient government, donors do not pursue these interests in a comparably direct way. If a government acts against donor interests but is democratically legitimate, no clear pattern of interest-driven confrontation emerges. This differentiation – donor interests in favour of the status quo have a continuous and direct effect, whereas donor interests against the status quo do not – thus involves a plausible assessment of interests: an interest-driven policy that supports the status quo on the recipient side immediately serves these interests; an interest-driven policy that tries to change the status quo on the recipient side has, by contrast, significantly lower prospects of success, and entails greater risk.

A 'purely' interest-driven policy may violate norms related to democracy promotion by, for example, suggesting a confrontation with an elected government. In this case, norms have a constraining effect. This does not, however, work the other way round. When there is interest in cooperating with an authoritarian government such cooperation is not significantly disturbed by counter-acting norms. Thus, again, there is a differentiation according to conditions in the recipient country. When norms 'protect' a recipient government because it is democratically elected, their constraining effect tends to prevent a policy of openly challenging the status quo in the recipient country. When, by contrast, norms related to democracy promotion require opposing a recipient government, an effect – that would counteract an interest in cooperation in the direction of regime change – can scarcely be detected. This differentiation is consistent with general norm theory-related considerations: actively contravening norms (of democracy promotion) is qualitatively different from passively disregarding them by not taking action. In addition, when donor interests call for a contravention of democracy promotion norms, traditional international norms (sovereignty and non-intervention) support the norm of democracy promotion. In the case of disregarding them, such 'traditional' norms clash with the 'liberal' norm of democracy promotion.[33]

The interaction between power-, interest-, and norm-based determinants can be summarized schematically. Vis-à-vis a democratically legitimated government that contravenes donor interests, the *normative prohibition* against openly confronting it constrains a donor from pursuing an *interest in changing the status quo*, which, even in a context of high power asymmetry, can only be realized in limited and risky ways. Vis-à-vis a non-democratic government that supports donor interests, the *interest in the status quo* can reliably be achieved against the *normative imperative* to work towards its change, which is further strengthened in cases of low levels of power asymmetry. Thus, depending on specific conditions in the recipient country, which define what is politically possible and normatively appropriate, double standards are revealed in regard to both donor interest and normative orientation: interest in the status quo is more important than per se equally strong interest in changing the status quo; a norm has a stronger effect against active infringements than against passive neglect.

Civilian Power and Freedom Fighter between interests and norms

The qualitative content analysis of government sources presented in Chapter 2 demonstrated that differing conceptions of democracy promotion are reflected in the official rhetoric employed by Germany and the United States. Comparative analysis of the case studies reveals that in their practices of democracy promotion too, Germany and the United States differ *grosso modo* according to the ideal-type conceptions of Civilian Power and Freedom Fighter. German policies largely correspond to the normative disposition of a Civilian Power. This, however, does not hold true to a comparable degree for the Freedom Fighter: US policies display elements of democracy promotion according to the normative guidelines of Civilian Power and Freedom Fighter, and violate, sometimes quite openly, both.

The expectation that the two ideal-type conceptions of democracy promotion approximately characterize the habitually and culturally embedded approaches of different democracy promoters could thus be only partially confirmed. The Civilian Power-type conception proved to be useful in characterizing an actually existing approach to democracy promotion. Regarding the Freedom Fighter, however, the results of this study suggest that most probably no approximations to this ideal type exist empirically. If not the United States, who else should come close to following the Freedom Fighter model? Still, this ideal-type conception remains helpful as a heuristic device for identifying the antithesis to the Civilian Power. It is, thus, relevant as a competing approach to democracy promotion, even if it does not represent characteristics that generally typify a specific democracy promoter, but tendencies that are put into practice under certain circumstances.

The correspondence between German policy and the Civilian Power conception can be attributed to a harmonious configuration of norms and interests. The logic of appropriateness of the Civilian Power ('culture of restraint') as a rule corresponds directly to German interests. The requirements of the specific pluralism of actors involved in German democracy promotion point in the same direction. The heterogeneity of the organizations involved as well as their respective individual logics require a broad, dialogue-oriented strategy of democracy promotion not too closely tied to politics. In addition, the normative premises of the Civilian Power correspond well to conflict situations on the recipient side that lead to sharply conflicting objectives on the donor side.

By contrast with Germany, the United States has the option to use the approach of the Freedom Fighter: its conception of democracy promotion and the specific pluralism of actors (limited political heterogeneity as well as division of labour; stronger foreign policy subordination of development cooperation) permit this in general. However, in actual practice, this option regularly runs counter to US interests.[34] In addition, the normative premises of the Freedom Fighter – which are linear, dichotomous and aimed at short-term effects – mean that this conception of democracy promotion depends upon highly specific conditions in the recipient country. The Freedom Fighter is consequently in a relatively poor position for dealing with conflicting objectives in democracy promotion.

This, then, does not lead to the theoretical conclusion that ideational (cultural, normative) factors are more important than material ones – even if, in the case of German democracy promotion, political practice corresponds quite well with the programmatic conception. On the one hand, the example of Germany shows that the Civilian Power approach to democracy promotion not only gives expression to a particular identity and role conception of democratic foreign policy that reflects specific historical experiences.[35] At the same time, this is closely linked with the 'material' foundations of German foreign policy (its position as a middle power, the specific shape of German 'national interests'). In this sense,

German self-perceptions as a Civilian Power and as a 'trading state' (Rosecrance 1987) go hand in hand.[36]

On the other hand, specific conceptions of democracy promotion cause policies only in the form of enabling and constraining – individual political decisions and reactions cannot be adequately explained by them. As the case studies clearly show, the conceptions of Civilian Power and Freedom Fighter offer relatively broad and not very discriminating ranges of possible responses to the various conflict situations. As a result, the forms in which the general logic of appropriateness for the respective conception of democracy promotion is converted into concrete patterns of perception and reaction are largely determined by the interests of the donor. This is also true the other way round: not only the interpretation of the recipient context but also the definition of one's own interests and of appropriate strategies for achieving them are marked by conceptual and normative preconceptions held by the donors.

The results of the investigation show that donors, as a rule, understand the challenges for donor interests and recipient democracy in such a way that the two do not contradict each other. A policy on the recipient side that threatens the donor's security or economic interests is mostly also regarded as harmful to recipient democracy, or at least as an indicator of a low level of liberal-democratic orientation in the government in question. This is because, from the donor's perspective, reliable foreign, economic and security policies, growing economic and security cooperation as well as protection of investors' rights all support democracy in the recipient country. In accordance with this, donor interests – for instance in security or economic cooperation – as a rule are not conceived as expressing egoistic 'national interests' but joint donor–recipient interests.

The ideational dimension of democracy promotion – as emphasized, for instance, in the 'conceptual politics of democracy promotion' approach (Hobson and Kurki 2012) – should thus not be understood in a culturalist way. From a configurational perspective, it is an empirical question how the complex interaction and reciprocal influence of ideational orientations and material interests 'produce' a certain policy of democracy promotion that, then, seems to the actor in question to be appropriate in the sense of both normative and utilitarian preferences. Unlike what the common analytic confrontation of 'hard' interests and 'soft' norms in democracy promotion research suggests, we are thus confronted with dynamic processes in which norms and interests, patterns of perception, and behavioural impulses are mutually co- and re-defined.

This mutual articulation of interests and norms also facilitates understanding a striking difference between the general role conception of Civilian Power developed by Hanns W. Maull (see Chapter 2) and Germany's conception of democracy promotion. In the original Civilian Power concept – and in Germany's overall foreign policy – multilateralism plays a preeminent role. Apart from electoral observation, nothing of this is to be seen in German democracy promotion. Taking the idea of Civilian Power seriously, one would have expected German democracy promotion to above all – or at least relatively strongly – make use of multilateral instruments and organizations. Multilaterally mediated democracy promotion could especially rely on these international organizations to whose norms both donor and recipient have subjected themselves. This would defuse many of the inherent tensions that characterize the Civilian Power conception of democracy promotion (for example, between value orientation and the aversion to unilateral export of models). The dominant bilateral conception and practice of German democracy promotion corresponds far better, however, to a way of promoting democracy in which altruistic goals and primarily economic interests coalesce.

A second difference between the Civilian Power ideal-type conception of democracy promotion as employed in this study and Maull's original concept was confirmed by the case studies. This is connected with the core topic itself: the orientation to democracy promotion. The general literature on Civilian Power suggests, in a rather undifferentiated way, that the promotion of 'good governance' and 'democratization' (Kirste and Maull 1996: 302) or of 'democracy and human rights' (Maull 2001: 125) is a central goal of Civilian Powers. Yet, as the theoretical derivation of the respective ideal-type conception in Chapter 2 showed, the general Civilian Power preference for democracy and human rights translates into a concrete commitment to democracy promotion only with significant modifications. Civilian Powers – according to the general normative guidelines formulated by Maull et al. – are sceptical about the unilateral export of models, are characterized by a 'culture of restraint', and rely on international norms and on the 'civilizing' of world politics through cooperative integration. This has repercussions for promoting democracy as it rules out openly rejecting the sovereignty claims of other states in the name of democracy, imposing democratic conditions and blocking the cooperative integration of autocracies.

Consequently, the German practice of democracy promotion proves much more nuanced and even ambiguous than the undifferentiated conclusion that Germany, as a Civilian Power, would be expected to assign democracy and human rights central importance. The politically cautious, decidedly non-proselytizing rhetoric and practice of German democracy promotion also corresponds to Germany's historical experiences with democracy and its failure. Going hand in hand with this – and supported by Germany's etatistic tradition – is the specific profile of German democracy assistance: its focus on the public sector and governance themes, as well as a kind of support for civil society – e.g. through the political foundations – that does not promote counterweights to the state but dialogue and consensus building.

Reflexive democracy promotion

Democracy promotion, as the analysis shows, can neither be understood as simply norm-guided nor as purely interest-driven. It is also not a fixed factor but a network of complex interacting processes. What we observe are processes of reflexive democracy promotion – reflexive in the sense that democracy promotion reflects interests that drive policies, normative dispositions and power relations that constrain and enable, and recipient-specific conditions that define the normatively appropriate and the pragmatically possible.

This de facto reflexivity of democracy promotion can be illustrated by the pattern of alternatively conditioned double standards: here, characteristics on the recipient side as perceived by the donor determine how normative dispositions (Is an infringement of norms forbidden? Is ignoring a norm acceptable?) and interests (Are securing the status quo and cooperation required? Are regime change and confrontation possible?) interact in case-specific ways. Further research should aim at investigating this 'reflexivity loop' more systematically. Theoretically and empirically, additional work is needed to clarify the interaction of interests and norms, constellations of actors on the donor side as well as contextual factors on the recipient side and in the international realm in the process of policy formation and implementation.

While democracy promotion is factually reflexive in this sense, it lacks the consciousness and the operational tools for deliberately processing this reflexivity. Across our case studies, there is no evidence of any attempt on the part of the donors to consider the interplay between goals and contextual factors in an explicit and organized way. This observation draws attention to the practical implications.

Practical implications

From the point of view of the practitioner, what is interesting about democracy promotion research are the findings concerning its effects as well as the factors and strategies affecting its success. The present study, which aimed at an analysis of democracy promoters, offers no direct answers. Yet, studying the determinants of democracy promotion is by no means 'purely academic': what is the use of the best strategy for effective democracy promotion offered by political science if it was designed without an understanding of the actors who are to make use of it, and consequently will be implemented at best in distorted form? Above all, however, the case studies compiled in this volume offer extensive evidence from which – through empirically based speculation – general conclusions for the future of democracy promotion in the twenty-first century can be worked out.

Probably the most important finding relates to the omnipresence of goal conflicts with which democracy promotion is confronted.[37] Even in the case of relatively 'friendly' recipient countries in which a democratic regime is basically established, the harmonizing assumption that 'all good things go together', which is a principle underlying democracy promotion, reveals itself as scarcely appropriate. With regard to extrinsic conflicts of objectives it is almost a platitude that the goal of democracy promotion regularly comes into conflict with other 'national interests'.

At the same time, there is no evidence in the case studies that any open exploration of this *problematique* exists on the donor side. Democracy promoters regularly present themselves as altruistic. Once their interests seem to be endangered, donors adapt their policy ad hoc and depict even a policy clearly driven by donor interests as normatively appropriate. The 'recipient', conversely, tends to regard donor statements about democracy (promotion) as a purely rhetorical cloak for power politics and interest-driven foreign policies. In this way, the potential for conflict that extrinsically conflicting objectives have for bilateral relations between donor and recipient is exacerbated rather than reduced, and the prospects of success for democracy promotion certainly not enhanced. A bit more honesty on the part of democracy promoters – internally as well as externally – would constitute important progress here.

This also applies to intrinsic conflicts of objectives. Since democracy promotion aims at supporting *internal* democratic self-determination *from abroad*, the basic contradiction between external intervention and self-determination pervades the whole project of democracy promotion (cf. Poppe and Wolff 2013). When recipient governments possess clear mandates from their population (as in Bolivia, Ecuador and Turkey) or can at least plausibly claim broad social support (as is still the case in Russia), this confronts any democracy promotion that goes beyond intergovernmental cooperation with difficult normative dilemmas. But even in cases in which systematic political repression openly contradicts the government's claim to collective self-determination (as in Belarus), the difficult question of appropriate means is not the only one raised: without appropriate partners for democracy promotion in the recipient country any support for democratic self-determination remains an illusion.

In addition, the conflict situations analysed show that neither the goal nor the pathway to democratic self-determination can be regarded as a given. Their differences notwithstanding, the transformation processes investigated in Bolivia and Ecuador, in Pakistan, Turkey and Russia call into question the assumption that there is a universal model of a just, liberal-democratic political order: a model towards which all human beings strive, that fits every society – and that forms the indisputable goal democracy promotion should strive towards always and everywhere.

The same is true regarding the idea that there is a linear path of political development that leads from autocratic rule to consolidated liberal democracy and thus defines the individual steps to democratization and the tasks of democracy promotion.[38] With regard to this question, too, there is no evidence of more than ad hoc answers from democracy promoters. This is scarcely appropriate for the difficult weighing-up processes called for when dealing with intrinsic conflicts of objectives – and with the moral dilemmas of democracy promotion entailed herein.

Such critical self-reflection on the foundations of democracy promotion, ideally, ought to take place between donors and recipients or in multilateral forums, but is urgent at least for the donor country. This requires willingness to critically assess the normative premises of democracy promotion. Instead of a clearly defined universal goal and a linear path, a form of democracy promotion would be needed that accompanies complex, contradictory and non-directed internal search processes. To the extent that democracy is based on collective self-determination, democracy promoters must accept that self-determining collectives have their own views and ideas as well as their own interests and values.

This raises difficult normative questions: where are the limits to such toleration or support of diverging approaches to and models of democratic self-determination? How much deviation from their own, particular conception of democracy should democracy promoters allow for? Within the framework of this study, we cannot offer answers to these questions. A procedural suggestion, a peace-related appeal and a deliberately utopian criterion will have to suffice here.

First, in an open dialogue, which should not be restricted to the level of governments, donor and recipient countries could put their respective conceptions of democracy, human rights and good governance up for discussion. The aim would be to jointly work out whether there are enough normative agreements to allow for cooperation in the area of democracy promotion. Until now, official political dialogues are all too often limited to unilateral donor appeals or to banal references to 'internationally recognized human rights' or 'the shared commitment to democracy'.

Second, from a normative peace studies perspective, it is important to draw attention to an alternative to the search for consensus on issues involving democracy and human rights. It would be significantly easier to reach an agreement on basic principles of civilized conduct of conflict that implies a taboo against the use of violence. Democratic foreign and development policies would, thus, be primarily guided by the aim to minimize the use of physical violence and systematic political repression, and not by objectives related to competitive elections or liberal constitutionalist principles. This would not only mitigate conflict between donors and recipients, but would also better respond to the uncertainties and risks that are inherent to processes of democratization (see Spanger 2012).

Third and finally, the 'strategy of non-profit publicity' (*gewinnfreie Werbung*) as proposed by Ernst-Otto Czempiel (1972: 95–101) could serve as a utopian standard for critical self-reflection.[39] According to this, a policy of seeking to support democracy in other parts of the world, in principle, should not be distorted by narrow donor interests and values, but must be conceptualized and carried out *as though no benefit is to be gained*. However, this is impossible because democracy promotion as part of democratic foreign and development policy is primarily accountable to one's own society. Strictly speaking, a policy that aims at externally promoting the democratic self-determination of independently constituted societies should be limited to passively presenting one's own model as an example; it would have to carry out *publicity as non-intervention*. Yet, every form of pro-democracy propaganda, let alone its active promotion, involves some kind of intervention. Finally, a policy that takes the guiding principle of democracy seriously should start by seeking to resolve the all too obvious problems of democracy actually existing in the promoter's own country; it should *try hard to perfect its own democracy*. External democracy promotion, however, is an advertising strategy directed outside one's own country, a strategy that unavoidably seeks to present its own model as a model for success. In sum, the standard of non-profit publicity offers a consciously utopian critical benchmark that constantly reminds practitioners and scholars of the contradictions of democratic democracy promotion.

Outlook: democracy promotion in the twenty-first century

In his essay *Losing 'the Force'? The 'Dark Side' of Democratization after Iraq*, Laurence Whitehead speculated whether the dramatic failure of the regime change imposed by military force in Iraq could become a historical turning point for the international promotion of democracy. Just as the successful transitions to democracy in Spain and South Africa, Poland and Hungary represented key events in the upsurge of external democracy promotion, the case of Iraq could become the symbol of a transition into a new historical era in which the promotion of democracy had to struggle against a noticeable headwind (Whitehead 2009: 215).

In any event, the boom era in the 1990s during which an undisputed liberal hegemony appeared to resolve the inherent contradictions of democracy promotion – as an external intervention aimed at self-determination – is now definitely over. Since the turn of the millennium, political and academic discussion is increasingly focused on new challenges and growing resistance against the project of worldwide democratization.[40] The conceptual underpinnings and normative premises of North-Western democracy promotion are the subject of increasingly critical discussion (cf. Goldsmith 2008. Hobson and Kurki 2012; Smith 2007). At the same time, scholars have (re-)turned their attention to potential ideological rivals to liberal democracy (Ottaway 2010) and to new forms of autocracy promotion (Burnell 2011: chapter 11).

The case studies collected in this volume confirm the notion that, after the short phase of liberal triumphalism in the 1990s, democracy promotion at the beginning of the twenty-first century has entered a new historical phase. It is by no means a new insight that the possibilities for working from outside to steer internal transformation processes are, as a general rule, extremely limited. However, this basic problem could be downplayed as long as such internal processes were (perceived as) moving in the direction of liberal democracy, as witnessed during the so-called 'third wave of democratization' (Huntington 1991).

In the cases investigated here, the notion of goal-directedness is clearly misleading: important differences between the countries notwithstanding, neither Bolivia nor Ecuador, neither Turkey nor Pakistan, neither Belarus nor Russia finds itself on a direct path towards liberal democracy, no matter how liberal democracy may be defined in detail. At the same time, these 'recipients' of North-Western democracy promotion – and in Bolivia, Ecuador and Turkey this refers by no means only to the incumbent governments – demand precisely this: their own pathway to a self-defined democratic goal. From a historical perspective this may seem hardly noteworthy. Still, for current democracy promotion, which is very strongly shaped by the scarcely questioned liberal hegemony of the 1990s, it is a serious challenge. The same is true for the limits of external democracy promotion and its inherent moral dilemmas, to which all the case studies draw attention.

The outcome is paradoxical. Whereas democracy promotion *per definitionem* aims at changing conditions in the recipient country, these local conditions, conversely, exert an important influence on the policies of democracy promotion. These conditions delineate the strategic options and spheres of external influence just as much as they determine their chances of success and the risks entailed. The scope of international democracy promotion in the twenty-first century is thus predictably limited, while continuously (re-)emerging, extrinsic and intrinsic conflicts of objectives must be reckoned with. There is no eluding this situation. Practitioners as well as scholars of democracy promotion cannot escape the need to systematically reflect upon the conceptual and material underpinnings as well as the ambivalences and limits of the project of global democratization. Making such processes of reflexion possible is democracy's primary advantage; actually doing it is democracy promotion's great opportunity.

Notes

1 In the cases of Bolivia, Ecuador and Turkey the German government acted in accordance with the general premise that free and fair elections were held.
2 In Belarus the United States acted against Lukashenko, in Bolivia in 2002 against Morales, and in Pakistan in 2008 in favour of a deal between Musharraf and Bhutto (see below).
3 USAID's relatively comprehensive democracy programme in Russia was an exception, but its magnitude was fostered as much by the US government as by Congress.
4 But even then the Bush government sought to block an unequivocal dismantling of the Musharraf regime, and preferred a controlled transition based on a treaty between Musharraf and Bhutto.
5 None of these measures was, of course, aimed at promoting democracy in the countries in question. But, nonetheless, they have implications for democracy: directly, they signify military support of the particular political regime (whether democratic or not); indirectly, which US (para-)military activities can contribute to the escalation of violent conflicts or conversely to freedom and stability obviously matters for democratic development in the recipient country.
6 In Bolivia, the case of an expropriated German company also meant that the aim to support an elected government collided with the protection of (minor) German economic interests.
7 The aim to support democracy in Turkey through the process of EU accession did collide with specific party or domestic policy preferences (held by the CDU/CSU). Nevertheless, this conflict did not concern the aim of promoting democracy per se, but only the EU enlargement process as a specific instrument of democracy promotion.
8 Germany's decision to tolerate the 'soft coup' against Erbakan in Turkey should be mentioned here too. In a broader sense, the suspension of a German development project in Bolivia, by which the government reacted to the pending compensation for an 'expropriated' German company, could also be mentioned. Here, however, the link to democracy (promotion) is at best indirect, while the German government could argue that the protection of German economic interests simultaneously supported the rule of law (property rights) in Bolivia.
9 This reference to the constitution, which was adopted under a military regime, meant

that the United States de facto supported the disputed, scarcely democratic role of the military in Turkish politics – but presented this as promotion of democracy (support of secular-democratic principles or of constitutional order).

10 Added to this was the relatively broad acceptance by the general population of the governments of Putin and Medvedev during the period in which the research was conducted. Criticism of the elections notwithstanding, this domestic support was reinforced by a certain electoral legitimacy.

11 At least until 2007, this was supported by the perception that the Musharraf government had been, on balance, relatively successful in terms of stabilization and governability (see below). In general, especially after 9/11, Musharraf was regarded not only as an anchor of stability, but also as a bulwark against Islamic forces in Pakistan – a perception that refers to the risk of destabilization and Islamization through democratization.

12 In the case of Bolivia, the aspiration of the Morales government to politically incorporate the indigenous majority was fundamentally democratic but contributed to polarization and destabilization. This increased the intensity of intrinsically conflicting aims. Specific circumstances in Ecuador, by contrast, reduced the intensity of intrinsic conflicts: measured against its predecessors, the Correa government promised improvements in stability and governability. In Turkey, intrinsically conflicting objectives were mitigated by the relative moderation of the AKP (in comparison with the RP). Still, they continued to be acute as a result of the recurring escalation of conflict between the AKP government and the Kemalists, as well as because of accusations of 'cloaked Islamization.'

13 As a rule, donors only resorted to open criticism of breaches of democratic standards when they regarded these breaches as in no way helpful for democracy, stability and governability, but simply as a means of retaining power for the incumbent government. Such breaches were, then, not perceived by the donors as giving rise to intrinsic conflicts of objectives. This was the case, for instance, with the electoral fraud and post-electoral repression in Belarus or with the restrictions on NGOs in Russia.

14 To be sure, the AKP represented (and represents) a significantly more moderate political form of Islam than the RP.

15 Especially for the United States, this was plausibly primarily a matter of integrating Belarus more tightly with the West (against Russia). In contrast with the basic pattern mentioned above, during a brief period US regional interests were, thus, in tension with a confrontational strategy of promoting democracy against Lukashenko.

16 The forms of such 'acceptance' ranged from toleration – in the sense of not adopting any active countermeasures – all the way to direct support.

17 The specific shape of German democracy promotion in Bolivia and Ecuador can, by contrast, scarcely be explained in terms of power: Despite large asymmetries, the former was cooperative and politically cautious. This plausibly reflects the absence of relevant German interests and/or Germany's political culture.

18 This was true for both German and US policy toward Pakistan and German policy toward Russia. US policy toward Russia was more ambivalent, but there was certainly no consistent policy of democracy promotion either.

19 Admittedly, the case studies identify polarizing and Freedom Fighter-like statements in debates in the German Federal Parliament too (relating to Bolivia and Russia as well as Belarus).

20 In accordance with this hypothesis, the tentative support by the US government for the (failed) *coup d'état* against Hugo Chávez in 2002 led to significant criticism in the United States and above all in the region, isolating the United States within the OAS. The debate in the Americas on an appropriate reaction to the *coup d'état* against President Zelaya in Honduras in 2009 was admittedly highly controversial, but there was an official consensus that the coup government itself should not be recognized – a consensus to which the United States adhered.

21 It is important to note, however, that domestic politics in this case are shaped by broader political and societal dynamics inside Germany, rather than by domestic special interests as defined in this volume, i.e. by groups or NGOs specifically interested in Turkey.
22 In this sense, the political foundations offer an ideal tool for Germany's Russia policy, which enables long-term, semi-official democracy promotion incorporating NGOs and political parties belonging to the opposition, without endangering the trusting relations between governments in the process. In regard to the Council of Europe, it could be argued that Germany has de facto delegated dealing with the politically sensitive reservations regarding the status of Russian democracy to this multilateral forum, in order to be able to concentrate on bilateral relations as a matter of normal protocol.
23 These are the dyads Germany/Bolivia, Germany/Ecuador, Germany/Belarus, and United States/Belarus.
24 These are the dyads Germany/Pakistan and United States/Pakistan (in each case after 9/11), Germany/Russia, and United States/Russia.
25 These are the dyads United States/Bolivia, United States/Ecuador, Germany/Turkey and United States/Turkey. But even in the pairs of states mentioned above (for example Germany/Russia, United States/Russia), as has been seen, important facets of democracy promotion lie outside the narrow rationalistic perspective.
26 This is especially the case for United States/Bolivia, United States/Ecuador and United States/Turkey (rationalistic: too cooperative, idealistic: too confrontational) or for Germany/Turkey, United States/Turkey, Germany/Russia, and United States/Russia (rationalistic: too strongly oriented to democracy promotion, idealistic: too restrained).
27 As in the case of US policy toward Bolivia and Ecuador.
28 Especially as in the case of the EU, which provides German democracy promotion with both an additional normative reference point and specific instruments.
29 In regard to, for example, Belarus, the EU context (in the case of Germany), or the rivalry with Russia (especially in the case of the United States) had a pro-democracy promotion effect. The role of Pakistan in the 'war on terror' and, in particular, for the war in Afghanistan had a clearly negative effect on democracy promotion.
30 In contrast with 'traditional' foreign policy analyses, in studies of democracy promotion, the level of implementation in the recipient country has to be added to the usual three levels of analysis: 'society, political system, and international environment' (Müller and Risse-Kappen 1993: 26).
31 A dimension that was not explored systematically in the present study, which is focused on democracy promotion in bilateral relations, is the global, systemic context in which democracy promotion by states is embedded.
32 In terms of political orientation, NDI and IRI are much more similar than Germany's political foundations; and politically USAID is more in line with the State Department than GTZ and BMZ are with the German Foreign Office.
33 The latter argument shows that the constraining effect of democracy promotion norms on interest-driven policies is not unconditional, but is shaped by its interaction with additional, potentially competing normative orientations. Just as during the Cold War anti-communism as a dominant normative orientation regularly 'permitted' contraventions against democratic norms, alternative orientations – for example, against Islam and/or terrorism – could be superimposed on the democratic frame. In the case of German and especially US policy on Turkey – in the 1990s in particular – certain tendencies in this direction were revealed, even more strongly in the case of Pakistan; so far, however, the 'fight against Islamism' has (fortunately) not become a dominant normative framework of Western policy, analogous to the 'fight against Communism.'
34 Here, Belarus – among our cases – is the exception confirming the rule.
35 This is, of course, just as true for the conception of the Freedom Fighter.

36 This is revealed with particular clarity in our case study on Russia, but is consistent with a general pattern of German foreign policy. A study that confirmed Germany's basically 'norm-consistent foreign policy that, at the same time, aims at enhancing its influence in the realm of high politics and seeks to achieve economic gains in the realm of foreign trade' (Rittberger and Wagner 2001: 300), concluded, for German foreign trade policy, that norms and interests were 'almost indistinguishably linked' (Rittberger and Wagner 2001: 319).
37 Only very recently, conflicting objectives have become an explicit topic of democracy promotion research (cf. Leininger *et al.* 2012).
38 The intrinsic conflicting objectives in democracy promotion and, in particular, the conflict situations in the countries analysed in this volume thus reinforce Carothers's critique of the transition paradigm (Carothers 2002).
39 Developed as a strategy for dealing peacefully with the East–West conflict, this approach aimed at perfecting 'political, economic and social democratization' in one's own country in order to then campaign globally for such a kind of peaceful order – in the sense of 'non-violent systemic change' and 'renouncing propaganda, the export of ideology and the transfer of one's own system via development aid' (Czempiel 1972: 95, 99).
40 See Carothers (2006); Diamond (2008: 56–87); Burnell and Youngs (2010).

References

Burnell, P. (2000) 'Democracy Assistance: Origins and Organizations', in: P. Burnell (ed.) *Democracy Assistance: International Co-operation for Democratization*, London: Frank Cass.

Burnell, P. (2011) *Promoting Democracy Abroad: Policy and Performance*, New Brunswick, NJ: Transaction Publishers.

Burnell, P. and Youngs, R. (eds) (2010) *New Challenges to Democratization*, London: Routledge.

Carothers, T. (1999) *Aiding Democracy Abroad: The Learning Curve*, Washington, DC: Carnegie Endowment for International Peace.

Carothers, T. (2002) 'The End of the Transition Paradigm', *Journal of Democracy*, 13 (1): 5–21.

Carothers, T. (2006) 'The Backlash against Democracy Promotion' *Foreign Affairs*, 85 (2): 55–68.

Czempiel, E.-O. (1972) *Schwerpunkte und Ziele der Friedensforschung*, München: Kaiser.

Diamond, L. (2008) *The Spirit of Democracy. The Struggle to Build Free Societies throughout the World*, New York, NY: Times Books.

Goldsmith, A.A. (2008) 'Making the World Safe for Partial Democracy? Questioning the Premises of Democracy Promotion', *International Security*, 33 (2): 120–47.

Hobson, C. and Kurki, M. (eds) (2012) *The Conceptual Politics of Democracy Promotion*, London: Routledge.

Huntington, S.P. (1991) *The Third Wave. Democratization in the Late 20th Century*, Norman, OK: University of Oklahoma Press.

Kirste, K. and Maull, H.W. (1996) 'Zivilmacht und Rollentheorie, *Zeitschrift für Internationale Beziehungen*, 3 (2): 283–312.

Leininger, J., Grimm, S. and Freyburg, T. (eds) (2012) *Do all Good Things Go Together? Conflicting Objectives in Democracy Promotion*, London: Routledge (Democratization Special Issue).

Maull, H.W. (2001) 'Germany's Foreign Policy, Post-Kosovo: Still a "Civilian Power" '?, in S. Harnisch and H.W. Maull (eds) *Germany as a Civilian Power? The Foreign Policy of the Berlin Republic*, Manchester: Manchester University Press.

Müller, H. and Risse-Kappen, T. (1993) 'From the Outside In and from the Inside Out: International Relations, Domestic Politics, and Foreign Policy', in D. Skidmore and V.M. Hudson (eds) *The Limits of State Autonomy: Societal Groups and Foreign Policy Formulation*, Boulder, CO: Westview Press.

Ottaway, M. (2010) 'Ideological Challenges to Democracy: Do they Exist?', in P. Burnell and R. Youngs (eds) *New Challenges to Democratization*, London: Routledge.

Poppe, A.E. and Wolff, J. (2013) 'The Normative Challenge of Interaction: Justice Conflicts in Democracy Promotion', *Global Constitutionalism*, forthcoming.

Rittberger, V. and Wagner, W. (2001) 'German Foreign Policy since Unification: Theories meet Reality', in V. Rittberger (ed.) *German Foreign Policy since Unification: Theories and Case Studies*, Manchester: Manchester University Press.

Rosecrance, R.N. (1987) *The Rise of the Trading State: Commerce and Conquest in the Modern World*, New York, NY: Basic Books.

Schraeder, P.J. (2003) 'The State of the Art in International Democracy Promotion: Results of a Joint European–North American Research Network', *Democratization*, 20 (2): 21–44.

Smith, T. (2007) *A Pact with the Devil: Washington's Bid for World Supremacy and the Betrayal of the American Promise*, New York, NY: Routledge.

Spanger, H.-J. (ed.) (2012) *Der demokratische Unfrieden. Über das spannungsreiche Verhältnis zwischen Demokratie und innerer Gewalt*, Baden-Baden: Nomos.

Spanger, H.-J. and Wolff, J. (2007) 'Universales Ziel – partikulare Wege? Externe Demokratieförderung zwischen einheitlicher Rhetorik und vielfältiger Praxis', in: A. Geis, H. Müller and W. Wagner (eds) *Schattenseiten des Demokratischen Friedens. Zur Kritik einer Theorie liberaler Außen- und Sicherheitspolitik*, Frankfurt a.M.: Campus.

Whitehead, L. (2009): 'Losing "the Force"? The "Dark Side" of Democratization after Iraq', *Democratization*, 16 (2): 215–42.

Index

Page numbers in *italics* denote tables, those in **bold** denote figures.

AA (Auswärtiges Amt) *see* German Foreign Office
AKP (Adalet ve Kalkınma Partisi, Justice and Development Party) 132–7, 140–3, 146–55, 258–61, 264, 268, 270–1, 285n12, 285n14

Bhutto, Benazir 162–3, 173, 175, 284n2, 284n4
BMZ (Bundesministerium für wirtschaftliche Zusammenarbeit und Entwicklung) *see* German Federal Ministry for Economic Cooperation and Development)
Bundestag *see* German parliament
Bush, George W./Bush Administration 3, 24n5, 43, 45, 50–1, 54n22, 91, 93, 98, 100n21, 119, 146, 148–9, 173–5, 179, 204–9, 213, 234–43, 245n17, 256, 259–60, 271–3, 284n4

capacity building 27n46, 44, 90, 122, 169, 262, 264
CDU/CSU (Christlich Demokratische Union, Christian Democratic Union/ Christlich Soziale Union, Christian Social Union) 84, 139–41, 154, 167, 212, 230, 232, 257, 265, 284n7
Center for International Private Enterprise (CIPE) 22, 89, 92, 117, 172, 236
Centre for International Migration and Development (CIM) 82, 112, 180n11
Chávez, Hugo 84, 90, 98, 118–19, 268, 285n20
Civilian Power 18, 23, 37, 39–41, 43–4, 47–8, 51–2, 53n9, 53n15, 53n17, 67, *69*, 97–8, 124, 154–5, 179, 213, 244, 260, 264–5, 267–70, 276–9

civil society 16, *22*, 28n49, 42, 44, 46, 79, 83, 94–5, 97, 116, 151, 192, 196, 198–9, 205, 210, 233; civil society promotion 82–3, 85, 92, 98, 100n11, 111–12, 114, 117, 121–2, 126n12, 126n14, 126n16, 127n31, 142, 145, 150, 166, 169–70, 176–7, 196–8, 200–3, 205, 209, 213, 236, 241, 246n28, 255, 265, 272
Clinton, William J./Clinton Administration 24n5, 43, 49–51, 144, 172, 203–4, 235–6, 238, 241, 245–6n18, 255
Conditionality 14, *21*, 43; *see also* sanctions
Consulting 83, 86, 93, 112, 115, 262; to parliament 33, 87; to government 196, 241
Correa, Rafael 107–10, 112–25, 125n3, 125n4, 125n5, 126n18, 127n24, 127n30, 128n36, 260–2, 265, 270, 285n12
Council of Europe 15, 68, 142, 209, 233, 254, 266, 270, 286n22

DED (Deutscher Entwicklungsdienst) *see* German Development Service
Department of Defense *see* Pentagon
Department of State *see* State Department
Drug Enforcement Administration (DEA) 88, 94–5, 263

economic interests 4, 9–10, 12–13, **19**, 20, 25n16, 44, 50, 61, 65, *69*, 70, 81, 89, 95, 97–8, 122–3, 128n36, 144, 171, 243, 258, 263, 271, 278–9, 284n6, 284n8
elections 9, 21, 39, 42, 44, 46, 79–80, 89, 91, 117, 121–3, 127n31, 137, 150, 153, 168, 176, 192–4, 200, 205, 209, 214n12, 224–5, 254–5, 282; election monitoring

elections *continued*
  22, 95, 101n28, 101n29, 117, 122, 127n31, 128n33, 128n34, 150–1, 172, 176–7, 183n43, 193–4, 199, 210, 213, 233, 241, 245n10, 254, 278
empowerment 51, 77, 80, 136, 236, 254–5
Erbakan, Necmettin 132–3, 136, 139, 143, 146, 151–2, 154, 256, 261, 284n8
Erdoğan, Recep Tayyip 133–6, 140, 146–7, 150, 152, 154, 256, 260, 265, 271
European Union (EU) 15, 25n11, 25n14, 27n41, 52n1, 53n10, 68, 70, 87–8, 95, 101n28, 109, 121–2, 125n10, 128n33, 132, 134–42, 146–7, 149, 151–5, 177, 183n43, 191, 195, 197, 199–203, 208–13, 213n1, 214n6, 214n12, 214n17, 215n24, 226, 228, 230, 232, 234, 254, 257, 262, 265–6, **267**, 268–9, 274, 284n7, 286n28

Freedom Fighter 23, 37, 39–40, *40*, 41–2, 47, 51–2, 53n9, 67, *69*, 98, 124, 155, 179, 213, 244, 264–5, 269–72, 276–8, 285n19
Friedrich-Ebert-Stiftung (FES) 21, 83–4, 87, 100n15, 100n18, 112–15, 126n15, 125n19, 139, 143, 166, 169, 197, 203, 228–9, 245n11
Friedrich-Naumann-Stiftung (FNS) 21, 139, 143, 166, 169, 197, 228–9, 244n5

German Agency for Technical Cooperation (Deutsche Gesellschaft für Technische Zusammenarbeit, GTZ) 21, 27n47, 43, 82–3, 85–7, 98–9, 100n10, 100n13, 112, 114–16, 126n13, 126n18, 138, 142, 166, 169–70, 181n17, 197, 202, 228, 255, 274, 286n32
German Development Service (Deutscher Entwicklungsdienst, DED) 21, 27n47, 82, 98, 111–12, 126n14, 166, 180n12
German Federal Ministry for Economic Cooperation and Development (Bundesministerium für wirtschaftliche Zusammenarbeit und Entwicklung, BMZ) 21, 28n48, 48–51, 54n23, 82, 84–6, 98, 99n5, 111, 113–14, 124, 125n9, 138–43, 170, 181n15, 182n24, 197, 228, 267, 286n32
German Foreign Office (Auswärtiges Amt, AA) 44, 83, 85–6, 98, 100n14, 115, 139–40, 142, 168, 181n15, 197, 202, 232, 268–9, 286n32

German government 38, 43, 45, 48, 50–1, 71n8, 83–5, 87–8, 94–6, 98, 114, 121, 126n10, 126n22, 139–40, 142, 151, 153–4, 165–9, 178, 181n20, 196, 200–2, 210, 213, 215n20, 215n24, 229, 231, 233, 245n11, 254–7, 259, 264–6, 269, 284n1, 284n8 ; *see also* Kohl; Merkel; Schröder
German parliament 27–8n48, 84, 116, 139, 142, 151, 167–8, 181n16, 198–200, 202, 215n24, 230
(good) governance 12, 39, 43–4, 48, 50, 81–3, 85, 89, 92, 94–6, 98, 110, 116–17, 121, 139, 145, 151, 166, 170, 172, 176–7, 182n25, 206, 225, 228, 236, 255, 257, 261, 264, 269, 279, 282

Hanns-Seidel-Stiftung (HSS) 21, 83, 87, 112, 125n8, 126n16, 126n21, 155n5, 167, 228–9, 244n5
Heinrich-Boell-Stiftung (HBS) 22, 139, 143, 166, 169, 228–9, 244n5, 245n11

International Military Education and Training (IMET) 90, 101n23, 118, 145–6, 149–50, 156n18
International Monetary Fund (IMF) 20, 78, 108–9, 148
International Republican Institute (IRI) 22, 89, 92–4, 98, 117, 121–2, 145, 148, 150, 172, 176–7, 205, 209, 236, 246n19, 255, 286n32
InWent (Internationale Weiterbildung und Entwicklung, Capacity Building International) 27n47, 112, 166, 228

KfW Development Bank 21, 82, 112, 138, 166, 197, 202, 228
Kohl, Helmut/Kohl Administration 139, 141, 227, 231–2; *see also* German government
Konrad-Adenauer-Stiftung (KAS) 21, 83–4, 87, 100n17, 100n18, 112–13, 126n17, 126n20, 139, 143, 167, 169, 181n19, 182n27, 197, 203, 215n26, 228–9, 245n11

labour unions 28n49, 79, 108, 125n5, 139, 166, 172, 216n42, 229
Lukashenko, Alexander 191–5, 197–213, 213n3, 214n5, 214n7, 214n11, 215n24, 215n28, 255, 257–8, 260, 262, 265–6, 269, 271, 284n2, 285n15

Medvedev, Dmitry 224, 226, 230–2, 242, 245n8, 270, 285n10

Merkel, Angela/Merkel Administration 88, 140, 200, 202, 210, 215n21, 226, 231–2, 242, 245n8; CDU-SPD coalition government 232; CDU/CSU-FDP coalition government 140, 230, 269; *see also* German government
military 108, 133–5, 140, 145–7, 149–51, 153, 155n3, 156n18, 161–6, 172–3; military aid 63–4, 138, 144, 171, 175, 183n40, 184n41; military cooperation 22, 64, 88, 90, 95, 118, 122, 149, 166, 171, 179, 183n36; military regime 163, 165, 172, 174–5, 177–8, 255–8, 260, 263, 271, 284n9
Millennium Challenge Account (MCA)/ Millennium Challenge Corporation (MCC) 94–5, 97–8, 257, 259
Morales, Evo 77–81, 83–94, 96–9, 100n14, 100n20, 255, 260–1, 263, 265, 267–8, 270, 284n2, 285n12
Musharraf, Pervez 161–5, 167–79, 180n1, 180n12, 181n19, 183n34, 255–61, 264, 266, 268–9, 271, 284n2, 284n4, 285n11

National Democratic Institute (NDI) 22, 89, 92–4, 98, 101n25, 117, 121, 145, 148, 150, 172, 177, 182n31, 205, 209, 236, 246n19, 246n20, 255, 286n32
National Endowment for Democracy (NED) 22, 28n49, 53n13, 89, 92, 94, 98, 117, 121, 145, 148, 150, 172, 176–7, 205, 209, 236, 245n17, 246n19, 255, 273
NATO 64, 68–9, 70n3, 71n9, 132–6, 138–9, 144–6, 151–2, 174, 191, 194, 204, 213n1, 226, 234, 238, 258, 263
nongovernmental organizations (NGO) 13, 27n41, 66, 92, 117, 121, 126n20, 155, 166, 169, 197–9, 204–5, 207–8, 212, 216n41, 229, 242, 245n11, 254, 259, 263, 285n13, 286n21, 286n22

Obama, Barack/Obama Administration 43, 94, 98, 120, 147, 149, 173, 175, 179, 208, 210, 234–8, 240–3, 256
Organization for Security and Cooperation in Europe (OSCE) 64, 68–9, 151, 192–4, 198–200, 204, 209–10, 212–13, 214n5, 215n30, 216n38, 233, 245n10, 266
Organization of American States (OAS) 15, 27n42, 68, 124, 266, 285n20

parties 78, 83, 87, 107–8, 132, 136–7, 148, 153, 167–8, 256, 259, 261, 286n22; cooperation with political parties 115, 121, 143, 150, 177, 229; party/political foundations 21, 27n48, 28n49, 53n17, 83–7, 100n10, 100n14, 112, 115, 139, 141, 143, 153, 166, 169–70, 177, 197, 203, 210, 228–9, 233, 236, 244n5, 245n11, 255, 262, 264, 270, 273–4, 277, 279, 281, 286n22, 286n32; party-strengthening 87, 89, 92–3, 100n17, 112, 117, 172, 176–7, 198, 204–5, 207–10, 236, 241, 254
Pentagon 88, 127n27, 146, 174, 183n37, 271
Putin, Vladimir 222–7, 229–35, 237–9, 243–4; Putinism 222, 224–5, 231, 233–4, 242

RP (Refah Partisi, Welfare Party) 132–4, 136–41, 143–4, 146–8, 150–5, 258, 285n12, 285n14
Rosa-Luxemburg-Stiftung (RLS) 22, 125n6, 155n5, 228–9, 244n5
rule of law 12, 44, 46, 47, 48, 50, 65, 81, 90, 96, 122, 124, 125n9, 139–40, 168, 200, 202, 225, 230–1, 239, 245n7, 255–6, 261, 284n8; rule of law programme 86, 89, 112, 145, 151, 169–70, 215n23, 228, 236

sanctions 6, 21, 22, 44; *see also* conditionality
Schröder, Gerhard/Schröder Administration 141, 167–8, 214n11, 226–7, 230–3, 242; *see also* German government
security interests 4, 9, 12, 18, 19, 61–3, 63, 69, 70, 96, 124, 135, 138, 148, 165, 178–9, 195, 201, 212–13, 225, 230, 243, 258, 260, 263, 266, 268–71
Solidarity Center/American Center for International Labor Solidarity 22, 172, 236
SPD (Sozialdemokratische Partei Deutschlands, German Social Democratic Party) 84, 140–1, 154, 167, 169, 181n13, 212, 215n24, 232, 269, 273
State Department 28n49, 45, 88, 91–2, 118–19, 127n27, 127n29, 145–7, 149–50, 172, 205, 209, 244, 246n26, 246n30, 274, 286n32

trade unions *see* labour unions

292 *Index*

United Nations (UN) 15, 67, 126n22, 170, 207
United States Agency for International Development (USAID) 21, 45, 48–9, 89–94, 98–9, 101n24, 101n29, 117, 120–1, 127n31, 145, 172, 176, 183n42, 205, 207, 209, *235*, 236, 240, 246n20, 255, 265, 274, 284n3, 286n32

White House 21, 147, 177, 205–6
World Bank 20, 78, 94, 108–9, 117